D0746670

THE
MICHELIN
GUIDE
HONG KONG
MACAU
2018

RESTAURANTS

& HOTELS

米芝蓮指南
香港 澳門 2018
餐廳及酒店

CONTENTS

目錄

3

DEAR READER

This year, the MICHELIN Guide Hong Kong and Macau celebrates its 10th anniversary as we publish the 10th selection of MICHELIN Guide for the cities. To mark the occasion, we commissioned the local illustration artist Flying Pig to create the cover art.

Hong Kong consists of Hong Kong Island, Kowloon Peninsula, New Territories and over 200 offshore islands. The proposed illustration by our artist is depicting the islands of Hong Kong as different dishes and the multitude of choices. People is joyfully enjoying the cuisines on these "food-islands"; in the middle of the first cover, have a look to the fisherman : he illustrates the origin of the Hong Kong local food. Nowadays, the fishing port-turned international metropolis takes advantage of its coastal location to specialize in fresh and sundried seafood on the menu.

From there, Hong Kong and its neighbouring Macau transformed themselves into the gourmet paradises they are now known as. Food and beverage industry flourishes in the cities just like what the cover art depicts. Everyone can indulge in the great variety of tasty food on offer regardless of your budget and personal tastes.

As always, all restaurants included in this Guide are cherry-picked by our full-time inspectors. Only the best in its category can make it to the list. Our inspectors visit all restaurants and shops anonymously to ensure their experience is the same with any other customer and to keep the reviews unbiased and objective.

Apart from the world-famous categories of Michelin Starred restaurants, Bib Gourmand restaurants, and street food that packs local charm and oomph, we added a new category known as the Plate – a list of the absolutely best restaurants featuring the freshest ingredients, impeccable cooking and the most divine taste.

Our inspectors also selected a myriad of quality hotels for our audience. From the fashionably hip, to the cosy elegance and the palatial luxury, we compiled the Guide across all classes and styles of hotels with one common thread that runs through them all – where good service, comfort and amenities meet.

We care about what you think and would love to hear from you. If you have any opinion or comment about our Guide, please write to:

michelinguide.hongkong-macau@michelin.com

Wish you a wonderful culinary and hotel experience in Hong Kong and Macau.

Bon appétit!

親愛的讀者

今年是香港澳門米芝蓮指南落戶香港和澳門的第十個年頭，本指南亦出版至第十版。為慶祝這個值得紀念的里程碑，我們特別邀請了本地藝術家Flying Pig為本版指南設計封面插圖。

香港由港島、九龍半島等逾二百個小島組成，眾所周知，香港初期是一個漁港，後來才發展至現在的國際都會，因利成便，沿海而居的優勢，捕漁業應勢而生，亦因此海鮮和生曬醃製海產成了本地一大特色。

迄今，不論是香港或是彼岸的澳門，均已成為世界知名的美食天堂，餐飲業百花盛放，就一如封面插圖上的景象:你、我、他和她都可以在這個美食小島上大快朵頤，享受各式各樣的美食。

一如既往，本指南內推薦的餐廳全部由全職米芝蓮評審員嚴格挑選，只有最優秀的食店才會獲推介。為確保體驗到與一般顧客同等的待遇，讓評審結果更客觀公正，我們的評審員會以匿名身份到訪各大食肆。

除了聞名遐邇的米芝蓮星級❀餐廳、車胎人⌾美食推介和充滿本地風味的街頭小吃外，今年我們還引入了米芝蓮餐盤⍟。米芝蓮餐盤推介的是評審員萬裏挑一的餐館，材料新鮮、烹調用心，美味的菜餚。

此外，評審員亦在芸芸酒店中挑選了一系列優質酒店，推薦給廣大讀者。從時尚型格到優雅舒適，以致豪華典雅，各個級別和風格的酒店，只要服務水準高、房間舒適及設備完善均會獲推薦。

我們向來重視讀者的回饋，渴望聆聽閣下的意見。如閣下對本指南有任何意見或提議，歡迎電郵至下列電子郵箱:

michelinguide.hongkong-macau@michelin.com

祝願閣下在香港和澳門擁有愉快的美食
和住宿體驗！
Bon appétit！

THE MICHELIN GUIDE'S COMMITMENTS

"This volume was created at the turn of the century and will last at least as long".

This foreword to the very first edition of the MICHELIN Guide, written in 1900, has become famous over the years and the guide has lived up to the prediction. It is read across the world and the key to its popularity is the consistency of its commitment to its readers, which is based on the following promises:

Anonymous inspections:
Our inspectors make regular and anonymous visits to restaurants and hotels to gauge the quality of the products and services offered to an ordinary customer. They settle their own bill and may then introduce themselves and ask for more information about the establishment. Our readers' comments are also a valuable source of information, which we can then follow up with another visit of our own.

Independence:
Our choice of establishments is a completely independent one, made for the benefit of our readers alone. The decisions to be taken are discussed around the table by the inspectors and the editor. Inclusion in the guide is completely free of charge.

Selection and choice:
Our guide offers a selection of the best restaurants and hotels. This is only possible because all the inspectors rigorously apply the same methods.

Annual updates:
All the practical information, the classifications and awards are revised and updated every single year to give the most reliable information possible.

Consistency:
The criteria for the classifications are the same in every country covered by the MICHELIN Guide.

...And our aim:
To do everything possible to make travel, holidays and eating out a pleasure, as part of Michelin's ongoing commitment to improving travel and mobility.

承諾

「這冊書於世紀交替時創辦，亦將繼續傳承下去。」

這是1900年首冊米芝蓮指南的前言，多年來享負盛名，並一直傳承下去。指南在世界各地均大受歡迎，關鍵在其秉承一貫宗旨，履行對讀者的承諾。

匿名評審

我們的評審員以匿名方式定期到訪餐廳和酒店，以一般顧客的身份對餐廳和酒店的食品和服務質素作出評估。評審員自行結賬後，在需要時會介紹自己，並會詳細詢問有關餐廳或酒店的資料。讀者的評語和推薦也是寶貴的資訊來源，我們會根據讀者的推薦到訪該餐廳。

獨立性

餐廳的評選完全是我們獨立的決定，純以讀者利益為依歸。經評審員和編輯一同討論後才作出決定，亦不會向收錄在指南內的餐廳和酒店收取任何費用。

選擇

全賴一眾評審員使用一致且嚴謹的評選方法，本指南才能向讀者推介一系列優質餐廳和酒店。

每年更新

每年都會修訂和更新所有實用資訊、分類及評級，務求為讀者提供最可靠的資料。

一致性

每個國家地區的米芝蓮指南均採用相同的評審和分類準則。

我們的目標

盡全力令旅遊、度假及在外用膳成為一大樂事，實踐米芝蓮一貫優化旅遊和生活的承諾。

ONCE UPON A TIME, IN THE HEART OF FRANCE...

It all started way back in 1889, in Clermont-Ferrand, when the Michelin brothers founded the Manufacture Française des Pneumatiques Michelin tyre company – this was at a time when driving was considered quite an adventure!

In 1900, fewer than 3,000 cars existed in France. The Michelin brothers hit upon the idea of creating a small guide packed with useful information for the new pioneers of the road, such as where to fill up with petrol or change a tyre, as well as where to eat and sleep. The MICHELIN Guide was born!

The purpose of the guide was obvious: to track down the best hotels and restaurants across the country. To do this, Michelin employed a veritable armada of anonymous professional inspectors to scour every region – something that had never before been attempted!

Over the years, bumpy roads were replaced by smoother highways and the company continued to develop, as indeed did the country's cuisine: cooks became chefs, artisans developed into artists, and traditional dishes were transformed into works of art. All the while, the MICHELIN Guide, by now a faithful travel companion, kept pace with – and encouraged – these changes. The most famous distinction awarded by the guide was created in 1926: the "étoile de bonne table" – the famous star which quickly established itself as the reference in the world of gastronomy!

Bibendum – the famous tyre-clad Michelin Man – continued to widen his reach and by 1911, the guide covered the whole of Europe.

In 2006, the collection crossed the Atlantic, awarding stars to 39 restaurants in New York. In 2007 and 2008, the guide moved on to San Francisco, Los Angeles and Las Vegas, and in 2011 it was the turn of Chicago to have its own Michelin guide – The Michelin Man had become truly American!

In November 2007, The Michelin Man took his first steps in Asia: in recognition of the excellence of Japanese cuisine, stars rained down on Tokyo, which was gripped by culinary fever! A guide to Kyoto, Kobe, Osaka and Nara followed, with Yokohama and Shonan then joining Tokyo. Thereafter the Michelin Man set his feet down in Southern China, with the publication in 2009 of a guide to Hong Kong and Macau.

The Red Guide was now firmly on the map in the Far East. The Michelin Man then explored Southeast Asia and China. In 2016 the first editions of MICHELIN Guide Singapore and MICHELIN Guide Shanghai was published. The MICHELIN guides collection now covers 29 titles in 28 countries, with over 30 million copies sold in a century. Quite a record!

Meanwhile, the search continues... Looking for a delicious pot-au-feu in a typical Parisian bistro, or a soothing bowl of congee in Hong Kong? The Michelin Man continues to span the globe making new discoveries and selecting the very best the culinary world has to offer!

從前，在法國中部⋯⋯

這一切始於1889年，米芝蓮兄弟在法國克萊蒙費朗 (Clermont-Ferrand) 創辦 Manufacture Française des Pneumatiques Michelin 輪胎公司 － 當年駕駛汽車仍被視為一大冒險。

在1900年，法國的汽車總數量少於3,000輛。米芝蓮兄弟靈機一觸，想到為道路駕駛的先驅提供含實用資訊的小指南，如補充汽油或更換輪胎，以至用餐和睡覺的好去處。米芝蓮指南就這樣誕生了！

指南的宗旨非常清晰：搜羅全國各地最好的酒店和餐廳。為達目的，米芝蓮招攬了一整隊神秘專業評審員，走遍全國每一個角落尋找值得推介的酒店和餐廳，這在當時是前所未有的創舉。

多年來，崎嶇不平的道路早已被平順的高速公路取代，米芝蓮公司持續茁壯成長。同時間，全國各地餐飲業的發展亦一日千里：廚子成為大廚、傳統手藝成為藝術，傳統菜餚亦轉化成為藝術傑作。現今米芝蓮指南已成為廣受信賴的旅遊夥伴，不僅與時並進，更致力推動這些轉變。指南中最著名的是早在1926年面世，並迅即成為美食界權威指標的「星級推介」。

❋ ✿ ✿

由米芝蓮車胎人必比登為代言人的米芝蓮指南，不斷拓展其版圖，到1911年已覆蓋全歐洲。

2006年，米芝蓮指南系列成功跨越大西洋，授予紐約39家餐廳星級推介。在2007及2008年，米芝蓮指南在三藩市、洛杉磯和拉斯維加斯出版，2011年已拓展至芝加哥，米芝蓮車胎人必比登也正式落戶美國。

2007年11月，米芝蓮車胎人首次踏足亞洲，在東京廣發星級推介，以表揚日本料理的卓越成就，同時亦掀起美食熱潮。其後，旋即推出京都、神戶、大阪及奈良指南，並繼東京之後推出橫濱和湘南指南。香港和澳門指南亦於2009年推出。

2016年，米芝蓮車胎人更涉足新加坡和中國，推出首本米其林新加坡指南及米其林上海指南，令這本以紅色為標誌的指南，在遠東地區的覆蓋範圍更見廣泛。

時至今日，米芝蓮指南系列共計29本，涵蓋28個國家，一個世紀以來，總銷量超過三千萬。這是個令人鼓舞的紀錄！

此時此刻，我們仍然繼續對美食的追尋……是巴黎餐廳的美味雜菜鍋，還是香港令人窩心的粥品？米芝蓮車胎人將會努力不懈，發掘全球美食，為你們挑選最出色的佳餚美饌！

HOW TO USE
THIS RESTAURANT GUIDE
如何使用餐廳指南

Map number / coordinates
地圖號碼 / 座標

New entry in the guide
新增推介

Cuisine type
菜式種類

Name of restaurant
餐廳名稱

Stars for good food
美食星級
🟢 to 🟢🟢🟢

Bib Gourmand
(Inspectors' favourite
for good value)
車胎人美食推介
😋

Plate
米芝蓮餐盤
🍽️

Restaurant classification
according to comfort
餐廳 — 以舒適程度分類
Particularly pleasant if in red
紅色代表上佳

🍽️	Simple shop 簡單的食店
X	Quite comfortable 頗舒適
XX	Comfortable 舒適
XXX	Very comfortable 十分舒適
XXXX	Top class comfort 高級舒適
XXXXX	Luxury 豪華

●CANTONESE 粵菜   MAP 地圖 16/B-1

Yuet Lai Shun Ⓝ
粵來順

Ceiling fans, window grilles, booth seats and faux-marble tables are reminiscent of the good old cha chaan teng in Hong Kong circa 1960s. The décor also chimes with the food it serves – retro Cantonese classics that are well-made and reasonably priced. Chicken poached in honey soy stands out, with juicy velvety meat and well-balanced sauce. Deep-fried shrimp balls with cheese filling and pork lung almond milk soup are among diners' favourites.

吊扇加鐵窗花、帶點茶餐廳味道的雲石方桌卡座，裝潢一如六、七十年代的酒樓，很有老香港風情。與其裝潢一樣，這兒主打的就是懷舊廣東菜。蜂蜜豉油雞，肉質嫩滑，與以蝦膠芝士作餡料的千絲芝心球和生磨杏汁白肺湯同屬招牌菜。

TEL. 2788 3078
Shop 10-12, GF Po Hang Building,
2-8 Dundas Street, Mong Kok
旺角登打士街 2-8號寶亨大廈地下 10-12號舖

SPECIALITIES TO PRE-ORDER 預訂食物
Double-boiled pork lung and almond milk soup 生磨杏汁白肺湯 /Steamed crab roe with glutinous rice in lotus leaf 蟳仔荷香糯米蒸蟹

■ PRICE 價錢
Lunch 午膳
set 套餐 $ 42-50
à la carte 點菜 $ 100-200
Dinner 晚膳
à la carte 點菜 $ 200-300

● OPENING HOURS 營業時間
11:30-23:00 (L.O.)

283

Restaurant symbols
餐廳標誌

CANTONESE 粵菜   MAP 地圖   31/C-2

Yee Tung Heen 怡東軒   🏵️

XXX   ⚅ 🅿 ⊕96 ☎⃠ 🍷

The first thing you'll notice is the Chinese ornaments and the second is how well Chinese screens and contemporary lighting go together. This elegant restaurant not only offers traditional Cantonese favourites but also serves specialities of a more creative persuasion. The enthusiastic chef and his team spend much time seeking out the best quality seasonal ingredients, whether that's from local markets or overseas.

踏入怡東酒店內的怡東軒中菜廳，馬上便會給精緻的中式擺設吸引。往內走，會發現四周的中式屏風與現代天花燈，配搭得十分別致。餐廳供應傳統粵菜，廚師及營運團隊充滿熱誠，專程由本地及世界各地搜羅各種高質素及時令食材，時有創新菜式或特別餐單推出。

TEL. 2837 6790
2F, The Excelsior Hotel,
281 Gloucester Road, Causeway Bay
銅鑼灣告士打道 281 號怡東酒店 2 樓

SPECIALITIES TO PRE-ORDER 預訂食物
Baked traditional salt-crusted chicken with
Chinese wine 古法酒香鹽焗雞

■ PRICE 價錢
Lunch 午膳
à la carte 點菜 $ 200-500
Dinner 晚膳
à la carte 點菜 $ 400-800

■ OPENING HOURS 營業時間
Lunch 午膳   12:00-14:30 (L.O.)
Dinner 晚膳   18:00-22:30 (L.O.)

💲	Cash only	只接受現金
♿	Wheelchair access	輪椅通道
⛱	Terrace dining	陽台用餐
<	Interesting view	上佳景觀
🛎	Valet parking	代客泊車
🅿	Car park	停車場
⊡	Private room with maximum capacity	私人廂房及座位數目
⊟	Counter	櫃枱式
☎	Reservations required	需訂座
☎⃠	Reservations not accepted	不設訂座
🍷	Interesting wine list	供應優質餐酒

HOW TO USE
THIS HOTEL GUIDE
如何使用酒店指南

Map number / coordinates
地圖號碼 / 座標

New entry in the guide
新增推介

Name of hotel
酒店名稱

Hotel classification
according to comfort
酒店 — 根據舒適程度分類

Particularly pleasant if in red
紅色代表上佳

🏠 Quite comfortable
頗舒適

🏠 Comfortable
舒適

🏠 Very comfortable
十分舒適

🏠 Top class comfort
高級舒適

🏠 Luxury
豪華

Restaurants
recommended in
MICHELIN Guide
米芝蓮指南內的推薦餐廳

MODERN 現代 　　　　　　　　　　　　　MAP 地圖　43/D-3

Wynn Palace
永利皇宮

Opened in 2016, with a striking flower motif and impressive pieces of art scattered around the vast hotel. Luxurious bedrooms are uncluttered, large and bright, with a Mandarin, Peacock or Gold theme; the caramel-coloured suites are also impressive. There's a host of dining choices, from noodles to steaks; show kitchens are a feature of several of the restaurants.

於2016年開業，以上萬朵花卉製作的巨型花卉雕塑、隨處可見的藝術作品，寬敞的酒店，典雅高貴。以橙、孔雀和金作主題陳設的豪華客房感覺整潔、寬敞及明亮，橙棕色作主調的套房尤為使人印象深刻。酒店內餐廳種類很廣，從簡單的麵食到高級的牛扒，一應俱全，開放式廚房似乎是這裏的餐廳特色。

TEL. 8889 8889
Avenida da Nave Desportiva, Cotai
路氹體育館大馬路
www.wynnpalace.com

🛏 = MOP 1,888-3,188
👥 = MOP 1,888-3,188
Suites 套房 = MOP 3,500-20,000
🍽 = MOP 220

Rooms 客房　845
Suites 套房　861

Cordis
康得思

The modern, luminous lobby of this 42-storey glass tower features contemporary Chinese paintings and sculpture – part of the collection of 1,500 pieces that you'll find dotted around the hotel. Good-sized rooms come with picture windows come with smart marble bathrooms and nice views. There's a pool on the top floor and an all-day buffet restaurant on the lobby floor.

康得思坐落於行人如鯽的旺角心臟地帶，連接地鐵站和購物商場。琉璃塔般的大樓高42層，不僅有科技發燒友夢寐以求的電子產品，還有超過1,500幅畫作、雕塑與裝置藝術品，是一個中國現代美術展覽館。客房的設計含蓄而時髦，窗外是五光十色的繁華市景；天台設室外恒溫游泳池，並有多間餐廳供客人選擇。

TEL. 3552 3388
555 Shanghai Street, Mong Kok
旺角上海街 555號
www.cordishotels.com/hong-kong

RECOMMENDED RESTAURANTS 餐廳推薦
Ming Court 明閣 ⏣⏣ ХуХу

♟ = $ 1,900-3,700
♟♟ = $1,900-3,700
Suites 套房 = $ 3,400-11,000
⛶ = $ 218

Rooms 客房 632
Suites 套房 32

Hotel symbols
酒店標誌

♿ Wheelchair access
輪椅通道

Interesting view
上佳景觀

Valet parking
代客泊車

P Car park
室外停車場

Garage
室內停車場

Non smoking rooms
非吸煙房室

Conference rooms
會議室

Outdoor/Indoor swimming pool
室外 / 室內游泳池

Spa
水療服務

Exercise room
健身室

Casino
娛樂場所

MICHELIN IS CONTINUALLY INNOVATING FOR SAFER, CLEANER, MORE ECONOMICAL, MORE CONNECTED... BETTER ALL-ROUND MOBILITY.

Tyres wear more quickly on short urban journeys.

TRUE!

You tend to accelerate and brake more often when driving around town so your tyres work harder!
If you are stuck in traffic, keep calm and drive slowly.

Tyre pressure only affects your car's safety.

FALSE!

Driving with underinflated tyres (0.5 bar below recommended pressure) doesn't just impact handling and fuel consumption, it will shave 8,000 km off tyre lifespan.
Make sure you check tyre pressure about once a month and before you go on holiday or a long journey.

Fitting **2 winter tyres** on my car guarantees maximum safety.

FALSE!

In the winter, especially when temperatures drop below 7°C, to ensure better road holding, all four tyres should be identical and fitted at the same time.

2 WINTER TYRES ONLY = risk of compromised road holding.

4 WINTER TYRES = **safer handling** when cornering, driving downhill and braking.

If you regularly encounter rain, snow or black ice, choose a **MICHELIN Alpin tyre**. This range offers you sharp handling plus a comfortable ride to safely face the challenge of winter driving.

MICHELIN

MICHELIN
IS COMMITTED

▶ MICHELIN IS **GLOBAL LEADER IN FUEL-EFFICIENT TYRES** FOR LIGHT VEHICLES.

▶ **EDUCATING OF YOUNGSTERS IN ROAD SAFETY,** NOT FORGETTING TWO-WHEELERS. LOCAL ROAD SAFETY CAMPAIGNS WERE RUN IN **16 COUNTRIES** IN 2015.

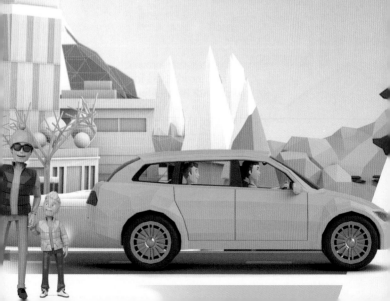

QUIZ

1 TYRES ARE BLACK SO WHY IS THE MICHELIN MAN WHITE?

Back in 1898 when the Michelin Man was first created from a stack of tyres, they were made of natural rubber, cotton and sulphur and were therefore light-coloured. The composition of tyres did not change until after the First World War when carbon black was introduced. But the Michelin Man kept his colour!

2 FOR HOW LONG HAS MICHELIN BEEN GUIDING TRAVELLERS?

Since 1900. When the MICHELIN guide was published at the turn of the century, it was claimed that it would last for a hundred years. It's still around today and remains a reference with new editions and online restaurant listings in a number of countries.

3 WHEN WAS THE "BIB GOURMAND" INTRODUCED IN THE MICHELIN GUIDE?

The symbol was created in 1997 but as early as 1954 the MICHELIN guide was recommending "exceptional good food at moderate prices". Today, it features on the MICHELIN Restaurants website and app.

If you want to enjoy a fun day out and find out more about Michelin, why not visit the l'Aventure Michelin museum and shop in Clermont-Ferrand, France:
www.laventuremichelin.com

HONG KONG
香港

RESTAURANTS
餐廳

STARRED RESTAURANTS
星級餐廳

Within this selection, we have highlighted a number of restaurants for their particularly good cooking. When awarding one, two or three Michelin Stars there are a number of factors we consider: the quality and compatibility of the ingredients, the technical skill and flair that goes into their preparation, the clarity and combination of flavours, the value for money and above all, the taste. Equally important is the ability to produce excellent cooking not once but time and time again. Our inspectors make as many visits as necessary, so that you can be sure of the quality and consistency.

A two or three star restaurant has to offer something very special that separates it from the rest. Three stars – our highest award – are given to the very best.

Cuisines in any style of restaurant and of any nationality are eligible for a star. The decoration, service and comfort levels have no bearing on the award.

在這系列的選擇裏,推薦的是食物質素特別出色的餐廳。給予一、二或三粒米芝蓮星時,我們考慮到以下因素:材料的質素和配搭、烹調技巧和特色、氣味濃度和組合、價錢是否相宜及味道層次。同樣重要的是該餐館的食物能恆常保持高水平。閣下對我們的推薦絕對可以放心!我們的評審員會因應需要多次到訪同一家餐館,以確認其食物品質恆常保持高水準。

二或三星餐廳必有獨特之處,比同類型其他餐廳更出眾。最高評級 – 三星 – 只會給予最出色的餐廳。

星級評定不會受到餐廳風格、菜式、裝潢陳設、服務及舒適程度影響。只要烹調技巧出色,食物品質特別優秀,都有機會獲得米芝蓮星星。

Exceptional cuisine, worth a special journey.
卓越的烹調，值得專程造訪。

Our highest award is given for the superlative cooking of chefs at the peak of their profession. The ingredients are exemplary, the cooking is elevated to an art form and their dishes are often destined to become classics.

獲得最高級別的餐館，其廚師的烹調技巧卓絕，選材用料堪稱典範，並將烹飪提升至藝術層次，菜式大多會成為經典。

Bo Innovation	XxX	Innovative 創新菜	71
L'Atelier de Joël Robuchon	XX	French contemporary 時尚法國菜	151
Lung King Heen 龍景軒	XxxX	Cantonese 粵菜	168
8 1/2 Otto e Mezzo - Bombana	XxxX	Italian 意大利菜	184
Sushi Shikon 志魂	X	Sushi 壽司	227
T'ang Court 唐閣	XxxX	Cantonese 粵菜	237

Excellent cooking, worth a detour.
烹調出色，不容錯過！

The personality and talent of the chef and their team is evident in the refined, expertly crafted dishes.

主廚的個人風格與烹飪天賦及其團隊的優秀手藝完全反映在精巧味美的菜式上。

Amber	XxxX	French contemporary 時尚法國菜	63
Caprice	XxXxX	French contemporary 時尚法國菜	77
Forum 富臨飯店	XX	Cantonese 粵菜	113
Kashiwaya 柏屋	XX	Japanese 日本菜	142
Pierre	XxxX	French contemporary 時尚法國菜	190
Ryu Gin 天空龍吟	XX	Japanese 日本菜	200
Shang Palace 香宮	XxxX	Cantonese 粵菜	207
Sun Tung Lok (Tsim Sha Tsui) 新同樂 (尖沙咀)	XxX	Cantonese 粵菜	223
Ta Vie 旅	XX	Innovative 創新菜	231

| Tin Lung Heen 天龍軒 | XXXX | Cantonese 粵菜 | 250 |
| Yan Toh Heen 欣圖軒 | XXXX | Cantonese 粵菜 | 271 |

High quality cooking, worth a stop!
優質烹調，不妨一試！

Within their category, these establishments use quality ingredients and serve carefully prepared dishes with distinct flavours.
此名單上的餐館，在同類型餐館中，其食材較具質素，烹調細緻用心、味道出色。

Ah Yat Harbour View (Tsim Sha Tsui) 阿一海景飯店 (尖沙咀)		XXX	Cantonese 粵菜	61
Akrame		XX	French contemporary 時尚法國菜	62
Arcane	ℑ	XX	European contemporary 時尚歐陸菜	65
Beefbar		XXX	Steakhouse 扒房	68
Celebrity Cuisine 名人坊		XX	Cantonese 粵菜	79
Duddell's 都爹利會館		XXX	Cantonese 粵菜	105
Épure		XXX	French contemporary 時尚法國菜	107
Fu Ho (Tsim Sha Tsui) 富豪 (尖沙咀)		XXX	Cantonese 粵菜	115
Guo Fu Lou 國福樓		XX	Cantonese 粵菜	125
Ho Hung Kee 何洪記		X	Noodles and Congee 粥麵	127
IM Teppanyaki & Wine		XX	Teppanyaki 鐵板燒	132
Imperial Treasure Fine Chinese Cuisine 御寶軒		XXX	Cantonese 粵菜	133
Jardin de Jade 蘇浙滙		XXX	Shanghainese 滬菜	137
Kaiseki Den by Saotome		XX	Japanese 日本菜	139
Kam's Roast Goose 甘牌燒鵝	℠		Cantonese Roast Meats 燒味	141
Lei Garden (Kwun Tong) 利苑酒家 (觀塘)		XX	Cantonese 粵菜	157
Lei Garden (Mong Kok) 利苑酒家 (旺角)		XX	Cantonese 粵菜	158
Lei Garden (North Point) 利苑酒家 (北角)		XX	Cantonese 粵菜	159
Loaf On 六福菜館		X	Cantonese 粵菜	164

Ⓝ   : New entry in the guide 新增推介

⤴   : Restaurant promoted to a Bib Gourmand or Star 評級有所晉升的餐廳

BIB GOURMAND RESTAURANTS
車胎人美食推介餐廳

This symbol indicates our inspectors' favourites for good value. These restaurants offer quality cooking for $400 or less (price of a 3 course meal excluding drinks).

車胎人標誌表示該餐廳提供具質素且經濟實惠的美食：費用在 400 元或以下（三道菜但不包括飲品）。

Ⓝ : New entry in the guide 新增推介

🍴 : Restaurant promoted to a Bib Gourmand or Star 評級有所晉升的餐廳

RESTAURANTS BY AREA
餐廳 — 以地區分類

Hong Kong Island 香港島

Admiralty 金鐘

Causeway Bay 銅鑼灣

N : New entry in the guide 新增推介

🔼 : Restaurant promoted to a Bib Gourmand or Star 評級有所晉升的餐廳

Sheung Wan 上環

Bibo	⑪○	XX	French 法國菜	70
Chan Kan Kee Chiu Chow (Sheung Wan) 陳勤記鹵鵝飯店 (上環)	⊕	X	Chiu Chow 潮州菜	81
Frantzén's Kitchen ⓝ	⑪○	XX	Scandinavian 北歐菜	114
Lin Heung Kui 蓮香居	⊕	🍴	Cantonese 粵菜	162
Moon Thai (Sheung Wan)	⑪○	X	Thai 泰國菜	178
Sun Yuen Hing Kee 新園興記	⊕	🍴	Cantonese Roast Meats 燒味	224
Sushi Shikon 志魂	✿✿✿ X		Sushi 壽司	227
Sushi Wadatsumi	✿	X	Sushi 壽司	230
Tate ⓝ	✿	XX	Innovative 創新菜	239
Tim's Kitchen (Sheung Wan) 桃花源小廚 (上環)	⑪○	XxX	Cantonese 粵菜	249
Upper Modern Bistro	⑪○	XX	French 法國菜	262

Tai Hang 大坑

IM Teppanyaki & Wine	✿	XX	Teppanyaki 鐵板燒	132

Tai Koo Shing 太古城

CIAK - All Day Italian	⊕	X	Italian 意大利菜	92

Tin Hau 天后

Shek Kee Kitchen 石記廚房	⊕	🍴	Cantonese 粵菜	209
Sister Wah (Tin Hau) 華姐清湯腩 (天后)	⊕	🍴	Noodles 麵食	216
Sushi Mori Tomoaki	⑪○	X	Sushi 壽司	226

Wan Chai 灣仔

Akrame	✿	XX	French contemporary 時尚法國菜	62
Atelier Vivanda	⑪○	X	Meat and Grills 烤肉小餐館	66
Bo Innovation	✿✿✿	XxX	Innovative 創新菜	71
Brass Spoon (Wan Chai)	⊕	🍴	Vietnamese 越南菜	74
Che's 車氏粵菜軒	⑪○	XX	Cantonese 粵菜	82
Chili Club 辣椒會	⑪○	X	Thai 泰國菜	84
Fook Lam Moon (Wan Chai) 福臨門 (灣仔)	⑪○	XxX	Cantonese 粵菜	112
Fu Sing (Wan Chai) 富聲 (灣仔)	⊕	XX	Cantonese 粵菜	117
Grand Hyatt Steakhouse	⑪○	XX	Steakhouse 扒房	123
Grissini	⑪○	XxX	Italian 意大利菜	124
Guo Fu Lou 國福樓	✿	XX	Cantonese 粵菜	125
Jardin de Jade 蘇浙滙	✿	XxX	Shanghainese 滬菜	137

Western District 西環

Kowloon 九龍

Cheung Sha Wan 長沙灣

Kwan Kee Bamboo Noodle (Cheung Sha Wan)
坤記竹昇麵（長沙灣）   🍴   Noodles 麵食   146

Hung Hom 紅磡

Qǐao Cuisine 巧饍坊		XX	Chinese 中國菜	195
Robatayaki 炉端燒	🍴O	X	Japanese 日本菜	199
Takeya 竹家			Japanese 日本菜	235
Wing Lai Yuen 詠藜園		X	Chinese 中國菜	267

Jordan 佐敦

Mak Man Kee 麥文記 **N**   Noodles 麵食   169

Yat Tung Heen (Jordan)
逸東軒（佐敦）   ✿   XX   Cantonese 粵菜   273

Yau Yuen Siu Tsui 有緣小敍   Shaanxi 陝西菜   274

Kowloon Bay 九龍灣

Lei Garden (Kowloon Bay)
利苑酒家（九龍灣）   🍴O   XX   Cantonese 粵菜   156

Siu Shun Village Cuisine (Kowloon Bay)
肇順名匯河鮮專門店（九龍灣）   X   Shun Tak 順德菜   217

Kwun Tong 觀塘

Dragon King (Kwun Tong)
龍皇（觀塘）   🍴O   XX   Cantonese 粵菜   103

Lei Garden (Kwun Tong)
利苑酒家（觀塘）   ✿   XX   Cantonese 粵菜   157

Lucky Indonesia 好運印尼餐廳   Indonesian 印尼菜   166

MIC Kitchen   ✿   X   Innovative 創新菜   174

Lei Yue Mun 鯉魚門

Hyde Park Garden
海德花園   **N**   🍴O   X   Seafood 海鮮   131

Kam Fai 金輝   **N**   🍴O   X   Seafood 海鮮   140

Mong Kok 旺角

Chuen Cheung Kui (Mong Kok)
泉章居（旺角）   X   Hakkanese 客家菜   90

Fung Shing (Mong Kok)
鳳城（旺角）   X   Shun Tak 順德菜   118

Good Hope Noodle (Fa Yuen Street) 好旺角麵家 (花園街)	⚉	占	Noodles and Congee 粥麵	122
Lei Garden (Mong Kok) 利苑酒家 (旺角)	✿	XX	Cantonese 粵菜	158
Ming Court 明閣	✿	XxX	Cantonese 粵菜	175
Yuet Lai Shun 粵來順 Ⓝ	⚉	占	Cantonese 粵菜	283

Prince Edward 太子

Ah Chun Shandong Dumpling 阿純山東餃子	⚉	占	Dumplings 餃子	60
Ju Xing Home 聚興家 Ⓝ	⚉	占	Cantonese 粵菜	138
Lan Yuen Chee Koon 蘭苑饎館	⚉	占	Cantonese 粵菜	150
Yung Kee 容記小菜王 Ⓝ	⚉	X	Cantonese 粵菜	284

Sham Shui Po 深水埗

Glorious Cuisine 增輝藝廚 Ⓝ	⚉	X	Cantonese 粵菜	120
Lau Sum Kee (Fuk Wing Street) 劉森記麵家 (福榮街)	ⅰ○	占	Noodles and Congee 粥麵	152
Thai Chiu (Sham Shui Po) 泰潮 (深水埗)	⚉	占	Thai 泰國菜	240
Tim Ho Wan (Sham Shui Po) 添好運 (深水埗)	✿	占	Dim Sum 點心	247

Tai Kwok Tsui 大角咀

Tim Ho Wan (Tai Kwok Tsui) 添好運 (大角咀)	⚉	占	Dim Sum 點心	248

Tsim Sha Tsui 尖沙咀

Above & Beyond 天外天	ⅰ○	XxX	Cantonese 粵菜	59
Ah Yat Harbour View (Tsim Sha Tsui) 阿一海景飯店 (尖沙咀)	✿	XxX	Cantonese 粵菜	61
Bostonian Seafood and Grill	ⅰ○	XX	Steakhouse 扒房	73
Celestial Court 天寶閣	ⅰ○	XxX	Cantonese 粵菜	80
Chesa 瑞樵閣	ⅰ○	XX	Swiss 瑞士菜	83
China Tang (Harbour City) 唐人館 (海港城)	ⅰ○	XX	Cantonese 粵菜	87
Come-Into Chiu Chow 金燕島	ⅰ○	XX	Chiu Chow 潮州菜	95
Cuisine Cuisine at The Mira 國金軒 (The Mira)	ⅰ○	XxX	Cantonese 粵菜	97
Din Tai Fung (Silvercord) 鼎泰豐 (新港中心)	⚉	X	Shanghainese 滬菜	100

New Territories 新界

Sai Kung 西貢

| Sai Kung Sing Kee 勝記 | ✿ | X | Seafood 海鮮 | 202 |

Sha Tin 沙田

Lei Garden (Sha Tin)

| 利苑酒家 (沙田) | ⵏ◯ | XX | Cantonese 粵菜 | 160 |

Sham Tseng 深井

| Yue Kee 裕記 | 🅐 | X | Cantonese 粵菜 | 282 |

Tseung Kwan O 將軍澳

| Tze Yuet Heen 紫粵軒 | ⵏ◯ | XX | Cantonese 粵菜 | 261 |

Tsuen Wan 荃灣

| Yin Yue 殷悅 | ⵏ◯ | XX | Cantonese 粵菜 | 277 |

Tuen Mun 屯門

Chinese Legend

廣東名門	Ⓝ	ⵏ◯	X	Cantonese 粵菜	88
Dragon Inn 容龍		🅐	XX	Seafood 海鮮	102
Hoi Tin Garden 海天花園	Ⓝ	ⵏ◯	X	Cantonese 粵菜	129
Yuè (Gold Coast) 粵 (黃金海岸)		ⵏ◯	XX	Cantonese 粵菜	280

Yuen Long 元朗

| Ho To Tai 好到底 | 🅐 | 🍜 | Noodles 麵食 | 128 |
| Tai Wing Wah 大榮華 | 🅐 | X | Cantonese 粵菜 | 232 |

RESTAURANTS BY CUISINE TYPE
餐廳 — 以菜式分類

Cantonese 粵菜

Above & Beyond 天外天	⑪○	XXX	Tsim Sha Tsui 尖沙咀	59
Ah Yat Harbour View (Tsim Sha Tsui) 阿一海景飯店 (尖沙咀)	✿	XXX	Tsim Sha Tsui 尖沙咀	61
Celebrity Cuisine 名人坊	✿	XX	Central 中環	79
Celestial Court 天寶閣	⑪○	XXX	Tsim Sha Tsui 尖沙咀	80
Che's 車氏粵菜軒	⑪○	XX	Wan Chai 灣仔	82
China Tang (Harbour City) 唐人館 (海港城)	⑪○	XX	Tsim Sha Tsui 尖沙咀	87
Chinese Legend 廣東名門 **N**	⑪○	X	Tuen Mun 屯門	88
Cuisine Cuisine at The Mira 國金軒 (The Mira)	⑪○	XXX	Tsim Sha Tsui 尖沙咀	97
Dragon King (Kwun Tong) 龍皇 (觀塘)	⑪○	XX	Kwun Tong 觀塘	103
Dragon Noodles Academy 龍麵館 **N**	⑪○	XX	Central 中環	104
Duddell's 都爹利會館	✿	XXX	Central 中環	105
Farm House 農圃	⑪○	XX	Causeway Bay 銅鑼灣	108
Fook Lam Moon (Wan Chai) 福臨門 (灣仔)	⑪○	XXX	Wan Chai 灣仔	112
Forum 富臨飯店	✿✿	XX	Causeway Bay 銅鑼灣	113
Fu Ho (Tsim Sha Tsui) 富豪 (尖沙咀)	✿	XXX	Tsim Sha Tsui 尖沙咀	115
Fu Sing (Causeway Bay) 富聲 (銅鑼灣)	㊛	XXX	Causeway Bay 銅鑼灣	116
Fu Sing (Wan Chai) 富聲 (灣仔)	㊛	XX	Wan Chai 灣仔	117
Glorious Cuisine 增輝藝廚 **N**	㊛	X	Sham Shui Po 深水埗	120
Golden Leaf 金葉庭	⑪○	XXX	Admiralty 金鐘	121
Guo Fu Lou 國福樓	✿	XX	Wan Chai 灣仔	125
Hoi Tin Garden 海天花園 **N**	⑪○	X	Tuen Mun 屯門	129
Imperial Treasure Fine Chinese Cuisine 御寶軒 **N**	✿	XXX	Tsim Sha Tsui 尖沙咀	133
Ju Xing Home 聚興家 **N**	㊛	🍜	Prince Edward 太子	138
Kwan Kee Clay Pot Rice 坤記煲仔小菜 **N**	㊛	🍜	Western District 西環	147
Lan Yuen Chee Koon 蘭苑饎館	㊛	🍜	Prince Edward 太子	150
Lei Garden (IFC) 利苑酒家 (國際金融中心)	⑪○	XX	Central 中環	155

N : New entry in the guide 新增推介

💱 : Restaurant promoted to a Bib Gourmand or Star 評級有所晉升的餐廳

Come-Into Chiu Chow 金燕島	◍	✗✗	Tsim Sha Tsui 尖沙咀	95
Pak Loh Chiu Chow (Hysan Avenue) 百樂潮州 (希慎道)	◍	✗✗	Causeway Bay 銅鑼灣	185
Pak Loh Chiu Chow (Times Square) 百樂潮州 (時代廣場)	◍	✗✗✗	Causeway Bay 銅鑼灣	186
Tak Kee 德記	Ⓝ	⌂	Western District 西環	234

Congee 粥品

Trusty Congee King (Wan Chai) 靠得住 (灣仔)	❀	⌂	Wan Chai 灣仔	255

Dim Sum 點心

Sheung Hei Dim Sum 囍囍點心皇	Ⓝ	⌂	Western District 西環	210
Tim Ho Wan (North Point) 添好運 (北角)	⌂	North Point 北角	246
Tim Ho Wan (Sham Shui Po) 添好運 (深水埗)	✿	Sham Shui Po 深水埗	247
Tim Ho Wan (Tai Kwok Tsui) 添好運 (大角咀)	⌂	Tai Kwok Tsui 大角咀	248

Dumplings 餃子

Ah Chun Shandong Dumpling 阿純山東餃子	⌂	Prince Edward 太子	60
Wang Fu (Central) 王府 (中環)	⌂	Central 中環	265

European 歐陸菜

Hugo's 希戈	◍	✗✗✗	Tsim Sha Tsui 尖沙咀	130

European contemporary 時尚歐陸菜

Arcane	❀	✿	✗✗	Central 中環	65
Café Gray Deluxe	◍	✗✗	Admiralty 金鐘	75
Felix	◍	✗✗	Tsim Sha Tsui 尖沙咀	109
Mandarin Grill + Bar 文華扒房+酒吧	✿	✗✗✗	Central 中環	171
Whisk	◍	✗✗	Tsim Sha Tsui 尖沙咀	266

French 法國菜

Bibo	◍	✗✗	Sheung Wan 上環	70
Cocotte	◍	✗	Central 中環	94
Gaddi's 吉地士	◍	✗✗✗	Tsim Sha Tsui 尖沙咀	119

Innovative 創新菜

Italian 意大利菜

Italian-American 美國意大利菜

Japanese 日本菜

Japanese contemporary 時尚日本菜

Korean 韓國菜

Malaysian 馬拉菜

Meat and Grills 烤肉小餐館

Middle Eastern 中東菜

Noodles 麵食

Noodles and Congee 粥麵

Shun Tak 順德菜

Sichuan 川菜

Singaporean and Malaysian 星馬菜

Spanish 西班牙菜

Steakhouse 扒房

Sushi 壽司

Xuan Sushi 玄鮨	⑩	✗	Central 中環	270

Swiss 瑞士菜

Chesa 瑞樵閣	⑩	✗✗	Tsim Sha Tsui 尖沙咀	83
The Swiss Chalet 瑞士餐廳 Ⓝ	⑩	✗	Tsim Sha Tsui 尖沙咀	245

Taiwanese 台灣菜

Qing Zuo 請坐 Ⓝ	㊐	🍴	Western District 西環	196

Tempura 天婦羅

Ippoh 一宝	⑩	✗	Central 中環	135

Teppanyaki 鐵板燒

IM Teppanyaki & Wine	✿	✗✗	Tai Hang 大坑	132

Thai 泰國菜

Chili Club 辣椒會	⑩	✗	Wan Chai 灣仔	84
Moon Thai (Sheung Wan)	⑩	✗	Sheung Wan 上環	178
Samsen 泰麵 Ⓝ	㊐	✗	Wan Chai 灣仔	203
Thai Chiu (Sham Shui Po) 泰潮（深水埗）	㊐	🍴	Sham Shui Po 深水埗	240

Vegetarian 素食

Kung Tak Lam (Causeway Bay) 功德林（銅鑼灣）	㊐	✗✗	Causeway Bay 銅鑼灣	145

Vietnamese 越南菜

Brass Spoon (Wan Chai)	㊐	🍴	Wan Chai 灣仔	74

Xinjiang 新疆菜

Ba Yi 巴依	㊐	✗	Western District 西環	67

RESTAURANTS WITH INTERESTING WINE LISTS
供應優質餐酒的餐廳

Ⓝ : New entry in the guide 新增推介

❦ : Restaurant promoted to a Bib Gourmand or Star 評級有所晉升的餐廳

RESTAURANTS WITH VIEWS
有景觀的餐廳

Ⓝ : New entry in the guide 新增推介

✿ : Restaurant promoted to a Bib Gourmand or Star 評級有所晉升的餐廳

quel cadre!

Looking for a taste of local life? Check out our top street food picks.
到哪兒尋找本土特色小食？請翻閱本年度的街頭小吃推介。

Read 'How to use this guide' for an explanation of our symbols, classifications and abbreviations.
請細閱「如何使用餐廳／酒店指南」，當中的標誌、分類等簡介助你掌握使用本指南的訣竅，作出智慧選擇。

STREET FOOD
街頭小吃

BRITISH CONTEMPORARY 時尚英國菜

MAP 地圖 24/B-2

Aberdeen Street Social

🍴 📶 🍽18 🕐🍷

It's now home to Hong Kong's creative industries but PMQ was originally built back in the '50s as Police married quarters. British chef Jason Atherton occupies two units inside, with a bar on the ground floor and a comfortable restaurant on the second which serves good looking modern dishes. From the private room you can look into the kitchen and admire the skills on show and from the small shop you can buy desserts, bread and chocolate.

原是已婚警察宿舍，獲列為三級歷史建築，保留下來後活化為現在的元創方。餐廳在靠近荷里活道那邊佔了兩層樓，地下是氣氛輕鬆的酒吧和露天座位，一樓是感覺舒適的餐室及一間能觀看廚房工作的私人房。精心炮製的時尚英國菜外形吸引。

TEL. 2866 0300
PMQ, 35 Aberdeen Street, Central
中環鴨巴甸街 35號元創方
www.aberdeenstreetsocial.hk

■ PRICE 價錢
Lunch 午膳
set 套餐 $ 158-288
Dinner 晚膳
à la carte 點菜 $ 550-850

■ OPENING HOURS 營業時間
Lunch 午膳　12:00-14:30 (L.O.)
Dinner 晚膳　18:00-22:30 (L.O.)

Above & Beyond
天外天

   ⛄30

HONG KONG 香港

When your restaurant has been designed by Sir Terence Conran, it's a racing certainty it will be a stylish place – and that is indeed the case here on the 28th floor of the Hotel Icon. What is somewhat unexpected is finding Cantonese food being served in such surroundings. Signature dishes include wok-fried sea cucumber with spring onion; crispy crab claw with shrimp mousse; and prawns with tangerine peel and fermented black beans.

由泰倫斯‧康爵 (Sir Terence Conran) 設計的唯港薈中菜廳，時尚典雅的酒吧大廳，是其一貫的設計風格，加上醉人的維港景致，叫人讚歎不已，臨窗的座位無疑是最佳選擇。在裝潢如此西化的餐廳，提供的是添有現代元素的粵菜，招牌菜包括陳皮豆豉炒蝦球、葱燒海參等。午市供應點心套餐。

TEL. 3400 1318
28F, Hotel Icon, 17 Science Museum Road,
East Tsim Sha Tsui
尖東科學館道 17號唯港薈 28樓
www.hotel-icon.com/dining/above-beyond

■ PRICE 價錢
Lunch 午膳
set 套餐 $ 198-298
à la carte 點菜 $ 250-2,100
Dinner 晚膳
set 套餐 $ 568-918
à la carte 點菜 $ 250-2,100

■ OPENING HOURS 營業時間
Lunch 午膳　11:00-14:30 (L.O.)
Dinner 晚膳　18:00-22:30 (L.O.)

Ah Chun Shandong Dumpling
阿純山東餃子

The shop has a traditional feel to it after renovation. Green wooden window frames on the wall are reminiscent of the old-time Hong Kong. Dumplings are handmade daily and only the freshest ingredients are used in the fillings. Try their most-ordered item lamb and Peking scallion dumplings. Or surprise yourself with the daily specialty, such as mackerel dumplings. Shandong roast lamb, meat pie and cuttlefish dumplings are also recommended.

翻新後的店子帶點傳統味道，牆上的綠色木窗框，很有老香港感覺。多款不同味道的傳統餃子以新鮮食材作餡料，每天在店內以人手包製，其中以京葱羊肉餃最受歡迎，此外，每日特色推介如馬鮫魚餃，常給顧客帶來驚喜！其他推介菜式還有山東紅燒羊肉和餡餅。最新推出的墨魚餃也值得一試。

TEL. 2789 9611
60 Lai Chi Kok Road, Prince Edward
太子荔枝角道 60 號

■ PRICE 價錢
à la carte 點菜 $ 30-100

■ OPENING HOURS 營業時間
11:00-22:30 (L.O.)

■ ANNUAL AND WEEKLY CLOSING 休息日期
Closed 6 days Lunar New Year and Wednesday
農曆新年 6 天及週三休息

Ah Yat Harbour View (Tsim Sha Tsui)
阿一海景飯店 (尖沙咀)

✗✗✗   ♿ ← 🛗 60 🔔

A large photo of chef-owner Yeung Koon Yat greets you as you come out of the lift – and he's enjoying his most famous dish: abalone. Ah Yat signature fried rice and stewed oxtail with homemade sauce and red wine casserole is also worth a try. The good value set lunch menu is a great way of experiencing many more of their Cantonese specialities. The contemporary dining room takes full advantage of the wonderful views; Table 11 is the best.

身處位於iSquare 29樓的阿一海景，當然要一嘗名廚老闆楊貫一的名菜：阿一鮑魚。此外，不妨試試其他馳名菜如一哥招牌砂窩炒飯及紅酒醬炆牛尾。飯店供應來自波爾多、加州、新西蘭和澳洲的高級紅酒。店內設有四間私人廂房，大部分座位都能欣賞宜人的維港兩岸美景，11號餐桌景觀最佳。

TEL. 2328 0983
29F, iSquare, 63 Nathan Road, Tsim Sha Tsui
尖沙咀彌敦道 63號 iSquare29樓

SPECIALITIES TO PRE-ORDER 預訂食物
Poached sliced fresh sea whelk 白灼響
螺盞 /Baked chicken filled with abalone matsutake mushroom and morchella mushroom 松茸羊肚菌吉濱鮮鮑魚焗雞 / Baked salty chicken 一哥鹽焗雞

■ PRICE 價錢
Lunch 午膳
set 套餐 $ 300-500
à la carte 點菜 $ 400-2,200
Dinner 晚膳
set 套餐 $ 800-1,500
à la carte 點菜 $ 400-2,200

■ OPENING HOURS 營業時間
Lunch 午膳   11:30-15:00 (L.O.)
Dinner 晚膳 18:00-22:30 (L.O.)

Akrame

✱

✗✗   ♿ ⊕10 ◐⚲

Chef Akrame Benallal turned his attention to Hong Kong after making his name in Paris. His eponymous, contemporary French restaurant comes in monochrome and is an understated yet comfortable space. The menus change monthly; if you decide on a set menu choose 3 or 4 courses at lunch and up to 8 courses at dinner. The emphasis is on seafood and the ingredients are sourced mainly from France. Sommeliers are on hand to recommend the best wine pairings.

總店設在巴黎的時尚法國菜餐廳,廚師Akrame Benallal選址船街開設香港分店, 室內空間以黑白色作主調,線條簡潔且具時尚魅力。午餐和晚餐均提供以海鮮 為主的套餐,大部分食材由法國購入,配合本地時令食材烹調,餐單平均每月 更新一次。你可讓侍酒師為你配搭餐酒用餐,饒有興味。

TEL. 2528 5068
9B Ship Street, Wan Chai
灣仔船街 9號 B
www.akrame.com.hk

■ PRICE 價錢
Lunch 午膳
set 套餐 $ 280-680
à la carte 點菜 $ 630-820

Dinner 晚膳
set 套餐 $ 888-1,188
à la carte 點菜 $ 630-820

■ OPENING HOURS 營業時間
Lunch 午膳   12:00-14:30 (L.O.)
Dinner 晚膳   18:30-22:00 (L.O.)

■ ANNUAL AND WEEKLY CLOSING 休息日期
Closed Monday 週一休息

Amber

❀❀

🌶🌶🌶🌶　　　♿ 🅿 ⬚16 📞🍴 ⚭

The cuisine of Dutch-born chef Richard Ekkebus is firmly rooted in classical French techniques but is made exceptional by its adventurous spirit and the quality of the ingredients, many of which come from Japan. The hanging ceiling sculpture, made up of over 3,500 copper tubes, provides a suitably striking backdrop to the cooking. The calm and comfortable restaurant is made more so by service that is well organised and detailed but also personable.

經Richard Ekkebus這位荷蘭廚師主理的菜式，糅合純熟的古典法國菜烹調技巧與大膽創新的精神製作而成，加上日本進口的食材，感覺就是與別不同。天花上懸着逾3,500條銅管，是充滿特色的美食之最佳陪襯。舒適的環境與組織嚴謹的服務，令食客倍感舒暢。

TEL. 2132 0066
7F, The Landmark Mandarin Oriental Hotel,
15 Queen's Road Central, Central
中環皇后大道中15號置地文華東方酒店 7樓
www.amberhongkong.com

■ PRICE 價錢
Lunch 午膳
set 套餐 $ 618-2,138
Weekend set 週末套餐 $ 1,028
à la carte 點菜 $ 1,600-2,500

Dinner 晚膳
set 套餐 $ 1,598-2,138
à la carte 點菜 $ 1,600-2,500

■ OPENING HOURS 營業時間
Lunch 午膳　12:00-14:30 (L.O.)
Public Holiday lunch 公眾假期午膳
12:00-14:00 (L.O.)
Dinner 晚膳　18:30-22:30 (L.O.)

HONG KONG 香港

Ancient Moon
古月

It was Singaporean and Malaysian street food enjoyed whilst travelling that inspired owners Fanni and Lico to open their fun little place. The small menu lists about 12 items and avoids serving the more standard dishes. Instead, it's one of the few places to offer Malaysian chilli pan mee (a flavoursome white noodles dish with dried fish and homemade chilli sauce) and Singaporean bak kut teh, made with pork ribs and garlic.

藏身於鬧市中，古月的位置確是有點隱蔽，你須從書局街進入方能找到。看着牆上帶有地方特色的卡通繪畫，不難猜中這裏提供的是星、馬兩地美食。餐單貴精不貴多，當中多是在香港較少見，甚或是首家供應的菜式，包括以胡椒和生蒜作湯底的星加坡肉骨茶及配自製辣椒乾進食非常惹味的馬來西亞板麵等。

TEL. 3568 4530
29A, Kam Ping Street, North Point
北角錦屏街 29號 A舖

■ PRICE 價錢
Lunch 午膳
set 套餐 $ 50-80
à la carte 點菜 $ 50-100
Dinner 晚膳
à la carte 點菜 $ 50-100

■ OPENING HOURS 營業時間
12:00-21:30 (L.O.)

■ ANNUAL AND WEEKLY CLOSING 休息日期
Closed 5 days Lunar New Year and Sunday 農曆新年 5 天及週日休息

Arcane

❀

🍴🍴 　　　　　　　　　　🛆 🕐🍷 ꙮ

Aussie chef Shane Osborn lets diners witness how quality ingredients turn into artistic culinary creations in the open kitchen. Simple recipes are done with a refined edge which allows authentic flavours to shine through. The affable manager and sommelier is more than happy to pair your food with their extensive cellar covering Europe, Oceania, Americas and a particularly lavish Burgundy selection.

開放式廚房讓食客能注視主廚Shane Osborn烹調時的專注、體會他的熱情，以簡易方式烹調日本海鮮、澳洲牛肉、意大利小牛肉和法國有機雞肉等食材，也反映了他對食材的尊重。經理兼紅酒總監的熱情招待，完滿了客人的用餐經驗，其挑選的餐酒涵蓋布根地、大洋洲和美國等地產物。

TEL. 2728 0178
3F, 18 On Lan Street, Central
中環安蘭街 18號 3樓
www.arcane.hk

■ PRICE 價錢
Lunch 午膳
set 套餐 $ 350
à la carte 點菜 $ 700-1,000
Dinner 晚膳
à la carte 點菜 $ 700-1,000

■ OPENING HOURS 營業時間
Lunch 午膳　12:00-14:30 (L.O.)
Dinner 晚膳　18:30-22:30 (L.O.)

■ ANNUAL AND WEEKLY CLOSING 休息日期
Closed Saturday lunch and Sunday
週六午膳及週日休息

MEAT AND GRILLS 烤肉小餐館

Atelier Vivanda

Akrame Benallal's third Atelier Vivanda was his first outside France and is in the same street as his eponymous restaurant. It specialises in meat – with an unlimited supply of potato – and, with chopping boards as tables, somewhat resembles a butcher's. Start with slices of 50-day matured beef and then try Black Angus flank or sirloin; chicken or duck breast; veal or pork rib – seasoned with a little salt and their own brand of peppered olive oil.

法籍廚師Akrame Benallal旗下法式概念小餐館，這是首家海外分店，以肉店作主題的砧板桌面、舊式切肉機及仿古羅馬款式餐刀，進餐時趣味頓添。其焦點有機草飼肉如黑安格斯牛、法國雞和鴨、伊比利亞豬肋骨，全以少許鹽及自家橄欖油調味後用紅外線爐烹煮。

TEL. 2109 1768
9A Ship Street, Wan Chai
灣仔船街9號A
www.ateliervivanda.com.hk

■ PRICE 價錢
Lunch 午膳
set 套餐 $298
à la carte 點菜 $350-1,000

Dinner 晚膳
set 套餐 $448
à la carte 點菜 $350-1,000

■ OPENING HOURS 營業時間
Lunch 午膳　12:00-14:00 (L.O.)
Dinner 晚膳　18:30-22:00 (L.O.)

■ ANNUAL AND WEEKLY CLOSING 休息日期
Closed Lunar New Year
農曆新年休息

Ba Yi
巴依

Lamb lovers will be glad they made the effort to find this somewhat out of the way Xinjiang restaurant. The special lamb dishes include traditional stewed lamb, roast leg and mutton skewers, with most of the meat being imported from Xinjiang. The handmade Xinjiang noodles are only available at lunchtime. The interior, dominated by a map of the Silk Route, has been refurbished and is now a little more up-to-date.

食店位置有點偏僻，但嗜羊的食客絕對不會後悔遠道而來。重新裝修後餐廳更富時代氣息，帶有標誌性的巨型絲路圖仍放置在店中央。大部分肉類均由新疆入口，羊肉特色菜包括手抓肉、烤羊腿和羊肉串燒等。三款新疆特色手打麵只於午餐時段供應。

TEL. 2484 9981
43 Water Street, Sai Ying Pun
西營盤水街 43號

■ PRICE 價錢
Lunch 午膳
set 套餐 $ 40-80
à la carte 點菜 $ 50-150
Dinner 晚膳
à la carte 點菜 $ 150-250

■ OPENING HOURS 營業時間
Lunch 午膳　12:00-14:30 (L.O.)
Dinner 晚膳　18:00-22:30 (L.O.)

■ ANNUAL AND WEEKLY CLOSING 休息日期
Closed 2 weeks Lunar New Year and Monday
農曆新年兩星期及週一休息

STEAKHOUSE 扒房

MAP 地圖　25/C-3

Beefbar

♿ 🪑20 ◐🍴

Gone are the days when restaurants had idiosyncratic names – now it's all about telling everyone what you do. Rare cuts of prime beef sourced from around the world are what this Monte Carlo based group, with branches around the world, offers. The room's design may use plenty of marble and leather but the style is more contemporary than masculine. The kitchen has a similarly light touch, which makes this steakhouse really stand out.

源自摩納哥的扒房在雪廠街開設的分店,是中環的新時尚熱點,主打頂級牛排:美國安格斯牛、澳洲安格斯牛、澳洲和牛及神戶牛,四大王牌牛肉、多種不同部位及一人或多人份量任你選擇。以白色雲石配搭黑色皮革裝潢的餐室別具型格。午餐供應六種主題各異的套餐,深得上班族喜愛。

TEL. 2110 8853
2F, Club Lusitano, 16 Ice House Street, Central
中環雪廠街 16號 Club Lusitano 2樓
www.beefbar.hk

■ PRICE 價錢
Lunch 午膳
set 套餐 $ 400-600
à la carte 點菜 $ 450-1,200

Dinner 晚膳
set 套餐 $ 800-1,200
à la carte 點菜 $ 450-1,200

■ OPENING HOURS 營業時間
Lunch 午膳　12:00-14:30 (L.O.)
Dinner 晚膳　18:30-22:30 (L.O.)

■ ANNUAL AND WEEKLY CLOSING 休息日期
Closed Sunday 週日休息

Belon

✕✕　　　　　　　　　🔲18　⚏　◑⍩

This neo-Parisian bistro has an understated décor because the chef wants the food and wine to be in the foreground. He rotates about 60% of the menu every week so that diners won't get tired of his offerings. Certain items can be ordered in flexible portions, customized to your party size. Precise and seamless service is another highlight – servers make every diner feel special by showing genuine interests in them without being pushy.

主廚一心專注於食材上，經他手處理的每道菜式都旨在突出食材原來的味道，並不會過於花巧。除特定菜式外，菜單上60%菜式會每星期更換一次。食物分量可隨食客的食量或人數而調校。優雅舒適的環境、親切利落且互動的服務，讓客人賓至如歸。

TEL. 2152 2872
41 Elgin Street, Soho, Central
中環蘇豪區伊利近街 41號
www.belonsoho.com

■ PRICE 價錢
Suncay lunch 週日午膳
set 套餐 $ 458
Dinner 晚膳
set 套餐 $ 888
à la carte 點菜 $ 700-1,100

■ OPENING HOURS 營業時間
Sunday lunch 週日午膳
12:00-14:30 (L.O.)
Dinner 晚膳　18:00-22:30 (L.O.)

■ ANNUAL AND WEEKLY CLOSING 休息日期
Closed Monday 週一休息

HONG KONG 香港

Bibo

🍴○

✕✕

🍽8 ◐🍷 ⊗⊗

As much an art gallery as a restaurant, Bibo serves modern French cuisine in remodelled 1930s heritage premises furnished with works by the hottest names in street and contemporary art such as Banksy, Basquiat, Murakami and Kaws. The exhaustive wine list is a fun read for connoisseurs. But before you get to appreciate the art, the food or the wine, you need to find the discreet button at the entrance that lets you in…

金色滑門後的樓梯通往這間感覺神秘、像藝廊般的餐廳。藝術品、街頭壁畫及雕塑遍佈整間餐廳。菜式結合傳統法國烹調藝術與世界不同地區食材，展現細膩且充滿時代感的法國風味。或許你的注意力也會隨着其他食客的目光一起遊走於藝術物件之上。

TEL. 2956 3188
163 Hollywood Road, Sheung Wan
上環荷李活道163號
www.bibo.hk

■ PRICE 價錢
Lunch 午膳
set 套餐 $ 280-380
à la carte 點菜 $ 650-1,500

Weekends & Public Holidays brunch
週末及公眾假期早午併餐 $ 680-780
Dinner 晚膳
à la carte 點菜 $ 650-1,500

■ OPENING HOURS 營業時間
Lunch 午膳 12:00-13:45 (L.O.)
Weekends & Public Holiday brunch
週末及公眾假期早午併餐 11:15-14:30 (L.O.)
Dinner 晚膳 18:30-22:15 (L.O.)

Bo Innovation

✿✿ ✿✿ ✿✿

🍴🍴🍴　　　　　　　　　　　　　🍽10　🚃　☂🍴　🎴

He may not have moved very far but in 2016 Alvin Leung found new, slightly bigger premises for his 'X-treme Chinese Cuisine'. It's an attractive space, with the decoration celebrating both the history of Hong Kong and important dates in the life of Alvin himself. What hasn't changed is his ambition and the highly imaginative and innovative cooking, which interprets traditional Chinese flavours in a bold, contemporary and theatrical way.

經過入口處以燈管砌成的地鐵路線圖，映入眼簾的是一幅由本地藝術家所繪、以香港過去重要事件為題的大型彩繪，加上各式本地特製的食具或古董，帶有濃濃的本土色彩。老闆兼主廚梁經倫熱衷為傳統食譜作全新演繹；餐廳大部分座位只供應套餐，只有吧枱座位的食客才能自選菜式。

TEL. 2850 8371
Shop 8, Podium 1F, J Senses,
60 Johnston Road, Wan Chai
灣仔莊士敦道 60 號
嘉薈軒一樓平台 8 號鋪
www.boinnovation.com

■ PRICE 價錢
Lunch 午膳
set 套餐 $630-800
Dinner 晚膳
set 套餐 $2,100-2,500

■ OPENING HOURS 營業時間
Lunch 午膳　12:00-14:00 (L.O.)
Dinner 晚膳　19:00-22:00 (L.O.)

■ ANNUAL AND WEEKLY CLOSING 休息日期
Closed 3 days Lunar New Year, Saturday
lunch and Sunday 農曆新年 3 天，週六午
膳及週日休息

Bombay Dreams

🍴🍴   📞🍽

Tucked away on the 4th floor of an unremarkable building is something of an institution – this Indian restaurant has been operating here since 2002. The jars of spices that line the shelves tell you this is a kitchen which takes spicing seriously. There's a great value lunch buffet but go for the à la carte for original, well-crafted dishes with an emphasis on northern India – specialities from the tandoor are a highlight.

這印度餐廳自2002年開始營業，雖然其位置不甚顯眼，卻一直不乏捧場客。一列列香料瓶置滿架上，說明了廚師對香料的重視。午市供應豐富的自助餐，如欲品嘗餐廳最出色、正宗的菜式，自選餐單是更佳選擇，以北印度泥爐炭火(Tandoor)烹調的菜式非試不可。

TEL. 2971 0001
4F, 75-77 Wyndham Street, Central
中環雲咸街 75-77號 4樓
www.diningconcepts.com

■ PRICE 價錢
Lunch 午膳
set 套餐 $158
à la carte 點菜 $200-400
Dinner 晚膳
à la carte 點菜 $200-400

■ OPENING HOURS 營業時間
Lunch 午膳   12:00-15:00 (L.O.)
Dinner 晚膳   18:00-23:00 (L.O.)

TREAT YOUR SENSES WITH EXQUISITE CULINARY MASTERPIECES

City of Dreams 新濠天地 • Studio City 新濠影滙 • Altira Macau 新濠鋒

MELCO RESORTS
& ENTERTAINMENT

EMBARK ON
A GASTRONOMIC JOURNEY

City of Dreams 新濠天地 · Studio City 新濠影滙 · Altira Macau 新濠鋒

MELCO RESORTS
& ENTERTAINMENT

Bostonian Seafood and Grill

      👨 💺 **P** 🍽16 🕐

The self-assured Bostonian is a handsome and sophisticated restaurant offering all the things you'd expect from an American restaurant: plenty of hearty salads, lots of lobster, oysters, assorted seafood and, of course, a huge choice of prime beef from the grill. The set lunch with the seafood buffet is particularly popular, as is brunch on a Sunday. It's unlikely anyone has ever left here still feeling hungry.

餐廳的高水準美食令人印象深刻，店內供應的菜式完全符合你對美式餐廳的期望；豐富的沙律和大量龍蝦、蠔及各類海鮮，當然少不了種類多樣的特級烤牛肉。在這裏進餐，沒人會空肚而回。這裏的半自助海鮮午市套餐及週日早午合餐非常受食客歡迎。

TEL. 2132 7898
BF, The Langham Hotel, 8 Peking Road, Tsim Sha Tsui
尖沙咀北京道 8號朗廷酒店地庫
www.langhamhotels.com/hongkong

■ PRICE 價錢
Lunch 午膳
set 套餐 $ 415
weekrnd set 週末套餐 $ 1,200
à la carte 點菜 $ 450-1,500

Dinner 晚膳
set 套餐 $ 628
weekend set 週末套餐 $ 1,200
à la carte 點菜 $ 450-1,500

■ OPENING HOURS 營業時間
Lunch 午膳　12:00-14:30 (L.O.)
Sunday lunch 週日午膳
11:00-14:30 (L.O.)
Dinner 晚膳　18:30-22:30 (L.O.)

HONG KONG 香港

Brass Spoon (Wan Chai)

The chef has barely had time to draw breath since he opened his small shop selling pho, Vietnam's national dish. He learnt to cook in France, where his family had a Vietnamese restaurant, and chose this small street to recreate the feeling you get when you come across a little ramen shop in Tokyo. He takes just 120 orders each day, uses US Angus beef and Danish pork and, for the noodles' soup base, slow-cooks beef shank bone for at least 16 hours.

這小小的越式河粉店選址於一條寧靜小街上，源於店東對日本街頭小巷拉麵店的嚮往。於法國學廚的主廚兼店東注重細節，湯底以牛小腿骨熬煮逾十六小時而成，確保味道濃郁；堅決不用味精、只選用最佳食材，如美國安格斯牛肉和自製麵條，且每日限量供應一百二十碗。種種堅持解釋了何以食客絡繹不絕。

TEL. 2877 0898
Shop B, GF, 1-3 Moon Street, Wan Chai
灣仔月街 1-3號地下 B鋪
www.thebrassspoon.com/

■ PRICE 價錢
à la carte 點菜 $ 90-220

■ OPENING HOURS 營業時間
12:00-18:45 (L.O.)

■ ANNUAL AND WEEKLY CLOSING 休息日期
Closed Sunday & Public Holidays
週日及公眾假期休息

Café Gray Deluxe

The fashionable Upper House hotel hosts this stylish bistro deluxe on its 49th floor and its great views, relaxed atmosphere and fluent, efficient service make it a very popular spot, especially at lunch. The kitchen uses plenty of modern techniques and adds its own twists to what are mostly European and American dishes. The speciality from consulting chef Gray Kunz is steak tartar ketjap. The restaurant also serves afternoon tea.

型格餐廳Café Gray Deluxe位處奕居酒店49樓，用餐的同時能欣賞維港的超凡美景，服務亦極為周到。新任的年輕主廚烹調技巧高超，在歐陸佳餚中混入獨特的材料變化，香草汁鮮茄車輪意粉、芥末汁牛小排等均值得一試。

TEL. 3968 1106
49F, The Upper House Hotel,
Pacific Place, 88 Queensway,
Admiralty
金鐘道 88號太古廣場奕居 49樓
www.cafegrayhk.com

■ PRICE 價錢
Lunch 午膳
set 套餐 $395-445
à la carte 點菜 $ 600-1,300
Dinner 晚膳
set 套餐 $725
à la carte 點菜 $ 600-1,300

■ OPENING HOURS 營業時間
Lunch 午膳   12:00-14:30 (L.O.)
Dinner 晚膳   18:00-22:30 (L.O.)

HONG KONG 香港

Café Hunan (Western District)
書湘門第 (西環)

The young Hunanese chef developed his skills while working in his
mother's restaurant and has a passion for the dishes of his home
town. To ensure authenticity he insists on using ingredients from
Hunan, like the different types of chilli and the smoked pickled
pork which is supplied directly by the farmer. Try the rich tasting
braised pork elbow – it involves 4 complicated stages and around
2 hours of cooking to get the texture just right.

廚師自小在母親的菜館幫忙，入廚經驗豐富。來自湖南的他對家鄉菜充滿熱
誠，最怕菜式不辣。此店大部分材料採購自湖南，如向農戶購買的煙燻臘肉及
各種辣椒，確保風味正宗。經四個工序以五個小時製作的霸王肘子，味道層次
豐富，紅黃二色辣椒蒸煮的鴛鴦魚頭王亦不遑多讓。

TEL. 2803 7177
420-424 Queen's Road West,
Western District
西環皇后大道西 420-424號

SPECIALITIES TO PRE-ORDER 預訂食物
Steamed fish head with diced red and
yellow pepper 鴛鴦魚頭王／Braised pork
elbow Hunan style 霸王肘子

■ PRICE 價錢
Lunch 午膳
set 套餐 $48　à la carte 點菜 $100-200
Dinner 晚膳
à la carte 點菜 $100-200

■ OPENING HOURS 營業時間
Lunch 午膳　11:00-14:30 (L.O.)
Dinner 晚膳　18:00-21:30 (L.O.)

■ ANNUAL AND WEEKLY CLOSING 休息日期
Closed 4 days Lunar New Year
農曆新年休息 4 天

Caprice

★ ★

♀♀♀♀♀   ♿ ◁ 🛏 🅿 🍽12 📞🍴 🎐

Supreme quality ingredients, classic French techniques and subtle Asian influences are the hallmarks of chef Guillaume Galliot's highly accomplished cuisine. Specialities include roasted pigeon with beetroot; crab laksa with confit egg; and 'Trilogie de Chocolat'. The handsome and comfortable room is run with considerable care and professionalism; you'll either enjoy stunning harbour vistas or a view of the chefs working in the raised open kitchen.

極高質素的食材、經典的法式烹調技巧及隱含的亞洲風味，是Guillaume Galliot的作品特色。招牌菜有烤乳鴿紅菜頭、蟹肉喇沙油封蛋黃及甜點朱古力三部曲。裝潢漂亮舒適的餐室、貼心及專業的服務，還有迷人海景與開放式廚房中的活潑氣氛，令進餐成為不一樣的享受。

TEL. 3196 8860
6F, Four Seasons Hotel,
8 Finance Street, Central
中環金融街 8 號四季酒店平台 6 樓
www.fourseasons.com/hongkong/
dining/restaurants/caprice/

■ PRICE 價錢
Lunch 午膳
set 套餐 ＄645-2,080
à la carte 點菜 ＄1,200-2,000
Dinner 晚膳
set 套餐 ＄1,320-2,080
à la carte 點菜 ＄1,200-2,000

■ OPENING HOURS 營業時間
Lunch 午膳 12:00-14:30 (L.O.)
Dinner 晚膳 18:30-22:30 (L.O.)

ITALIAN-AMERICAN 美國意大利菜 MAP 地圖 26/B-2

Carbone

🍴24 ☎🍴

As with the original Carbone in Greenwich Village, this colourful restaurant pays homage to the Italian-American eateries of the 1950s. Tiles, wood panelling, red armchairs and a counter bar all help to create that typical Manhattan feel. The menu features classics like Caesar salad, spicy rigatoni vodka and veal parmesan – and the regulars would never allow the meatballs to be removed. From the dessert trolley, choose the lemon cheesecake.

色彩明艷式樣懷舊的地磚、牆上的木窗框裝飾、懷舊天花、紅色扶手靠背椅和入口處的小吧枱，將你帶進五十年代的紐約。餐單以美國意大利菜為主，凱撒沙律、辣伏特加酒汁通心粉和肉丸等是招牌菜。餐後侍應會推着載有意大利芝士蛋糕、檸檬芝士蛋糕等甜品的餐車服務顧客。酒單上羅列的均是意國佳釀。

TEL. 2593 2593
9F, LKF Tower, 33 Wyndham Street, Central
中環雲咸街 33號 LKF Tower 9樓
www.carbone.com.hk

■ PRICE 價錢
Lunch 午膳
set 套餐 $ 388
à la carte 點菜 $ 480-1,200

Dinner 晚膳
à la carte 點菜 $ 480-1,200

■ OPENING HOURS 營業時間
Lunch 午膳 12:00-14:30 (L.O.)
Dinner 晚膳 18:00-23:30 (L.O.)
Friday and Saturday dinner
週五及週六晚膳 18:00-00:00 (L.O.)

■ ANNUAL AND WEEKLY CLOSING 休息日期
Closed Sunday lunch 週日午膳休息

Celebrity Cuisine
名人坊

XX P ⊟14 ⊙▯

Having just six tables and a host of regulars makes booking ahead vital at this very discreet and colourful restaurant concealed within the Lan Kwai Fong hotel. The Cantonese menu may be quite short but there are usually plenty of specials; highlights of the delicate, sophisticated cuisine include whole superior abalone in oyster sauce; baked chicken with Shaoxing wine and, one of the chef's own creations, 'bird's nest in chicken wing'.

這家隱藏於蘭桂坊酒店內的餐廳，看似不甚出眾但別具魅力，地方雖小卻常客眾多，故此必須提早預約。這裏的廣東菜餐牌頗為精簡，但全是大廚富哥的特選菜式，精美菜餚推介包括富哥頂級鮑魚、花雕焗飛天雞及自創菜式燕窩釀鳳翼。

TEL. 3650 0066
1F, Lan Kwai Fong Hotel, 3 Kau U Fong, Central
中環九如坊 3號蘭桂坊酒店 1樓

SPECIALITIES TO PRE-ORDER 預訂食物
Baked chicken with Shaoxing wine 花雕焗飛天雞 / Whole duck stuffed with eight goodies 八子全鴨

■ PRICE 價錢
Lunch 午膳
à la carte 點菜 $ 200-400

Dinner 晚膳
à la carte 點菜 $ 350-1,000

■ OPENING HOURS 營業時間
Lunch 午膳　12:00-14:30 (L.O.)
Dinner 晚膳　18:00-22:30 (L.O.)

■ ANNUAL AND WEEKLY CLOSING 休息日期
Closed 3 days Lunar New Year
農曆新年休息 3 天

CANTONESE 粵菜

Celestial Court
天寶閣

& 🖐 **P** 🛋96 ☎🍴

The room may be windowless but that at least puts the emphasis on the decoration – which features plenty of wood veneer – and, of course, onto the food. The chef has over 40 years of Cantonese culinary experience and also spent time in Japan – and his cooking is informed by his travels. Specialities include roasted whole suckling pig with pearl barley and black truffles; and deep-fried prawns with spicy termite mushrooms and crispy rice toast.

天寶閣位於喜來登酒店內，雖然餐室欠窗戶，但典雅堂皇的裝潢和具水準的菜餚足以彌補。主廚於不同粵菜餐廳和日本打拼超過四十年，遊歷於不同城市也豐富了他的創作，黑松露薏米燒釀乳豬和飯焦雞樅菌鳳尾蝦是其得意之作。

TEL. 2732 6991
2F, Sheraton Hotel, 20 Nathan Road,
Tsim Sha Tsui
尖沙咀彌敦道 20 號喜來登酒店 2 樓
www.sheratonhongkonghotel.com

SPECIALITIES TO PRE-ORDER 預訂食物
Roasted whole suckling pig, pearl barley,
black truffles, glutinous rice, Yunnan ham
黑松露薏米燒釀乳豬

■ PRICE 價錢
Lunch 午膳
set 套餐 $ 350-2,150
à la carte 點菜 $ 200-3,300
Dinner 晚膳
set 套餐 $ 650-5,850
à la carte 點菜 $ 200-3,300

■ OPENING HOURS 營業時間
Lunch 午膳　11:30-15:00 (L.O.)
Dinner 晚膳　18:00-23:00 (L.O.)

Chan Kan Kee Chiu Chow (Sheung Wan)
陳勤記鹵鵝飯店 (上環)

Ms Chan's grandfather set up this family business in 1948 in Sheung Wan; it moved to its current location in 1994 and was completely refurbished in 2010, when the kitchen was also expanded. Chiu Chow goose, cooked in a secret family recipe, remains the main event here, but there are other Chiu Chow specialities on offer such as pan fried baby oyster with egg, steamed goby fish with salted lemon, and double-boiled pig's lung and almond soup.

此店始創於1948年，由陳小姐的祖父於上環開創，1994年遷至現址，及後於2010年大規模翻新，除了廚房規模加以擴充，樓面亦一改容貌。以家傳秘方炮製的潮州鹵鵝仍然是招牌菜，另外還提供其他潮州特色美食，如潮州蠔仔粥、檸檬蒸烏魚和杏汁燉白肺湯等。

TEL. 2858 0033
11 Queen's Road West, Sheung Wan
上環皇后大道西 11號

SPECIALITIES TO PRE-ORDER 預訂食物
Chiu Chow crab 潮州凍花蟹 /Steam sliced
eel with plum in soy sauce 豉汁梅子蒸白鱔

■ PRICE 價錢
Lunch 午膳
set 套餐 $ 50-80
à la carte 點菜 $ 100-400
Dinner 晚膳
à la carte 點菜 $ 100-400

■ OPENING HOURS 營業時間
10:30-22:00 (L.O.)

■ ANNUAL AND WEEKLY CLOSING 休息日期
Closed 3 days Lunar New Year
農曆新年休息 3 天

HONG KONG 香港

Che's
車氏粵菜軒

🖐 🍽35 📵🍴

This unremarkable-looking little restaurant is popular with the local businessmen who come here in their droves for speedy service of the house speciality - crispy pork buns. But there are other reasons to visit: the dim sum at lunch; the extensive menu of classic dishes like crispy chicken or crab and dry scallop soup with bitter melon; simpler offerings such as congee or braised claypot dishes; and the blueberry pudding with which to end.

這家小餐館看似不起眼，但在本地商界人士間卻享負盛名，選擇豐富的經典粵菜如脆皮炸子雞，簡單卻美味的粥品和煲仔菜，還有午市點心，都使一眾食客趨之若鶩。服務快速且有效率，午餐時分往往座無虛席。

TEL. 2528 1123
4F, The Broadway,
54-62 Lockhart Road, Wan Chai
灣仔駱克道 54-62號博匯大廈 4樓

SPECIALITIES TO PRE-ORDER 預訂食物
Braised duck stuffed with eight types of delicacies 蓮子八寶鴨 /Baked chicken in rock salt 古法鹽焗雞

■ PRICE 價錢
Lunch 午膳
à la carte 點菜 $ 120-350
Dinner 晚膳
à la carte 點菜 $ 200-750

■ OPENING HOURS 營業時間
Lunch 午膳 11:00-14:30 (L.O.)
Dinner 晚膳 18:00-22:30 (L.O.)

Chesa
瑞樵閣

An imposing wood door leads into an intimate Swiss-style chalet with wooden objects left, right and centre – for over forty years this charming spot has played host to the cuisine of Switzerland. Traditional dishes sit alongside the cheese specialities: fondue moitié-moitié (gruyère and vacherin cheese fondue) or raclette du Valais (hot melted cheese with potatoes, pickled onions and gherkins). For dessert: chocolate fondue or Swiss chocolate mousse.

瑞士美食在香港佔一席位超過四十年。氣派莊嚴的木門後是親切的瑞士農舍，四處都有木製裝飾。傳統瑞士菜式與特選芝士系列互相輝映：瑞士芝士火鍋或瓦萊斯烤芝士(熱熔的芝士配馬鈴薯、醃洋葱及青瓜)。至於甜品，巧克力火鍋或瑞士巧克力慕絲是兩大必吃之選！

TEL. 2696 6769
1F, The Peninsula Hotel,
Salisbury Road, Tsim Sha Tsui
尖沙咀梳士巴利道半島酒店 1 樓
www.hongkong.peninsula.com/zh/
fine-dining/chesa-swiss-restaurant

■ PRICE 價錢
Lunch 午膳
set 套餐 $ 300-500
à la carte 點菜 $ 500-1,000
Dinner 晚膳
set 套餐 $ 1,000-1,800
à la carte 點菜 $ 500-1,000

■ OPENING HOURS 營業時間
Lunch 午膳 12:00-14:30 (L.O.)
Dinner 晚膳 18:30-22:30 (L.O.)

Chili Club
辣椒會

It's fair to say that customers aren't attracted to Chili Club by its looks. However, if you're strolling along Lockhart Road in search of sustenance you'll find yourself drawn inexorably into this Thai restaurant by the enticing aromas emanating from it. Proving further than one shouldn't judge by appearance, the kitchen is less preoccupied with presentation and instead focuses on delivering authentic and very satisfying flavours.

每次經過駱克道這幢大廈門前，都會嗅到陣陣香味，有時是混着椰香的泰式咖喱、有時是烤豬沙嗲的肉香。推門進去經過曲折的樓梯，是這家開業逾二十年的辣椒會。菜式雖無佳美的外形，卻有正宗而味道層次豐富的泰國風味。室內裝潢亦很簡樸，透過巨幅玻璃窗能一覽駱克道的繁華景象。

TEL. 2527 2872
1F, 88 Lockhart Road, Wan Chai
灣仔駱克道 88 號 1 樓

■ PRICE 價錢
Lunch 午膳
à la carte 點菜 $ 150-350
Dinner 晚膳
à la carte 點菜 $ 150-350

■ OPENING HOURS 營業時間
Lunch 午膳　12:00-14:30 (L.O.)
Dinner 晚膳　18:00-22:30 (L.O.)

Chilli Fagara
麻辣燙

The name will be known to all fans of Sichuan cooking as this is their second site and replaces the original one in Graham Street which closed in 2016. It's quite a large space and is moodily dark at night. Dishes are classified 'Ma', 'La' and 'Tang' according to their level of spiciness – it's best to end with a 'La' dish. Chilli crab always delivers, but you won't regret ordering the glazed beef with caramelised garlic and ginger-infused sauce.

店如其名，裝潢離不開火辣辣的紅色，昏暗的燈光，並沒影響食客在此品嘗美食的興致，為免白行一趟，請預訂座位。以麻、辣、燙作為分類的主餐單，供應的是辣度不同的四川小菜，建議從辣度較低的燙菜單開始，嗜辣者不妨挑戰一下辣菜單。麻菜單的霸王登格斯辣蟹和辣菜單的薑焗蒜片牛肉均不能錯過。

TEL. 2796 6866
GF, 7 Old Bailey Street, Central
中環奧卑利街 7 號地下
www.chillifagara.com

■ PRICE 價錢
Lunch 午膳
set 套餐 $ 108-168
à la carte 點菜 $ 200-400
Dinner 晚膳
à la carte 點菜 $ 300-500

■ OPENING HOURS 營業時間
Lunch 午膳　11:30-14:30 (L.O.)
Dinner 晚膳　17:00-23:30 (L.O.)

■ ANNUAL AND WEEKLY CLOSING 休息日期
Closed 4 days Lunar New Year
農曆新年休息 4 天

CHINESE 中國菜

China Tang (Central)
唐人館 (中環)

P ⇔24 ☾|

Decorated with a mix of traditional Chinese art and contemporary Western design, this handsome restaurant was conceived and designed by Sir David Tang as a sister to the London branch. Tables are set closely together and there are several private rooms. Dishes from Beijing, Sichuan and Canton feature and dim sum is popular. The most recently appointed chef hasn't tinkered too much with the menu, although he has introduced a more modern element.

由鄧永鏘爵士構思及設計，是其繼倫敦唐人館後又一傑作。人手刺繡的牆紙、獨特的鏡飾、古董燈飾及線裝中式排版菜譜，中式傳統藝術與西方美學結合得天衣無縫，流露出典雅貴氣。菜單涵蓋粵、京、川等地美食及精製南北點心：老北京傳統掛爐烤鴨、唐人館叉燒和琉璃蝦球等，滋味無窮。

TEL. 2522 2148
Shop 411-413, 4F, Landmark Atrium,
15 Queen's Road Central, Central
中環皇后大道中 15 號
置地廣場 4 樓 411-413 號舖
www.chinatang.hk

SPECIALITIES TO PRE-ORDER 預訂食物
Traditional Beijing roasted duck 老北京傳統掛爐烤鴨 / Hangzhou Vagabond chicken 火焰杭州富貴雞

■ PRICE 價錢
Lunch 午膳
à la carte 點菜 $300-1,000
Dinner 晚膳
à la carte 點菜 $800-1,200

■ OPENING HOURS 營業時間
Lunch 午膳 12:00-14:30 (L.O.)
Dinner 晚膳 18:00-22:30 (L.O.)

■ ANNUAL AND WEEKLY CLOSING 休息日期
Closed 3 days Lunar New Year
農曆新年休息 3 天

China Tang (Harbour City)
唐人館 (海港城)

In 2016 Hong Kong got its second China Tang, this time in Harbour City. A bar and lounge with pretty embroidery and chinoiserie fabrics leads into the colourful, comfortable dining room. Some appetizers are prepared by a chef from Hangzhou; traditional Beijing roast duck comes courtesy of a Beijinese chef. Recommendations include marinated shrimps with 'Hua Diao' wine, crystal prawns with lobster bisque, and wok-fried dried beef with onions.

唐人館在香港的第二家分店，同樣由鄧永鏘爵士設計。他巧妙地將歐陸式裝潢和中式元素融合，色彩繽紛的布料配搭優雅的花卉圖案，雅緻舒適。餐單以粵菜為主，也有南北點心、佐酒小食和大筒地爐端燒菜式；廚師團隊包括杭州的涼菜師傅和北京的烤鴨師傅。陳年花雕話梅蝦和琥珀水晶大蝦球值得一試。

TEL. 2157 3148
Shop 4101, 4F, Gateway Arcade,
Harbour City, 17 Canton Road,
Tsim Sha Tsui
尖沙咀廣東道 17 號
海港城港威商場 4 樓 4101 號舖
www.chinatang.hk

SPECIALITIES TO PRE-ORDER 預訂食物
Hangzhou Vagabond chicken 杭州富貴雞

■ PRICE 價錢
Lunch 午膳
à la carte 點菜 $ 300-800
Dinner 晚膳
à la carte 點菜 $ 400-1,000

■ OPENING HOURS 營業時間
Lunch 午膳　12:00-15:00 (L.O.)
Weekends & Public Holiday lunch
週末及公眾假期午膳　11:30-15:00 (L.O.)
Dinner 晚膳　18:00-22:30 (L.O.)

Chinese Legend
廣東名門

Located right opposite the seafood market, this popular glass-clad restaurant not only cooks the critters you get from the market, but also serves their own famous Cantonese roast meat, such as lychee wood-roasted goose, available in limited quantity daily. Despite its plain interior, antique pieces add some interest and there is even a stone grinder hidden underneath each round table.

門上刻有「廣東名門」的牌匾是店主從廣東運來，是菜館名字的由來。位處海鮮市場，客人會先購買海鮮，再拿到菜館前台的籃子量重並作記號。每晚都人頭湧湧輪候入座，不僅是為了烹調出色的海鮮，還為了以荔枝柴燻烤的各款燒味，如限量供應的荔枝柴燒鵝。店內有許多古董傢具，連圓形桌子底部都藏了一個石磨，煞是有趣。

TEL. 2955 1313
Shop 1, GF, Sam Shing Market,
Sam Shing Estate, Tuen Mun
屯門三聖村三聖市場 1 號地下
www.kingmen.com.hk

SPECIALITIES TO PRE-ORDER 預訂食物
Roasted duck with Lychee wood (Dinner only) 荔枝柴燒鵝（晚市供應）

■ PRICE 價錢
Lunch 午膳
à la carte 點菜 $200-300
Dinner 晚膳
à la carte 點菜 $300-400

■ OPENING HOURS 營業時間
11:00-22:00 (L.O.)

■ ANNUAL AND WEEKLY CLOSING 休息日期
Closed 1 day Lunar New Year 農曆新年休息一天

HONG KONG 香港

Chiuchow Delicacies
潮樂園

Walls covered in photos the chef took with celebrities speak loads about the popularity of this no-frills shop. Velvety goose meat steeped in its signature spiced marinade, baby oyster porridge, oyster omelette, and pork blood curd with chives keep the regulars coming. Sourced from a local fish farm, the fatty grey mullet is juicy but without a muddy taste. It also serves rare traditional Chiu Chow gems, such as raw marinated red ark clams.

簡樸的店子，牆上滿是東主與廚師和名人的合照，其受歡迎程度不言而喻。滷水汁的香料成分有特定比例，因此，每天供應的滷水食物味道絕無差異。不含味精的滷汁令鵝肉更嫩滑。採用的烏頭是元朗楊氏烏頭，帶黃油且沒泥味。還供應時下較罕見的潮式生醃蜊蚶。蠔仔粥、蠔餅及韭菜豬紅很受常客歡迎。

TEL. 3568 5643
GF, Ngan Fai Building,
84-94 Wharf Road, North Point
北角和富道 84-94 號銀輝大廈地下

SPECIALITIES TO PRE-ORDER 預訂食物
Cold crab in Chiu Chow style 潮州凍花蟹

■ PRICE 價錢
Lunch 午膳
à la carte 點菜 $ 40-150
Dinner 晚膳
à la carte 點菜 $ 100-250

■ OPENING HOURS 營業時間
11:00-22:30 (L.O.)

■ ANNUAL AND WEEKLY CLOSING 休息日期
Closed 3 days Lunar New Year
農曆新年休息 3 天

Chuen Cheung Kui (Mong Kok)
泉章居 (旺角)

This two-storey restaurant has been owned by the same family since the 1960s. It moved to this location in 2004 and has been jam-packed at night ever since. Diners line up to enjoy its traditional Hakkanese fare, including the unmissable salt-baked chicken and braised pork belly with dried mustard greens. The ground floor is smaller in size and rice plates that are less complicated to prepare are served there during lunch hours.

菜館自六十年代起一直由同一家族經營，直至2004年才遷至現址。雖然餐廳樓高兩層，但晚上經常座無虛席，門外排隊等候的客人，為的都是這裏的傳統客家菜，不能錯過的有鹽焗雞和梅菜扣肉。下層地鋪面積較小，下午時分主要供應烹調工序較簡單的碟頭飯。

TEL. 2396 0672
Lisa House, 33 Nelson Street,
Mong Kok
旺角奶路臣街 33號依利大廈

■ PRICE 價錢
à la carte 點菜 $ 100-300

■ OPENING HOURS 營業時間
11:00-23:15 (L.O.)

■ ANNUAL AND WEEKLY CLOSING 休息日期
Closed 4 days Lunar New Year
農曆新年休息 4 天

Chuen Kee Seafood
全記海鮮菜館

🍴　🛆　🍽50　📞🍴

Two family-run restaurants overlook a pleasant harbour to distant islands; choose the one with the rooftop terrace and the quayside plastic seats. An extraordinary range of seafood is available from adjacent fishmongers: cuttlefish, bivalve, crab and lobster, mollusc, shrimps, prawns…Go to the tank, select your meal, and minutes later it appears in front of you: steamed, poached, or wok-fried. Then settle back and watch the boats go by.

兩家相連的餐廳是家族生意，位置優越，可選擇有陽台的那一家，坐在碼頭邊的膠座椅上觀賞宜人海灣及離島景致。魚缸內的海鮮種類繁多，包括墨魚、貝類、蟹、龍蝦、瀨尿蝦、大蝦小蝦等等，任你隨意挑選。蒸、灼、炒也好，不一會就奉到餐桌上，然後你便可輕鬆地邊品嘗海鮮邊細覽海上景色。

TEL. 2791 1195
53 Hoi Pong Street, Sai Kung
西貢海傍街53號

■ PRICE 價錢
à la carte 點菜 $250-500

■ OPENING HOURS 營業時間
11:00-22:30 (L.O.)

HONG KONG 香港

CIAK - All Day Italian

Tai Koo Shing was the chosen location for the second CIAK, which opened its doors in 2016 – and, as the name suggests, rarely closes them. The Italian food is fresh and invigorating, with many of the ingredients imported from Italy; the bread and pasta really standout, as does the homemade sausage. Many of the dishes come in two sizes so you can try more things and there is also a takeaway counter.

CIAK的分店取名All Day Italian，並一如其名全日為食客提供意大利美食。餐廳特別注重食材品質，除了自製麵包和麵條，亦自行培養發酵用的酵母，所用的麵粉和礦泉水都由意大利進口，其中豬肉腸仔拼蘑菇芝士薄餅值得一試。大部分食物設小及正常兩種份量，讓食客多嘗幾道菜。設有外賣區。

TEL. 2116 5128
Shop 265, 2/F, Cityplaza,
18 Taikoo Shing Road, Tai Koo Shing
太古太古城道18號
太古城中心2樓265號舖
www.ciakconcept.com

■ PRICE 價錢
Lunch 午膳
set 套餐 $98-340
Weekend set 套餐 $280
à la carte 點菜 $150-500
Dinner 晚膳
à la carte 點菜 $150-500

■ OPENING HOURS 營業時間
11:30-21:30 (L.O.)

ITALIAN 意大利菜 MAP 地圖 25/C-3

CIAK - In The Kitchen

&   ⌖6   ⛽   ᠁

There are four sections to this casual eatery in the Landmark Atrium which comes courtesy of celebrity chef Umberto Bombana: the kitchen, bakery, charcoal grill, and pasta bar. The decoration is simple yet contemporary and the atmosphere is bustling and busy. The food focuses on the tastes of an Italian home and the produce is available to take away. Afternoon tea is popular.

此間以地道意大利市集風味作主題的餐廳，設計簡約時尚，置身其中猶如在家中般舒適自在，適合與三五知己共膳閒談。店內分為廚房、麵包店、炭燒食品及意粉吧四個區域，食客可以享受不同烹調風格的意大利家常美食。下午茶套餐格外受歡迎。

TEL. 2522 8869
Shop 327-333, 3F, Landmark Atrium,
15 Queen's Road Central, Central
中環皇后大道中 15 號置地廣場 3 樓
327-333號舖
www.ciakconcept.com

■ PRICE 價錢
Lunch 午膳
set 套餐 $ 298-358
à la carte 點菜 $ 300-400
Dinner 晚膳
à la carte 點菜 $ 600-700

■ OPENING HOURS 營業時間
Lunch 午膳　11:30-15:00 (L.O.)
Dinner 晚膳　18:30-22:30 (L.O.)

93

Cocotte

Tucked away on a quaint pedestrian street, Cocotte reinvents French classics with meticulous execution and the freshest seasonal ingredients. The brightly lit dining room has a modern Parisian feel to it, adorned by exquisite wallpaper, marble-topped tables and chairs covered in tweed and velvet. While the presentation is contemporary, traditional flavours underpin every recipe. Portion size is usually generous enough for sharing.

黑色鐵框玻璃門後是一個空間狹長的餐室。花俏的牆紙、雲石餐桌、橡木地板和綠色絲絨長沙發，創造出亮麗的環境與輕鬆的氣氛。喜歡法國菜的食客定會享受這裏的美食。廚師選用時令食材並以精細的烹調方式製作傳統菜，展現出時尚法國口味。分量較大的分享菜式，適合多人聚會，感覺更親密。

TEL. 2568 8857
9 Shin Hing Street, Central
中環善慶街 9號
www.cocotte.hk

■ PRICE 價錢
Lunch 午膳
set 套餐 $ 150-180
à la carte 點菜 $ 240-370
Dinner 晚膳
à la carte 點菜 $ 450-650

■ OPENING HOURS 營業時間
Lunch 午膳　12:00-15:00 (L.O.)
Dinner 晚膳　18:00-23:00 (L.O.)
Weekends & Public Holiday brunch
週末及公眾假期早午併餐　11:00-16:00 (L.O.)

Come-Into Chiu Chow
金燕島

HONG KONG 香港

The restaurant may have moved in 2014 but that hasn't stopped all the regulars coming along for their regular fix of Chiu Chow dishes. The team spirit of the staff, many of whom have been working together for over three decades, is clear to see and the restaurant itself has quite a grand feel and comes complete with assorted calligraphy and paintings. The standout Chiu Chow dishes include bird's nest and soyed meat such as goose web and wings.

餐廳在2014年遷至現址，共佔兩層，二樓有多間設備齊全的廂房，一樓的主餐室飾以書畫作品，裝潢甚具中式大宅氣派。由早年在星光行開業起，此店一直以高級潮州菜馳名，共事已久的員工默契十足，熟客也追隨至今。馳名潮州美食有燕窩菜式和滷味如滷水鵝掌翼。

TEL. 2322 0020
1F & 2F, Guang Dong Hotel,
18 Prat Avenue, Tsim Sha Tsui
尖沙咀寶勒巷 18號粵海酒店 1-2樓
www.come-into.com.hk

■ PRICE 價錢
Lunch 午膳
à la carte 點菜 $ 150-200
Dinner 晚膳
à la carte 點菜 $ 300-500

■ OPENING HOURS 營業時間
Lunch 午膳   11:00-14:30 (L.O.)
Dinner 晚膳 17:30-22:30 (L.O.)

■ ANNUAL AND WEEKLY CLOSING 休息日期
Closed 3 days Lunar New Year
農曆新年休息 3 天

HONG KONG 香港

Congee and Noodle Shop
粥麵館

Hidden in a glass-clad office tower, this simple shop has no ambiance or décor to speak of, but guests come for the creamy congee made by a chef with over 30 years of experience. Bestsellers include fresh crab congee and salted pork ribs congee with bitter melon. Regulars also customize with their favourite ingredients such as fish belly and beef. Expect to sit on plastic chairs and share a table with strangers.

隱藏在充滿藝術氣息的嘉里中心內，店內裝潢卻並不講究，食客全是慕粥品之名而來。為了品嘗逾三十年經驗老師傅精心炮製的傳統靚粥，客人都不介意坐塑膠椅及跟陌生人拼桌。暢銷粥品有原味蟹皇粥及涼瓜鹹排骨粥，但食客通常會自選配粥材料，如魚腩及牛肉等，魚片頭撈麵等麵食也是不錯的選擇。

TEL. 2750 0208
Shop 2A, 2F, Kerry Centre,
683 King's Road, Quarry Bay
鰂魚涌英皇道 683 號
嘉里中心 2 樓 2A 號鋪

■ PRICE 價錢
à la carte 點菜 $ 50-150

■ OPENING HOURS 營業時間
10:30-20:15 (L.O.)

■ ANNUAL AND WEEKLY CLOSING 休息日期
Closed 3 days Lunar New Year
農曆新年休息 3 天

Beast of the Green Hell.

The all-new Mercedes-AMG GT R. Handcrafted by Racers.
mercedes-amg.com/beastofthegreenhell

AMG

DRIVING PERFORMANCE

CANTONESE 粵菜

MAP 地圖　18/B-1

Cuisine Cuisine at The Mira
國金軒 (The Mira)

♿ 🍴 **P** ⟷44 ☎🍷 ⚬⚬

Striking crystal orbs hanging down from above make quite a statement at this stylish dining room on the 3rd floor of the equally fashionable Mira hotel. It'll come as little surprise to learn that the Cantonese cooking also comes with modern touches. Dim sum is good but to see the kitchen at its best try specialities like soft shell crab, pumpkin soup with winter melon, and Peking duck – given a twist with three flavoured pancakes.

這家充滿現代感的型格餐廳位於同樣時尚的The Mira酒店三樓，圓球狀的水晶吊燈引人注目，在此享受融入精巧現代元素的廣東美食，可謂相得益彰。午市供應精美點心，然而自選菜式更能體驗廚房的功力，東方夜明珠和芝麻桔子軟殼蟹都值得一試，北京片皮鴨兩食配以三款特色薄餅，口味創新。

TEL. 2315 5222
3F, The Mira Hotel, 118 Nathan Road, Tsim Sha Tsui
尖沙咀彌敦道118號 The Mira 3樓
www.themirahotel.com

SPECIALITIES TO PRE-ORDER 預訂食物
Roasted Peking duck served two ways
北京烤鴨（一鴨兩吃）

■ PRICE 價錢
Lunch 午膳
set 套餐　$ 250-300
à la carte 點菜　$ 400-2,500
Dinner 晚膳
set 套餐　$ 500-700
à la carte 點菜　$ 400-2,500

■ OPENING HOURS 營業時間
Lunch 午膳　11:30-14:30 (L.O.)
Sunday lunch 週日午膳　10:30-15:00 (L.O.)
Dinner 晚膳　18:00-22:30 (L.O.)

Da Ping Huo
大平伙

HONG KONG 香港

The Sichuan couple who founded this somewhat hidden restaurant have a more consultative role these days but their restaurant remains as charming and as popular as ever. An 11 course menu is offered at dinner; at lunch there is a 6 course menu plus an à la carte. The signature dishes include Da Ping Huo braised beef brisket and the special chilled rice noodles.

這家獨具魅力的餐廳由來自四川的王先生夫婦創辦。時尚典雅的餐室由本身是藝術家的王先生親自設計，曾為歌手的太太負責統籌廚房團隊的運作，為客人烹調正宗四川家常小菜。中午除了套餐外，還提供自選餐單，晚上則只供應十多道菜的套餐。

TEL. 2559 1317
LG, Hilltop Plaza, 49 Hollywood Road, Central
中環荷李活道 49 號鴻豐商業中心地下低層

■ PRICE 價錢
Lunch 午膳
set 套餐 $ 120
à la carte 點菜 $ 200-680
Dinner 晚膳
set 套餐 $ 380

■ OPENING HOURS 營業時間
Lunch 午膳 12:00-14:00 (L.O.)
Dinner 晚膳 18:30-22:30 (L.O.)

■ ANNUAL AND WEEKLY CLOSING 休息日期
Closed 3 days Lunar New Year 農曆新年休息 3 天

Din Tai Fung (Causeway Bay)
鼎泰豐 (銅鑼灣)

🍴   🛋14 ⊘🍽

Queuing can be a tiresome bind but occasionally the reward for waiting in line makes it worthwhile. Din Tai Fung's Xiao Long Bao are so terrific you'll find it hard not to re-order a second basket – and you can even watch them being made while waiting for a table. Other standouts are double-boiled chicken soup and braised beef brisket noodle soup. The place is bigger than the Tsim Sha Tsui branch and is run with impressive efficiency.

這間位於銅鑼灣的分店不但更摩登，而且佔地更廣，也同樣備受追捧，很多時都需要輪候入座。菜牌包括上海小菜與點心，小籠包是其重點所在。熱賣菜式有原盅雞湯與紅燒牛肉湯麵。飯店還為初次光顧的客人提供進食馳名小籠包的說明，非常周到。

TEL. 3160 8998
Shop G3-G11, GF, 68 Yee Woo Street, Causeway Bay
銅鑼灣怡和街 68號地下 G3-G11號舖
www.dintaifung.com.hk

■ PRICE 價錢
à la carte 點菜 $ 150-280

■ OPENING HOURS 營業時間
11:30-22:00 (L.O.)

■ ANNUAL AND WEEKLY CLOSING 休息日期
Closed 3 days Lunar New Year
農曆新年休息 3 天

Din Tai Fung (Silvercord)
鼎泰豐 (新港中心)

🍴

💬12 🚫🍴

Mr Yang opened up his dumpling shop in Taiwan back in 1958 and focused on delivering service, price and quality; there are now branches in all major Asian cities. Fresh, handmade Shanghai dumplings are their speciality and they are extremely good; the steamed pork ones being especially tasty. Queues are the norm here, but don't worry: a team of 130 smart and efficient staff serve at least 1000 people a day and take it all in their stride.

楊先生在1958年於台灣開辦首家小籠包店，特別注重服務、價格及品質；如今，在所有主要亞洲城市均有分店。新鮮、以人手炮製的上海小籠包是主打，餡料充足，令人食指大動。店前常擠滿排隊輪候的食客，由一百三十名員工組成的服務團隊非常有效率。

TEL. 2730 6928
Shop 130 & Restaurant C,
3F Silvercord, 30 Canton Road,
Tsim Sha Tsui
尖沙咀廣東道 30號新港中心 3樓 C130號舖
www.dintaifung.com.hk

■ PRICE 價錢
à la carte 點菜 $ 150-280

■ OPENING HOURS 營業時間
11:30-22:30 (L.O.)

■ ANNUAL AND WEEKLY CLOSING 休息日期
Closed 3 days Lunar New Year
農曆新年休息 3 天

Dong Lai Shun
東來順

The first Dong Lai Shun was founded in 1903 in Peking, and has been successfully transplanted to the basement of the Royal Garden hotel. Its décor is contemporary with distinct Asian nuances, panels and paintings; there's also a water feature which creates a relaxing atmosphere. The mix of Beijing and Huaiyang recipes includes hotpot, Peking duck and 'shuan yang rou': paper thin slices of Mongolian black-headed mutton.

餐廳的裝修揉合了現代和傳統格調；鮮明細緻的亞洲特色，從牆板和壁畫便可略知一二；人工噴泉替餐廳添了些閒適氣氛。食物方面，餐廳的北京和淮陽菜共冶一爐，包括火鍋、北京填鴨及涮羊肉：採用蒙古黑頭白羊的上乘部分，肉質薄如紙，軟如棉。

TEL. 2733 2020
B2F, The Royal Garden Hotel,
69 Mody Road, East Tsim Sha Tsui
尖東麼地道69號帝苑酒店地庫2樓
www.rghk.com.hk

SPECIALITIES TO PRE-ORDER 預訂食物
Roasted Beijing duck 烤北京填鴨 / Roasted chicken fillet with wild mushrooms and black truffles 黑松露野生菌烤雞柳 / Baked beggar's chicken 叫化雞

■ PRICE 價錢
Lunch 午膳
set 套餐 $120-300
à la carte 點菜 $200-700
Dinner 晚膳
set 套餐 $300-600
à la carte 點菜 $200-700

■ OPENING HOURS 營業時間
Lunch 午膳 11:30-14:30 (L.O.)
Sunday lunch 週日午膳 11:00-14:30 (L.O.)
Dinner 晚膳 18:00-22:30 (L.O.)

HONG KONG 香港

Dragon Inn
容龍

✗✗   ♿ 🅿 🪑72 ☎️🍴

This restaurant is known by almost everyone in the neighbourhood and was revamped in 2017 to include more private rooms alongside the main dining hall. Most guests pick their seafood from the nearby wet market for the chefs here to cook up; others choose from their catch of the day without looking at the menu. Baked baby lobster with cheese and baked oysters with port are not to be missed. It also serves dim sum during the day.

容龍海鮮酒家在本區可謂無人不曉，今年裝修後增添更多房間，讓客人可享私人空間。不少客人會自來海鮮加工，但個別食客完全不看主菜牌，而是直接從海鮮單上挑選食物。芝士焗龍蝦與砵酒焗生蠔是必然之選。日間有點心供應。

TEL. 2450 6366
Castle Peak Road, Miles 19, Tuen Mun
屯門青山公路 19 咪

■ PRICE 價錢
à la carte 點菜 $ 200-500

■ OPENING HOURS 營業時間
10:00-22:30 (L.O.)

■ ANNUAL AND WEEKLY CLOSING 休息日期
Closed 2 days Lunar New Year
農曆新年休息 2 天

Dragon King (Kwun Tong)
龍皇 (觀塘)

  ♿   **P**   ⊟60   ☏

Creative Cantonese dishes with a seafood slant are the draw at this contemporary dining room owned by famous local chef Wong Wing Chee. Standout dishes include Australian Tiger Jade abalone double-boiled with herbs, and Mantis prawns steamed in a bamboo basket. From time to time the chefs enter group culinary competitions to aid their cooking skills and creative thinking – the results can be seen in some of the more innovative dishes on the menu.

這家富現代感的中菜館，提供以海鮮為主的創新廣東菜式，東主為香港著名廚師黃永幟。在芸芸美食中，最出眾的有石決明燉老虎鮑和清蒸斑馬富貴蝦。所屬集團會定期舉行廚藝比賽，讓各分店主廚施展實力與創意，同時亦會將配搭新穎的得獎菜式上市供食客品嘗。

TEL. 2955 0668
2F, Yen Sheng Centre,
64 Hoi Yuen Road, Kwun Tong
觀塘開源道 64 號源成中心 2 樓
www.dragonkinggroup.com

SPECIALITIES TO PRE-ORDER 預訂食物
Australian Tiger Jade abalone double-boiled with herbs 石決明燉老虎鮑 /
Mantis prawns steamed in a bamboo basket 清蒸斑馬富貴蝦

■ PRICE 價錢
Lunch 午膳
à la carte 點菜 $ 80-100
Dinner 晚膳
à la carte 點菜 $ 150-200

■ OPENING HOURS 營業時間
Lunch 午膳 11:00-16:00 (L.O.)
Sunday & Public Holiday lunch
週日及公眾假期午膳 10:00-16:00 (L.O.)
Dinner 晚膳 18:00-23:00 (L.O.)

CANTONESE 粵菜

Dragon Noodles Academy
龍麵館

✗✗   ♿ 🅿 ⇌24 🚇 ☏🍽

The wooden dummies, weapon racks, lion dance heads and hand-carved golden dragon pay homage to Hong Kong pop culture and kung fu studios circa 1970s. Apart from noodles, such as the Lanzhou variety, one of the most-ordered items, it also showcases an array of Chinese cooking with the creative use of western ingredients and cooking techniques. Diners get to enjoy the performance of hand-pulling noodles in the open kitchen while sipping cocktails.

以70年代武館概念加中國特色陳設的裝潢：木人樁、兵器架、舞獅頭、手工雕刻金龍及舊式涼茶壺等，帶有濃濃的中國特色。菜式卻採用西化食材和加入了創新烹調風格，手打蘭州拉麵是常獲食客點選的食品。開放式廚房，讓拉麵師傅的製麵和拉麵絕技毫無保留地展現在食客眼前。店內還有供應雞尾酒。

TEL. 2561 6688
Shop G04, GF, Man Yee Arcade, Man Yee Building, 68 Des Voeux Road Central, Central
中環德輔道中68號萬宜大廈萬宜廊地下G04號舖
www.dragon-noodles.com

■ PRICE 價錢
Lunch 午膳
à la carte 點菜 $ 200-250
Dinner 晚膳
à la carte 點菜 $ 350-400

■ OPENING HOURS 營業時間
11:30-22:30 (L.O.)

SPECIALITIES TO PRE-ORDER 預訂食物
8 Treasure beggar's chicken 荷葉八寶富貴雞 / Wood-oven whole Peking duck 京城即燒片皮鴨

Duddell's
都爹利會館

❀

✕✕✕   ⇄24 ☏❚ ⅋

Not many restaurants come with their own 'Art Manager' but then Duddell's has always been about more than just serving food and hosts regular art exhibitions and screenings. The upstairs bar is a cool spot for a pre-dinner drink, while the restaurant itself is a stylish and contemporary space. In contrast to the surroundings, the Cantonese menu keeps things fairly traditional, with ingredients very much from the luxury end of the scale.

都爹利會館是少數設有藝術項目經理的餐館,除了專營傳統粵菜,餐館會定期舉行藝術展覽、電影欣賞和藝術沙龍等活動。閣樓酒吧宜於餐前歇息淺酌。主餐室布置時尚且風格獨特,餐牌上所見均是傳統菜式,選用的是高級矜貴食材。

TEL. 2525 9191
Level 3, Shanghai Tang Mansion,
1 Duddell Street, Central
中環都爹利街 1 號上海灘 3 樓
www.duddells.co

■ PRICE 價錢
Lunch 午膳
set 套餐 $ 380-680
à la carte 點菜 $ 450-1,000
Dinner 晚膳
set 套餐 $ 1,480
à la carte 點菜 $ 450-1,000

■ OPENING HOURS 營業時間
Lunch 午膳　12:00-14:30 (L.O.)
Dinner 晚膳　18:00-22:30 (L.O.)

HONG KONG 香港

Eng Kee Noodle Shop
英記麵家

For 23 years, this tiny shop has been feeding hungry locals with Cantonese soup noodles. The family business prides itself on its signature beef brisket – braised one night ahead and steeped in a spiced marinade overnight for silky tenderness and deep flavours. Instead of shoulder, their oven-grilled cha siu is made with pork neck, characterised by fine marbling, succulence and springiness. Most-wanted items also include deep-fried wantons.

開業23年，以住家風味的潮式和廣東麵食小吃作招徠。招牌牛腩以牛坑腩製作，每天晚上開始燜煮，以滷水浸泡一晚，開舖前再燜煮，確保牛腩軟腍入味。用焗爐烹調的自家製叉燒棄胸頭肉而取豬頸肉，因其肥瘦肉分佈的比例使油分均勻滲透，叉燒吃起來肉爽且多汁。淨牛腩、叉燒湯麵和炸雲吞最受食客歡迎。

TEL. 2540 7950
GF, 32 High Street, Sai Ying Pun
西營盤高街 32號地下

■ PRICE 價錢
à la carte 點菜 $ 40-110

■ OPENING HOURS 營業時間
09:00-18:30 (L.O.)

■ ANNUAL AND WEEKLY CLOSING 休息日期
Closed 7 days Lunar New Year 農曆新年
休息 7 天

Épure

✗✗✗   P ⛶18 ⬤ 𓎩

Avert your eyes as you approach or you'll be distracted by the temptations of the patisserie by the entrance – this elegant and strikingly decorated French restaurant deserves your full attention. To best experience the contemporary French cuisine, order the 6 or 8 course Chef's Inspiration Menu and let the kitchen decide what you're eating. Expect creative dishes like vol-au-vent with langoustine and a terrific Grand Marnier soufflé.

別讓入口前的糕點甜品分了心，法籍大廚精湛的烹調功夫絕對遠超你的期望。曾於各地星級餐廳工作的他選用法國時令食材，製作細膩味美的現代法國佳餚。點選含六或八道菜的廚師精選套餐，可以品嘗大蝦海鮮酥盒、干邑橙酒梳乎厘等創意菜式。半圓廂座適合浪漫約會，臨窗的餐桌則可欣賞如畫的維港美景。

TEL. 3185 8338
Shop 403, Level 4,
Ocean Centre Harbour City,
Canton Road, Tsim Sha Tsui
尖沙咀廣東道海港城海洋中心 4樓 403號舖
www.epure.hk

■ PRICE 價錢
Lunch 午膳
set 套餐 $ 368-568
Dinner 晚膳
set 套餐 $ 988-1,588
à la carte 點菜 $ 700-1,200

■ OPENING HOURS 營業時間
Lunch 午膳   12:00-14:30 (L.O.)
Dinner 晚膳   18:30-21:30 (L.O.)

Farm House
農圃

🍴○

✕✕

👐 🍽24 🕐🍴

HONG KONG 香港

Set in a sleek business building, this contemporary dining room has private rooms leading off it as well as an eye-catching aquarium running the entire length of one wall. A highlight of the Cantonese menu is the deep-fried chicken wing stuffed with glutinous rice, while other specialities include the baked sea whelk with goose liver, and steamed rice with abalone and dried chicken. Many of the ingredients are also available to buy.

飯店裝潢時尚，進門便可看到數間貴賓房和一個延伸整道牆的巨型水族箱，非常引人注目。農圃的粵菜選用特級新鮮材料炮製而成，著名菜式有古法糯米雞翼、鵝肝焗釀響螺和瑤柱鮑魚雞粒飯。飯店亦出售一些難於家中烹調的食物如鮑魚及海參。

TEL. 2881 1331
1F, China Taiping Tower,
8 Sunning Road, Causeway Bay
銅鑼灣新寧道 8號中國太平大廈 1樓
www.farmhouse.com.hk

■ PRICE 價錢
Lunch 午膳
set 套餐 $ 428-788
à la carte 點菜 $ 200-900
Dinner 晚膳
set 套餐 $ 428-788
à la carte 點菜 $ 200-900

■ OPENING HOURS 營業時間
Lunch 午膳　11:00-14:45 (L.O.)
Dinner 晚膳　18:00- 22:30 (L.O.)

Felix

There are views and there are breathtaking views – and the Peninsula's top floor restaurant certainly provides diners with the latter. That being said, your attention will be equally drawn to the room itself, which is magnificently futuristic and was designed by Philippe Starck. The inventive menus are a good match for the surroundings, with dishes cleverly blending European and Asian ingredients, albeit at prices as vertiginous as the views.

著名設計師Philippe Starck匠心獨運，讓半島酒店的頂樓餐廳盡顯不凡。廚房配合整體環境，運用現代技巧創作新穎精緻的佳餚。餐廳收費大概如酒店的裝潢令人目眩，但亦有提供收費合理的特惠晚餐時段菜單。全球只有少數餐廳能與之匹敵的醉人景色，與舞台般的室內設計完美配合。

TEL. 2696 6778
28F, The Peninsula Hotel,
Salisbury Road, Tsim Sha Tsui
尖沙咀梳士巴利道半島酒店 28樓
www.hongkong.peninsula.com/zh/
fine-dining/felix

■ PRICE 價錢
Dinner 晚膳
set 套餐 $ 400-1,800
Friday & Saturday set 週五及週六套餐
$ 1,000-1,800
à la carte 點菜 $ 700-1,750

■ OPENING HOURS 營業時間
Dinner 晚膳 17:30-22:30 (L.O.)

Fish School

& ⌷24 🚉 ◎🍴

There's an experienced team behind this small restaurant whose focus is locally sourced, top quality seafood offered at affordable prices – the only challenge facing the customer is finding its discreet entrance. The kitchen brings a modern sensibility to the cooking, while the infectious ebullience of the service team adds to the atmosphere of the room. The counter seats are best if you want to really feel part of the action.

由富經驗的廚師主理,他希望顧客能以不太高昂的價格嘗到高質素的海鮮,因此對食材也有些許堅持,例如只用本地漁獲,而且只用海魚等。如想多嘗幾款菜式,可點選有八道菜的Tasting Menu。喜歡觀看烹調過程的食客,不妨要求吧台座位。親切有禮的服務員會主動介紹菜式,令餐廳更富生氣。

TEL. 2361 2966
G/F, 100 Third Street, Sai Ying Pun, Western District
西環西營盤第三街 100號地舖
www.fishschool.hk/

■ PRICE 價錢
Dinner 晚膳
set 套餐 $ 750
à la carte 點菜 $ 300-900

■ OPENING HOURS 營業時間
Dinner 晚膳　18:00-22:30　(L.O.)

■ ANNUAL AND WEEKLY CLOSING 休息日期
Closed 3 days Lunar New Year 農曆新年休息 3 天

Fofo by el Willy

Fofo means 'chubby' and, judging by the look on the faces of the plump pig and penguin figures dotted around the room, therein lies contentment. For those eating here, three of the authentic Spanish dishes for each person, plus a little rice, should bring equal joy. The appealing tapas range from the popular suckling pig, which is slow-roasted overnight, to fried croquettes of Iberian ham and fried gambas with garlic and chilli. Try the roof terrace for even better views.

Fofo是圓胖之意。小豬與企鵝裝飾臉上滿足的表情，與店名非常相配。在這兒，每位食客能享用三道傳統西班牙菜和少許飯，那份滿足，非筆墨能形容。從以慢火通宵烤製的脆皮乳豬，到脆炸伊比利亞火腿丸子和蒜椒炸蝦等，全是令人垂涎的西班牙小菜。可選擇在屋頂露台用餐。

TEL. 2900 2009
20F, M88, 2-8 Wellington Street, Central
中環威靈頓街 2-8號 M88 20樓
www.fofo.hk

■ PRICE 價錢
Lunch 午膳
set 套餐 $268-298
à la carte 點菜 $300-600

Dinner 晚膳
à la carte 點菜 $300-600

■ OPENING HOURS 營業時間
Lunch 午膳 12:00-14:30 (L.O.)
Dinner 晚膳 18:00-22:30 (L.O.)

■ ANNUAL AND WEEKLY CLOSING 休息日期
Closed 3 days Lunar New Year and Sundays 農曆新年 3 天及週日休息

CANTONESE 粵菜

Fook Lam Moon (Wan Chai)
福臨門 (灣仔)

XXX   ♿ 🍷 🛋150 ☎️🍴

Run with considerable passion by the third generation of the same family, Fook Lam Moon is one of the best known restaurants around and attracts many regulars. Decoration of the two large dining rooms is based around a colour scheme of gold, silver and bronze which seems appropriate as there are so many luxury items on the menu. The respect for the ingredients is palpable and signature dishes include baked stuffed crab shell and roast suckling pig.

福臨門意指好運來到你家門，現由創業家族的第三代經營，是城中享負盛名的酒家之一，深受一眾食家愛戴。店內兩個大堂以金、銀、銅色系裝潢，映襯着菜單上的珍饈百味。食材明顯經過精心處理，招牌菜包括釀焗鮮蟹蓋與大紅片皮乳豬。

TEL. 2866 0663
35-45 Johnston Road, Wan Chai
灣仔莊士敦道 35-45號
www.fooklammoon-grp.com

SPECIALITIES TO PRE-ORDER 預訂食物
Barbequed suckling pig (whole) 大紅片皮乳豬全體 / Double-boiled whole chicken stuffed with bird's nest 上湯鳳吞燕

■ PRICE 價錢
Lunch 午膳
à la carte 點菜 $ 300-1,000
Dinner 晚膳
à la carte 點菜 $ 800-2,000

■ OPENING HOURS 營業時間
Lunch 午膳 11:30-14:30 (L.O.)
Dinner 晚膳 18:00-22:30 (L.O.)

■ ANNUAL AND WEEKLY CLOSING 休息日期
Closed 2 days Lunar New Year
農曆新年休息 2 天

Forum
富臨飯店

☪ 🍴48 ○🍽

★★

Everyone knows the name of Yeung Koon Yat, the owner chef of Forum; indeed, his signature dish of Ah Yat abalone has rapidly acquired iconic status and some have even been known to travel to Hong Kong from overseas just to try his delicacy. The new premises are more comfortable and contemporary than the old address and thankfully all the kitchen team made the move too. As well as abalone, you can try other options like pan-fried star garoupa.

各位對餐廳老闆楊貫一的大名一定不會陌生。多年來不論是本地食客或世界知名人士，全是他的座上客，其招牌菜阿一鮑魚更是天下聞名。此店搬至現址後，面積更廣、裝潢更豪華兼具時代感。滿有默契的幕後團隊聚首一堂為食客炮製美食。日本乾鮑製作的砂鍋鮑魚和海鮮類如生煎東星斑等均不可錯過。

TEL. 2869 8282
1F, Sino Plaza,
255-257 Gloucester Road,
Causeway Bay
銅鑼灣告士打道 255-257 號信和廣場 1 樓

■ PRICE 價錢
Lunch 午膳
set 套餐 $ 500
à la carte 點菜 $ 200-600
Dinner 晚膳
à la carte 點菜 $ 500-2,000

■ OPENING HOURS 營業時間
Lunch 午膳 11:00-14:45 (L.O.)
Sunday lunch 週日午膳
10:30-14:45 (L.O.)
Dinner 晚膳 17:30-22:30 (L.O.)

Frantzén's Kitchen

Bjorn Frantzén's first restaurant outside Sweden aims to bring Nordic cooking with an Asian influence to Hong Kong. He gave the head chef full autonomy on its concept, from the menu to the interior. A sleek but cosy warmth characterises the décor. Every course has a story to tell and matches perfectly with their exciting wine list and Scandinavian craft beers. Food comes in moderate portions so that diners can try more variety.

東主在瑞典以外首家海外分店，主打斯堪的納維亞菜，亦是本地暫時唯一一家供應該菜式的餐廳。每道菜式都是一個故事。廚師帶着對食材的尊重，以簡單的方式炮製美食，務使食客品嘗到食材的原汁原味，分量亦較少，讓食客可嘗試更多菜式。店內還供應斯堪的納維亞雞尾酒和手工啤酒。

TEL. 2559 8508
11 Upper Station Street, Sheung Wan
上環差館上街 11 號
www.frantzenskitchen.com

■ PRICE 價錢
Dinner 晚膳
à la carte 點菜 $ 600-1,000

■ OPENING HOURS 營業時間
17:30-00:00

■ ANNUAL AND WEEKLY CLOSING 休息日期
Closed Sunday and Monday
週日及週一休息

Fu Ho (Tsim Sha Tsui)
富豪 (尖沙咀)

 ⌕36 ◯❡

Thanks to its authentic cooking, diners have been coming to this Cantonese restaurant on a hidden floor of the Miramar shopping centre for over a decade. Among the specialities that appeal to these scores of regulars are the signature abalone dishes, the bird's nest with almond cream and the fried rice 'Ah Yung'. The most recent refurbishment gave this comfortable and relaxing restaurant a contemporary and elegant look.

這家粵菜酒家憑著正宗的烹調方式打響名堂，即使位於美麗華商場不太起眼的一層，十多年來依然吸引無數饕客。招牌菜有阿翁鮑魚、杏汁官燕、阿翁炒飯。布置時尚優雅，予人舒適悠閒感覺。

TEL. 2736 2228
Shop 402, 4F FoodLoft, Mira Place One,
132 Nathan Road, Tsim Sha Tsui
尖沙咀彌敦道 132號美麗華廣場一期
食四方 4樓 402號舖

■ PRICE 價錢
Lunch 午膳
à la carte 點菜 $ 250-1,500
Dinner 晚膳
à la carte 點菜 $ 600-1,500

■ OPENING HOURS 營業時間
Lunch 午膳　11:00-15:00 (L.O.)
Dinner 晚膳　18:00-22:00 (L.O.)

Fu Sing (Causeway Bay)
富聲 (銅鑼灣)

✗✗✗

🍽32 ⚫🍴

With its modern interior, attentive service and accessible location, it is little wonder that this large second Fu Sing restaurant has proved so successful. The dim sum selection is comprehensive and the prices are suitably appealing to allow for much over-ordering. Specialities include steamed crab in Chinese wine and soy sauce chicken in Fu Sing style, but we also recommend the garoupa with preserved vegetables and fish head soup in Shun Tak style.

富現代感的裝潢，細心的服務，加上地點便利，難怪這間富聲第二分店會如此成功！點心選擇多且價錢合理，除了招牌菜富聲花雕蒸蟹和鮑汁豉油雞外，甜菜三葱炒斑球及順德無骨魚雲羹同樣值得一試。何不多點幾道菜，與良朋好友共享美食？

TEL. 2504 4228
1F, 68 Yee Wo Street, Causeway Bay
銅鑼灣怡和街 68 號 1 樓
■ PRICE 價錢
Lunch 午膳
à la carte 點菜 $ 150-600
Dinner 晚膳
à la carte 點菜 $ 200-600

■ OPENING HOURS 營業時間
Lunch 午膳　11:00-14:30 (L.O.)
Weekend lunch 週末午膳　11:00-15:30 (L.O.)
Dinner 晚膳　18:00-22:30 (L.O.)

■ ANNUAL AND WEEKLY CLOSING 休息日期
Closed 2 days Lunar New Year
農曆新年休息 2 天

Fu Sing (Wan Chai)
富聲 (灣仔)

✗✗   ⛁40   ◔⏹

Located in a commercial building in Wan Chai, the dining room of Fu Sing is modern and benefits from having a glass roof. The service team are attentive and the cooking, with its broad repertoire of Cantonese dishes, is undertaken with equal care. Dim sum is recommended, as is fish head soup in Shun Tak style, soy sauce chicken Fu Sing style, and steamed crab in Chinese wine.

富聲位處時尚大樓之中，升降機可帶你直達這富麗堂皇、佔地寬廣的酒家，採用玻璃天花的餐室設計風格富現代感。侍應服務非常周到，選擇多元化的粵菜餐單，全屬精心炮製之作。除了點心以外，推介菜式包括順德無骨魚雲羹、富聲鮑汁豉油雞及花雕蒸蟹。

TEL. 2893 2228
3F, Sunshine Plaza, 353 Lockhart Road,
Wan Chai
灣仔駱克道 353號三湘大廈 3樓

■ PRICE 價錢
Lunch 午膳
à la carte 點菜 $ 130-600
Dinner 晚膳
à la carte 點菜 $ 200-600

■ OPENING HOURS 營業時間
Lunch 午膳　11:00-14:45 (L.O.)
Dinner 晚膳　18:00-22:15 (L.O.)

■ ANNUAL AND WEEKLY CLOSING 休息日期
Closed 2 days Lunar New Year
農曆新年休息 2 天

HONG KONG 香港

Fung Shing (Mong Kok)
鳳城 (旺角)

This family business has been going since 1954; and their story has been published along with assorted recipes. Owner-chef Mr Tam looks to the region of Shun Tak for inspiration for his tasty Cantonese cooking – must try dishes are stir-fried milk with egg whites and roasted suckling pig. The two-storey restaurant is always busy, so it's well worth booking in advance.

這個由家族經營的生意始於1954年，位於旺角的這家總店共有兩層，其歷史與部分食譜已輯錄成書出版。主廚兼老闆譚國景從順德菜中尋找烹調美味廣東菜的靈感，大良炒鮮奶及馳名燒乳豬絕對值得一試。

TEL. 2381 5261
1-2F, 749 Nathan Road, Mong Kok
旺角彌敦道 749號 1-2樓

■ PRICE 價錢
Lunch 午膳
à la carte 點菜 $ 100-350
Dinner 晚膳
à la carte 點菜 $ 150-350

■ OPENING HOURS 營業時間
Lunch 午膳 09:00-15:00 (L.O.)
Dinner 晚膳 18:00-22:30 (L.O.)

■ ANNUAL AND WEEKLY CLOSING 休息日期
Closed 4 days Lunar New Year
農曆新年休息 4 天

Gaddi's
吉地士

When you see the splendour of the room you understand why they insist on men wearing a jacket and tie. This paean to 'fine dining' really is the jewel in the Peninsula's crown and is home to a 17C Coromandel screen, a George Chinnery painting and Christofle candelabras brought over from Shanghai in the 1920s. The French menus have a classical base but cooking has a light, modern style with fine European ingredients flown in daily.

專用電梯把你帶到這個享譽數十載的餐飲傳奇食店，典雅餐室內盡是半島酒店的珍藏品——價值連城的17世紀科羅曼德屏風、George Chinnery畫作和1920年代從上海帶來的昆庭燭台，難怪男士須帶上一件西裝外套到此用膳。餐單上是融入了現代元素的傳統法國菜，上乘的材料每天從歐洲空運到港。

TEL. 2696 6763
1F, The Peninsula Hotel,
Salisbury Road, Tsim Sha Tsui
尖沙咀梳士巴利道半島酒店 1 樓
www.hongkong.peninsula.com/zh/
fine-dining/gaddis-french-restaurant

■ PRICE 價錢
Lunch 午膳
set 套餐 $ 500-900
à la carte 點菜 $ 1,000-3,500
Dinner 晚膳
set 套餐 $ 1,000-3,000
à la carte 點菜 $ 1,000-3,500

■ OPENING HOURS 營業時間
Lunch 午膳   12:00-14:30 (L.O.)
Dinner 晚膳   18:30-22:30 (L.O.)

CANTONESE 粵菜

Glorious Cuisine
增煇藝廚

🍴 🪑 14 ☎️🍽️

The live fish tank at the entrance is itself a spectacle – Hokkaido scallops, Thai marble goby, and even rare hanasaki crab if you're lucky, all to be cooked and served on your dining table. Apart from fish, the signature braised chicken stuffed with abalone and sea cucumber has also won the hearts of many. It is also worth pre-ordering their roasted-to-order suckling pig and chicken marinated in first-press soy sauce.

北海道帶子、泰國筍殼魚⋯⋯門外的魚缸內是來自各地的海鮮，幸運的話，或能吃到日本花咲蟹。曾經營賣雞生意的老闆，優勢在能取得新鮮食材。自創的鮑魚海參雞，以鮑魚和海參釀入雞中，煮後再把汁液浸雞，令其均勻入味，是他引以為傲之作。即燒BB乳豬及頭抽雞同樣受歡迎，每晚限量供應，需預訂。

TEL. 2778 8103
31-33 Shek Kip Mei Street,
Sham Shui Po
深水埗石硤尾街 31-33號

SPECIALITIES TO PRE-ORDER 預訂食物
Chicken stuffed with fresh abalone and braised sea cucumber 鮑魚海參雞 / Instant barbecue piglet 即燒 BB 乳豬

■ PRICE 價錢
à la carte 點菜 $ 200-300

■ OPENING HOURS 營業時間
18:00-01:30 (L.O.)

■ ANNUAL AND WEEKLY CLOSING 休息日期
Closed 3 days Lunar New Year
農曆新年休息 3 天

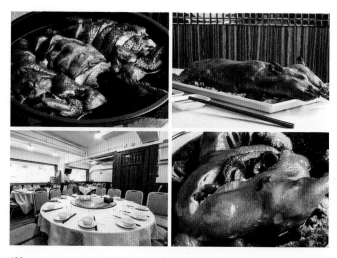

NEVER BLAND,
FOREVER BOLD.

UNCAGE
是敢的

Golden Leaf
金葉庭

Teak, rosewood, antique vases, lanterns and silks combine to make this very smart dining room as elegant as it is intimate. With no views to draw away your gaze, the Cantonese cuisine is allowed to take centre stage. Expect barbecued specialities like suckling pig, and pork with queen's honey, alongside seafood dishes like prawns in Chinese wine, and baked lobster with ginger. To dream of golden leaves is indeed a good omen.

金葉庭位於港麗酒店之內，飾以屏風、柚木樹、古董花瓶、燈籠和絲綢畫作的餐室，感覺高貴典雅。在充滿東方情調的環境下，客人可以享受一系列傳統廣東菜餚，太白醉翁鴿、化皮乳豬件、蜜糖汁叉燒都叫人垂涎不已。

TEL. 2822 8570
5F, Conrad Hotel, Pacific Place,
88 Queensway, Admiralty
金鐘道 88號太古廣場港麗酒店 5樓
www.conraddining.com

SPECIALITIES TO PRE-ORDER 預訂食物
Beggar's chicken 杭州富貴雞 / Poached
whole pigeon with soya sauce 豉油皇浸
乳鴿

■ PRICE 價錢
Lunch 午膳
set 套餐 $ 420-585
à la carte 點菜 $ 400-1,500
Dinner 晚膳
set 套餐 $ 558-800
à la carte 點菜 $ 400-1,500

■ OPENING HOURS 營業時間
Lunch 午膳　11:30-14:30 (L.O.)
Sunday lunch 週日午膳
11:00-14:30 (L.O.)
Dinner 晚膳　18:00-22:30 (L.O.)

Good Hope Noodle (Fa Yuen Street)
好旺角麵家 (花園街)

Mong Kok residents will know the name, as Good Hope Noodle has been around for 47 years, but now they have a more comfortable spot in which to enjoy their favourite dishes. The brightly lit dining room is neatly furnished with booths and tiles. Food is prepared in the open kitchen, with noodles, congee and snacks served all day. Try the distinctive flavour of Zha Jiang Mian (fried noodles).

好旺角麵家在旺角區開業至今四十七載，街坊對這名字一定不會陌生。新店以卡座為主，開放式廚房、光潔的牆身、地磚和明亮的燈光，為顧客提供了一個整潔的環境。店家全日供應粥品、粉麵和各式小吃。這兒的炸醬麵別具風格，不容錯過。

TEL. 2384 6898
18 Fa Yuen Street, Mong Kok
旺角花園街 18號

■ PRICE 價錢
Lunch 午膳
set 套餐 $ 55-66
à la carte 點菜 $ 40-80
Dinner 晚膳
à la carte 點菜 $ 40-80

■ OPENING HOURS 營業時間
11:00-00:45 (L.O.)

■ ANNUAL AND WEEKLY CLOSING 休息日期
Closed 3 days Lunar New Year
農曆新年休息 3 天

Grand Hyatt Steakhouse

Accessed via its own elevator, this decidedly masculine steakhouse is divided into three areas; the best spot is the moodily lit bar which has both counter seats and small tables for two by the windows. The prime cuts of beef are sourced from Canada, Nebraska and Japan; be sure to add the chunky chips cooked in duck fat to your order. The wine list contains a large selection of champagne. There is also a cigar room as well as smart private rooms.

顧客需乘搭專屬升降機到達這帶陽剛味的扒房，餐廳分為三個區，最佳位置在富情調的酒吧區，設吧枱座位及靠窗的二人桌。廚師深諳烹調肉類的法門，以來自加拿大、內布拉斯加和日本的特級牛扒作材料。別忘了點鴨油炮製的厚切薯條作配菜。酒單內含多款香檳，餐廳有多間設計優雅的私人廂房和雪茄房。

TEL. 2584 7722
MF, Grand Hyatt Hotel,
1 Harbour Road, Wan Chai
灣仔港灣道 1 號君悅酒店閣樓
www.hongkong.grand.hyatt.com

■ PRICE 價錢
Dinner 晚膳
à la carte 點菜 $480-2,200

■ OPENING HOURS 營業時間
Dinner 晚膳　18:00-22:30 (L.O.)

Grissini

The young chef of this smart, candlelit restaurant hails from Italy's south but regions the length and breadth of his country are represented. There's also a good balance struck between traditional dishes, such as homemade pastas, and more innovative creations such as burrata with Mediterranean prawns and anchovies; homemade potato gnocchi with smoked provola cheese and crispy pork cheeks; and herb-roasted lamb loin with Neapolitan rice cake.

如欲在醉人夜景下享受燭光晚餐，這兒是必然之選。來自南意的年輕主廚除了帶來傳統的意國風味，亦不忘將自家風格和創作加到餐單中，部分菜式融合了地中海特色，如香草烤羊柳、地中海紅蝦配普利亞水牛芝士、自家製薯糰等。作為店名的Grissini麵包於午餐及晚餐時段新鮮焗製，水準毋庸置疑。

TEL. 2584 7722
2F, Grand Hyatt Hotel,
1 Harbour Road, Wan Chai
灣仔港灣道 1 號君悅酒店 2 樓
www.hongkong.grand.hyatt.com

■ PRICE 價錢
Lunch 午膳
set 套餐 $ 468
à la carte 點菜 $ 450-900
Dinner 晚膳
set 套餐 $ 800
à la carte 點菜 $ 450-900

■ OPENING HOURS 營業時間
Lunch 午膳　12:00-14:30 (L.O.)
Dinner 晚膳　19:00-22:30 (L.O.)

■ ANNUAL AND WEEKLY CLOSING 休息日期
Closed Saturday lunch and Sunday
週六午膳及週日休息

Guo Fu Lou
國福樓

🚫 🧼 ⊟16 ◐♨

✕✕

Moving from the 31st floor of iSquare TST to the basement of a hotel in Wan Chai may have resulted in more space for the restaurant's celebrity clientele but there's been no change in the quality of the cooking. The chef demonstrates his respect for Cantonese cuisine by adopting traditional cooking methods as well as by using top quality ingredients. Try the baked stuffed crab shell or the fried lobster with black bean chilli sauce.

從尖沙咀iSquare遷至灣仔，國福樓或許不像昔日受關注，然而卻為一眾低調的名人食客帶來方便。環境雖稱不上瑰麗豪華，卻不失優雅舒適，設有多間廂房供私人宴會之用。廚師堅守以頂級食材精心烹調傳統粵菜的宗旨。釀焗鮮蟹蓋及豉椒炒龍蝦球是其得意之作。

TEL. 2861 2060
LG2, The Empire Hotel,
33 Hennessy Road, Wan Chai
灣仔軒尼詩道33號皇悅酒店LG2

SPECIALITIES TO PRE-ORDER 預訂食物
Roasted crispy goose 明爐燒鵝 / Deep-fried stuffed crab claw with shrimp paste 百花炸釀蟹鉗 / BBQ suckling pig 大紅袍乳豬 / Traditional baked chicken in rock salt 正宗鹽焗雞

■ PRICE 價錢
Lunch 午膳
set 套餐 $700-2,900
à la carte 點菜 $200-1,800
Dinner 晚膳
à la carte 點菜 $500-1,800

■ OPENING HOURS 營業時間
Lunch 午膳　11:00-14:30 (L.O.)
Dinner 晚膳　18:00-22:30 (L.O.)

■ ANNUAL AND WEEKLY CLOSING 休息日期
Closed 2 days Lunar New Year
農曆新年休息2天

SEAFOOD 海鮮

MAP 地圖 18/B-1

Hing Kee
避風塘興記

It started two generations ago in Causeway Bay but the family's reputation for Boat People style cuisine was made in Tsim Sha Tsui; further testimony comes from the celebrity signatures lining the walls. Elder sister heads the serving team; younger brother runs the kitchen. They are famous for their stir-fry crabs with black beans and chilli, roast duck and rice noodles in soup and congee. Guests aren't seated until everyone in the party has arrived.

由祖父輩創辦，原址在銅鑼灣，其後才遷到尖沙咀現址，主打的仍是避風塘特色小菜。現由第三代經營，服務團隊由大家姐領導，弟弟則主理廚房炊事。店內的牆上貼滿明星簽名，是此店名聞遐邇的明證。招牌菜包括避風塘炒蟹、燒鴨湯河及艇仔粥。座位有限，食客須人齊方能入座。

TEL. 2722 0022
1F, Bowa House, 180 Nathan Road,
Tsim Sha Tsui
尖沙咀彌敦道 180 號寶華商業大廈 1 樓

■ PRICE 價錢
Dinner 晚膳
à la carte 點菜 $ 300-700

■ OPENING HOURS 營業時間
Dinner 晚膳 18:00-02:30 (L.O.)

■ ANNUAL AND WEEKLY CLOSING 休息日期
Closed 2 days Lunar New Year
農曆新年休息 2 天

Ho Hung Kee
何洪記

HONG KONG 香港

No discussion about Hong Kong's historic noodle shops would be complete without mentioning Ho Hung Kee, which originally opened in Wan Chai in the 1940s and is famed for its springy wonton noodles and fresh, sweet soup. More elements have been added here at its new address – dim sum and some Cantonese dishes are now served too. For the interior, they've adopted a more contemporary, western style aesthetic.

要數香港歷史悠久的麵家，怎少得何洪記？此店自四十年代起在灣仔區營業，多年來其招牌雲吞麵憑着麵條彈牙、湯底鮮甜而口碑載道；其粥品也很出色。遷至現址後的新店，設計加入了不少現代西方元素，華麗而舒適。為滿足食客需求，增加了食物種類，除粥麵外，還供應點心和廣東小菜。

TEL. 2577 6028
Shop 1204-1205, Level 12, Hysan Place,
500 Hennessy Road, Causeway Bay
銅鑼灣軒尼詩道 500 號希慎廣場 12 樓
1204-1205 號舖

■ PRICE 價錢
à la carte 點菜 $ 100-200

■ OPENING HOURS 營業時間
11:30-22:45 (L.O.)
Weekends & Public Holidays
週末及公眾假期
11:00-22:45 (L.O.)

■ ANNUAL AND WEEKLY CLOSING 休息日期
Closed 2 days Lunar New Year
農曆新年休息 2 天

Ho To Tai
好到底

Traditional shops that make their own noodles from scratch are hard to come by. Founded in 1946, this household name is among the remaining few. The nostalgic two-storey shop has the quintessential Cantonese dumplings on the menu – the must-try wanton soup and fish skin dumplings. Those craving more carbs can order the hugely popular tossed noodles with shrimp roe. The owner also runs a dried noodle factory with retail outlets all over town.

自家製麵的傳統店舖愈來愈少,這家於1946年開業、位處元朗的老字號麵家是其中之一。樓高兩層的店舖內是濃濃的懷舊氣氛。蝦子撈麵和特製魚皮水餃向來是最受歡迎的食物,而雲吞更是非試不可!麵店附近設有製麵工場,店主同時在市區設立多個麵食銷售店,出售自製乾麵。

TEL. 2476 2495
67 Fau Tsoi Street, Yuen Long
元朗阜財街67號

■ PRICE 價錢
à la carte 點菜 $30-70

■ OPENING HOURS 營業時間
10:00-20:00 (L.O.)

■ ANNUAL AND WEEKLY CLOSING 休息日期
Closed 10 days Lunar New Year
農曆新年休息10天

Hoi Tin Garden
海天花園

One of the biggest and best known restaurants on the seafood street in Sam Shing, this three-storey establishment, complete with its own parking lot, has been in business for over 30 years. Seafood lovers travel from around town to shop for their favourite catch at the wet market nearby and ask their chefs to cook it up. Dim sum is served in the morning. A private room on the third floor caters to bigger parties.

位於三聖村海鮮街入口，稱得上是該處規模最大的酒家，樓高三層且設有停車場，街坊對海天這個名字一定不會感到陌生，概因她已在區內開業逾三十年。與海鮮街毗鄰的便利，食客都會在市場購買海鮮後帶到酒家內由廚師烹調處理。上午有早茶點心供應。一大班朋友聚餐，可選擇在三樓的廂房。

TEL. 2450 6331
5 Sam Shing Street, Castle Peak Bay, Tuen Mun
屯門青山灣三聖街 5 號

■ PRICE 價錢
à la carte 點菜 $ 400-500

■ OPENING HOURS 營業時間
11:00-22:00 (L.O.)

HONG KONG 香港

Hugo's
希戈

There aren't many restaurants in Hong Kong with a medieval theme, complete with swords and suits of armour, but then Hugo's is all about the charms of yesteryear. The European menu includes plenty of French classics like Dover sole meunière and escargot à la bourguignonne; there are also plenty of dishes finished at the table, like steak tartare and steak au poivre. At lunch, desserts and a large hors d'oeuvre selection are served from a trolley.

完整的銀鎧甲、大型金屬燭台加上兵器裝飾，令這餐廳瀰漫着不一樣的中世紀懷舊風情。餐單提供的是具濃厚法國特色的傳統歐洲菜，如法式洋葱湯、布根地式焗田螺等，部分菜式如生牛肉他他或法式黑胡椒牛柳，更是席前調製，帶來多一重享受。午市的套餐提供大量餐前開胃菜和甜品選擇。

TEL. 3721 7733
Lobby F, Hyatt Regency Tsim Sha Tsui,
18 Hanoi Road, Tsim Sha Tsui
尖沙咀河內道 18 號凱悅酒店 - 尖沙咀大堂
www.hongkongtsimshatsui.regency.
hyatt.com

■ PRICE 價錢
Lunch 午膳
set 套餐 $ 385-540
weekend set 週末套餐 $ 738
à la carte 點菜 $ 700-1,700
Dinner 晚膳
set 套餐 $ 888-1,388
à la carte 點菜 $ 700-1,700

■ OPENING HOURS 營業時間
Lunch 午膳　12:00-14:30 (L.O.)
Sunday lunch 週日午膳　11:30-15:00 (L.O.)
Dinner 晚膳　18:30-23:00 (L.O.)

Hyde Park Garden
海德花園

🍴   🛎20   🕐🍴

Precise cooking time is crucial to seafood and no one knows better than the chef here – his stir-fried razor clams in chilli black bean sauce boasts tender flesh seared in a scorching wok for the right period of time. The signature fish soup is simmered with freshwater fishes and tofu for over 2 hours, made fresh every day. Other recommended dishes include ginger and scallion abalones in clay pot and tofu skin sweet soup with pearl barley.

海鮮全由同一老闆的明月海鮮檔提供，品質俱佳。師傅對於烹調海鮮的時間掌控得十分好，如鮮甜爽脆豉椒炒鯉子這道菜就火喉十足。淡水鮮魚湯用了大量淡水魚加入豆腐，熬煮兩個小時或以上，每天新鮮烹調。薑葱鮑魚煲以秘方炮製。招牌菜包括腐竹洋薏米糖水、炸茄子皇和無添加人造色素的咕嚕肉。

TEL. 2717 6381
44 Hoi Pong Road Central,
Lei Yue Mun
鯉魚門海傍道中 44 號
www.hydeparkdeli.com

■ PRICE 價錢
Dinner 晚膳
à la carte 點菜 $ 500-1,000

■ OPENING HOURS 營業時間
Lunch 午膳   11:30-14:30 (L.O.)
Dinner 晚膳   16:30-22:00 (L.O.)

■ ANNUAL AND WEEKLY CLOSING 休息日期
Closed 4 days Lunar New Year
農曆新年休息 4 天

IM Teppanyaki & Wine

🍴🍴 ⊟8 ⟷ ☎🍷

Less a meal, more a full multi-sensory experience. Sit at the teppanyaki bar, admire the cooking show and enjoy contemporary Japanese flavours that make great use of prime ingredients like lobster and premium quality Wagyu. You also get to hear all about owner-chef Lawrence Mok's extraordinary triathlon experiences straight from his own mouth while he prepares your food. There is a private room available for small groups.

到這兒光顧的客人，十有八九是慕主廚莫師傅之名而來。坐在鐵板燒桌前，欣賞莫師傅用精湛廚藝為你炮製龍蝦和頂級和牛等美食，確是賞心樂事！莫師傅偶爾會與客人分享其參加鐵人賽的體驗，令你在一頓飯的時間得到多重感觀享受。餐室設計糅合了和風與時尚概念。小廂房適合私人聚會之用。

TEL. 2570 7088
134 Tung Lo Wan Road, Tai Hang
大坑銅鑼灣道134號
www.imteppanyaki.com

■ PRICE 價錢
Lunch 午膳
set 套餐 $ 280-380
à la carte 點菜 $ 1,000-2,000
Dinner 晚膳
set 套餐 $ 1,480-1,800
à la carte 點菜 $ 1,000-2,000

■ OPENING HOURS 營業時間
Lunch 午膳　12:00-14:30 (L.O.)
Dinner 晚膳　18:00-22:30 (L.O.)

Imperial Treasure Fine Chinese Cuisine
御寶軒

XXX   ♿ ⟨ P ⌂20 ☺♨

Finding success in Singapore and Shanghai, Imperial Treasure opened its first Hong Kong branch in the sky-scrapping landmark, with panoramic views of the harbour. The stylish dining room is embellished with subtle Chinese touches, such as the ceramic Koi carps and calligraphy. A fish tank in the kitchen ensures live seafood is available every day. Poached garoupa in fish soup with crispy rice and stuffed crab shell are worth a try.

繼新加坡、上海後，御寶飲食集團終於落戶香港。選址在九龍半島地標北京道1號，坐擁無敵維港兩岸景色，加上時尚中帶點中國風的設計 —— 水泥牆上的3D陶瓷鯉魚和梁柱上的書法-令人悠然神往！廚房內附設有魚缸，每天都有鮮活的海鮮供應，脆米海鮮浸東星、糯米釀脆皮乳豬及法式蟹蓋是招牌菜。

TEL. 2613 9800
10F, One Peking, 1 Peking Road, Tsim Sha Tsui
尖沙咀北京道 1 號 10 樓
www.imperialtreasure.com

■ PRICE 價錢
Lunch 午膳
set 套餐 $238-438
à la carte 點菜 $200-300
Dinner 晚膳
set 套餐 $438
à la carte 點菜 $500-1,000

■ OPENING HOURS 營業時間
Lunch 午膳 11:30-14:30 (L.O.)
Dinner 晚膳 18:00-22:30 (L.O.)

Involtini

The young chef of this fairly diminutive Italian restaurant is an alumnus of both Otto e Mezzo and CIAK. The speciality of the house is homemade pasta, served with a variety of good quality, imported seasonal ingredients ranging from seafood to truffles. Recommendations include orecchiette in tomato sauce with homemade sausage, and black truffle tagliolini. The open kitchen adds plenty of animation to the simply furnished, monochrome room.

餐廳面積不大,以白色為主調配上簡樸的裝飾。揀選開放式廚房邊上的座位,能盡情注視廚師為你炮製美食的過程。每天鮮製的手造意粉是這裏的主打食品,配以時令進口食材如新鮮海產和松露等,黑松露幼麵和配上自家製香腸的貓耳意粉值得一試。午市供應的意粉套餐,味美且價錢實惠,適合上班族。

TEL. 2658 2128
11F, The L. Square,
459-461 Lockhart Road, Causeway Bay
銅鑼灣駱克道 459-461號
The L. Square 11樓
www.involtiniconcept.com

■ PRICE 價錢
Lunch 午膳
set 套餐 $ 68-138
à la carte 點菜 $ 250-500

Dinner 晚膳
set 套餐 $ 328- 468
à la carte 點菜 $ 290-600

■ OPENING HOURS 營業時間
Lunch 午膳　11:30-15:00 (L.O.)
Dinner 晚膳　18:00-22:00 (L.O.)

■ ANNUAL AND WEEKLY CLOSING 休息日期
Closed 3 days Lunar New Year
農曆新年休息 3 天

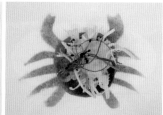

Ippoh
一宝

These experts in tempura have been in Japan for over five generations – and their Hong Kong branch manages to maintain that friendly, family atmosphere for which they are known. All the seafood is flown in daily from Tokyo's Tsukiji Market, they use safflower oil to ensure that the natural taste of ingredients is not overpowered, and the sauce is made to a special secret recipe. The omakase is the best way to go.

這家天婦羅餐館由大廚兼東主的家族經營，至今已傳至第五代。餐館規模不大，所以能保持穩定水準，服務親切友善，令人感到猶如在家用膳。這裏的天婦羅選用時令的日本海產和蔬菜，放在較輕純的紅花油中以明火烹調，進食時再配上每天鮮製的醬汁。要盡嘗最時令美食，建議點選廚師套餐。

TEL. 2468 0641
39 Aberdeen Street, Central
中環鴨巴甸街 39 號
www.ippoh.com.hk

■ PRICE 價錢
Lunch 午膳
set 套餐 $ 480-1,100
Dinner 晚膳
set 套餐 $ 900-1,500

■ OPENING HOURS 營業時間
Lunch 午膳　12:00-14:00 (L.O.)
Dinner 晚膳　18:00-21:30 (L.O.)

■ ANNUAL AND WEEKLY CLOSING 休息日期
Closed mid-August, late December to early January and Wednesday
八月中、十二月尾至一月初及週三休息

Iwanami
岩浪

♿ ⛶12 🍽 ☎🍴

The building hosts quite a number of Japanese restaurants but it's worth seeking out the tempura and sashimi served at Iwanami. The head chef is a local and he adds his own creative touches while at the same time using techniques based on traditional Japanese methods – ask for a counter seat so you can chat with him while he prepares something special for you. Signature dishes include abalone tempura and tuna roll.

各式天婦羅和新鮮高質的刺身均非常受歡迎，熟客都會點選天婦羅鮑魚和以混和吞拿魚油脂烤香的飯糰所製的吞拿魚油卷等招牌菜式。大廚擅於運用不同食材，巧妙配搭製成一系列創意壽司。建議訂座時選擇壽司吧座位，可直接與廚師溝通，讓他為你度身製作特別美食。

TEL. 2591 1159
9F, Macau Yat Yuen Centre,
525 Hennessy Road, Causeway Bay
銅鑼灣軒尼詩道 525 號澳門逸園中心 9 樓

■ PRICE 價錢
Lunch 午膳
set 套餐 $ 160-880
à la carte 點菜 $ 300-800
Dinner 晚膳
set 套餐 $ 1,000-1,500
à la carte 點菜 $ 300-800

■ OPENING HOURS 營業時間
Lunch 午膳   12:00-14:30 (L.O.)
Dinner 晚膳   18:00-22:30 (L.O.)

■ ANNUAL AND WEEKLY CLOSING 休息日期
Closed 3 days Lunar New Year
農曆新年休息 3 天

Jardin de Jade
蘇浙滙

✗✗✗   ♿ 🅿 ⇆16 ◖🍴

HONG KONG 香港

The first Hong Kong venture from this renowned Shanghai restaurant group is certainly not lacking in grandeur, thanks to its double-height ceiling and striking chandelier. The kitchen naturally focuses on Shanghainese cooking and makes good use of traditional recipes but presents the dishes in a more modern style. High quality ingredients are sourced from the mainland for delicious dishes like steamed reeves shad and braised whole sea cucumber.

作為上海著名餐飲集團落戶香港的首家分店，餐廳的裝潢雅致，特高樓底配上引人注目的吊燈，別具氣派。餐館以時尚包裝演繹傳統上海菜式，味美且外形精緻。集團從內地搜羅優質食材，炮製出多款如清蒸鰣魚及蔥燒大烏參等美食。

TEL. 3528 0228
GF, Sun Hung Kai Centre,
30 Harbour Road, Wan Chai
灣仔港灣道 30 號新鴻基中心地下
www.jade388.com

SPECIALITIES TO PRE-ORDER 預訂食物
Eight-treasure duck with spicy salt
椒鹽八寶鴨

■ PRICE 價錢
Lunch 午膳
set 套餐 $ 148
à la carte 點菜 $ 200-800
Dinner 晚膳
à la carte 點菜 $ 200-800

■ OPENING HOURS 營業時間
Lunch 午膳 11:30-14:30 (L.O.)
Dinner 晚膳 17:30-22:30 (L.O.)

Ju Xing Home
聚興家

This hole-in-the-wall with only seven tables is always jam-packed – because of its food, not because of its décor or service. Regulars range from hotel chefs to local stars. Chef-owner Ng gets hands on in the kitchen and tries out new recipes with other cooks. The menu was mostly Cantonese at first, but now comes with a few Sichuan options. His succulent salt-baked chicken is a must-try. Reservations are highly recommended.

沒有豪華裝修，亦沒有五星級服務，小店內只有七張餐桌，卻經常爆滿，且是許多酒店大廚和明星的飯堂，因此想在此用餐，請務必訂座。店東兼主廚吳師傅喜歡親自下廚，亦愛與各大廚師交流並學習新菜式，由最初主攻粵菜到現在店內添加了少量川菜。用鮮雞炮製的新鮮鹽焗雞是招牌菜。

TEL. 2392 9283
GF, 418 Portland Street, Prince Edward
太子砵蘭街 418號地下

■ PRICE 價錢
à la carte 點菜 $ 250-350

■ OPENING HOURS 營業時間
17:00-01:00 (L.O.)

■ ANNUAL AND WEEKLY CLOSING 休息日期
Closed 1 day Lunar New Year 年初一休息

Kaiseki Den by Saotome

Formerly a hip and glitzy space in Sheung Wan, the Japanese haute cuisine restaurant embraces a zen-inspired aesthetic with bamboo, grass green and birch panels at this new location opened in 2017. Only the freshest food in season prepared flawlessly makes it to the table. Seats at the counter let you observe chef Saotome and his term's artistic touch. Try their signature dishes of sea urchin truffle rice and chargrilled wagyu beef.

從上環舊店遷至現址，以深淺啡色配搭木材的裝潢，很強烈的時尚日式風格。店內仍設有開放式廚房，令你可以觀賞廚師埋首製作食物的過程。由大廚決定的廚師發辦懷石料理，一如既往，食材會隨着時令轉變而更新，炭烤和牛及黑松露海膽飯是招牌菜。

TEL. 2851 2820
Shop 3-4, the Oakhill, 28 Wood Road,
Wan Chai
灣仔活道 28號 3-4號鋪

■ PRICE 價錢
Dinner 晚膳
set 套餐 $ 2,280-3,380

■ OPENING HOURS 營業時間
Dinner 晚膳 18:30-21:30 (L.O.)

■ ANNUAL AND WEEKLY CLOSING 休息日期
Closed 3 days Lunar New Year and Sunday
農曆新年 3 天及週日休息

139

Kam Fai
金輝

　　　　　　　　　　　　　🏠 ⟷20 ☎

With over 50 years of history, this family business is managed by the father while the kitchen is headed by his son with 40 years of cooking experience under his belt. They embrace personalized service and you may specify how you want your seafood cooked. Do you want your deep-fried oysters lightly floured, tempura-battered, or breadcrumbed? Try also their virgin crabs baked in salt and oil, and deep-fried mantis shrimps in peppered salt.

開業逾五十年，歷史悠久之餘更向以信譽和品質見稱。父親羅先生是店舖的掌舵，有四十年入廚經驗的兒子則為廚房主帥，其烹調海鮮的技術毋庸置疑。靈活的經營模式，服務以客為本，如酥炸生蠔可應客人要求以不同作法烹調。招牌菜包括油焗奄仔蟹及火喉充足的椒鹽瀨尿蝦。

TEL. 2347 7434
10 Hoi Pong Road Central, Lei Yue Mun
鯉魚門海傍道中 10號

■ PRICE 價錢
à la carte 點菜 $ 600-1,100

■ OPENING HOURS 營業時間
12:00-22:30 (L.O.)

■ ANNUAL AND WEEKLY CLOSING 休息日期
Closed 4 days Lunar New Year 農曆新年休息 4 天

Kam's Roast Goose
甘牌燒鵝

The Kam family name is synonymous with their famous roast goose restaurant. This little place is owned by the third generation of the family and he wisely hired his father's former chef to ensure the goose is as crisp and succulent as ever. There's also suckling pig, goose neck and head, and goose blood pudding available. With only 30 seats, don't be surprised to see a queue.

從祖父輩創業至今歷七十多年，甘氏出品的燒鵝早已遠近馳名，現由第三代傳人在灣仔開設全新餐館，承傳父輩廚藝。與父輩共事多年的老師傅以甘氏家傳秘方炮製的燒鵝，掛在窗前令人垂涎欲滴。燒乳豬、鵝頭和鵝紅也非常美味。小店僅有三十個座位，故常見輪位或買外賣的人龍。

TEL. 2520 1110
226 Hennessy Road, Wan Chai
灣仔軒尼詩道 226號
www.krg.com.hk

■ PRICE 價錢
Lunch 午膳
set 套餐 $ 60-80
à la carte 點菜 $ 50-150
Dinner 晚膳
à la carte 點菜 $ 50-150

■ OPENING HOURS 營業時間
11:30-21:15 (L.O.)

HONG KONG 香港

Kashiwaya
柏屋

🏵 🏵

✕✕   ♿ ⌷6 ⇌ ☏

The head chef worked for twenty years at the much celebrated, original Kashiwaya restaurant in Osaka before being charged with opening their Hong Kong branch here in Central. It's a predictably discreet, impeccably run operation with around 80% of the menu the same as the original. For the kaiseki cuisine, all the fiercely seasonal ingredients are flown in from Japan, including the soft water for the cooking of the rice.

柏屋在大阪的總店享負盛名，這家首間海外分店於2015年開業，在這兒食客可嘗到與日本店相同水準的懷石料理，餐單上的菜式有八成跟日本總店相同，且主廚曾於總店工作長達二十年，食材更全部來自日本，當中包括用於製作煮物、飯和上湯的軟水。

TEL. 2520 5218
8F, 18 On Lan Street, Central
中環安蘭街18號8樓
jp-kashiwaya.com/hongkong/

■ PRICE 價錢
Lunch 午膳
set 套餐 $ 680-4,000
Dinner 晚膳
set 套餐 $ 1,800-4,000

■ OPENING HOURS 營業時間
Lunch 午膳 12:00-13:30 (L.O.)
Dinner 晚膳 18:30-21:00 (L.O.)

■ ANNUAL AND WEEKLY CLOSING 休息日期
Closed Sunday 週日休息

Kau Kee
九記

Kau Kee has been trading since the 1930s and has consequently built up a huge following that you'll probably have to line up in the street first to eat here. It's all very basic and you'll have to share your table but the food is delicious. Beef noodles are the speciality; different cuts of meat with a variety of noodles in a tasty broth or spicy sauce. Try the iced milk tea too.

九記自三十年代開始營業，支持者眾，門外經常看見人龍，午飯時間尤其擠擁，要在此用膳或許要提早到來。店內陳設比較簡單，進餐時要和其他人共用餐桌，但食物極具水準。牛腩麵是九記的特色；不同部位的肉塊配以各式粉麵，無論是上湯或咖喱，均滋味無窮。奶茶亦值得一試。

TEL. N/A
21 Gough Street, Central
中環歌賦街 21 號

■ PRICE 價錢
à la carte 點菜 $40-90

■ OPENING HOURS 營業時間
12:30-22:30 (L.O.)

■ ANNUAL AND WEEKLY CLOSING 休息日期
Closed 10 days Lunar New Year, Sunday
and Public Holidays
農曆新年 10 天、週日及公眾假期休息

MAP 地圖 22/B-2

Kaum

A coffee shop, a boutique, a bar-lounge, a restaurant and even a secret Music Room combine to celebrate all things Indonesian. The attractive main dining room comes with beautiful Toraja tiles and communal tables at which to share and enjoy the appealingly priced and generously sized dishes. The menu covers many different styles of the vibrant indigenous cuisine, with bamboo dishes being particularly good.

店名Kaum在印尼文有宗族、部落之意，店子也一如其名分成五部分，包括咖啡室、衣物手工藝店、酒吧和兩個風格截然不同的主餐室。其中位處店子最深處的餐室以五、六十年代風格的家具布置，綴以由印尼少數民族製造的天花鑲板、布藝品和裝飾，饒富特色。餐單羅列印尼各地佳餚，參巴或竹筒菜式均值得一試。

TEL. 2858 6066
GF, 100 Third Street, Sai Ying Pun
西營盤第三街 100號地下
www.kaum.com

■ PRICE 價錢
Lunch 午膳
set 套餐 $ 88-186
weekend and public holiday set
週末及公眾假期套餐 $ 398
Dinner 晚膳
à la carte 點菜 $ 200-450

■ OPENING HOURS 營業時間
12:00-22:45 (L.O.)
Monday dinner 週一晚膳
18:00-22:45 (L.O.)

■ ANNUAL AND WEEKLY CLOSING 休息日期
Closed Monday lunch 週一午膳休息

Born naturally sparkling, Badoit's fine bubbles subtly awaken flavours of meals and fine wine.

1778
SAINT GALMIER
France
BADOIT.
SPARKLING NATURAL MINERAL WATER

NATURAL MINERAL WATER

Unique mineral composition and pure as nature intended.

The perfect accompaniment for fine dining.

Customer Service Hotline: (852) 2663 1012

Kung Tak Lam (Causeway Bay)
功德林 (銅鑼灣)

XX

← ⏱24 ◎♨

As befits a vegetarian restaurant, Kung Tak Lam boasts a fresh, green look. Based on traditional Shanghainese cuisine but with less salt and oil, the dishes are not only healthy and good looking but also deliver some punchy flavours. Don't be alarmed to see words like 'pork' and 'chicken'– they merely show what can be done with soy bean products. Standout dishes include braised vegetarian 'meatball' in casserole and cold noodles.

翠綠配上淺色系的裝潢，予人清新自然的感覺，功德林素食菜館，為食客帶來印象深刻的綠色體驗。店家以傳統上海菜作藍本，配合少鹽少油的烹調方式製作出外形精緻且風味獨特的健康素食。雖然菜單上出現豬、雞等菜式，但其實全是大豆製品。特別推介菜式有砂鍋獅子頭及上海冷麵。

TEL. 2881 9966
10F, World Trade Centre,
280 Gloucester Road, Causeway Bay
銅鑼灣告士打道 280號世貿中心 10樓

■ PRICE 價錢
Lunch 午膳
à la carte 點菜 $ 150-250
Dinner 晚膳
à la carte 點菜 $ 250-500

■ OPENING HOURS 營業時間
11:00-22:30 (L.O.)

Kwan Kee Bamboo Noodles (Cheung Sha Wan)
坤記竹昇麵 (長沙灣)

It's inside a local market but easy to spot, thanks to the big yellow sign above the entrance. All the noodles here are made using the traditional bamboo method, which may be labour intensive but leaves them tasting great as the noodles are freshly made each day; don't miss the signature dried shrimp roe mix with noodles. A glass wall allows you to watch each step of the noodle making process.

麵店位處住宅區的市集內,大門上的黃色招牌顯眼易認。與店東在廣州的家族麵店一脈相承,這裏的麵條均於店門旁的小工房中經人手以傳統竹竿壓法打製,每日鮮製、新鮮彈牙。蝦子撈麵是招牌菜式,萬不可錯過。

TEL. 3484 9126
1E Wing Lung Street, Cheung Sha Wan
長沙灣永隆街 1E號

■ PRICE 價錢
à la carte 點菜 $ 50-70

■ OPENING HOURS 營業時間
10:00-22:45 (L.O.)

Kwan Kee Clay Pot Rice
坤記煲仔小菜

Its gigantic yellow sign, typical greasy spoon-style interior and the traditional stir-fries it serves all point to an authentic Hong Kong culinary experience. Its famous clay pot rice is only served at night, and features a blend of three types of rice enrobed in oil brushed on the bottom of the clay pot. The rice itself is chewy and fragrant, with a crispy crust on the bottom perfectly scorched with the right amount of heat and time.

巨型淡黃色招牌、親切而熟悉的飯店大門，是地道的香港風味，飯店供應的是傳統港式小炒。只在晚上供應的馳名煲仔飯，飯底用上了三種米混合而成，均勻地塗在瓦煲底的油滲透於飯內，米飯吃起來特別香滑軟糯；控制得宜的時間與火候，令飯焦變得十分香脆。一口飯、一啖茶，幸福竟是如此簡單！

TEL. 2803 7209
Shop 1, GF, Wo Yick Mansion,
263 Queen's Road West, Sai Ying Pun
西營盤皇后大道西 263號和益大廈地下 1
號舖

■ PRICE 價錢
Lunch 午膳
à la carte 點菜 $ 50-100
Dinner 晚膳
à la carte 點菜 $ 80-150

■ OPENING HOURS 營業時間
Lunch 午膳　11:00-14:30 (L.O.)
Dinner 晚膳　18:00-23:00 (L.O.)

■ ANNUAL AND WEEKLY CLOSING 休息日期
Closed 7 days Lunar New Year and Sunday
lunch 農曆新年 7 天及週日午膳休息

HONG KONG 香港

Kyoku
旭

⊡12

Opened in 2016, this sophisticated Japanese restaurant comes divided into two, with a sushi bar on one side and a teppanyaki station on the other. There's also a high table in the middle for those having a drink and a couple of private dining rooms. If you're at the sushi counter you have a choice of three omakase, while teppanyaki is à la carte. The wild tuna sashimi is a memorable dish, and good use is made of the Japanese Wagyu.

在熙來攘往的銅鑼灣一隅，可找到這家高級日式餐廳。室內分為兩部份：一邊是壽司吧，提供三種價錢的廚師發辦套餐；另一邊則供應鐵板燒。另設私人廂房供小型聚會。在此用餐不得不試其野生吞拿魚壽司或刺身，肉質上乘入口即溶，且魚味突出，叫人齒頰留香欲罷不能。用餐前可於門口的高枱淺酌一番。

TEL. 2156 9888
Shop 2, GF, 38 Haven Street,
Causeway Bay
銅鑼灣希雲街38號地下2號舖

■ PRICE 價錢
Lunch 午膳
à la carte 點菜 $ 300-1,000
Dinner 晚膳
à la carte 點菜 $ 1,000-1,500

■ OPENING HOURS 營業時間
Lunch 午膳　12:00-14:30 (L.O.)
Dinner 晚膳　18:00 -22:30 (L.O.)

■ ANNUAL AND WEEKLY CLOSING 休息日期
Closed 2 days Lunar New Year 農曆新年休息2天

La Bombance

🍴12 🕐🍴

HONG KONG 香港

La Bombance is celebrated in Tokyo for its creative 'new Japanese cuisine' and opened its first overseas branch here in V Point in 2016. Dinner sees just one monthly-changing, 10-course kaiseki menu – although there are more menu options at lunch. Nearly all the produce is flown in from Japan but don't be surprised to see certain ingredients more associated with French cuisine, like foie gras, as well as some French cooking techniques.

東京La Bombance首家海外分店。以和風裝潢的餐室內最顯眼的是中央的長木餐桌，座位皆面向窗戶，窗外是動人的維港景色。餐廳以日本直送的時令食材奉客，菜式走日法融和路線，晚膳只供應十道菜的套餐；午膳除了壽司、魚生及和牛套餐，也可預訂迷你懷石料理套餐。餐單每月更新，供應多款清酒和葡萄酒。

TEL. 3188 3326
30F, V Point, 18 Tang Lung Street,
Causeway Bay
銅鑼灣登龍街 18號 V Point 30樓
www.labombance.com.hk

SPECIALITIES TO PRE-ORDER 預訂食物
Lunch Mini Kaiseki 午膳迷你懷石料理套餐

■ PRICE 價錢
Lunch 午膳
set 套餐 $ 260-680
Dinner 晚膳
set 套餐 $ 1,280

■ OPENING HOURS 營業時間
Lunch 午膳　12:00-14:00 (L.O.)
Dinner 晚膳　18:00-21:30 (L.O.)

■ ANNUAL AND WEEKLY CLOSING 休息日期
Closed Monday and Tuesday lunch
週一及週二午膳休息

HONG KONG 香港

Lan Yuen Chee Koon
蘭苑饎館

The Chan's first place opened back in '84; they moved here in '98 to premises with a proper kitchen and now offer Cantonese claypots, healthy home-style steamed dishes, noodles and deliciously sweet puddings. Fine Chinese furniture is a feature of the small dining room, where Mrs Chan does the cooking and her husband the serving. The set menus at dinner prove particularly popular so be prepared to queue outside. It only serves dessert on Mondays.

陳氏夫婦創辦的這家食館，原店在1984年開業，並於1998年遷到有正規廚房的現址；雅致的中式家具是餐廳的特色。廚房由陳太掌舵，供應各種粵式煲仔菜、健康家常蒸煮菜式、麵食、美味糕點和糖水。陳先生則負責招呼客人。晚飯時間的套餐特別受歡迎。週一只供應甜品。

TEL. 2381 1369
318 Sai Yeung Choi Street North,
Prince Edward
太子西洋菜北街 318號

■ PRICE 價錢
set 套餐 $ 90-108
à la carte 點菜 $ 100-150

■ OPENING HOURS 營業時間
12:00-21:00 (L.O.)
Sunday 週日   12:00-21:30 (L.O.)

■ ANNUAL AND WEEKLY CLOSING 休息日期
Closed 9 days Lunar New Year and Chinese
festivals 農曆新年 9 天及中國節日休息

L'Atelier de Joël Robuchon

☙☙☙

✗✗　　　　　　　　　　⊟8 ⊞ ☏⅋ ⸰⸰

Dedicated escalators lead you up to this sleek and impeccably run restaurant. The familiar red and black colour scheme and atmospheric lighting set the tone. Seats at the counter are for those who want to feel at the centre of things; if you'd prefer a table ask for Le Jardin which looks out onto a large terrace. The highly accomplished contemporary French cuisine uses sublime ingredients and the wine list has enormous depth and range.

專屬電梯將你帶到這家管理完善、井然有序的餐廳。熟悉的紅黑配搭與滿有情調的燈飾設計帶出了餐廳的獨一風格。喜歡身處中心的你，可選擇開放式廚房前的櫃枱座位；喜歡坐在一旁，可要求能看到露台的位置。精細的法國菜用料上乘，厚甸甸的餐酒牌內可供挑選的品牌與級別種類繁多。

TEL. 2166 9000
Shop 401, 4F, The Landmark,
15 Queen's Road Central, Central
中環皇后大道中 15 號置地廣場 4 樓 401
號舖
www.robuchon.hk

■ PRICE 價錢
Lunch 午膳
set 套餐 $ 498-2,080
à la carte 點菜 $ 800-2,000
Dinner 晚膳
set 套餐 $ 1,180-2,080
à la carte 點菜 $ 800-2,000

■ OPENING HOURS 營業時間
Lunch 午膳　12:00-14:30 (L.O.)
Dinner 晚膳　18:30-22:30 (L.O.)

HONG KONG 香港

Lau Sum Kee (Fuk Wing Street)
劉森記麵家 (福榮街)

This is one noodle shop that is not afraid of the competition. In a street overflowing with alternatives, Lau Sum Kee (and its sister shop around the corner) are packed with customers buzzing in and out. It is run by the third generation of the family, the noodles are pressed by bamboo and the wontons are freshly made at the shop. Recommendations include wonton noodles, dry prawn roe mix with noodles and pork knuckles mixed with noodles.

這家麵店可謂競爭力強勁！在滿是麵店的街道上，劉森記麵家及其轉角位的姊妹店仍然擠滿食客。此家由家族經營的麵店已傳到第三代，全部竹昇麵及雲吞均在店內新鮮人手製造。推薦麵食包括雲吞麵、蝦子撈麵及豬手撈麵。

TEL. 2386 3583
82 Fuk Wing Street, Sham Shui Po
深水埗福榮街 82 號

■ PRICE 價錢
à la carte 點菜 $ 30-50

■ OPENING HOURS 營業時間
12:30-22:00 (L.O.)

■ ANNUAL AND WEEKLY CLOSING 休息日期
Closed 3 days Lunar New Year
農曆新年休息 3 天

Le Souk

Le Souk brings a little exotic spice to the streets of SoHo and is owned by two friendly and hospitable Egyptian brothers who make time to ensure that everyone is having a good time. Trinkets, jewels and lanterns add plenty of colour to the intimate room, while the kitchen prepares Moroccon and Middle Eastern cuisine with care and attention. Tender and aromatic lamb tagine is a standout dish, as is the roasted fig salad.

由兩位友善好客的埃及兄弟開設的 Le Souk 坐落於蘇豪內，為區內帶來一點獨特的中東味道。餐廳內的空間以色彩繽紛的小飾物、珠寶和燈籠點綴；大廚則在廚房精心烹調摩洛哥和中東美食。嫩滑又香氣洋溢的羊肉煲是出色之作，香燒無花果沙律亦不可錯過。

TEL. 2522 2128
4 Staunton Street, Central
中環士丹頓街 4 號

■ PRICE 價錢
Dinner 晚膳
à la carte 點菜 $ 200-400

■ OPENING HOURS 營業時間
Dinner 晚膳　17:00-23:30 (L.O.)

FRENCH 法國菜

Le 39V

An outpost of the Parisian establishment helmed by the renowned chef Frederic Vardon, it serves haute cuisine in a relaxed atmosphere alongside unobstructed harbour view. The menu syncs with its Paris sister branch and some of the items change according to the season. Most fish and meat are flown in from France. Culinary highlights include oven-grilled macaroni with truffle ragout, blue lobster ravioli and 'French style' roasted pigeon.

氣氛浪漫、服務周到的高級餐廳，餐牌內的菜式以法國總店作藍本，再按時令食材的質素定期更換。魚類大多從法國直送而來，也有來自日本的海產如帶子和紅鯛魚等，還有澳洲的黑松露，簡言之，若非優質食材絕不使用。招牌菜包括薄切帶子、藍龍蝦意大利餛飩和烤乳鴿。

TEL. 2977 5266
Shop A, 101F, International Commerce Centre, 1 Austin Road West, Tsim Sha Tsui
尖沙咀柯士甸道西 1 號環球貿易廣場 101 樓 A 舖

■ PRICE 價錢
Lunch 午膳
set 套餐 $ 380-480
Dinner 晚膳
set 套餐 $ 1,200-1,880

■ OPENING HOURS 營業時間
Lunch 午膳 12:00-14:30 (L.O.)
Dinner 晚膳 18:00-22:30 (L.O.)

Lei Garden (IFC)
利苑酒家 (國際金融中心)

🍴🔘

✗✗　　　　　　　　　　　　♿ 🍽16 ☎🍴

Forward planning is advisable here – not only when booking but also when selecting certain roast meat dishes and some of their famous double-boiled soups which require advance notice. The extensive menu features specialist seafood dishes and the lunchtime favourites include shrimp and flaky pastries filled with shredded turnip. All this is served up by an efficient team, in clean, contemporary surroundings.

到這間利苑分店用餐，無論座位，還是食物如燒味或受歡迎的燉湯，均須提早預約。這裏菜式種類繁多，其中以海鮮炮製的佳餚最具特色，而午市時段的美食首推巧製點心如銀蘿千層酥。格局設計富時代氣息，潔淨雅致，服務效率亦十分高。

TEL. 2295 0238
Shop 3008-3011, Podium Level 3,
IFC Mall, 1 Harbour View Street, Central
中環港景街 1 號國際金融中心商場第 2期
3 樓 3008-3011號舖
www.leigarden.com.hk

SPECIALITIES TO PRE-ORDER 預訂食物
Dried abalone in oyster sauce 蠔皇乾鮑 /
Baked chicken with sea salt in casserole 古仿鹽甑雞

■ PRICE 價錢
Lunch 午膳
à la carte 點菜　$ 150-300
Dinner 晚膳
à la carte 點菜　$ 200-600

■ OPENING HOURS 營業時間
Lunch 午膳　11:30-14:30 (L.O.)
Dinner 晚膳　18:00-22:30 (L.O.)

■ ANNUAL AND WEEKLY CLOSING 休息日期
Closed 3 days Lunar New Year
農曆新年休息 3 天

HONG KONG 香港

Lei Garden (Kowloon Bay)
利苑酒家 (九龍灣)

P ⊟40 ◐❙

Service is one of the strengths of this Lei Garden, located in a shopping mall near the MTR station. Signature dishes include the 10 different varieties of double-boiled tonic soups (to be ordered in advance), sautéed scallops with macadamia nuts and yellow fungus, and braised boneless spare-ribs with sweet and sour sauce. Those who like to eat lunch early or at pace are rewarded with a discount if they vacate their tables before 12:45pm.

這家利苑分店位於地鐵站附近的商場內，服務周到是其強項。招牌菜包括多款須提前預訂的燉湯；米網黃耳夏果炒帶子、宮庭醬烤骨。中午12:45前離席有折扣優惠，對於喜歡提早吃午飯或能於短時間內吃畢午飯的顧客而言，這待遇確實吸引。

TEL. 2331 3306
Shop Unit F2, Telford Plaza 1,
33 Wai Yip Street, Kowloon Bay
九龍灣偉業街33號德福廣場一期F2號舖
www.leigarden.com.hk

SPECIALITIES TO PRE-ORDER 預訂食物
Dried abalone in oyster sauce 蠔皇乾鮑 /
Braised whole fish maw 蠔皇香扣原隻繁肚公
/Braised goose web with Kanto spiky sea
cucumber 關東遼參扣玉掌 /Baked chicken
with sea salt in casserole 古仿鹽甑雞

■ PRICE 價錢
Lunch 午膳
à la carte 點菜 $ 100-400
Dinner 晚膳
à la carte 點菜 $ 150-750

■ OPENING HOURS 營業時間
Lunch 午膳　11:30-15:00 (L.O.)
Dinner 晚膳　18:00-23:00 (L.O.)

■ ANNUAL AND WEEKLY CLOSING 休息日期
Closed 3 days Lunar New Year
農曆新年休息3天

Lei Garden (Kwun Tong)
利苑酒家 (觀塘)

🍴🍴

P 🪑20 ◐🍴

Avoid the escalators and use the shuttle lift to get to the fifth floor in this confusingly arranged shopping mall. Once there, the set up will seem familiar if you've experienced other Lei Garden branches: dishes are standard Cantonese but are reliably cooked using fresh ingredients. The place is as frantic as the others but has been partitioned into different seating areas by smart trellises. Try not to sit near the entrance as it's noisy.

如欲更易找到和更快搭達此酒家，請直接乘搭升降機到5樓。如你曾光顧其他利苑分店，對此店絕不會感到陌生：清一色的廣東菜與可靠的美食及新鮮的材料。當然，這裏同樣擠滿利苑的忠實顧客，簡潔的屏風巧妙地將餐廳分隔成不同用餐區。

TEL. 2365 3238
L5-8, Level 5, apm, Millennium City 5,
418 Kwun Tong Road, Kwun Tong
觀塘觀塘道 418號創紀之城第 5期
apm5樓 L5-8
www.leigarden.com.hk

SPECIALITIES TO PRE-ORDER 預訂食物
Dried abalone in oyster sauce 蠔皇乾鮑 /
Braised whole fish maw 蠔皇香扣原隻繁肚公
/Braised goose web with Kanto spiky sea
cucumber 關東遼參扣玉掌 /Baked chicken
with sea salt in casserole 古仿鹽瓹雞

■ PRICE 價錢
Lunch 午膳
à la carte 點菜 $ 100-400
Dinner 晚膳
à la carte 點菜 $ 150-750

■ OPENING HOURS 營業時間
Lunch 午膳   11:30-15:00 (L.O.)
Dinner 晚膳   18:00-23:00 (L.O.)

■ ANNUAL AND WEEKLY CLOSING 休息日期
Closed 3 days Lunar New Year
農曆新年休息 3 天

CANTONESE 粵菜

Lei Garden (Mong Kok)
利苑酒家 (旺角)

XX

 🕸30 ◑❙|

This is the original Lei Garden, which opened back in the 1970s; it's still as busy as ever so it's always worth booking ahead. The contemporary restaurant is spread over two floors and the upper space has views out onto the busy street. The long and varied Cantonese menu certainly represents good value; recommendations include tonic soups like double-boiled teal with Cordyceps militaris and fish maw.

由於這家餐廳實在太受歡迎，食客必須預先訂座。此店是利苑總店，開業於七十年代。富時代感的餐廳共分為兩層，樓上可看到旺角繁華的街景。以廣東菜為主的菜單花樣多變令人目不暇給，絕對物有所值。特別推薦各式燉品如蛹蟲草鬚燉花膠水鴨。

TEL. 2392 5184
121 Sai Yee Street, Mong Kok
旺角洗衣街 121 號
www.leigarden.com.hk

SPECIALITIES TO PRE-ORDER 預訂食物
Dried abalone in oyster sauce 蠔皇乾鮑 /
Braised whole fish maw 蠔皇香扣原隻繁肚公
/ Baked chicken with sea salt in casserole 古仿鹽甑雞

■ PRICE 價錢
Lunch 午膳
à la carte 點菜 $ 100-750
Dinner 晚膳
à la carte 點菜 $ 150-750

■ OPENING HOURS 營業時間
Lunch 午膳   11:30-15:00 (L.O.)
Dinner 晚膳   18:00-22:30 (L.O.)

■ ANNUAL AND WEEKLY CLOSING 休息日期
Closed 3 days Lunar New Year
農曆新年休息 3 天

Lei Garden (North Point)
利苑酒家 (北角)

✕✕　　　　　　　　　　　　　　🍽16 ◷🍴

Discreetly tucked away on the first floor of a residential block and overlooking a pleasant courtyard garden is this branch of the popular chain. Things here can certainly get quite frenetic as it accommodates up to 200 people. The lengthy Cantonese menu mirrors what's available at other branches, but particular dishes worth noting here are the double-boiled soups and the daily seafood specialities.

這家深受歡迎的連鎖酒家分店，隱藏在住宅大廈一樓。從酒家外望是屋苑的翠綠庭園，寬敞的空間可容納多達二百人，氣氛往往極為熱鬧。這裏的菜單與其他利苑分店大致相同，除了各式燉湯之外，亦可嘗試每日海鮮精選。

TEL. 2806 0008
1F, Block 9-10, City Garden, North Point
北角城市花園 9-10座 1樓
www.leigarden.com.hk

SPECIALITIES TO PRE-ORDER 預訂食物
Dried abalone in oyster sauce 蠔皇乾鮑 /
Braised whole fish maw 蠔皇香扣原隻繁肚公
/Braised goose web with Kanto spiky sea
cucumber 關東遼參扣玉掌 /Baked chicken
with sea salt in casserole 古仿鹽甑雞

■ PRICE 價錢
Lunch 午膳
à la carte 點菜 $ 80-200
Dinner 晚膳
à la carte 點菜 $ 150-750

■ OPENING HOURS 營業時間
Lunch 午膳　11:30-14:30 (L.O.)
Dinner 晚膳　18:00-22:30 (L.O.)

■ ANNUAL AND WEEKLY CLOSING 休息日期
Closed 3 days Lunar New Year
農曆新年休息 3 天

HONG KONG 香港

Lei Garden (Sha Tin)
利苑酒家 (沙田)

It may have been in town for over 20 years, however, refurbishment has kept this Lei Garden feeling fresh. It is located in New Town Plaza Sha Tin, which means that it can get especially busy at weekends when everyone needs refuelling after a day spent shopping. The menu largely follows the theme of others in the group; always ask for the daily special. Pre-ordering the seasonal double-boiled tonic soup is particularly recommended.

位於沙田新城市廣場的利苑分店已開業超過二十年，憑着精心烹調的正宗粵菜及舒適的室內環境，在區內蠻受食客歡迎，常常座無虛席。細心的服務員會在你致電訂座時提醒你預訂老火湯或時令特色小菜。

TEL. 2698 9111
Shop 628, 6F, Phase I New Town Plaza, Sha Tin
沙田新城市廣場第 1 期 6 樓 628 號舖
www.leigarden.com.hk

SPECIALITIES TO PRE-ORDER 預訂食物
Dried abalone in oyster sauce 蠔皇乾鮑 /
Braised whole fish maw 蠔皇香扣原隻鱉肚公
/Braised goose web with Kanto spiky sea cucumber 關東遼參扣玉掌 /Baked chicken with sea salt in casserole 古仿鹽甑雞

■ PRICE 價錢
Lunch 午膳
à la carte 點菜 $ 100-750
Dinner 晚膳
à la carte 點菜 $ 150-750

■ OPENING HOURS 營業時間
Lunch 午膳 11:30-14:45 (L.O.)
Dinner 晚膳 18:00-23:00 (L.O.)

■ ANNUAL AND WEEKLY CLOSING 休息日期
Closed 3 days Lunar New Year
農曆新年休息 3 天

Lei Garden (Wan Chai)
利苑酒家 (灣仔)

P ⌗18 ☯️⏰

An inventory of restaurants in Wan Chai wouldn't be complete without a Lei Garden. This branch is bigger than most and boasts a busy, bustling atmosphere, particularly at lunchtime. It follows the group's tried-and-tested formula by offering an extensive menu of dishes with luxurious dishes alongside less elaborate but classic Cantonese specialities. Seafood enthusiasts should consider pre-ordering the Alaskan king crab or Brittany blue lobster.

論灣仔區的出色食肆，當然少不了利苑的份兒。菜單包含珍饈百味與經典粵式小菜，種類繁多，加上巧手精製的點心和便利的地點，難怪總是座無虛席。食客可於訂位時跟店方預訂特別海鮮如亞拉斯加蟹和法國藍龍蝦等。

TEL. 2892 0333
1F, CNT Tower, 338 Hennessy Road, Wan Chai
灣仔軒尼詩道 338號北海中心 1樓
www.leigarden.com.hk

SPECIALITIES TO PRE-ORDER 預訂食物
Dried abalone in oyster sauce 蠔皇乾鮑 / Braised whole fish maw 蠔皇香扣原隻繁肚公 /Braised goose web with Kanto spiky sea cucumber 關東遼參扣玉掌 /Baked chicken with sea salt in casserole 古仿鹽焗雞

■ PRICE 價錢
Lunch 午膳
à la carte 點菜 $ 150-800
Dinner 晚膳
à la carte 點菜 $ 200-800

■ OPENING HOURS 營業時間
Lunch 午膳　11:30-14:45 (L.O.)
Dinner 晚膳　18:00-22:45 (L.O.)

■ ANNUAL AND WEEKLY CLOSING 休息日期
Closed 3 days Lunar New Year
農曆新年休息 3 天

Lin Heung Kui
蓮香居

This huge two-floor eatery opened in 2009 with the aim of building on the success of the famous Lin Heung Tea House in Wellington Street. It's modest inside but hugely popular and the dim sum trolley is a must, with customers keen to be the first to choose from its extensive offerings. The main menu offers classic Cantonese dishes with specialities such as Lin Heung special duck. Don't miss the limited offered pig lungs soup with almond juice. The pastry shop below is worth a look on the way out.

蓮香居於2009年開業，樓高兩層，延續威靈頓街蓮香樓的輝煌成績。樸素的內部裝潢掩不住鼎沸的人氣，以傳統點心車盛載着各式各樣經典點心，讓人急不及待從中選擇心頭好，限量供應的杏汁白肺湯不能錯過。菜單上羅列了傳統廣東菜及特色小菜，如蓮香霸王鴨。離開時不妨逛逛樓下的中式餅店。

TEL. 2156 9328
2-3F, 40-50 Des Voeux Road West,
Sheung Wan
上環德輔道西 40-50號 2-3樓

SPECIALITIES TO PRE-ORDER 預訂食物
Eight-treasure duck 八寶鴨 / Roast suckling
pig 乳豬

■ PRICE 價錢
Lunch 午膳
à la carte 點菜 $ 50-150
Dinner 晚膳
à la carte 點菜 $ 100-400

■ OPENING HOURS 營業時間
06:00-22:30 (L.O.)

Liu Yuan Pavilion
留園雅敍

XX   ⊖24 ⦿¶

Authentic Shanghainese specialities served in a room where you'll hear plenty of Shanghainese speakers really will make you think you're in Shanghai. Along with dim sum, you shouldn't miss the stir-fried shrimps, Mandarin fish with sweet and sour sauce, braised meatballs with vegetables or braised pig knuckle. A recent renovation has given the restaurant a look of understated elegance; the booths are the prized seats and it's worth pre-booking.

重新裝修後的留園雅敍素淨優雅，靠窗的卡座尤為舒適。開業多年的店子，擁有不少忠心擁躉。有趣的是，店內大部分食客和侍應，都會以上海話交談，當然，大家最關注的，還是這兒的正宗滬菜。不論是清炒蝦仁、松子桂魚、砂鍋獅子頭或紅燒元蹄等經典小菜，還是點心均值得一試。

TEL. 2804 2000
3F, The Broadway,
54-62 Lockhart Road, Wan Chai
灣仔駱克道 54-62號博匯大廈 3樓

SPECIALITIES TO PRE-ORDER 預訂食物
Smoked pomfret with tea leaves
煙燻倉魚

■ PRICE 價錢
Lunch 午膳
à la carte 點菜 $ 150-250
Dinner 晚膳
à la carte 點菜 $ 250-750

■ OPENING HOURS 營業時間
Lunch 午膳   12:00-14:30 (L.O.)
Dinner 晚膳   18:00-22:30 (L.O.)

■ ANNUAL AND WEEKLY CLOSING 休息日期
Closed 3 days Lunar New Year
農曆新年休息 3 天

HONG KONG 香港

Loaf On
六福菜館

🍴 🛏36 ⏰🍴

Spread over three floors and hidden behind a strip of seafood restaurants in Sai Kung is this neat little spot. The daily soup depends on what the owner buys from local fishermen; you can even bring your own fish and have it prepared by the kitchen. Besides seafood, Loaf On also offers simple but flavoursome Cantonese dishes like chilli and garlic bean curd, Loaf On-style chicken, and steamed sea fish with salt.

這家佔了三層樓的小菜館，藏身於西貢海鮮餐廳一帶後街。店主每天從當地漁民處搜購最新鮮的食材炮製是日魚湯，你亦可自行攜帶海鮮，交由廚師為你烹調。除了海鮮和魚湯，椒鹽奇脆豆腐和鹽蒸海魚也必須一試，別忘了預訂一客風沙雞。

TEL. 2792 9966
49 See Cheung Street, Sai Kung
西貢市場街 49號

SPECIALITIES TO PRE-ORDER 預訂食物
Crispy skin chicken 脆皮風沙雞 /Fish soup 西貢地道魚湯 /Minced fish in pumpkin soup 金湯魚蓉羹

■ PRICE 價錢
Lunch 午膳
à la carte 點菜 $ 200-500
Dinner 晚膳
à la carte 點菜 $ 200-500

■ OPENING HOURS 營業時間
11:00-22:30 (L.O.)

■ ANNUAL AND WEEKLY CLOSING 休息日期
Closed 2 days Lunar New Year
農曆新年休息 2 天

Lobster Bar and Grill
龍蝦吧

The room is dominated by the bar, and it's one for big hitters – cocktails are very popular and how many places serve Château Lafite by the glass? The mood is pretty sober at lunch but things warm up at night, thanks to the live jazz. It would be easy to overlook the food but the seafood dominated menu has great appeal. The seafood platter is popular, as are the Maine lobster and Alaskan crab; they also serve dishes from the grill.

晚間的現場爵士樂演奏無疑是餐廳一大特點，然而食物該獲得同等關注，以海鮮為主的餐單惹人垂涎，海鮮拼盤一直深得食客歡心，因為可一次過品嘗龍蝦、阿拉斯加蟹腳等海鮮，品種更定期更新。此外，烤美國牛柳及澳洲和牛也是不錯的選擇。顯眼的酒吧餐酒選擇良多，甚至包括單杯的Chateau Lafite。

TEL. 2820 8560
6F, Island Shangri-La Hotel, Pacific Place,
Supreme Court Road, Admiralty
金鐘法院道太古廣場港島香格里拉酒店 6樓
www.shangri-la.com/island

■ PRICE 價錢
Lunch 午膳
set 套餐 $468
à la carte 點菜 $600-1,400
Dinner 晚膳
set 套餐 $888
à la carte 點菜 $600-1,400

■ OPENING HOURS 營業時間
Lunch 午膳　12:00-14:30 (L.O.)
Dinner 晚膳　18:30-22:30 (L.O.)

Lucky Indonesia
好運印尼餐廳

One's first impression of this small dining room, with its wooden furniture and traditional wall hangings, is that it's a little dated, but you'll soon feel as though you have been transported to the Indonesian countryside. The Middle Java cuisine is not unlike the décor – there's no fancy presentation, just authentic and tasty flavours. Satay is charcoal roasted which creates a lovely aroma; also try the Nasi Kuming and Mee Goreng.

細小的用膳區、木製的家具及傳統的掛牆吊飾,室內裝潢予人點點懷舊感覺,令食客感到身處印尼郊區。一如其裝潢,此店的食物不賣弄花巧,只用真材實料炮製出正宗美味的爪哇中部菜式。炭燒沙嗲烤肉風味特別,而印尼黃薑飯和印尼炒麵更不容錯過。

TEL. 2389 3545
46 Tung Ming Street, Kwun Tong
觀塘通明街 46號

■ PRICE 價錢
à la carte 點菜 $ 55-85

■ OPENING HOURS 營業時間
11:00-21:00 (L.O.)

■ ANNUAL AND WEEKLY CLOSING 休息日期
Closed 10 days Lunar New Year
農曆新年休息 10 天

Luk Yu Tea House
陸羽茶室

🍽 14 🍴

Large numbers of both regulars and tourists come to Luk Yu Tea House for the traditionally prepared and flavoursome dim sum, and its three floors fill up quickly. The animated atmosphere and subtle colonial decoration are appealing but no one really stays too long; the serving team in white jackets have seen it all before and go about their work with alacrity. Popular dishes are fried prawns on toast and fried noodles with sliced beef.

陸羽茶室以傳統方法製作的美味點心，不光招徠本地常客，更令不少外地遊客慕名而至，所以樓高三層的茶室經常滿座。生氣盎然的環境和帶點殖民地色彩的裝潢別具特色，穿着白色外套的侍應敏捷而專注地工作。除點心外其他菜式，如窩貼蝦及乾炒牛河也值得一試。

TEL. 2523 5464
24-26 Stanley Street, Central
中環士丹利街 24-26號

■ PRICE 價錢
Lunch 午膳
à la carte 點菜 $ 200-350
Dinner 晚膳
à la carte 點菜 $400-550

■ OPENING HOURS 營業時間
07:00-22:00 (L.O.)

■ ANNUAL AND WEEKLY CLOSING 休息日期
Closed 4 days Lunar New Year
農曆新年休息 4 天

CANTONESE 粵菜

Lung King Heen
龍景軒

✗✗✗✗　　　　 ♿ ≤ 🖐 **P** ⊡16 ☏ 🍴 ⚭

Your first and only challenge will be attempting to secure a reservation at this most popular of restaurants. Chef Chan Yan Tak is one of Hong Kong's most experienced and respected chefs and every one of his dishes is as delicately crafted as it is tantalizingly presented. The name means 'view of the dragon' and the large room offers great views of the harbour but your attention will rarely wander from the stunning Cantonese food in front of you.

要在此家極受歡迎的餐廳用餐，最大最難的挑戰是訂座！經驗充足、深受業內人士敬重的行政總廚陳恩德師傅掌管廚房命脈，他處理的菜式，每一道都是精緻誘人的藝術品。偌大的空間，典雅時尚的布置，配上無敵維港海景，令人心曠神怡。然而，優美的環境從不曾將你的專注力從精美的食物上移離。

TEL. 3196 8880
4F, Four Seasons Hotel,
8 Finance Street, Central
中環金融街 8號四季酒店 4樓
www.fourseasons.com/hongkong/
dining/restaurants/lung_king_heen/

SPECIALITIES TO PRE-ORDER 預訂食物
Roast Peking duck 北京烤鴨

■ PRICE 價錢
Lunch 午膳
set 套餐 $ 580-2,980
à la carte 點菜 $ 600-2,400
Dinner 晚膳
set 套餐 $ 1,980-2,980
à la carte 點菜 $ 600-2,400

■ OPENING HOURS 營業時間
Lunch 午膳　12:00-14:30 (L.O.)
Weekend and Public Holiday lunch
週末及公眾假期午膳　11:30-15:00 (L.O.)
Dinner 晚膳　18:00-22:30 (L.O.)

9 letters for "incomparable"

Nespresso Boutiques: ifc shop 1058. Elements shop 1093. Festival Walk shop LG2-70
YOHO MALL I shop 1042A

Customer Hotline: 800 968 821

Business Solutions Enquiry: 800 905 486

Order online at www.nespresso.com or **Nespresso** mobile app

NESPRESSO.
What else ?

Mak Man Kee
麥文記

No one is here for the no-frills interior, typical of any noodle shop in Hong Kong. This 40-year-old establishment is all about Cantonese wanton soup noodles – firm and bouncy prawns, visible through the paper-thin translucent skin, with springy duck egg noodles swimming in a flavourful broth. The serving size isn't the most filling so you may want to order their pork knuckles braised in red taro curd on the side.

麵店已有逾四十年歷史，裝潢簡單樸素，是典型港式麵食店的陳設。鮮蝦雲吞是這兒最具人氣的食物，薄薄的雲吞皮內包着的就只有滿滿的蝦肉，用料十足吃起來很爽口。南乳豬手同樣是必吃之選。店家用的生麵並非用雞蛋而是用鴨蛋製作，蛋味香而麵質爽彈。

TEL. 2736 5561
51 Parkes Street, Jordan
佐敦白加士街 51 號

■ PRICE 價錢
à la carte 點菜 $50-100

■ OPENING HOURS 營業時間
12:00-00:30 (L.O.)

Man Wah
文華廳

XXX ← ⇱14 ◑❙ 🖐

Ceiling lamps resembling birdcages; original, ornate silk paintings; and local rosewood combine to create the striking interior of this Cantonese restaurant on the 25th floor of the Mandarin Oriental hotel. Tsui Yin Ting is their private room for 14 people and is styled on an old Chinese pavilion. The chef's specialities include steamed garoupa with crispy ginger and crabmeat, and roast goose puff with yanmin sauce.

位於文華東方酒店25樓的文華廳裝潢華麗典雅，一盞盞仿鳥籠中式吊燈、牆上古色古香的絲綢畫與紫檀木的運用帶來了雅致的古中國情調。裝飾一如中國古時涼亭的廂房聚賢亭能容納十四人。酥薑珊瑚蒸星斑球及仁稔燒鵝酥皆為這兒的招牌菜。

TEL. 2825 4003
25F, Mandarin Oriental Hotel,
5 Connaught Road, Central
中環干諾道中 5號文華東方酒店 25樓
www.mandarinoriental.com/hongkong/
fine-dining/

■ PRICE 價錢
Lunch 午膳
à la carte 點菜 $ 500-1,600
Dinner 晚膳
à la carte 點菜 $ 500-1,600

■ OPENING HOURS 營業時間
Lunch 午膳　12:00-14:30 (L.O.)
Dinner 晚膳　18:30-22:30 (L.O.)

Mandarin Grill + Bar
文華扒房+酒吧

XXXX   🦽 💱14 🍽 🕕🍴 🎱

This is one of those restaurants in which you instantly feel that you're going to be well looked after. This bright and comfortable room is run with consummate professionalism and it's easy to see why it's so busy, especially at lunch. The kitchen specialises in contemporary European cuisine and the appealing menu offers something for everyone – and that includes seasonal classic dishes and tasting menu.

這家典雅明亮的餐廳是著名室內設計師Sir Terence Conran的作品，注重舒適與休閒。如果你想增添一點娛樂，可預訂吧枱位置，觀賞廚師準備餐廳提供的多種生蠔。選擇餐廳的另一邊，你可看到廚房團隊用心準備令人垂涎三尺的歐洲菜和時令經典菜式；點選試食餐單，能更完滿地體驗時尚歐陸風味。

TEL. 2825 4004
1F, Mandarin Oriental Hotel,
5 Connaught Road, Central
中環干諾道中 5號文華東方酒店 1樓
www.mandarinoriental.com/hongkong/
fine-dining/

■ PRICE 價錢
Lunch 午膳
set 套餐 $ 538-638
à la carte 點菜 $ 1,000-1,600

Dinner 晚膳
à la carte 點菜 $ 1,000-1,600

■ OPENING HOURS 營業時間
Lunch 午膳　12:00-14:30 (L.O.)
Dinner 晚膳　18:30-22:30 (L.O.)

■ ANNUAL AND WEEKLY CLOSING 休息日期
Closed Weeknd lunch
週末午膳休息

Megan's Kitchen
美味廚

Those who like a little privacy while they eat will appreciate the booth seating with sliding screens – the restaurant underwent a renovation in 2016. The choice of Cantonese dishes is considerable and includes specialities like steamed minced beef with dried mandarin peel – and all dishes come with complimentary rice, soup and dessert. The restaurant is also known for its hotpots, which are made with good quality ingredients.

在廣東菜和火鍋中難以選擇？美味廚讓你不再苦惱。這兒除了有各式廣東小菜如陳皮蒸手剁牛肉和美味煲仔飯外，火鍋亦同樣聞名，更有海鮮、和牛等高級火鍋配料。點選小菜奉送湯、白飯和甜品，經濟實惠。餐廳內的卡座設備齊全，拉下布幕即成私密度高的私人廂座。

TEL. 2866 8305
5F, Lucky Centre,
165-171 Wan Chai Road, Wan Chai
灣仔灣仔道 165-171號基樂基中心 5樓
www.meganskitchen.com

■ PRICE 價錢
Lunch 午膳
set 套餐 $60-150
à la carte 點菜 $200-500
Dinner 晚膳
à la carte 點菜 $200-500

■ OPENING HOURS 營業時間
Lunch 午膳　12:00-14:30 (L.O.)
Dinner 晚膳　18:00-23:00 (L.O.)

Mercato

Having established Mercato as a very popular spot in Shanghai, Jean-Georges Vongerichten brought this Italian restaurant to Hong Kong. It comes with a fun, easy-going vibe, along with a bar and a terrace. The menu focuses largely on pasta and pizza, with the emphasis on simplicity and freshness; from the other dishes on offer it's well worth ordering the crispy beef short rib for two. Prices are fair and the location's good.

Mercato從上海來到香港，簡約風格始終如一。進餐前不妨到近門口的酒吧享用特色雞尾酒或到陽台與三五知己淺酌的聊天，餐廳的葡萄酒選擇良多，還供應由侍酒師精挑細選的杯裝酒。餐單選擇較集中，但亦包含各式薄餅和意粉。推介可供二人享用的Crispy beef short rib，外脆內軟的口感令人回味無窮。

TEL. 3706 8567
8F, California Tower,
30-32 D'Aguilar Street,
Lan Kwai Fong, Central
中環蘭桂坊德己立街 30-32號
加州大廈 8樓
www.mercato-international.com/

■ PRICE 價錢
Lunch 午膳
set 套餐 $ 228-278
à la carte 點菜 $ 400-900
Dinner 晚膳
à la carte 點菜 $ 400-900

■ OPENING HOURS 營業時間
Lunch 午膳 12:00-14:30 (L.O.)
Weekend lunch 週末午膳
12:00-15:00 (L.O.)
Dinner 晚膳 18:00-23:00 (L.O.)

MIC Kitchen

X   P 🚌 ⏱

'Demon chef' Alvin Leung, of Bo Innovation fame, brings his innovative style of cooking to a new building in Kwun Tong. Here at MIC kitchen his team uses creative touches along with superlative cooking skills to mix and match Chinese and Western food – the resulting flavours are bound to surprise you. The interior is relaxed yet contemporary; ask for a seat at the counter if you want to watch the chefs work their magic while you eat.

廚魔Alvin Leung繼續發揮無窮創意，配合精湛廚藝和現代化的處理食物方法，糅合中西食材的特點，炮製出令人驚喜兼讚歎的美食。餐廳位於觀塘一棟新建成的大廈內，設計時尚簡約，感覺舒適。建議預訂開放式廚房前的座位，品嘗美食之餘能觀賞廚師的手藝。

TEL. 3758 2239
GF, AIA Kowloon Tower,
100 How Ming Street, Kwun Tong
觀塘巧明街100號友邦九龍大樓地下

■ PRICE 價錢
Lunch 午膳
set 套餐 $ 248-566
à la carte 點菜 $ 350-500
Dinner 晚膳
set 套餐 $ 498-846
à la carte 點菜 $ 700-1,000

■ OPENING HOURS 營業時間
Lunch 午膳   12:00-14:30 (L.O.)
Dinner 晚膳   18:30-22:30 (L.O.)

■ ANNUAL AND WEEKLY CLOSING 休息日期
Closed 3 days Lunar New Year, Sunday and Public Holidays 農曆新年 3 天、週日及公眾假期休息

Ming Court
明閣

    👨‍🦽 🫕 🅿 🍽36 🕐🍴 🐚

There are two distinct dining areas in this elegant Cantonese restaurant on the 6th floor of the Cordis hotel: if you want a cosy, more intimate setting ask for Ming Sum, with its collection of Ming Dynasty bronzes; if you're coming in a larger group go for Ming Moon. Drunken sea prawns with Shao Xing wine, and roasted crispy chicken are among the specialities. The impressive wine list includes suggested pairings for your barbecued meat or abalone.

位於康得思6樓、裝潢典雅的明閣分為兩個截然不同的餐室：擺設着青銅器、充滿古風的明日適合小型聚餐，一大班朋友相聚則可選擇裝潢較現代時髦的明月。此店提供多種餐酒，侍應還會協助顧客揀選適當佳釀配合菜餚佐吃。其招牌菜太白醉翁蝦、明閣炸子雞不容錯過。

TEL. 3552 3028
6F, Cordis Hotel, 555 Shanghai Street, Mong Kok
旺角上海街 555 號康得思酒店 6 樓
www.cordishotels.com/en/hong-kong

■ PRICE 價錢
Lunch 午膳
set 套餐 $ 428-528
weekend set 週末套餐 $ 308-338
à la carte 點菜 $ 480-1,200
Dinner 晚膳
set 套餐 $ 888-1,288
à la carte 點菜 $ 480-1,200

■ OPENING HOURS 營業時間
Lunch 午膳   11:00-14:30 (L.O.)
Dinner 晚膳   18:00-22:30 (L.O.)

Don't confuse the rating 🍴 with the Stars ✿! The first defines comfort and service, while Stars are awarded for the best cuisine.

千萬別混淆了餐具 🍴 和星星 ✿ 標誌！餐具標誌表示該餐廳的舒適程度和服務質素，而星星代表的是食物質素與味道非常出色而獲授為米芝蓮星級餐廳的餐館。

An important business lunch? The symbol ⇔ indicates restaurants with private rooms.

需要一個合適的地點享用商務午餐？可從注有這個 ⇔ 標誌的餐廳中選一間有私人廂房又合你心意的餐館。

Momojein

Adorned with sleek wood furniture and industrial chic softened by plants and flowers, this modern and cosy restaurant puts a new spin on traditional Korean cooking. Chefs are all Korean and the celebrity head chef often appears on cooking shows. Most ingredients are shipped from Korea and all sauces are made from scratch. Allergic to MSG himself, the head chef makes sure none is used in his kitchen. Brunch menu available on weekends.

不同的鮮花植物和簡單的木桌與木餐具，氣氛輕鬆舒適。時尚韓國菜由全是韓國人的廚師團隊處理，主廚在韓國更是赫赫有名，他不時會研究新菜式，選用的食材大部分來自韓國，醬汁也是由他親手調製，確保食物內沒有任何味精。週末有早午合餐菜牌。

TEL. 2789 1949
23F, QRE Plaza, 202 Queen's Road
East, Wan Chai
灣仔皇后大道東 202號 QRE Plaza 23樓
www.momojein.hk

■ PRICE 價錢
Lunch 午膳
set 套餐 $ 88-138
à la carte 點菜 $ 180-280
Dinner 晚膳
à la carte 點菜 $ 300-350

■ OPENING HOURS 營業時間
Lunch 午膳 12:00-14:20 (L.O.)
Dinner 晚膳 18:00-21:30 (L.O.)

■ ANNUAL AND WEEKLY CLOSING 休息日期
Closed 2 days Lunar New Year 農曆新年休息 2 天

Moon Thai (Sheung Wan)

HONG KONG 香港

🏠 🍽 14 🕐

Secreted on the second floor of the Holiday Inn Express, Moon Thai is led by an experienced Thai chef who insists on using the freshest ingredients. Seafood dishes are the ones that stand out and he is known particularly for his own creation of fried crab with tom yum paste. Get in the mood by beginning your evening with a lemongrass martini. There is also an Indian chef in the kitchen preparing some Indian specialities.

經驗老到的泰籍主廚統領的泰國廚師團隊，以本地新鮮食材與泰國進口香料、菜蔬，炮製正宗高級泰菜，尤擅長以海鮮入饌，主廚獨創的芭堤雅蟹逅是代表作。此店還提供小量印度菜如即烘印度酵餅和薄餅，由印裔廚師主理。

TEL. 2851 1288
2F, Holiday Inn Express,
83 Jervois Road, Sheung Wan
上環蘇杭街 83 號
香港蘇豪智選假日酒店 2 樓

■ PRICE 價錢
Lunch 午膳
set 套餐 $ 168-188
à la carte 點菜 $ 210-860
Dinner 晚膳
à la carte 點菜 $ 210-860

■ OPENING HOURS 營業時間
12:00-22:30 (L.O.)

New Shanghai
新滬坊

♿ ⊓ 14 ◐🍴

Glass walls and exquisite Chinese art combine to create a strikingly contemporary interior here on the first floor of the Convention & Exhibition Centre. The menu offers a light, healthy style of Shanghainese cooking and mixes the traditional and the innovative, with dim sum coming from the open kitchen in the middle of the room. Specialities include stir-fried barley with air-dried pork and braised duck stuffed with glutinous rice.

玻璃牆結合精緻的中國藝術，為這家位於香港會議展覽中心一樓的餐廳，營造出極時尚的風格。新滬坊提供以輕盈健康為主、糅合傳統和創新意念的上海菜式，廚師在店中央的開放式廚房內為食客製作各款美味點心。馳名菜式包括豐年藏珍寶和江南八寶鴨。

TEL. 2582 7332
1F, Hong Kong Convention and
Exhibition Centre,
1 Harbour Road, Wan Chai
灣仔港灣道 1 號香港會議展覽中心 1 樓

SPECIALITIES TO PRE-ORDER 預訂食物
Braised duck stuffed with glutinous rice
江南八寶鴨 /Baked beggar chicken 宮庭
富貴雞 /Steamed fresh shad 清蒸鰣魚

■ PRICE 價錢
Lunch 午膳
set 套餐 $ 220
à la carte 點菜 $ 200-800
Dinner 晚膳
à la carte 點菜 $ 200-800

■ OPENING HOURS 營業時間
Lunch 午膳　12:00-15:00 (L.O.)
Dinner 晚膳　18:30-22:00 (L.O.)

■ ANNUAL AND WEEKLY CLOSING 休息日期
Closed 2 days Lunar New Year
農曆新年休息 2 天

JAPANESE 日本菜

Nishiki
錦

Nishiki is concealed within the Regal Kowloon hotel but is owned and run by its Japanese chef. Tradition runs deep here, as demonstrated by the fact that the decorative style has remained largely unchanged for over 20 years. The atmosphere and the style of food are typical of an izakaya. Chicken meatball and tofu hotpot, BBQ eel and BBQ chicken are the recommendations. Booking is strongly advised – when doing so, ask for seats at the counter.

位於富豪九龍酒店內的這家餐廳，多年來見證着尖沙咀的變遷亦擁有一眾忠實追隨者，內部裝潢由始至今沒甚改變，很典型的居酒屋格局，氣氛總是熱鬧非常。食客最喜愛這裏的燒烤，如燒鱔、兔治雞肉棒，而雞肉丸豆腐鍋亦美味非常。建議預先訂座，開放式廚房邊上的座位能觀賞廚師的技藝，氣氛更佳。

TEL. 2723 8660
Shop 103, 1F Regal Kowloon Hotel,
71 Mody Road, Tsim Sha Tsui
尖沙咀麼地道 71號富豪九龍酒店 1樓 103室

■ PRICE 價錢
Lunch 午膳
set 套餐 $ 85-110
à la carte 點菜 $ 200-450
Dinner 晚膳
set 套餐 $ 360-380
à la carte 點菜 $ 200-450

■ OPENING HOURS 營業時間
Lunch 午膳   12:00-14:00 (L.O.)
Dinner 晚膳 18:00-22:00 (L.O.)

JAPANESE CONTEMPORARY 時尚日本菜   MAP 地圖   19/C-3

Nobu

This branch of the über-trendy, international Nobu brand boasts an impressive ceiling fashioned from sea urchin spines and images of cherry blossom behind the bar. At lunch, bento boxes are the popular choice. At dinner, Mr Matsuhisa's beguiling blend of Japanese and South American tastes continues to work its magic by featuring sushi and sashimi, good quality seafood and fine salsas.

這家享譽國際的Nobu餐廳分店有着以海膽刺裝飾的天花，讓人印象深刻，背景更配有櫻花美景裝飾。午餐時間最受歡迎的是便當。而晚餐方面，主廚融合日本和美洲烹調風格炮製的嶄新口味更是迷人。菜式包括壽司、刺身和優質海鮮。

TEL. 2313 2323
2F, Intercontinental Hotel,
18 Salisbury Road, Tsim Sha Tsui
尖沙咀梳士巴利道18號洲際酒店2樓
www.hongkong-ic.intercontinental.
com

■ PRICE 價錢
Lunch 午膳
set 套餐 $ 220-888
à la carte 點菜 $ 300-2,000
Dinner 晚膳
set 套餐 $ 1,088-1,488
à la carte 點菜 $ 300-2,000

■ OPENING HOURS 營業時間
Lunch 午膳   12:00-14:30 (L.O.)
Dinner 晚膳   18:00-22:30 (L.O.)

FRENCH 法國菜

ON

XX   ⌂ ⟨ ♨12 ☕ ⅋

With its panoramic terrace and floor to ceiling windows, the lounge makes you feel you're on a luxury cruise ship; a red carpeted staircase then brings you up to the soberly decorated restaurant which comes from the same team who brought you Upper Modern Bistro. From the open kitchen comes French cuisine with colourful Mediterranean influences. There are around 500 labels on the wine list and cheese lovers will want to check out the cheese room.

餐館於2014年12中開業，由Jéremy Evrard、Philippe Orrico和其他合伙人經營；Philippe Orrico負責領導廚師團隊，主要供應混合了地中海風味的法國菜；睡蟹龍蝦生蠔薯仔沙律、白汁帕爾瑪腿火腿雲吞均是招牌菜。食客還可到芝士房挑選喜歡的芝士。餐酒單上羅列約五百款餐酒，大部分源自法國和意大利。

TEL. 2174 8100
29F, 18 On Lan Street, Central
中環安蘭街 18號 29樓
www.ontop.hk

■ PRICE 價錢
Lunch 午膳
set 套餐 $ 388-428
à la carte 點菜 $ 650-1,200
Dinner 晚膳
set 套餐 $ 1,288
à la carte 點菜 $ 650-1,200

■ OPENING HOURS 營業時間
Lunch 午膳   12:00-14:30 (L.O.)
Dinner 晚膳   18:00-22:30 (L.O.)

■ ANNUAL AND WEEKLY CLOSING 休息日期
Closed 4 days Lunar New Year and Sunday
農曆新年 4 天及週日休息

One Harbour Road
港灣壹號

One Harbour Road may be set in a hotel, but its graceful ambience will make you think you're on the terrace of an elegant 1930s Taipan mansion. Split-level dining adds to the airy feel, there are views of the harbour, and the sound of the fountain softens the bold statement of the huge pillars. Cantonese menus offer a wide variety of well-prepared meat and fish dishes. Private parties should consider booking the Chef's Table.

這裏的氣氛，令你仿如置身三十年代的優雅大班府第。分層用餐，空間感較大，且能飽覽維港景色。大型蓮花池及潺潺的流水聲，使感覺硬朗的大柱子變得柔和。這裏的粵菜包括精心準備、種類繁多的肉類和魚類菜式。如想一睹烹調過程，可考慮預訂「廚師餐桌」。

TEL. 2584 7722
8F, Grand Hyatt Hotel,
1 Harbour Road, Wan Chai
灣仔港灣道 1 號君悅酒店 8 樓
www.hongkong.grand.hyatt.com

■ PRICE 價錢
Lunch 午膳
set 套餐 $ 518-738
à la carte 點菜 $ 300-800

Dinner 晚膳
set 套餐 $ 1,068-1,588
à la carte 點菜 $ 450-800

■ OPENING HOURS 營業時間
Lunch 午膳　12:00-14:30 (L.O.)
Sunday and Public Holiday lunch
週日及公眾假期午膳　11:30-15:00 (L.O.)
Dinner 晚膳　18:30-22:30 (L.O.)

ITALIAN 意大利菜   MAP 地圖 25/D-3

8 1/2 Otto e Mezzo - Bombana

XXXX   ⊖18 📞🍴 🐮

Chef-owner Umberto Bombana enjoys a stellar reputation in Hong Kong and, thanks to his flagship restaurant here in Alexander House, it's easy to see why. It's not just the talented and accomplished kitchen brigade who share his passion and his pride – the charming front of house team are equally enthusiastic and knowledgeable. The acclaimed Italian cooking is underpinned by impeccable ingredients and dishes are all about flavour and taste.

位於中環的這家店子，是店東兼主廚Umberto Bombana最引以為傲的旗艦店。充滿天賦且無懈可擊的烹飪團隊、熱情主動兼知識豐富的服務員團隊，難怪Otto E Mezzo成績斐然。廣受好評的意大利菜，與一絲不苟的選材用料不無關係。色、香、味，是每道佳餚的精粹。

TEL. 2537 8859
Shop 202, 2F, Alexandra House,
18 Chater Road, Central
中環遮打道18號歷山大廈2樓202號舖
www.ottoemezzobombana.com

■ PRICE 價錢
Lunch 午膳
set 套餐 $ 580-1,380
à la carte 點菜 $ 760-1,060

Dinner 晚膳
set 套餐 $ 1,380
à la carte 點菜 $ 760-1,060

■ OPENING HOURS 營業時間
Lunch 午膳　12:00-14:30 (L.O.)
Dinner 晚膳　18:30-22:30 (L.O.)

■ ANNUAL AND WEEKLY CLOSING 休息日期
Closed Sunday 週日休息

Pak Loh Chiu Chow (Hysan Avenue)
百樂潮州 (希慎道)

✕✕   ⎆16 ◑⅋

There are now four branches of this Chiu Chow restaurant in Hong Kong, but this is the original – which was founded in 1967. For lunch try the baby oyster congee or the fried noodle with sugar and vinegar; in the evening you can go for something a little heavier like soyed goose liver. It's also worth pre-ordering a speciality, like deep-fried king prawn with bread noodles, and finishing with the classic Chiu Chow dessert of fried taro with sugar.

自1967年於銅鑼灣開業，發展至今已有多間分店，而希慎道這間老店的受歡迎程度始終如一。食客最愛的菜式包括各式鹵水食物如鵝肝及鵝，還有高質凍蟹，或者預訂特別菜式如子母龍躉蝦、薑米乳鴿及荷包豬肚雞湯等等。

TEL. 2576 8886
GF, 23-25 Hysan Avenue, Causeway Bay
銅鑼灣希慎道 23-25號地下

■ PRICE 價錢
Lunch 午膳
set 套餐 $ 98
à la carte 點菜 $ 100-200
Dinner 晚膳
à la carte 點菜 $ 200-400

■ OPENING HOURS 營業時間
11:00-22:30 (L.O.)

Pak Loh Chiu Chow (Times Square)
百樂潮州 (時代廣場)

✕✕✕ ⊟14 ◎⫯

A vaulted ceiling, clever lighting, woods and leather all combine to create a striking contemporary restaurant on the 10th floor of Times Square. The chiu chow cuisine is prepared in a traditional way using authentic ingredients, although the presentation – like the room – is modern. For lunch try dim sum or something light, such as sliced pomfret or baby oyster congee; for dinner the stewed, dried Oma abalone is a must.

由本地年輕設計師操刀的室內設計，燈光、線條和空間構成出色的視覺效果，令人留下深刻印象。百樂這家分店提供一眾傳統潮州美食，配以精美外形，且份量較小巧容你可嘗味更多。煎鯧魚和鹵水鵝當然不能少，想試點特別的食物可預先通知店家，讓大廚為你炮製潮州燒盞。

TEL. 2577 1163
10F, Times Square, 1 Matheson Street, Causeway Bay
銅鑼灣勿地臣街 1 號時代廣場 10 樓

■ PRICE 價錢
Lunch 午膳
à la carte 點菜 $ 200-300
Dinner 晚膳
à la carte 點菜 $ 300-400

■ OPENING HOURS 營業時間
11:00-22:30 (L.O.)

■ ANNUAL AND WEEKLY CLOSING 休息日期
Closed 1 day Lunar New Year 年初一休息

Pang's Kitchen
彭慶記

Anyone living in Happy Valley will be familiar with Pang's Kitchen as it has been packing them in since it opened back in 2001. Its reputation is largely down to its Cantonese cuisine which comes in a decidedly homestyle, traditional style, with dishes such as baked fish intestines in a clay pot, whole superior abalone in oyster sauce, and snake soup. It is not a huge place so it's worth booking ahead.

跑馬地的街坊必定不會對彭慶記感到陌生，店舖自2001年開業以來一直服務該區。其馳名粵式佳餚主要是家常小菜和傳統菜式，如缽仔焗魚腸、蠔皇原隻吉品鮑及太史五蛇羹。由於食店面積不大，食客宜預先訂座。

TEL. 2838 5462
25 Yik Yam Street, Happy Valley
跑馬地奕蔭街 25號

■ PRICE 價錢
Lunch 午膳
set 套餐 $ 80
à la carte 點菜 $ 250-500
Dinner 晚膳
à la carte 點菜 $ 250-500

■ OPENING HOURS 營業時間
11:00-22:30 (L.O.)

PEKINGESE 京菜

Peking Garden (Central)
北京樓 (中環)

✗✗✗   ⊡48 ◐ⓘ

The signature Peking duck is not to be missed – they serve upwards of 60 of them here every night. They arrive plump and glossy at the table, where they are carved with some ceremony by a waiter in white gloves. The restaurant is comprised of two rooms: the more traditional one is best, as it's here the noodle-making demonstration happens each night at 8:30; the more modern dining room, next to the private rooms, is aimed at bigger groups.

毫無疑問，精心炮製的北京填鴨是這家京菜館的招牌菜，每天售出超過六十隻！戴上白手套的侍應會在食客面前將飽滿油亮的填鴨切割片肉，仿如莊嚴的儀式。餐廳劃分為兩個大廳；風格較為傳統的一邊，每晚八時半設拉麵製作示範；較為時尚的一邊則適合大伙兒聚餐。

TEL. 2526 6456
BF, Alexandra House, 18 Chater Road,
Central
中環遮打道 18號歷山大廈地庫
www.maxims.com.hk

■ PRICE 價錢
Lunch 午膳
à la carte 點菜 $ 200-1,000
Dinner 晚膳
à la carte 點菜 $ 200-1,000

■ OPENING HOURS 營業時間
Lunch 午膳   11:30-14:30 (L.O.)
Dinner 晚膳   18:00-22:15 (L.O.)

Petrus
珀翠

Restaurants don't come more opulent than this – crystal chandeliers blend with elaborately draped curtains; tables are immaculately set; and a pianist adds a sense of occasion. The most recent chef has brought a more modern interpretation to the classical French menu and the best ingredients are sourced from around the world to create visually appealing dishes. The stunning wine list includes 45 vintages of Château Pétrus dating back to 1928.

閃爍奪目的水晶吊燈、高貴的絨布簾幕配上能欣賞無敵海景的巨幅玻璃窗與一絲不苟的餐桌佈置,如此環境令人感到賞心悅目,晚飯時間的現場鋼琴演奏,更添幾分情調。主廚以現代手法演繹的經典法國菜,賣相吸引。酒單上有二千多款餐酒,包括自1928年起產自珀翠酒莊的多個年份葡萄酒。

TEL. 2820 8590
56F, Island Shangri-La Hotel, Pacific Place,
Supreme Court Road, Admiralty
金鐘法院道太古廣場
港島香格里拉酒店 56 樓
www.shangri-la.com/island

■ PRICE 價錢
Lunch 午膳
set 套餐 $ 528-618
Dinner 晚膳
set 套餐 $ 980-1,480
à la carte 點菜 $ 800-1,200

■ OPENING HOURS 營業時間
Lunch 午膳　12:00-14:30 (L.O.)
Dinner 晚膳　18:30-22:30 (L.O.)

Pierre

XXXX   🦽 ⪡ 🛎14 ☕🍴 🐝

The top floor of the Mandarin Oriental provides suitably chic surroundings for celebrated French chef Pierre Gagnaire's culinary pyrotechnics. The intricate and innovative dishes and their component parts arrive in a number of vessels, all carefully explained by the charming staff. The views are absolutely terrific and the room itself is stylish, moodily lit and very comfortable. The focus here is on enjoyment with an atmosphere free from pomposity.

文華東方酒店頂樓的環境，與法國名廚Pierre Gagnaire讓人驚歎的美味菜式非常合襯。精緻創新的菜式與配菜以不同容器盛載著，殷勤細心的侍應會仔細為你講解每道菜式。餐廳景觀迷人，裝潢也甚有現代感，配合富情調的燈光，非常舒適。

TEL. 2825 4001
25F, Mandarin Oriental Hotel,
5 Connaught Road, Central
中環干諾道中 5 號文華東方酒店 25 樓
www.mandarinoriental.com/hongkong/
fine-dining/pierre/

■ PRICE 價錢
Lunch 午膳
set 套餐 $ 538-1,998
à la carte 點菜 $ 1,800-2,100

Dinner 晚膳
set 套餐 $ 1,998
à la carte 點菜 $ 1,800-2,100

■ OPENING HOURS 營業時間
Lunch 午膳   12:00-14:30 (L.O.)
Dinner 晚膳   18:30-22:30 (L.O.)

■ ANNUAL AND WEEKLY CLOSING 休息日期
Closed Saturday lunch, Sunday dinner and Monday 週六午膳、週日晚膳及週一休息

Po Kee
波記

Po Kee is familiar to anyone who's lived in Western District as it's been a feature here for over 40 years and for many local residents a bowl of rice noodles (Lai Fan) with roasted duck leg remains a cherished childhood memory. To prepare his own roast meats, the owner built a factory behind the shop when he moved it to the current address. Regulars know to come before 2pm which is about the time the pork sells out each day.

西環的居民對波記一定不會陌生，此店在區內已有逾四十年歷史，一碗美味的燒鴨腿瀨粉是許多人的童年回憶。遷至現址後，店主在店舖後自設工場，炮製多款燒味。區內居民對店內各款美食了若指掌，燒肉往往在下午二時前售罄，欲試其燒鵝，最好在四時前到達。

TEL. N/A
425P Queen's Road West,
Western District
西環皇后大道西 425P號

■ PRICE 價錢
à la carte 點菜 $ 30-90

■ OPENING HOURS 營業時間
11:30-19:30 (L.O.)

■ ANNUAL AND WEEKLY CLOSING 休息日期
Closed Sunday 週日休息

HONG KONG 香港

Putien (Causeway Bay)
莆田 (銅鑼灣)

🍴🍴

🅿 ⌗14 ◑🍴

The original restaurant was founded in Singapore in 2000 and named after a coastal city in Fujian province – the owner's home town. This branch comes with an easy-going atmosphere and its Fujian cuisine is respectful of tradition, with the focus on natural flavours. There's much to recommend, like stewed yellow crocker, seaweed with shrimps, and braised pig intestine; and don't miss their homemade chilli sauce – a perfect match for fried bean curd.

莆田於2000年在星加坡開業，後擴展至香港，老闆以其家鄉福建內的城市為餐廳命名，堅守忠於原味、鮮味自然的原則，做出一道道美味菜式；無論是清鮮嫩滑的燜黃花魚、回味悠長的九轉小腸，以至香酥的炒芋頭等都令人留下深刻印象，自家秘製的辣椒醬更是非試不可。

TEL. 2111 8080
Shop A, 7F, Lee Theatre Plaza,
99 Percival Street, Causeway Bay
銅鑼灣波斯富街99號利舞臺廣場7樓A號舖

■ PRICE 價錢
Lunch 午膳
à la carte 點菜 $ 150-300
Dinner 晚膳
à la carte 點菜 $ 150-300

■ OPENING HOURS 營業時間
Lunch 午膳　11:30-14:30 (L.O.)
Dinner 晚膳　17:30-22:00 (L.O.)

Qi (Tsim Sha Tsui)
呇 (尖沙咀)

Carved dark wood, dragon wall paintings and chilli-shaped light fixtures provide plenty of clues that you're in a Sichuan restaurant. This sister to the original branch in Wan Chai also makes the most of its top floor location by providing diners with great harbour views. The must-try dishes include sugar-glazed ginger beef, and fish fillet in chilli oil soup; it's also well worth pre-ordering the chilli-fried Dungeness crab.

置身於尖沙咀一幢商廈的頂層，室內是深啡色刻花木飾板和飛龍壁畫，配上仿似紅色辣椒的燈具，與川菜相當匹配；玻璃窗外則是維港景致，食客更可登上天台露天園用膳。這裏的新派川菜賣相吸引，蘊含甜、酸、麻、辣、苦、香、鹹等多種滋味，其中薑牛及油潑香水魚為必試菜式，也值得預訂霸王辣蟹。

TEL. 2799 8899
20F, Prince Tower, 12A Peking Road,
Tsim Sha Tsui
尖沙咀北京道 12號 A太子集團中心 20樓
www.qi-ninedragons.hk

SPECIALITIES TO PRE-ORDER 預訂食物
Chili Dungeness crab 霸王辣蟹

■ PRICE 價錢
Lunch 午膳
set 套餐 $ 120-165
à la carte 點菜 $ 250-800
Dinner 晚膳
set 套餐 $ 100-695
à la carte 點菜 $ 250-800

■ OPENING HOURS 營業時間
Lunch 午膳 12:00-14:15 (L.O.)
Dinner 晚膳 18:00-22:15 (L.O.)

Qi (Wan Chai)
呇 (灣仔)

The word 'Qi' means 'shining star' and the idea for the name was inspired by the shape of star anise – an important component of Sichuan cooking. This is a hip, moody and atmospherically lit restaurant where the coolness of the look contrasts with the heat of the food. Blacks and reds and opera-inspired paintings help create the striking room while in the kitchen sauces, herbs and chillies from Sichuan are used to prepare hot, spicy dishes.

呇意謂明亮的星星，餐廳以此命名意在比喻四川菜常用的香料八角。室內裝潢別具一格，紅與黑的鮮明對比，昏暗的燈光配上川劇壁畫，時尚中蘊含中式韻味。廚師採用自四川運來的醬汁、香料和辣椒，以傳統烹調方法做出正宗的麻、辣、鮮和香的四川風味，配合不同地區的食材，令人驚喜。

TEL. 2527 7117
2F, J Senses , 60 Johnston Road, Wan Chai
灣仔莊士敦道 60 號 2 樓
www.qi-sichuan.hk

SPECIALITIES TO PRE-ORDER 預訂食物
Chili Dungeness crab 霸王辣蟹

■ PRICE 價錢
Lunch 午膳
set 套餐 $ 120-240
à la carte 點菜 $ 200-750
Dinner 晚膳
à la carte 點菜 $ 200-750

■ OPENING HOURS 營業時間
Lunch 午膳　12:00-14:15 (L.O.)
Dinner 晚膳　18:00-22:15 (L.O.)

Qïao Cuisine
巧饍坊

There's nothing quite like a culinary remedy when you're feeling down. From the same owner and management as Wing Lai Yuen – famous for dandan noodles – comes this restaurant guided by theories of Chinese medicine. The food is mostly Shanghainese and vegetarian and the menu explains which dish is good for what ails you. For example, vegetarian sweet and sour is great for those suffering from indigestion yet unsuitable for anyone with gout.

有着奪目的綠色門面，巧饍坊與隔壁的詠藜園源自同一集團。主要供應上海菜及素菜，更結合中醫藥知識傳承藥食同源的中醫理論，餐單上甚至列出個別菜式的食用宜忌。此外餐廳更聘有國家級廚師，為預訂國宴菜的客人籌備多達二十三道菜的套餐。

TEL. 3152 2162
Shop 106-107, 1F, Site 8,
Whampoa Garden, Hung Hom
紅磡黃埔花園第 8期 1樓 106-107號舖

■ PRICE 價錢
Lunch 午膳
set 套餐 $ 60
à la carte 點菜 $ 150-400
Dinner 晚膳
à la carte 點菜 $ 150-400

■ OPENING HOURS 營業時間
Lunch 午膳 11:00-15:30 (L.O.)
Dinner 晚膳 18:00-22:30 (L.O.)

Qing Zuo
請坐

Two Taiwanese mothers opened this shop to fulfil their cravings for authentic homey food and it turns out to be a hit among diners. You don't come for the ambiance – it reminds one of the street stalls in Taipei. But the food is the real deal. Taiwanese omelette roll comes with various condiments. Braised pork rice looks small, but is quite generously and tightly packed. Soup noodles with braised beef shin exude a hint of Sichuan spiciness.

兩位來自台灣的媽媽為了一解鄉愁而開設。店舖商標由份屬老顧客的一位學生設計，簡簡單單兩張椅子，實為兩個「人」字，點出了「以人為本」的主題。店東推崇的不光是家鄉的古早味，更是一份人情味和健康文化。招牌菜包括有多款口味、充滿蛋香的嫩滑蛋餅，滷肉飯和帶川辣味的紅燒牛肉麵。

TEL. 2677 2888
Shop No. 2-3, Wah Fai Court,
1-6 Ying Wah Terrace, Sai Ying Pun
西營盤英華台 1-6號華輝閣 2-3號舖

■ PRICE 價錢
Lunch 午膳
set 套餐 $ 33-68
à la carte 點菜 $ 40-80
Dinner 晚膳
à la carte 點菜 $ 40-120

■ OPENING HOURS 營業時間
Lunch 午膳   12:00-15:00 (L.O.)
Dinner 晚膳   16:30-21:00 (L.O.)

■ ANNUAL AND WEEKLY CLOSING 休息日期
Closed 3 days Lunar New Year and
Monday 農曆新年 3 天及週一休息

Ramen Jo (Causeway Bay)
拉麵Jo (銅鑼灣)

Named after the owner's favourite manga character, this lively noodle joint serves pork cha siu ramen in 10 different flavours alongside gyoza dumplings and other seasonal specials. From the mild miso-based variety to the fiery spicy type, the rich and flavourful pork bone broth simmered for over 16 hours is the soul of every bowl. Those ordering dipping noodles are given a card illustrating the dipping steps in comic form.

東主以心愛的漫畫人物名字為店子命名。餐單內提供十款拉麵及小食如餃子，花上十六個小時精心熬製的豬骨湯底是此店拉麵的精髓所在，味濃而不膩，再配上特製的麵條和醬汁，令人回味無窮。若點選沾麵，服務員會給你一張「沾麵食法」卡片，其上是以漫畫形式展示的正確沾麵進食方法。

TEL. 2885 0638
3 Caroline Hill Road, Causeway Bay
銅鑼灣加路連山道 3號

■ PRICE 價錢
Lunch 午膳
à la carte 點菜 $ 80-110
Dinner 晚膳
à la carte 點菜 $ 80-110

■ OPENING HOURS 營業時間
Lunch 午膳　12:00-14:30 (L.O.)
Dinner 晚膳　18:00-22:00 (L.O.)
Weekends 週末　12:00-22:00 (L.O.)

SEAFOOD 海鮮

Rech

The famous Parisian seafood restaurant was acquired by the world-famous chef Alain Ducasse in 2007 and this is its first international outpost. The modern space with unobstructed harbour views complements the fresh fish on the menu, mostly shipped from France. Classics like seafood platter, raw oysters, sole meunière and Baba au rhum are served alongside creative offerings such as marinated raw fish and shrimps with nuts, herbs and seaweed.

於1925年在法國開業的Rech是巴黎有名的海鮮餐館，自2007年後由Alain Ducasse接手經營，此店是海外首家分店。採用的海產全由法國進口，每星期三至四次直送到店，確保食材質素。從生蠔、生醃海鮮冷盤、香煎牛油龍脷柳至法式冧酒蛋糕，一應俱全。明媚的維港景色，讓眼福跟肚腹同等滿足。

TEL. 2313 2323
1F Intercontinental Hotel,
18 Sailsbury Road, Tsim Sha Tsui
尖沙咀梳士巴利道18號洲際酒店1樓
www.hongkong-ic.intercontinental.com

■ PRICE 價錢
Lunch 午膳
Sunday set 週日套餐 $888

Dinner 晚膳
set 套餐 $1,188
à la carte 點菜 $700-1,200

■ OPENING HOURS 營業時間
Sunday lunch 週日午膳
12:00-14:30 (L.O.)
Dinner 晚膳 18:00-23:00 (L.O.)

■ ANNUAL AND WEEKLY CLOSING 休息日期
Closed Monday 週一休息

Robatayaki
炉端燒

Run by the Harbour Grand Kowloon hotel and set on the ground floor of an office building opposite is, as the name tells you, a restaurant specialising in robatayaki. This busy spot has counter seats on three sides of the grills, and dishes are passed from chefs to diner via long paddles. The ingredients include seasonal vegetables and seafood from Japan, and Wagyu from Kobe and Australia. The snacks, like the crispy chicken wing, are excellent.

餐廳由九龍海逸君綽酒店營運,位處酒店正門對面。兩個爐端燒燒爐佔去餐室大部分空間,櫃台中陳列了琳瑯滿目的時令蔬菜和海產,廚師就坐在當中為你燒煮食物,由蔬菜、海鮮到和牛,選擇豐富。除爐端燒外還提供魚生、壽司和天婦羅。

TEL. 2996 8438
GF, Harbourfront Two,
Harbour Grand Kowloon Hotel,
22 Tak Fung Street, Whampoa Garden,
Hung Hom
紅磡黃埔花園德豐街 22號九龍海逸君綽酒店
海濱廣場 2期地下
www.harbourgrand.com/kowloon

■ PRICE 價錢
Lunch 午膳
set 套餐 $ 175-365
weekend set 週末套餐 $ 458
à la carte 點菜 $ 200-1,500

Dinner 晚膳
set 套餐 $ 750
à la carte 點菜 $ 500-1,500

■ OPENING HOURS 營業時間
Lunch 午膳   12:00-14:00(L.O.)
Weekend & Public Holiday lunch
週末及公眾假期午膳   12:00-14:30 (L.O.)
Dinner 晚膳   18:00-22:30 (L.O.)

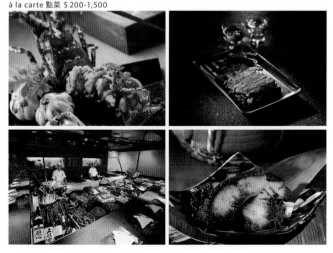

Ryu Gin
天空龍吟

✕✕　

The views are spectacular from its position on the 101st floor of the ICC Tower and the interior is gracefully understated, but it's the food that'll live longest in the memory. Seiji Yamamoto is owner-chef of the celebrated Ryugin in Tokyo and his team here prepare a 10-12 course menu which changes every six weeks. It offers a mix of traditional flavours and modern touches, with 95% of the ingredients flown in daily from Japan.

環球貿易廣場101樓壯麗的景觀叫人屏息靜氣，超凡的食物水準更令人對龍吟再三回味。主廚兼東主山本征治先生和其團隊主理的懷石料理最少包含十道精緻菜餚，巧妙地將傳統與現代風味及創意融合，來自日本的上等食材每天新鮮運到，菜單更每隔六星期更換一次。

TEL. 2302 0222
Shop B, 101F, International Commerce Centre, 1 Austin Road West, Tsim Sha Tsui
尖沙咀柯士甸道西1號環球貿易廣場101樓B舖
www.ryugin.com.hk

■ PRICE 價錢
Dinner 晚膳
set 套餐 $ 2,180

■ OPENING HOURS 營業時間
Dinner 晚膳　18:00-21:30 (L.O.)

■ ANNUAL AND WEEKLY CLOSING 休息日期
Closed 2 days Lunar New Year
農曆新年休息 2 天

Sabah (Wan Chai)
莎巴 (灣仔)

Sabah is one of the few Malaysian restaurants to have served authentic Malaysian food for many years. It may have an unremarkable façade, but at least it's easy to find thanks to the huge horizontal neon sign. The kitchen staff are all Malaysian and the care they take is palpable, as is the skill they show in preparing the dishes. Satay, king prawns with butter and deep-fried egg yolk, beef Rendang and Hainanese chicken rice are some of the highlights.

這家餐廳的外觀也許毫不起眼,但是靠着巨大的霓虹燈招牌,我們可輕易找到它。內部裝潢與外觀一樣平凡,但吸引眾多食客的並不是餐廳的室內設計,而是正宗的馬拉菜。精選菜式包括沙嗲、金絲奶油大蝦、巴東牛肉與海南雞飯。主廚秘方炮製的炸香蕉也十分惹味。

TEL. 2143 6626
98-102 Jaffe Road, Wan Chai
灣仔謝菲道 98-102號

■ PRICE 價錢
Lunch 午膳
set 套餐 $ 75
à la carte 點菜 $ 100-150
Dinner 晚膳
à la carte 點菜 $ 150-350

■ OPENING HOURS 營業時間
11:00-22:30 (L.O.)
Sunday and Public Holidays
週日及公眾假期 12:00-22:00 (L.O.)

■ ANNUAL AND WEEKLY CLOSING 休息日期
Closed 4 days Lunar New Year
農曆新年休息 4 天

HONG KONG 香港

Sai Kung Sing Kee
勝記

🍴   ⊡36 ☎❙❙

At first sight, this brightly coloured seafood restaurant may not seem too dissimilar to others in Sai Kung. However, there is something special here and that's the abalone menu. The abalone are prepared in various ways, from deep-fried to steamed; try the stewed abalone in oyster sauce. The building has 12 variously sized dining rooms spread over its three floors, all differently decorated; the most contemporary are on the 1st and 2nd floors.

這棟建築物樓高三層，備有十二個大小不一、裝飾各異的房間，一樓和二樓的餐室裝潢較時尚，驟眼看來，跟西貢其他餐廳並沒兩樣。但是，它真正特別的地方，在於扣鮑魚菜式。這裏提供多種以不同方式烹調的鮑魚菜式，由酥炸到蒸煮式式俱備，特別推介古法扣兩頭鮑魚。

TEL. 2791 9887
39 Sai Kung Tai Street, Sai Kung
西貢西貢大街 39號
www.singkee.ecomm.hk

SPECIALITIES TO PRE-ORDER 預訂食物
Crispy chicken 金牌炸子雞 /
Stewed abalone in oyster sauce 古法扣鮑魚

■ PRICE 價錢
Lunch 午膳
à la carte 點菜 $300-950
Dinner 晚膳
à la carte 點菜 $400-950

■ OPENING HOURS 營業時間
11:00-22:00 (L.O.)

■ ANNUAL AND WEEKLY CLOSING 休息日期
Closed 2 days Lunar New Year
農曆新年休息 2 天

Samsen
泰麵

Adam Cliff, who once worked for the Aussie chef David Thompson, opened this casual Thai noodle shop next to the historic Blue House. Aptly named after an area in Bangkok where the Chinese traded with the Thais, the restaurant emulates the authentic street-stall vibe and flavours. Rattan blinds, bare concrete walls and distressed wood furniture add to the old-time charm. Most ingredients are shipped from Thailand daily.

Samsen是過去華人仕泰國與泰國人做貿易生意和會面之地，在泰文中有三麵之意。在著名的藍屋旁邊，以復古風格裝飾：舊家具、古老泰國小販檔陳設、泰國鐵標牌，充滿懷舊與泰風情。熱愛泰菜的主廚旨在透過湯河及泰國街頭小吃，讓香港人品嘗地道泰國風味。超過六成食材每天由泰國直送到店。

TEL. 2234 0001
68 Stone Nullah Lane, Wan Chai
灣仔石水渠街68號地下

■ PRICE 價錢
Lunch 午膳
set 套餐 $108-128
à la carte 點菜 $140-200
Dinner 晚膳
à la carte 點菜 $200-400

■ OPENING HOURS 營業時間
Lunch 午膳　12:00-14:30 (L.O.)
Dinner 晚膳　18:30-23:00 (L.O.)

■ ANNUAL AND WEEKLY CLOSING 休息日期
Closed Sunday 週日休息

Sang Kee
生記

Having stood here proudly for over 40 years, Sang Kee is a true symbol of Wan Chai and remains refreshingly impervious to modernisation. The owner insists on buying the seafood herself each day and the Cantonese dishes are prepared using traditional methods. You'll find yourself thinking about their classic dishes like fried snapper, fried minced pork with cuttlefish, and braised fish with bitter melon long after you've sampled them.

現在許多粵菜餐廳都以雷同的裝潢和新派菜單作招徠，令生記這類傳統酒家讓人感到特別親切！開業逾四十年，店主一直堅持每天親自採購優質海鮮，以傳統烹調方式製作一道道經典廣東菜：用時令材料炮製的乾煎海鱺，家常菜如土魷煎肉餅和涼瓜燜魚等，令人回味無窮。

TEL. 2575 2236
1-2F, Hip Sang Building,
107-115 Hennessy Road, Wan Chai
灣仔軒尼詩道 107-115號協生大廈 1-2樓
www.sangkee.com.hk

SPECIALITIES TO PRE-ORDER 預訂食物
Fried snapper 乾煎海鱺 /Baked fish intestine 焗魚腸

■ PRICE 價錢
Lunch 午膳
set 套餐 $ 88
à la carte 點菜 $ 100-200
Dinner 晚膳
à la carte 點菜 $ 200-500

■ OPENING HOURS 營業時間
Lunch 午膳　12:00-14:15 (L.O.)
Dinner 晚膳　18:00-22:15 (L.O.)

■ ANNUAL AND WEEKLY CLOSING 休息日期
Closed first Monday of each month
每月第一個週一休息

Serge et le Phoque

Thanks to its large glass façade, discreet sign and understated, faux industrial interior, it's pretty apparent that the refreshingly relaxed Serge and The Seal is unlike many of the city's French restaurants. The appealingly minimalist surroundings contrast somewhat with the cooking, which is detailed and innovative. The set menus can change daily, depending on what's in the market, and are made up of small, elaborately constructed dishes.

小巧精緻的賣相和配搭創新的烹調，讓這家餐廳的食物有別於一般法國菜館，不光每道菜式都經過主廚精心設計和鑽研，餐單亦按每天市場上供應的食材更新。店內裝潢與時尚創新的烹調風格貫徹如一，落地玻璃窗與工業風陳設，透出一分灑脫，錯落有致的圓吊燈透着抽象表現主義，不羈中帶點藝術色彩。

TEL. 5465 2000
GF, Shop B2, The Zenith,
3 Wan Chai Road, Wan Chai
灣仔道 3號尚翹峰地下 B2號舖

■ PRICE 價錢
Dinner 晚膳
set 套餐 $ 850
à la carte 點菜 $ 500-1,000

■ OPENING HOURS 營業時間
Dinner 晚膳　18:00-22:30 (L.O.)

Seventh Son
家全七福

♿ 🍽 ⊟20 🍴

There was a change of venue for this Cantonese restaurant in 2016 – it is now housed on the 3rd floor of the Wharney Guang Dong Hotel. Its new surroundings are smart and contemporary, with gold and yellow colours adding warmth to the comfortable room. The standard of the traditional Cantonese cuisine remains as was, with the kitchen making good use of quality ingredients. The specialities are barbecued suckling pig and crispy chicken.

餐廳名稱包含了東主父親的名字及其在兄弟中的排序，也有傳承父親廚藝之意。從杜老誌道遷至華美粵海酒店，新店以深色木地板配金黃色的日式裝潢，感覺時尚。自十四歲隨父習廚、擅長高級功夫粵菜的東主，以時令食材、最少的調味料和精細的烹調，帶出食物真味。大紅片皮乳豬和炸子雞是招牌菜。

TEL. 2892 2888
3F, The Wharney Guang Dong Hotel HK,
57-73 Lockhart Road, Wan Chai
灣仔駱克道 57-73號香港華美粵海酒店 3樓
www.seventhson.hk

■ PRICE 價錢
Lunch 午膳
à la carte 點菜 $ 200-3,000
Dinner 晚膳
à la carte 點菜 $ 350-3,000

■ OPENING HOURS 營業時間
Lunch 午膳　11:30-14:30 (L.O.)
Dinner 晚膳　18:00-22:30 (L.O.)

■ ANNUAL AND WEEKLY CLOSING 休息日期
Closed 2 days Lunar New Year
農曆新年休息 2 天

CANTONESE 粵菜

Shang Palace
香宮

❀❀

✕✕✕✕   ♿ 🛁 🅿 ⇹24 ◐

Lobster prepared in 35 different ways is just one of the specialities here at this sumptuously decorated room at the Shangri-La hotel. The kitchen is overseen by Chef Mok Kit Keung, and his longstanding brigade prepares the traditional Cantonese cuisine with considerable skill and obvious pride. Equal care goes into the charming and thoughtful service. The pretty room is decorated with a mix of antique Chinese window frames and Sung-style paintings.

35種龍蝦烹調方式是香宮一大特色，華麗的室內布置是另一特色。由富經驗的莫傑強師傅領軍的廚房團隊，以經歷練的烹調造詣，每道傳統菜式均是細緻與自信的結晶。體貼細心的服務同樣叫人喜悅。古中國窗框與宋代風格油畫，陳設漂亮的餐室變得更有韻味。

TEL. 2733 8754
Lower level, Kowloon Shangri-La Hotel,
64 Mody Road, East Tsim Sha Tsui
尖東麼地道64號九龍香格里拉酒店地庫1樓
www.shangri-la.com/kowloon

SPECIALITIES TO PRE-ORDER 預訂食物
Beggar's chicken 富貴雞 /Deep-fried
whole boneless chicken filled with fried
glutinous rice 脆皮糯米雞

■ PRICE 價錢
Lunch 午膳
set 套餐 $398-1,388
à la carte 點菜 $350-1,000
Dinner 晚膳
set 套餐 $628-1,388
à la carte 點菜 $350-1,000

■ OPENING HOURS 營業時間
Lunch 午膳   12:00-14:00 (L.O.)
Weekend & Public Holiday lunch
週末及公眾假期午膳   10:30-14:30 (L.O.)
Dinner 晚膳   18:30-22:45 (L.O.)

CANTONESE 粵菜

MAP 地圖 30/B-2

She Wong Yee
蛇王二

Their signature snake soup has long been renowned and on a typical winter's day over 1,000 bowls are served. Regulars are quick to occupy one of the few tables for this memorable experience and it is no surprise that the recipe has remained unchanged for years. These days, those regulars come also for the famed barbecued meats and homemade liver sausages; the roast goose and double-boiled soups are good too.

此店位於銅鑼灣的中心地帶，以傳統方法烹調的蛇羹多年來口碑載道，秋冬高峰期更每日出售逾千碗。除此之外，其自製潤腸也同樣令食客趣之若鶩，而盅頭滋補燉湯是不少本地市民的最愛。店內氣氛熱鬧，需與其他人拼桌用膳。

TEL. 2831 0163
24 Percival Street, Causeway Bay
銅鑼灣波斯富街 24號

■ PRICE 價錢
à la carte 點菜 $ 60-160

■ OPENING HOURS 營業時間
11:00-22:45 (L.O.)

■ ANNUAL AND WEEKLY CLOSING 休息日期
Closed 3 days Lunar New Year
農曆新年休息 3 天

Shek Kee Kitchen
石記廚房

🍲 || 　🍽10 🕐🍴

It serves ordinary Cha Chaan Teng fare during the day, but turns into a dining hotspot specialising in home-style Cantonese dishes at night. The owner-chef sources the freshest ingredients from wet markets daily. Regulars also call him directly to pre-order certain dishes, including the signature fried chicken with toasted garlic that needs to be ordered one day ahead. Menu changes regularly to reflect the seasonal produce available.

餐廳在日間供應普通茶餐廳食物，而晚間卻是人氣鼎盛、主打家庭式廣東小菜的菜館。大廚兼東主每天會親自往街市選購最新鮮的食材，部分熟客更會直接致電預訂當晚的菜式，石記風沙雞需要提前一天預訂。菜單經常更新，確保所用的是最當造的時令食材。

TEL. 2571 3348
GF, 15-17 Ngan Mok Street, Tin Hau
天后銀幕街 15-17 號地下

SPECIALITIES TO PRE-ORDER 預訂食物
Crispy chicken 炸子雞 /Roast chicken with fermented bean curd 南乳吊燒雞

■ PRICE 價錢
Lunch 午膳
set 套餐 $ 48-56
à la carte 點菜 $ 80-100
Dinner 晚膳
à la carte 點菜 $ 100-300

■ OPENING HOURS 營業時間
Lunch 午膳　11:30-15:00 (L.O.)
Dinner 晚膳　18:00-23:00 (L.O.)

HONG KONG 香港

Sheung Hei Dim Sum
嚐囍點心皇

A quick fix for your dim sum cravings whatever the time, this 24-hour shop boasts its own bite-sized MSG-free Cantonese snacks made from scratch and steamed to order. Shrimp dumplings and the steamed bun with diced chicken & mushroom are worth a try. A set lunch menu is also available between 11am to 3pm, while dinner with clay pot rice and stir-fries is served from 6pm to 9:30pm. A lively spot to meet friends, without breaking the bank.

簡約的店子以24小時全天候供應點心作招徠，點心全是自家製作，即點即蒸，全無味精。推介水晶鮮蝦餃，特色點心懷舊雞大包也值得一試。除點心外，早上11時至下午3時還供應午市套餐，晚上6時至9時30分更有煲仔飯和小菜可供選擇。價錢相宜，是不錯的聚腳點。

TEL. 2817 0838
GF, 25 North Street, Western District
西環北街 25號地下

■ PRICE 價錢
Lunch 午膳
set 套餐 $ 42-50
à la carte 點菜 $ 100-120
Dinner 晚膳
à la carte 點菜 $ 100-120

■ OPENING HOURS 營業時間
24 Hours 24 小時

Sheung Hei Claypot Rice
嚐囍煲仔小菜

Most claypot rice in town is cooked to order. But this shop takes it one step further and does it on a charcoal stove. The rice has a characteristic with smoky scent with a crispy crust at the bottom. Order the one with eel and pork ribs for the rich aroma of the fish and the luscious pork grease that coats every grain. The owner also runs a dim sum shop next door where you may order some Cantonese bite-size munchies to go with your claypot rice.

即點即煮並非這兒的特別之處，倒是其碳烤煲仔飯的方法使人印象深刻。以碳火烹煮米飯時香氣已撲鼻而來，煮熟後的飯焦更加香味誘人。推介白鱔排骨飯，能吃到鱔的香味之餘，排骨內的油分滲進飯內令米飯變得更香軟。隔鄰的點心店是姊妹店，食客可以選些點心佐餐。

TEL. 2819 6190
GF, 25 North Street, Western Dsitrcit
西環北街 25號地下

■ PRICE 價錢
Lunch 午膳
à la carte 點菜 $ 40-50
Dinner 晚膳
à la carte 點菜 $ 60-160

■ OPENING HOURS 營業時間
Lunch 午膳　11:00-15:00 (L.O.)
Dinner 晚膳　18:00-22:30 (L.O.)

■ ANNUAL AND WEEKLY CLOSING 休息日期
Closed Lunar New Year Eve and 3 days
Lunar New Year 年夜及農曆新年休息 3 天

Shiba

On a quiet street not far from the sea, and hidden behind a modest façade, is this intimate izakaya-style dining room – a good choice if you're meeting up with friends. It serves mainly yakitori and barbecued seafood; with shiso minced chicken, and scallop being two popular dishes. Most of the produce is imported from Japan, along with about 50 different sake, as well as shochu, fruit liqueurs and Japanese beers.

這小店子位於士美菲路靠海一帶，離新啟用的港鐵堅尼地城站並不遠。低調的門面，十分平易近人的居酒屋餐室，最適宜和朋友邊吃燒肉串，邊品嘗清酒。這裏的清酒有五十種之多，而食物方面除燒雞肉之外，尚有其他肉類和多種海鮮；自家製的紫蘇兔治雞肉和燒帆立貝最受歡迎。

TEL. 3568 2425
11 Smithfield, Kennedy Town
堅尼地城士美菲路 11 號

■ PRICE 價錢
à la carte 點菜 $ 350-550

■ OPENING HOURS 營業時間
18:00-23:30 (L.O.)

Shugetsu Ramen (Central)
麵鮮醬油房周月 (中環)

The queues form early for the ramen here, with many of the customers coming for the Tsukemen ramen, as well as the Abura and special soup ramen. The shop makes its own noodles – which you can have thick or thin – but it is the sauce at the base of the slow-cooked soup that really makes the difference: it's fermented for 18 months in a 100 year old wooden basket and adds richness and depth.

周月與別不同之處，在其以醬油為湯底的神髓：採用有逾一百四十年歷史的愛媛縣梶田商店特製的醬油，配入沙丁魚粉、鯖魚粉及海帶長時間慢火熬製，味道更醇厚豐富。與日本店一樣，香港店設有製麵房，每天新鮮製造兩款粗幼不同的麵條。除了湯拉麵外，還供應沾麵。

TEL. 2850 6009
5 Gough Street, Central
中環歌賦街 5號
www.shugetsu.com.hk

■ PRICE 價錢
à la carte 點菜 $ 89-150

■ OPENING HOURS 營業時間
11:30-20:50 (L.O.)
Sunday 週日　12:00-19:00 (L.O.)
Sunday before Public Holiday
公眾假期前週日　11:30-20:50 (L.O.)

■ ANNUAL AND WEEKLY CLOSING 休息日期
Closed New Year's Day and 1 day
Lunar New Year 元旦及年初一休息

Shugetsu Ramen (Quarry Bay)
麵鮮醬油房周月 (鰂魚涌)

This was the second branch of Shugetsu to open in Hong Kong. It's the freshly made noodles and the soy sauce base that make them so popular. The broth is prepared with sardines, mackerel and kelp, and soy sauce that is produced by a longstanding factory in Ehime. The popular choice is Tsukemen, for which they use thick noodles to absorb the sauce's taste more easily – you decide how large a portion you want.

這是周月在香港的第二間分店，以鮮製麵條和醬油湯為賣點的拉麵店，湯底用放在百年木桶內經十八個月發酵而成的醬油，加上沙丁魚粉、鯖魚粉及海帶煮成，美味且味道特別。除了湯拉麵外，沾麵也頗受歡迎，選用的麵條較粗但掛湯力強，能盡吸醬汁精華。食客可選擇麵的分量。

TEL. 2336 7888
30 Hoi Kwong Street, Quarry Bay
鰂魚涌海光街 30號
www.shugetsu.com.hk

■ PRICE 價錢
à la carte 點菜 $ 90-120

■ OPENING HOURS 營業時間
11:30-20:50 (L.O.)
Sunday 週日 12:00-19:00 (L.O.)
Sunday before Public Holiday
公眾假期前週日 11:30-20:50 (L.O.)

■ ANNUAL AND WEEKLY CLOSING 休息日期
Closed New Year's Day and 1 day
Lunar New Year 元旦及年初一休息

Sing Kee (Central)
星記 (中環)

 ♿ 👱 ♺16 ☎

HONG KONG 香港

The second branch of Sing Kee is a bright, tidy spot serving classic Cantonese food – something that's proving increasingly hard to find in Central. You'll find only traditional recipes using chicken, pork and seafood here, free of gimmicks or fancy presentation. Many specialities need pre-ordering, like chicken with ginger in clam sauce, or almond juice with fish maw and pig's lung. Come at lunch to take advantage of some reasonable prices.

想在中環區找到提供樸實高質的傳統粵菜且環境乾淨整潔的餐館，星記便是你的選擇。選用新鮮肉類如豬、雞及生猛海鮮等食材加上扎實的烹調技術，自然不乏支持者。午市提供一系列價錢實惠的小菜，甚得中環人士歡心。建議預訂燉湯如杏汁花膠燉豬肺。

TEL. 2970 0988
2F, 1 Lyndhurst Tower,
1 Lyndhurst Terrace, Central
中環擺花街 1號一號廣場 2樓

SPECIALITIES TO PRE-ORDER 預訂食物
Roasted cripsy chicken 脆皮炸子雞 /
Salt baked chicken in secret sauce 秘製
鹽焗雞

■ PRICE 價錢
Lunch 午膳
set 套餐 $ 78
à la carte 點菜 $ 100-200
Dinner 晚膳
à la carte 點菜 $ 200-400

■ OPENING HOURS 營業時間
Lunch 午膳　11:30-14:15 (L.O.)
Dinner 晚膳　18:00-22:15 (L.O.)

■ ANNUAL AND WEEKLY CLOSING 休息日期
Closed Sunday lunch 週日午膳休息

Sister Wah (Tin Hau)
華姐清湯腩 (天后)

With just six round tables, Sister Wah's diminutive dimensions are in direct contrast to the size of its reputation – this is one of the most famous beef brisket noodle shops. This family-run shop is always full and it is easy to see why: there are around 20 items on the menu which include Dan Dan noodles and Drunken chicken, but chief among them is the beef brisket in a clear soup.

這間家庭式經營的小店是最馳名的牛腩麵家之一，全店卻只有六張圓桌，難怪經常滿座，其規模與名氣有着鮮明對比。餐牌上約有二十種食品，包括擔擔麵和醉雞，但招牌菜還是清湯牛坑腩。

TEL. 2807 0181
Shop A1, 13 Electric Road, Tin Hau
天后電氣道 13號 A1號舖

■ PRICE 價錢
à la carte 點菜 $ 35-65

■ OPENING HOURS 營業時間
11:00-23:00 (L.O.)

■ ANNUAL AND WEEKLY CLOSING 休息日期
Closed 6 days Lunar New Year
農曆新年休息 6 天

SHUN TAK 順德菜

MAP 地圖   9/A-2

Siu Shun Village Cuisine (Kowloon Bay)
肇順名匯河鮮專門店 (九龍灣)

  P 🍽32

Not only do the river fish swim in the fish tanks at the entrance, but also in the waterways under the tempered glass floor - diners might even be under the illusion that they are dining in a glass-bottom boat on a river. It specialises in Shunde regional cooking and river fish dishes, including fried giant prawns with ginger and spring onion, stir-fried beef tenderloin strips with mushrooms in XO sauce, and braised fish lips casserole.

門外大大小小的魚缸放滿各式各樣的河鮮，走到店內亦不難發現腳下有水道和強化玻璃，魚兒在客人的腳下游來游去，特別的設計彷彿要提醒客人這裏的河鮮不能錯過。很多本地食客特意到此品嘗順德菜及河鮮菜式，招牌菜包括薑葱大蝦球、XO醬雙菇牛柳條和瓦罉煎焗魚咀等。

TEL. 2798 9738
Shop 6, 7F, MegaBox,
38 Wang Chiu Road, Kowloon Bay
九龍灣宏照道 38號 MegaBox7樓 6號舖

■ PRICE 價錢
Lunch 午膳
Dinner 晚膳

■ OPENING HOURS 營業時間
Lunch 午膳   09:00-16:15 (L.O.)
Dinner 晚膳 18:00-22:15 (L.O.)

SHANGHAINESE 滬菜

Snow Garden
雪園

❌❌   🍽16 📞🍴

Established in 1992 at this sleek business address and known for its traditional Shanghainese cuisine, this is a restaurant that operates like clockwork and whose staff are warm and attentive. The long-standing chef's specialities are steamed herring and deep-fried chicken skin with four spices; braised sea cucumber with shrimp roe; and yellow fish with sweet and sour sauce. Dishes arrive carefully prepared and bursting with flavour.

餐廳於1992年於此商業區熱點開始營業，以精心烹調的上海菜馳名，人流絡繹不絕，員工態度親切熱誠。清蒸鰣魚、四寶片皮雞、蝦子大烏參及糖醋黃魚都是歷久不衰的廚師精選。每道菜式都經過精心製作，色香味俱全。

TEL. 2881 6837
2F, China Taiping Tower,
8 Sunning Road, Causeway Bay
銅鑼灣新寧道 8號中國太平大廈 2樓
www.snow-garden.com

■ PRICE 價錢
Lunch 午膳
à la carte 點菜 $ 150-250
Dinner 晚膳
à la carte 點菜 $ 250-700

■ OPENING HOURS 營業時間
Lunch 午膳　11:30-14:30 (L.O.)
Dinner 晚膳　18:00-22:00 (L.O.)

■ ANNUAL AND WEEKLY CLOSING 休息日期
Closed 3 days Lunar New Year
農曆新年休息 3 天

Sorabol (Causeway Bay)
新羅寶 (銅鑼灣)

❌❌   ⬭35 ◎🍴

This branch of the successful restaurant group opened here in 1995. Its aesthetic is based on a traditional and elegant Korean house and uses lotus flower patterned doors, wood carvings and brick walls to good effect. The authentic cuisine is prepared using quality ingredients and includes a special menu of Jeonju dishes, which is the owner's homeland. Hoengseong Hanwoo is a good choice for barbecuing; also try the short ribs soup with rice.

其隻團於1995年在銅鑼灣開設此店，並於2011年搬至現址，店內裝潢取材自傳統韓國的精緻房舍，採用蓮花圖案的門、木雕和磚牆。食店選用優質食材製作正宗韓式料理。橫城韓牛是燒烤的最佳選擇，牛排骨湯飯及時令特別餐單也值得一試。

TEL. 2881 6823
Shop B, 18F, Lee Theatre Plaza,
99 Percival Street, Causeway Bay
銅鑼灣波斯富街 99號利舞臺廣場 18樓 B號舖
www.sorabol.com.hk

■ PRICE 價錢
Lunch 午膳
set 套餐 $ 78-108
à la carte 點菜 $ 200-650
Dinner 晚膳
à la carte 點菜 $ 200-650

■ OPENING HOURS 營業時間
Lunch 午膳   11:30-14:30 (L.O.)
Dinner 晚膳   17:30-22:30 (L.O.)

■ ANNUAL AND WEEKLY CLOSING 休息日期
Closed 1 day Lunar New Year
年初一休息

Spring Moon
嘉麟樓

XXX　　　　　　　　　　　　　& 🥢 P 🍽48 ©🍴 🐚

Oriental rugs, sepia prints of colonial life, teak floors and art deco styled stained glass all summon the spirit of a 1920s Shanghainese dining room here at The Peninsula hotel. Specialities are bird's nest soup, wok-fried lobster, and roasted Peking duck. The tea bar offers over 25 regularly-changing teas and staff, many of whom are sent to China for training, are hugely knowledgeable and happy to make recommendations.

餐室設計以半島酒店開業時的二十年代老上海為藍本，古典風格的柚木地板，配襯東方地氈、殖民地時代舊相片和帶裝飾藝術風格的彩色玻璃，充滿懷舊氣息。餐單上全是深受歡迎的經典菜式，包括千絲官燕羹、北京片皮鴨等等。店內提供的二十五種茶定期更換，曾到中國受訓的侍應樂於回答茗茶知識。

TEL. 2696 6760
1F, The Peninsula Hotel, Salisbury Road, Tsim Sha Tsui
尖沙咀梳士巴利道半島酒店 1 樓
www.hongkong.peninsula.com/zh/fine-dining/spring-moon-chinese-restaurant

SPECIALITIES TO PRE-ORDER 預訂食物
Hangzhou beggar's fortune chicken
杭州富貴雞

■ PRICE 價錢
Lunch 午膳
set 套餐 $ 500-800
à la carte 點菜 $ 400-800
Dinner 晚膳
set 套餐 $ 1,000-2,000
à la carte 點菜 $ 500-1,500

■ OPENING HOURS 營業時間
Lunch 午膳　11:30-14:30 (L.O.)
Sunday and Public Holiday lunch
週日及公眾假期午膳　11:00-14:30 (L.O.)
Dinner 晚膳　18:00-22:30 (L.O.)

Summer Palace
夏宮

♿ 🍽 **P** ⇆20 ◎📶

There's a timeless, exotic feel to this room whose decoration of gilt screens, golden silk wall coverings and lattice panels is inspired by the palace in Beijing. The menu is a roll-call of Cantonese classics; double-boiled soups are a speciality; dim sum is a highlight; and signature dishes include marinated pig's trotters, braised '23-head' Yoshihama abalone in oyster sauce, and Peking duck. They also offer a good selection of teas.

高聳的餐室以北京故宮為設計靈感，以華麗的水晶吊燈、大紅色餐桌，配以傳統中國屏風、金色絲綢畫作及雕塑，營造了迷人的情調。菜譜羅列各款傳統廣東名菜，招牌菜包括沙薑豬腳仔、蠔皇吉品鮑魚、北京片皮鴨等，燉湯也是其專長，部分需提早預訂。午市時點心是不俗的選擇。可供選擇的茶飲也很多。

TEL. 2820 8552
5F, Island Shangri-La Hotel, Pacific Place,
Supreme Court Road, Admiralty
金鐘法院道太古廣場港島香格里拉酒店 5樓
www.shangri-la.com/island

SPECIALITIES TO PRE-ORDER 預訂食物
Double-boiled soups 燉 湯 /Eight treasure duck 夏 宮 八 寶 鴨 /Beggar's chicken 富 貴 雞 /Poached fresh sliced sea-whelk 堂灼嚮螺片

■ PRICE 價錢
Lunch 午膳
à la carte 點菜 $350-1,500
Dinner 晚膳
à la carte 點菜 $350-1,500

■ OPENING HOURS 營業時間
Lunch 午膳　11:30-14:30 (L.O.)
Dinner 晚膳　18:30-22:30 (L.O.)

Sun Fook Kee
新福記

XX   🍽18 ◐🍴

Fujian cuisine is the draw here and in particular, dishes one rarely finds, like a shredded vegetable pancake which uses 12 different ingredients; many dishes require special skills and cooking techniques. It's a small place, albeit with three private rooms, so the chef – who is from Fujian province himself – buys his produce on a daily basis from the market; ask about the day's special and pre-order dishes when you make your reservation.

要品嘗高級懷舊福建菜，新福記是個好選擇。餐單上提供不少坊間難得一見的功夫菜，例如以十二種食材切幼絲烹煮、配上特製麵餅進食的潤餅菜；招牌菜還有滷大麵。為確保食材新鮮，廚師每天都會從市場採購。餐廳共三間廂房，適合大伙兒聚餐，建議訂座時查詢當日時令材料並預留菜式。

TEL. 2566 5898
1F, Circle Court, 3-5 Java Road,
North Point
北角渣華道 3-5 號永光閣 1 樓

■ PRICE 價錢
Lunch 午膳
à la carte 點菜 $ 350-500
Dinner 晚膳
à la carte 點菜 $ 500-700

■ OPENING HOURS 營業時間
Lunch 午膳 11:00-15:00 (L.O.)
Dinner 晚膳 18:00-22:00 (L.O.)

Sun Tung Lok (Tsim Sha Tsui)
新同樂 (尖沙咀)

XXX ⌂48 ☏

After 40 years in Happy Valley, Sun Tung Lok is now comfortably ensconced on the fourth floor of the Miramar shopping centre. A contemporary colour palette of grey, brown and beige is used to good effect in this stylish restaurant; ask for one of the three booths for extra privacy. The majority of the menu is Cantonese and dishes include rib of beef with house gravy, stuffed crab shell, and roast suckling pig; the abalone is a must.

在跑馬地駐紮四十年後，新同樂現在於美麗華商場4樓繼續營業。充滿時代感的灰色、咖啡色與米色的巧妙配搭讓店子看起來較摩登。店內設有三個廂座，以滿足需要私人空間的客人。八成菜式是粵菜，包括燒汁乾熘牛肋骨、鮮蘑菇焗釀蟹蓋及燒乳豬件。這裏的鮑魚是必試之選。

TEL. 2152 1417
4D, 4F, Miramar Shopping Centre,
132 Nathan Road, Tsim Sha Tsui
尖沙咀彌敦道132號美麗華商場4樓 D
www.suntunglok.com.hk

■ PRICE 價錢
Lunch 午膳
set 套餐 $ 298-428
à la carte 點菜 $ 300-500
Dinner 晚膳
à la carte 點菜 $ 500-800

■ OPENING HOURS 營業時間
Lunch 午膳 11:30-15:00 (L.O.)
Dinner 晚膳 18:00-22:30 (L.O.)

CANTONESE ROAST MEATS 燒味

Sun Yuen Hing Kee
新園興記

Located next to Sheung Wan market, this traditionally styled, simple but well maintained barbecue shop has been run by the same family since the mid-1970s. Over the years they've built up an appreciative following so the small place fills quickly. The appetising looking suckling pigs are not the only draw: roast pork, duck and pigeon all have their followers, as do the soft-boiled chicken, the homemade sausages and the preserved meats.

位於上環街市旁邊，這間格調傳統簡單的燒味店自七十年代中一直由同一家族經營。多年來，累積了不少忠實顧客，小小的地方往往座無虛席。這裏受歡迎的不僅是掛在廚房旁邊，賣相令人垂涎欲滴的乳豬，燒肉、烤鴨和乳鴿都各有忠實擁躉。白切雞、臘腸及臘肉亦十分吸引。

TEL. 2541 2207
327-329 Queen's Road Central,
Sheung Wan
上環皇后大道中 327-329號

■ PRICE 價錢
Dinner 晚膳
à la carte 點菜 $ 40-150

■ OPENING HOURS 營業時間
08:00-19:45

■ ANNUAL AND WEEKLY CLOSING 休息日期
Closed 3 days Lunar New Year
農曆新年休息 3 天

Sushi Masataka

Named after its executive chef, the former Sushi Rozan reopened in a wood-clad interior that reflects the roots of its cuisine. The nine seats in front of an open counter allow diners to watch the chefs in action. Only prix-fixe omakase menus are available, featuring quality seafood flown straight from Japan daily, such as golden-eye snapper and white sea urchin. Lunch is by reservation only and requires a minimum of 4 people.

從原來的名字鮨魯山(Sushi Rozan)易名後，店子亦重新裝修過。淺啡色木板裝潢，極有日本風味。從十二個櫃台座位減至九個座位，容納的人數少了，但廚師能更專注地服務每位客人。菜單仍是只供應廚師發辦套餐，食材和分量會按食客的需求調整。金目鯛和白海膽等高級食材每天從日本直送到店。

TEL. 2574 1333
GF, Oak Hill, 18 Wood Road, Wan Chai
灣仔活道 18號萃峯地下

■ PRICE 價錢
Dinner 晚膳
set 套餐 $ 2,080-2,980

■ OPENING HOURS 營業時間
Dinner 晚膳　18:00-20:00/20:30-22:30

■ ANNUAL AND WEEKLY CLOSING 休息日期
Closed 3 days Lunar New Year and Monday
農曆新年 3 天及週一休息

SUSHI 壽司 MAP 地圖 33/B-1

Sushi Mori Tomoaki

✗ 🍽8 ⏣ ◐🍴

The daily delivery of seafood at this sushi restaurant comes from Kyushu and Hokkaido. The rice is seasoned with red vinegar and each sushi has its own unique seasoning – for example nodoguro comes with yuzu pepper, and engawa with garlic soy sauce. For dinner it's best to go for the omakase which includes sashimi and assorted small dishes before the nigiri. There are two lunch sessions which are 12:00-13:30 and 13:30-15:00.

餐廳環境雅淨。中日混血兒廚主廚年紀輕輕卻具多年製作傳統壽司經驗，且喜愛鑽研烹調技法，其壽司以每日由日本運到之新鮮食材，加上混和紅醋的米飯製成。晚市可嘗嘗由十六道不同款壽司和魚生組合而成，梅花間竹式上菜的廚師套餐。午市分為12:00-13:30和13:30-15:00兩個時段。

TEL. 2979 5977
Shop D, GF, 9-23 Shell Street, Tin Hou
天后蜆殼街 9-23號地下 D鋪

■ PRICE 價錢
Lunch 午膳
set 套餐 $ 380-620
Dinner 晚膳
set 套餐 $ 2,000

■ OPENING HOURS 營業時間
Lunch 午膳　12:00-15:00 (L.O.)
Dinner 晚膳　18:30-22:30 (L.O.)

■ ANNUAL AND WEEKLY CLOSING 休息日期
Closed Mid-August, late December to early January and Sunday 八月中、十二月尾至一月初及週日休息

Sushi Shikon
志魂

✽✽ ✽✽ ✽✽

HONG KONG 香港

✂   ♿ ⛁6 ⛩ ◑♼

The owner wants his Hong Kong customers to enjoy the same superb quality sushi that he serves in his Tokyo restaurant – so the fish arrives daily from Tsukiji market and the rice comes from Niigata. The secret is in the vinegar, made from two kinds of sake sediment and aged for four years. The tiger prawn, the tender octopus and the egg custard with blue crab are just some of the stand-outs. Lunch is reservation only for a minimum of four people.

志魂堅持提供優質食物的宗旨多年保持不變，繼續堅持每天由日本築地市場運來鮮魚及選用由新潟運來頂級日本米。這兒的壽司烹調秘訣是以兩種成熟度達四年的清酒糟製造的醋入饌，鮮魚的鮮與米飯的醋香配搭出完美的味道。午膳時段只接受四人或以上的預訂。

TEL. 2643 6800
Citadines Mercer Hong Kong,
29 Jervois Street, Sheung Wan
上環蘇杭街 29號馨樂庭尚圓服務公寓
www.sushi-shikon.com

■ PRICE 價錢
Dinner 晚膳
set 套餐 $ 3,500

■ OPENING HOURS 營業時間
Dinner 晚膳　18:00-20:00, 20:30-22:30

■ ANNUAL AND WEEKLY CLOSING 休息日期
Closed Christmas; New Year Day;
Lunar New Year; Easter and Sunday
聖誕節、元旦、農曆新年、復活節及週日休息

Sushi Ta-ke
竹 寿司

🍴10 ⚐ ☀🍴

Sushi Ta-ke presents traditional Edomae sushi using the freshest ingredients. Along with sashimi, it also serves hot dishes like grilled swordfish and Wagyu beef – try too the Japanese pickle salad and boiled golden-eye snapper. The striking and artfully lit interior comes as no surprise when one considers the expertise of the three owners: one is an interior designer, one a lighting designer and the third a restaurateur.

竹寿司的室內設計特別且有藝術氣息，這跟三位東主的背景不無關係：一個室內設計師、一個燈光設計師，一個飲食業專家。餐廳以正宗傳統方式製作的壽司作賣點，魚生均每天由日本空運到港。除壽司外，還供應各款煮物和燒酒。可供選擇的清酒款式也很多。

TEL. 2577 0611
12F, Cubus, 1 Hoi Ping Road,
Causeway Bay
銅鑼灣開平道 1 號 Cubus12樓
www.sushitake.com.hk

■ PRICE 價錢
Lunch 午膳
set 套餐 $ 228-1,500
à la carte 點菜 $ 300-1,800

Dinner 晚膳
set 套餐 $ 1,200-1,680
à la carte 點菜 $ 300-1,800

■ OPENING HOURS 營業時間
Lunch 午膳　12:00-14:30 (L.O.)
Dinner 晚膳　18:30-22:30 (L.O.)

■ ANNUAL AND WEEKLY CLOSING 休息日期
Closed 1 day Lunar New Year 年初一休息

Sushi Tokami

The owner-chef not only runs the original Tokami in Tokyo but is also the founder of a speciality tuna supplier in Tsukiji market, so the quality of the ingredients that he gets flown in daily to his Hong Kong branch is a given. For the Edomae sushi he uses Tanada rice from Yamagata, cooked with red vinegar from sake lees in a traditional claypot, to accompany the various cuts of tuna which comes from Oma, Aomori and Uchiura Bay.

來自銀座，以吞拿魚壽司享負盛名，店主兼營日本築地市場一家吞拿魚專門店，每日均獲得優質新鮮的吞拿魚，在食材上佔盡優勢。另外，這兒依照江戶前傳統方法製作壽司，並選用礦物質豐富的山形縣和鹿兒島的溫泉水，配以傳統土鍋烹煮，再混入以酒粕發酵的赤醋，醋味特別香醇。以頸部製作的吞拿魚手卷非試不可。

TEL. 2771 3938
Shop 216A, Level 2, Ocean Centre,
Harbour City, 17 Canton Road,
Tsim Sha Tsui
尖沙咀廣東道 17號
海港城海洋中心 2樓 216A號鋪
www.tokami.com.hk

■ PRICE 價錢
Lunch 午膳
set 套餐 $ 800-1,200
Dinner 晚膳
set 套餐 $ 2,200

■ OPENING HOURS 營業時間
Lunch 午膳　12:00-15:00 (L.O.)
Dinner 晚膳　18:00-21:00 (L.O.)

SUSHI 壽司

Sushi Wadatsumi

🍴   🛋8   ⊙🍴

There were two major changes in 2016: firstly, the name changed from Sushi Ginza Iwa to Sushi Wadatsumi and secondly, the restaurant moved from Asia Pacific Centre to a new home in the Grand Millennium Plaza. The warm, softly lit room provides the perfect environment in which to enjoy the carefully crafted sushi. What hasn't changed is that the fish and seafood are still flown in daily from Tokyo's Tsukiji market.

從中環遷至上環、由Sushi Ginza Iwa易名為Sushi Wadatsumi，除了地址和名字不同和餐室環境更時尚淡雅外，店內的一切仍然與在日本銀座的總店相同。銀色的壽司盛器、每日從築地市場直送到港的鮮魚和海產，依然帶給你置身東京銀座總店的感覺。

TEL. 2619 0199
Shop 201, 2F,
Grand Millennium Plaza,
181 Queen's Road Central,
Sheung Wan
上環皇后大道中181號新紀元廣場201室

■ PRICE 價錢
Lunch 午膳
set 套餐 $ 480-1,380
Dinner 晚膳
set 套餐 $ 2,000-2,800

■ OPENING HOURS 營業時間
Lunch 午膳　12:00-14:30 (L.O.)
Dinner 晚膳　18:30-22:00 (L.O.)

Ta Vie
旅

❀❀

🍴🍴   ♿ 📷10 ◔🍴

After three years at Ryu Gin, Chef Sato Hideaki now displays his skills on the 2nd floor of the Pottinger Hotel. In an elegantly dressed restaurant he serves his own unique style of cuisine which fuses together Japanese and French techniques while using Asian ingredients. He serves an 8 course tasting menu, with most of the seafood coming directly from Tokyo. Along with French wine, Japanese wine and sake are three specially selected teas.

在龍吟工作數年後，日籍大廚佐藤秀明在中環石板街酒店開店再度獻藝，以其純熟的法日混合烹調技術，將從日本及其他亞洲地區精心搜購的食材炮製成佳餚；一些被濫用的熱門食材一定不會出現在套餐之中，保證給你一個不平凡的美食之旅。除葡萄酒及清酒外，店方更精選了三款清茶以供佐餐。

TEL. 2668 6488
2F, The Pottinger Hotel,
21 Stanley Street, Central
中環士丹利街 21號石板街酒店 2樓
www.tavie.com.hk

■ PRICE 價錢
Lunch 午膳
set 套餐 $ 450-790
Dinner 晚膳
set 套餐 $ 1,880

■ OPENING HOURS 營業時間
Lunch 午膳　12:00-13:30 (L.O.)
Dinner 晚膳　19:00-21:30 (L.O.)

■ ANNUAL AND WEEKLY CLOSING 休息日期
Closed Monday, Friday and Saturday lunch; and Sunday
週一、週五及週六午膳和週日休息

HONG KONG 香港

Tai Wing Wah
大榮華

✗   ♿ ⟆30

A refit in 2016 resulted in this Cantonese restaurant, located in the north of New Territories, looking a little brighter and feeling a little fresher. It serves dim sum and 'Walled Village' cuisine, alongside assorted classic Cantonese dishes. Try the roast duck with bean paste and coriander; claypot rice with lard and premium soy sauce; and, above all, the steamed sponge cake.

很多人長途跋涉來到元朗，只有一個原因：光顧大榮華。此酒家除了供應點心外，還提供近百款圍村小菜及經典粵式名菜如香茜燒米鴨及缽仔豬油頭抽撈飯等，還有奶黃馬拉糕。翻新過的餐廳用上五彩繽紛的地磚和明亮的燈光，配上傳統裝飾，感覺煥然一新。

TEL. 2476 9888
2F, 2-6 On Ning Road, Yuen Long
元朗安寧路 2-6號 2樓

■ PRICE 價錢
à la carte 點菜 $ 80-300

■ OPENING HOURS 營業時間
06:45-22:00 (L.O.)

Tai Woo (Causeway Bay)
太湖海鮮城 (銅鑼灣)

🍽 24　📞🍴

One of the district's most famous names, Tai Woo moved to these more comfortable surroundings in 2011 and, while the restaurant may be smaller than before, business is better than ever, with over 1,000 customers served every day. What hasn't changed is the quality of the service or the cooking – along with a menu of Cantonese seafood dishes, such as crunchy shrimp ball and mini lobster casserole, are favourites like sesame chicken baked in salt.

於八十年代開業的太湖是區內馳名酒家，尤擅海鮮菜式，2011年才搬遷到更新更舒適的現址。多年來食物質素維持不變，生意昌旺每天服務逾千名食客，即便如此，服務依然周到。這裏提供多款廣東菜式，招牌菜有芝麻鹽焗雞、奇脆明珠伴金龍及薑米鮮魚炒飯等。

TEL. 2893 0822
9F, Causeway Bay Plaza 2,
463-483 Lockhart Road, Causeway Bay
銅鑼灣駱克道 463-483號
銅鑼灣廣場第二期 9樓
www.taiwoorestaurant.com

■ PRICE 價錢
Lunch 午膳
set 套餐 $ 428-568
à la carte 點菜 $ 100-250
Dinner 晚膳
set 套餐 $ 428-568
à la carte 點菜 $ 300-500

■ OPENING HOURS 營業時間
10:30-02:30 (L.O.)

■ ANNUAL AND WEEKLY CLOSING 休息日期
Closed 1 day Lunar New Year 年初一休息

Tak Kee
德記

🍜⏐　　　　　　　　🥡16 📞⏐

It started out as a street-side hawker stall in the 1980s and still retains the casual, vibrant vibe. The second-generation hands-on owner shops for groceries every day and sometimes helps the experienced chefs with kitchen chores. Pork tripe and peppercorn soup is a culinary highlight, using berries from Malaysia and Indonesia. Regulars also come for its spiced marinated goose liver, crispy chitterlings stuffed with glutinous rice and oyster omelette.

於八十年代開業，早期為大排檔，現由第二代經營。店東凡事親力親為，每天親自到菜市場採購新鮮食材，間或會在廚房幫忙潮州老師傅打點廚務。這兒的胡椒豬肚湯獨特之處是採用馬來西亞和印尼兩種胡椒，滷水大鵝肝、脆皮糯米釀大腸及馳名蠔仔餅深得食客喜愛。傳統荷包鱔，需最少八位或以上才接受預訂。

TEL. 2819 5568
GF, 3 G Belcher's Street,
Western District
西環卑路乍街 3 號 G 地舖

SPECIALITIES TO PRE-ORDER 預訂食物
Double-boiled preserved mustard wrapped eel soup　荷包鱔 / Double-boiled pork lung soup with almond 杏汁白肺湯 / Joyful dumplings 繡球藏白玉

■ PRICE 價錢
Lunch 午膳
à la carte 點菜　$ 150-300
Dinner 晚膳
à la carte 點菜　$ 150-300

■ OPENING HOURS 營業時間
Lunch 午膳　11:00-15:00 (L.O.)
Dinner 晚膳　17:30-22:30 (L.O.)

■ ANNUAL AND WEEKLY CLOSING 休息日期
Closed Monday 週一休息

Takeya
竹家

The Japanese owner-chef was originally posted to Hong Kong as an engineer but, having settled here and married a local girl, he switched careers and together they opened this little yakitori shop in Hung Hom. Seating just 15, it's an intimate spot, made warmer with lots of bamboo. There's extensive choice, with seasonal specialities available. Try the special selections of Japanese wine or the high quality homemade umeshu.

日籍店主兼大廚在香港工作多年，其後與太太定居香港並展開新生活，一起經營這間以竹子為主題的串燒小店，小小的店子只有十五個座位卻予人親密溫暖的感覺。店內串燒種類繁多，時有特別食物推介。供應的日本酒較別的店子獨特，尤以自家浸製的梅酒更是不俗。

TEL. 2365 8878
Shop 1, On Wah Building,
31C1 Tak Man Street, Whampoa Estate,
Hung Hom
紅磡黃埔新村德民街 31C1安華樓 1號舖

■ PRICE 價錢
Dinner 晚膳
à la carte 點菜 $150-400

■ OPENING HOURS 營業時間
Dinner 晚膳 18:30-22:30 (L.O.)

■ ANNUAL AND WEEKLY CLOSING 休息日期
Closed 14 days Lunar New Year and
Monday 農曆新年 14 天及週一休息

Takumi by Daisuke Mori

Revamped and renamed after its new executive chef from Japan, the interior features beige panelling, dark marble and soft lighting, imparting effortless European chic. Chef Mori specialises in French haute cuisine made with seasonal Japanese produce. The prix-fixe 9-course menu includes his critically acclaimed chargrilled wagyu beef tenderloin. There are only 11 counter seats around the open kitchen. Reservation recommended.

以米白色木牆板與黑底白紋雲石配搭柔和燈光，翻新後的餐室更時尚，亦帶點西化，與櫃台座位相連的開放式廚房仍然屹立於店中央。日籍大廚採用來自日本的時令食材，烹調出帶有個人風格的菜式。晚市套餐重點在炭燒近江和牛。店內供應的清酒質素尤佳。全店只有十一個座位，建議訂座。

TEL. 2574 1299
GF, Oak Hill, 16 Wood Road, Wan Chai
灣仔活道 16號萃峯地下

■ PRICE 價錢
Lunch 午膳
set 套餐 $ 780-980
Dinner 晚膳
set 套餐 $ 2,080-2,680

■ OPENING HOURS 營業時間
Lunch 午膳 12:00-14:00 (L.O.)
Dinner 晚膳 18:00-21:30 (L.O.)

■ ANNUAL AND WEEKLY CLOSING 休息日期
Closed 3 days Lunar New Year; Sunday and Monday lunch 農曆新年 3 天及週日和週一午膳休息

T'ang Court
唐閣

Sautéed prawns with asparagus, deep-fried taro puffs with shrimps, and lobster with spring onions are just some of the delicate and refined Cantonese classics you can expect at this discreet and professionally run restaurant. It comes divided into two: upstairs has a more subdued, intimate feel, while the traditional style of the more appealing first floor room is broken up by contemporary artwork; tables 23 & 25 are best.

以中國史上最強盛的唐朝命名，呈獻各種粵式珍饈佳餚，露皇金銀蝦、荔芋寶盒、三葱爆龍蝦等，光聽名字已垂涎不已。這格調典雅的餐廳共佔兩層，一樓融合傳統裝潢與現代藝術裝飾，23及25號枱位置最佳；二樓較私密，適合情侶用餐或商務聚會，並設有以唐代詩人命名的貴賓廳。服務專業稱心。

TEL. 2132 7898
1F, The Langham Hotel, 8 Peking Road, Tsim Sha Tsui
尖沙咀北京道 8號朗廷酒店 1樓
www.langhamhotels.com/hongkong

SPECIALITIES TO PRE-ORDER 預訂食物
Baked Blue Point oysters with port wine
砵酒焗美國蠔

■ PRICE 價錢
Lunch 午膳
set 套餐 $ 500
à la carte 點菜 $ 400-1,700
Dinner 晚膳
set 套餐 $ 1,200
à la carte 點菜 $ 400-1,700

■ OPENING HOURS 營業時間
Lunch 午膳　12:00-14:30 (L.O.)
Weekend and Public Holiday lunch
週末及公眾假期午膳　11:00-14:30 (L.O.)
Dinner 晚膳　18:00-22:30 (L.O.)

HONG KONG 香港

Tasty (IFC)
正斗粥麵專家 (國際金融中心)

Be prepared to queue and share a table because over 1,000 customers a day, many of whom work in IFC, crowd into this Tasty. They mostly come for the trademark shrimp wonton or the much-loved beef and rice noodle stir fry; congee with prawns and dim sum are also recommended from the vast choice on offer. The last redecoration left the interior looking a lot more contemporary.

坐落於機鐵站上蓋，這裏每日有逾千個顧客，當中大部分在IFC工作，繁忙時間到訪，便要做好排隊和拼桌的準備。熱門食品包括招牌鮮蝦雲吞麵和極受歡迎的乾炒牛河。此外，生猛大蝦粥及精美點心亦值得一試。

TEL. 2295 0101
Shop 3016 - 3018, Podium Level 3,
IFC Mall, 1 Harbour View Street, Central
中環港景街 1 號國際金融中心商場 3樓
3016-3018號舖
www.tasty.com.hk

■ PRICE 價錢
à la carte 點菜 $ 60-200

■ OPENING HOURS 營業時間
11:00-22:45 (L.O.)

Tate

Moved from Elgin Street to a bigger, more versatile space on Hollywood Road, where the bleached timber and muted pink interior is laced with warm greys and brushed gold to impart sensuous elegance. Japanese kaiseki marries French haute cuisine – designer turned owner-chef Vicky Lau cares as much for the creative juxtaposition of ingredients and seasoning as the artistic mise en place. Carefully matched wine pairings are also available.

遷址後，新店以柔和的灰褐、淡粉紅和磨砂金作色調，感覺優雅中帶着女性的細膩纖柔。新的烹調意念，旨在反璞歸真，還原食材的本相。運用個人創意在基本的烹調基礎上對食材進行重塑，希望食客品嘗每一口食物時，都能喚起他們的熱誠與靈感。完美體驗，怎少得了與菜餚相輔相成的餐酒配對。

TEL. 2555 2172
210 Hollywood Road, Sheung Wan
上環荷李活道 210號
www.tate.com.hk

■ PRICE 價錢
Dinner 晚膳
set 套餐 $ 1,380-1,580

■ OPENING HOURS 營業時間
Dinner 晚膳　18:30-22:00 (L.O.)

■ ANNUAL AND WEEKLY CLOSING 休息日期
Closed Sunday 週日休息

Thai Chiu (Sham Shui Po)
泰潮 (深水埗)

Hainanese chicken; tom yum kung with seafood; fried egg with herbs and the various different styles of curry are just some of the highlights from an extensive menu prepared by native Thai chefs at this simple little restaurant. It's made up of two modest dining rooms, both decorated in bright green and yellow, with plastic tables and small stools. Simple it may be, but the food is good and the prices are competitive.

海南雞、冬蔭功海鮮湯、香草煎蛋及一系列咖喱只是種類繁多的菜單的一部分，全店食物一律由這家簡樸小餐廳的泰籍廚師主理，味道美味，價錢相宜。餐廳由兩個餐室組成，兩間房都以亮綠及黃色裝潢，配以膠桌和小板凳，感覺樸實自然。

TEL. 2314 3333
101-103 Fuk Wing Street, Sham Shui Po
深水埗福榮街 101-103號

■ PRICE 價錢
set 套餐 $ 30-60
à la carte 點菜 $ 60-150

■ OPENING HOURS 營業時間
11:30-22:30 (L.O.)

The Chairman
大班樓

🍽30 🕐🍴

The Chairman looks to small suppliers and local fishermen for its ingredients and much of the produce used is also organic. Showing respect for the provenance of ingredients, and using them in homemade sauces and flavoursome dishes such as steamed crab with aged Shaoxing, crispy chicken stuffed with shrimp paste and almond sweet soup, has attracted a loyal following. The restaurant is divided into four different sections and service is pleasant and reassuringly experienced.

大班樓的食材來自小型供應商和本地漁民，大部分都是有機材料，且將精挑細選的材料用來製作醬料和烹調美味菜式，如雞油花雕蒸大花蟹、香煎百花雞件配魚露、生磨杏仁茶等，吸引不少忠實擁躉。餐廳分成四個不同用餐區，服務令人賓至如歸。

TEL. 2555 2202
18 Kau U Fong, Central
中環九如坊 18號
www.thechairmangroup.com

SPECIALITIES TO PRE-ORDER 預訂食物
Pan fried crispy chicken stuffed with shrimp meat 香煎百花雞件配魚露 /
Crabmeat sticky rice 蟹肉糯米飯

■ PRICE 價錢
Lunch 午膳
set 套餐 $ 208-228
à la carte 點菜 $ 500-800
Dinner 晚膳
à la carte 點菜 $ 500-800

■ OPENING HOURS 營業時間
Lunch 午膳　12:00-14:00 (L.O.)
Dinner 晚膳　18:00-22:00 (L.O.)

■ ANNUAL AND WEEKLY CLOSING 休息日期
Closed 3 days Lunar New Year
農曆新年休息 3 天

The Ocean

 HONG KONG 香港

Warm birch with turquoise accents, an ocean theme with unobstructed sea views set the mood for a dining experience by the sea, from the sea. Renowned French chef Olivier Bellin's first venture outside Brittany cooks up seafood such as langoustine, sea urchin and scallops as creatively as he does back home. Five- and eight-course prix fixe aside, an à la carte menu also offers pigeon on top of fish. Blue lobster in curry sauce is a must-try.

尊重食材、還原食材的味道，是主廚的理念。透過食物和服務帶給客人歡樂是餐廳的宗旨。五道菜和八道菜的套餐以海洋為主題，每道菜式的食材均以海洋食材組合配搭如Brittany龍蝦、海膽、帶子等，乳鴿是店內唯一非海產類食材。Ocean breeze及great reef是招牌菜。

TEL. 2889 5939
Shop 302, 28 Beach Road, Repulse Bay
淺水灣海灘道 28號 302號舖
www.theocean.hk

■ PRICE 價錢
Dinner 晚膳
set 套餐 $ 1,088-1,288
à la carte 點菜 $ 900-1,200

■ OPENING HOURS 營業時間
Dinner 晚膳　18:30-22:30 (L.O.)

■ ANNUAL AND WEEKLY CLOSING 休息日期
Closed Monday 週一休息

The Square
翠玉軒

     ♿   ⇔48   ☎︎⏰

To retain the food's natural flavour, the chef insists on using fresh, seasonal produce – he also cooks in a healthy way. Delicacies such as poached spotted garoupa in soya milk broth, and crispy fried boneless chicken stuffed with minced prawn purée are worth a try. Climbing the small staircase up to The Square always adds to the sense of anticipation and this is all the greater these days as the last makeover left the room looking very handsome.

每次踏上往翠玉軒的梯級，內心總會惦念着其美味佳餚和貼心服務，不期然便加快了步伐。這兒的粵菜烹調甚具心思，大廚選用當造食材，加上細膩健康的烹調方式，保留並突出了食材原味。美食包括鮮豆漿浸海星石斑及脆皮江南百花雞等。

TEL. 2525 1163
Shop 401, 4F, Exchange Square Podium, Central
中環交易廣場平臺 4樓 401號舖
www.maxims.com.hk

SPECIALITIES TO PRE-ORDER 預訂食物
Steamed crab claw with Huadiao wine
花雕蒸蟹拑

■ PRICE 價錢
Lunch 午膳
à la carte 點菜 $ 250-300
Dinner 晚膳
à la carte 點菜 $ 300-500

■ OPENING HOURS 營業時間
Lunch 午膳   11:00-14:30 (L.O.)
Dinner 晚膳   18:00-22:30 (L.O.)

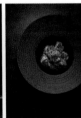

The Steak House Winebar + grill

One of the most sophisticated grill rooms in town comes with its own colourful wine bar and an impressive wine list – it's 70% American and includes a large number of top Californian wines. The ingredients used here are unimpeachable: beef sourced from Australia, the U.S. and Canada is supplemented by great seafood. You even get to choose your knife from 10 different models. Service is professional but also has personality.

作為城中最著名的扒房之一，它擁有出色的酒吧及令人眼花繚亂的餐酒名單，當中70%產自美國，更包括了許多頂級加州葡萄酒。這裏採用的全是一流食材：來自澳洲、美國與日本的牛肉，配合鮮美的海鮮。你還可以從十種餐刀中挑選最心儀的款式作餐具！服務專業友善。

TEL. 2313 2323
LF, InterContinental Hotel,
18 Salisbury Road, Tsim Sha Tsui
尖沙咀梳士巴利道18號洲際酒店地庫1樓
www.hongkong-ic.intercontinental.
com

■ PRICE 價錢
Weekrnds lunch 週末午膳
set 套餐 $698-898
Dinner 晚膳
set 套餐 $888
à la carte 點菜 $1,000-2,500

■ OPENING HOURS 營業時間
Weekends lunch 週末午膳   12:00-14:30 (L.O.)
Dinner 晚膳   18:00-22:30 (L.O.)

The Swiss Chalet
瑞士餐廳

    12

It was relocated next door, but you may not have noticed, because the same ambiance of a quaint and homely Alpine chalet is retained at this new location – wood furniture and beams set against white washed walls. The menu is classic Swiss with a variety of cured meats and sausages, over 20 different cheeses, and of course the unmissable fondue made with five cheeses and kirsch, to be paired with their extensive selection of Swiss wines.

遷到隔鄰舖位後，裝潢仍然保留原店的樣子：木傢俱、小窗戶，像極了瑞士高山上的小木屋。店東兼主廚與全店職員共事二十年，食物和服務水準一直維持不變。選用的瑞士香腸、芝士、醃肉和小牛肉等質素都很好。牛面沙律、炸牛仔肉和五種芝士混合櫻桃酒而成的芝士火鍋不可錯過。多款瑞士美酒任你挑選。

TEL. 2191 9197
GF, 8 Hart Avenue, Tsim Sha Tsui
尖沙咀赫德道 8號地下

■ PRICE 價錢
Lunch 午膳
set 套餐 $ 118-168
à la carte 點菜 $ 250-650
Dinner 晚膳
à la carte 點菜 $ 250-650

■ OPENING HOURS 營業時間
Lunch 午膳 12:00-14:30 (L.O.)
Dinner 晚膳 18:00-22:30 (L.O.)

Tim Ho Wan (North Point)
添好運 (北角)

The residents of North Point appear mighty glad that Tim Ho Wan finally opened a branch on Hong Kong Island. The soberly furnished dining room is always packed and at peak hours there'll even be a queue outside. The atmosphere is typical of a local tea house and hums with general contentment. There are over twenty different dim sum choices, along with a few desserts, and the menu changes each month.

添好運自從在港島區開設分店以來，一直深受北角區街坊喜愛；裝修雖簡約但客源不絕，每逢繁忙時段更會大排長龍；店內氣氛與一般本地茶樓無異，熱鬧而略嫌擠逼。餐牌上雖只列有二十多款點心及數款甜品，但餐單上的食物款式會每月更新一次。

TEL. 2979 5608
2-8 Wharf Road, North Point
北角和富道 2-8號

■ PRICE 價錢
à la carte 點菜 $ 30-50

■ OPENING HOURS 營業時間
10:00-21:30 (L.O.)

■ ANNUAL AND WEEKLY CLOSING 休息日期
Closed 3 days Lunar New Year
農曆新年休息 3 天

Tim Ho Wan (Sham Shui Po)
添好運 (深水埗)

The second branch of Tim Ho Wan is able to accommodate a few more customers than the original and is located in a more residential area; but don't be surprised to find a queue of expectant diners outside here too. The 25 different dim sum choices are reasonably priced and carefully prepared. Highlights include steamed shrimp dumpling, baked bun with barbecue pork and steamed beef balls. There are four small private rooms on the first floor.

這家添好運的第二分店，坐落於人口稠密的住宅區內，儘管能容納更多人客，但若看到店外等候入座的人龍，你不需要感到意外。供應25款由廚師巧手製作、價錢實惠的點心，不可不試的包括蝦餃、酥皮焗叉燒包和陳皮牛肉球。一樓設有四間小型貴賓房。

TEL. 2788 1226
9-11 Fuk Wing Street, Sham Shui Po
深水埗福榮街 9-11號

■ PRICE 價錢
à la carte 點菜 $30-50

■ OPENING HOURS 營業時間
10:00-21:30 (L.O.)
Weekends 週末 09:00-21:30 (L.O.)

■ ANNUAL AND WEEKLY CLOSING 休息日期
Closed 3 days Lunar New Year
農曆新年休息 3 天

Tim Ho Wan (Tai Kwok Tsui)
添好運 (大角咀)

Mention dim sum and many people will instantly think of the bustling Tim Ho Wan shop in Mong Kok. Here, at their new place, the crowds still flock in but the place is more spacious and feels even bigger, thanks to the high ceilings and bright lights. The reason for its popularity is the twenty different kinds of traditional Cantonese dim sum – made by hand with fresh ingredients – and the reasonable prices charged.

想到添好運的美味點心，便會想起旺角舊店的擠擁。新店位於大角咀一大型屋苑內，比舊店寬敞，高聳的樓底配搭白色主調的裝潢，舒適明淨。然而，主角還是那二十多款廣式點心。沒有花巧的外形、創新的配搭，有的是傳統手藝加上新鮮食材，價廉味美，難怪經常座無虛席。

TEL. 2332 2896
Shop G, 72A-C, Olympian City2,
18 Hoi Ting Road, Tai Kwok Tsui
大角咀海庭道 18號奧海城 2期 G72A-C鋪

■ PRICE 價錢
à la carte 點菜 $30-50

■ OPENING HOURS 營業時間
10:00-21:30 (L.O.)

■ ANNUAL AND WEEKLY CLOSING 休息日期
Closed 3 days Lunar New Year
農曆新年休息 3 天

Tim's Kitchen (Sheung Wan)
桃花源小廚 (上環)

⌑26

Success lead to Tim's Kitchen moving to these premises in 2010 – it's in the same area as before but, with two floors and a capacity of 100, is much larger; chef-owner Tim's son designed the colourful, modern room. Plenty of choice is offered, including popular specialities like Crystal prawn, pomelo skin and pork stomach, which showcase the kitchen's respect for the ingredients.

桃花源小廚遷至現址後，共有兩層，可容納一百人。店主兼廚師黎先生的兒子設計了色彩豐富兼時尚的房間。新店比舊店提供更多粵菜，當然，鎮店菜如玻璃蝦球、柚皮及豬肚仍然羅列在菜單上，每款食品都證明廚房對優質材料的高度重視。

TEL. 2543 5919
84-90 Bonham Strand, Sheung Wan
上環文咸東街 84-90號
www.timskitchen.com.hk

SPECIALITIES TO PRE-ORDER 預訂食物
Steamed whole fresh crab claw with winter melon 冬瓜蒸原隻鮮蟹鉗

■ PRICE 價錢
Lunch 午膳
à la carte 點菜 $ 150-300
Dinner 晚膳
à la carte 點菜 $ 300-1,000

■ OPENING HOURS 營業時間
Lunch 午膳　10:30-16:00 (L.O.)
Dinner 晚膳　18:00-22:30 (L.O.)

■ ANNUAL AND WEEKLY CLOSING 休息日期
Closed 4 days Lunar New Year
農曆新年休息 4 天

CANTONESE 粵菜

Tin Lung Heen
天龍軒

& ⮜ 🖾 P ⟷12 ◑🍴 ⚒

'Dragon in the sky' is a very apposite name as this good looking Cantonese restaurant occupies a large part of the 102nd floor of the Ritz-Carlton hotel. The vast windows bring in plenty of daylight at lunch and make it a good spot from which to watch the sun go down. Among the signature dishes are barbecued Iberian pork with honey, and double-boiled chicken soup with fish maw in coconut. There are also several charming private rooms.

位於香港麗思卡爾頓酒店102樓，這間極具氣派的粵菜餐館以氣勢十足的天龍命名。樓高兩層的設計令餐廳光線充沛，格外舒適，殷勤的服務人員讓你倍感親切。另設有多個精緻的私人包廂。菜單着重傳統菜式，值得一試的有蜜燒西班牙黑豚肉叉燒和原個椰皇花膠燉雞。

TEL. 2263 2150
102F, The Ritz-Carlton Hotel,
1 Austin Road West, Tsim Sha Tusi
尖沙咀柯士甸道西 1 號
麗思卡爾頓酒店 102 樓
www.ritzcarlton.com/en/hotels/
china/hong-kong/dining/tin-lung-
heen

■ PRICE 價錢
Lunch 午膳
set 套餐 $ 658-2,098
à la carte 點菜 $ 450-1,300

Dinner 晚膳
set 套餐 $ 1,888-2,098
à la carte 點菜 $ 450-1,300

■ OPENING HOURS 營業時間
Lunch 午膳 12:00-14:30 (L.O.)
Weekend and Public Holiday lunch
週末及公眾假期午膳 11:30-15:00 (L.O.)
Dinner 晚膳 18:00-22:30 (L.O.)

Toritama
酉玉

8

There appears to be no end to the number of Tokyo restaurants opening branches in Hong Kong and this time here in LKF it's all about yakitori. Seating is limited so it's worth booking ahead and asking for the bar counter to watch the expert preparation in the semi-open kitchen. 40-day old chickens are used and 28 different parts of the chicken are offered – all you have to do is decide how many skewers you want.

室內座位數量不多，建議預先訂座。餐廳選用的雞隻只有四十天大，確保肉質鮮嫩，供應超過二十八種由不同部位製作的雞串。由日籍和來自南非的大廚共同主理的串燒，每一件都烤得恰到好處。廚師會因應食客的進食速度預備每一道食物，並會親自送到食客面前。

TEL. 2388 7717
G/F, Greenville, 2 Glenealy, Central
中環己連拿利 2號翠怡閣地舖
www.toritama.hk/

■ PRICE 價錢
Dinner 晚膳
set 套餐 $ 288-588
à la carte 點菜 $ 200-600

■ OPENING HOURS 營業時間
Dinner 晚膳   18:00-23:00 (L.O.)

■ ANNUAL AND WEEKLY CLOSING 休息日期
Closed 7 days Lunar New Year and
Sunday 農曆新年 7 天及週日休息

ITALIAN 意大利菜

Tosca

XXXX　　　　　　　　　　 ⬅ ⛱ **P** ⟷16 ◎ℍ 🕸

Vast ceilings, an open kitchen in the centre of the room, huge Murano chandeliers and, of course, stunning views from its position on the 102nd floor of the Ritz-Carlton hotel really make this a striking Italian restaurant. What really sets it apart, however, is the cuisine of Puglia-born chef Pino Lavarra. His dishes let the ingredients speak for themselves; plates are never overcrowded and strike the right balance between tradition and innovation.

閣落的天花、店中央的開放式廚房、巨型穆拉諾吊燈，替這家在102樓層上擁有迷人海景的餐廳錦上添花。然而，與別不同的，是來自意大利南部普利亞的主廚 Pino Lavarra，他對傳統與創新之間的平衡拿捏得恰到好處，而其烹調的優勝之處在於突出食材原來的味道，讓食材「自己說話」，分量從不會過多。

TEL. 2263 2270
102F, The Ritz-Carlton Hotel,
1 Austin Road West, Tsim Sha Tsui
尖沙咀柯士甸道西 1號麗思卡爾頓酒店 102樓
www.ritzcarlton.com/en/hotels/china/
hong-kong/dining/tosca

■ PRICE 價錢
Lunch 午膳
set 套餐 $438-698
à la carte 點菜 $1,000-1,500
Dinner 晚膳
set 套餐 $1,280-1,680
à la carte 點菜 $1,000-1,500

■ OPENING HOURS 營業時間
Lunch 午膳　12:00-14:30 (L.O.)
Dinner 晚膳　18:00-22:30 (L.O.)

Town

🍴8 ⏱🍴

Bryan Nagao, the chef-owner of this chic yet relaxed urban eatery, is a name familiar to Hong Kong food lovers. Here he has created a menu that reflects his international background by using Japanese and Hawaiian influences along with French and Italian flavours, in dishes like suckling pig with clams and miso broth, and short rib with black garlic-cabbage and miso sweet potato. Lunch is a simpler affair and includes an hors d'oeuvres buffet.

混凝土和紅磚牆、櫟木地板、藍或淺咖啡色靠背椅與面向繁忙街道的落地玻璃窗塑造出活潑、現代的感覺。主廚兼東主Bryan Nagao設計的菜單帶有日本、夏威夷、法國和意大利風格；其拿手菜包括西西里蝦配黑松露魚子醬薄肉片及味噌甜薯牛仔骨。午餐供應較簡約的餐單和自助頭盤。

TEL. 2568 8708
10F, Cubus, 1 Hoi Ping Road,
Causeway Bay
銅鑼灣開平道 1號 Cubus10樓
www.townrestauranthk.com

■ PRICE 價錢
Lunch 午膳
set 套餐 $ 198-278
à la carte 點菜 $ 500-800
Dinner 晚膳
set 套餐 $ 648-822
à la carte 點菜 $ 500-800

■ OPENING HOURS 營業時間
Lunch 午膳   12:00-14:30 (L.O.)
Dinner 晚膳   18:30-22:30 (L.O.)

BALINESE 峇里菜

TRi

Borrowing its name from the Balinese concept of a balance between man, nature and divinity, this place exudes otherworldly serenity. The show-stopping 10-metre-long century table carved from one piece of wood seats 16 people. Lotus bud-shaped pods over water pools house round booth seating with sea views. Traditional Balinese fare is done with a touch of finesse and slightly less heat here. Try their Sapi Marangi, slow-cooked beef in sweet soy.

人工湖上是以竹竿與木材打造而成的半圓形卡座，家具全是從峇里運來，10米長的木餐桌，帶着純樸的大自然味道。餐廳供應的峇里菜雖傳統，味道卻並不太辣，餐單上的菜式貴精不貴多。招牌菜Sapi Marangi(慢煮牛肉)經過48個小時慢煮後再以秘製醬汁烹調，值得一試。

TEL. 2515 0577
The Pulse, 28 Beach Road, Repulse Bay
淺水灣海灘道 28號 The Pulse
www.tri.hk

■ PRICE 價錢
Lunch 午膳
set 套餐 $680
à la carte 點菜 $450-800

Dinner 晚膳
set 套餐 $680
à la carte 點菜 $450-1,000

■ OPENING HOURS 營業時間
Lunch 午膳　12:00-15:00 (L.O.)
Dinner 晚膳　18:30-22:00 (L.O.)
Weekends and Public Holidays
週末及公眾假期　11:30-22:00 (L.O.)

■ ANNUAL AND WEEKLY CLOSING 休息日期
Closed Monday 週一休息

Trusty Congee King (Wan Chai)
靠得住 (灣仔)

As suggested by its name, you can really trust the quality of the food served in this long-standing congee shop. The menu has become more versatile in recent years with congee, noodles and snack sets available. All congee is cooked in fish broth that gives an extra dimension of flavour. Many rave about the pork liver and scallop congee, sticky rice dumpling with salted egg yolk and pork, and poached grass carp skin.

位於灣仔多年的靠得住出品一如其名，從不令人失望。食物的種類愈來愈多元化，精選套餐有不同的配搭。採用魚湯作粥底的粥是其一大特色，不容錯過的有心肝寶貝粥、咸肉糉和皇牌魚皮。

TEL. 2882 3268
7 Heard Street, Wan Chai
灣仔克街 7號

■ PRICE 價錢
set 套餐 $ 54-107
à la carte 點菜 $ 50-120

■ OPENING HOURS 營業時間
11:00-22:45 (L.O.)

■ ANNUAL AND WEEKLY CLOSING 休息日期
Closed 2 days Lunar New Year
農曆新年休息 2 天

Trusty Gourmet
信得過

The owner also runs a supplying company of pork so that he has an edge on sourcing the freshest pork at competitive prices. He believes the quality of the food speaks louder than fame and doesn't allow MSG in the kitchen. The signature stir-fried pork offal with salted mustard greens boasts offal from 12- to 14-month-old pigs for the tenderness. Diners also rave about thickly sliced pork liver and pork lung soup with almond milk.

豬肉供應商的家族背景，令店東在貨源上佔有優勢，確保豬肉新鮮和有質素。注重食品質素多於名氣的店東不僅實行無味精烹調方式，還選用12-14個月大的中豬作豬雜材料，肉質較幼嫩。厚切豬肝是此店的特色食品，較受食客喜愛的有杏汁白肺湯、鹹菜炒豬雜、彩椒炒肥牛腸和奇妙肚絲炒蛋鉢。

TEL. 2838 7373
Shop A, Fasteem Mansion,
307-311 Jaffe Road, Wan Chai
灣仔謝斐道 307-311號快添大廈 A舖

■ PRICE 價錢
Lunch 午膳
set 套餐 $ 58-88
à la carte 點菜 $ 100-150
Dinner 晚膳
à la carte 點菜 $ 100-150

■ OPENING HOURS 營業時間
11:30-22:00 (L.O.)

■ ANNUAL AND WEEKLY CLOSING 休息日期
Closed 5 days Lunar New Year
農曆新年休息 5 天

Tsim Chai Kee (Wellington Street)
沾仔記 (威靈頓街)

HONG KONG 香港

This highly regarded, simple noodle shop has been here since 1998 and is easy to spot – just look for the lunchtime queues. The staff are as bright as their aprons; the popular side booths are quickly snapped up; and the regulars know to eat outside peak times when the pace is less frenetic. The attraction is the handmade fish balls, the generously filled wontons and the beef; ordering a three topping noodle is the way to go.

享負盛名的沾仔記於1998年開業,裝修簡單但整潔舒適。侍應制服明亮潔淨,設有卡位及經常滿座;熟客會在非繁忙時間光顧,因氣氛較悠閒。著名食品包括自製鮮鯪魚球、餡料豐富的招牌雲吞及鮮牛肉麵;你可以來一碗三拼湯麵,一次過品嘗以上三種美食。

TEL. 2850 6471
98 Wellington Street, Central
中環威靈頓街 98號

■ PRICE 價錢
à la carte 點菜 $25-50

■ OPENING HOURS 營業時間
09:00-22:00 (L.O.)

■ ANNUAL AND WEEKLY CLOSING 休息日期
Closed 4 days Lunar New Year
農曆新年休息 4 天

Tsui Hang Village (Tsim Sha Tsui)
翠亨邨 (尖沙咀)

  👨‍🦽 **P** 🪑60 📞🍴

Many in Tsim Sha Tsui will recognise the name, as Tsui Hang Village opened in this shopping mall in the 1970s, before moving upstairs in 2011 into more contemporary surroundings. The menu is largely traditional Cantonese, supplemented by the head chef's own creations. Through the large window watch the chefs prepare specialities like braised beef ribs, shredded chicken and honey-glazed barbecued pork – their best seller; the dim sum is also good.

尖沙咀坊眾大都會認識翠亨邨，因為它早在1970年代已經在這個購物商場開業。菜式以傳統粵菜為主，再加上一些大廚自家創作。透過大玻璃窗，你可以看到廚師烹調各式佳餚，如醬燒牛肋排、翠亨邨靚一雞及最暢銷的蜜汁叉燒；這兒的點心也非常出色。

TEL. 2376 2882
Shop 507, 5F, Mira Place 1,
132 Nathan Road, Tsim Sha Tsui
尖沙咀彌敦道132號美麗華廣場一期5樓
507號舖
www.miradining.com

■ PRICE 價錢
Lunch 午膳
set 套餐 $ 180-250
à la carte 點菜 $ 150-350

Dinner 晚膳
set 套餐 $ 280-350
weekend set 週末套餐 $ 300-400
à la carte 點菜 $ 200-500

■ OPENING HOURS 營業時間
Lunch 午膳　11:30-14:30 (L.O.)
Dinner 晚膳　18:00-22:00 (L.O.)
Sunday and Public Holiday lunch
週日及公眾假期午膳 10:30-14:30 (L.O.)
Dinner 晚膳　18:00-22:00 (L.O.)

Tsuta (Causeway Bay)
蔦 (銅鑼灣)

The dining room is styled after a traditional ramen house, but updated to look modern and sleek. Every morning, the chefs make the revered broth by simmering chicken, dried fish and Japanese soy sauce for hours. Noodles are also freshly made daily from scratch, in a machine programmed by the head chef of its Tokyo flagship store to ensure they taste exactly the same across all branches. Most ingredients are flown in straight from Japan.

日式拉麵店的裝潢風格中添了點時尚元素，簡約、整齊。清湯底以雞、魚乾和日本醬油熬煮，每天新鮮烹調，絕不含味精。麵條也是每天在店內即製，製麵機內的程式由日本總店的總廚親自設定，確保麵質與總店無異。大部分材料均由日本進口，熬湯用的魚乾更是每隔三天從日本直送過來。

TEL. 3188 2639
Shop 2, GF, V Point,
18 Tang Lung Street, Causeway Bay
銅鑼灣登龍街 18號 V Point地下 2號舖

■ PRICE 價錢
à la carte 點菜 $98-200

■ OPENING HOURS 營業時間
11:30-22:45 (L.O.)

Tulsi (North Point)
羅勒 (北角)

The baby sister to Tulsi in Quarry Bay is next to North Point MTR's Exit B4 and comes with tightly packed tables that ensure there's always a warm, convivial atmosphere. You'll find the aromas coming from the clean, compact kitchen will quickly stimulate your appetite. The colourful, tasty Indian specialities are made using quality ingredients; signature dishes are butter chicken using marinated and barbecued chicken, and rogan josh.

Tulsi在北角港鐵站附近開設了這家分店。小小的店子內，牆壁懸着油畫、天花上的吊燈帶有古典味，簡約的設計風格營造出和諧溫馨的氣氛。友善親切的服務和香氣四溢、令人垂涎的亞洲風味美食如牛油雞、印度烤雞和咖喱羊肉等，讓食客賓至如歸。

TEL. 2568 3806
GF, Fairview Court,
5-13 Tsat Tze Mui Road, North Point
北角七姊妹道 7號昌輝閣後座地下
www.tulsi.com.hk

■ PRICE 價錢
Lunch 午膳
set 套餐 $ 68-128
à la carte 點菜 $ 200-300
Dinner 晚膳
à la carte 點菜 $ 200-300

■ OPENING HOURS 營業時間
Lunch 午膳　11:30-14:45 (L.O.)
Dinner 晚膳　18:00-23:00 (L.O.)

Tze Yuet Heen
紫粵軒

The main restaurant of the Crowne Plaza Kowloon East hotel is this smart Cantonese restaurant. It uses a water theme as the inspiration behind its design and its painted screens and artwork are brought to life by judicious lighting. Over 100 Cantonese dishes are on offer, including plenty of vegetarian options and healthy delicacies, and preparation methods are largely traditional. The set menus are particularly appealing.

紫粵軒提供過百款依照傳統烹調方法炮製的廣東菜，還有一系列美味健康素菜。選擇午、晚市套餐，可一次過品嘗多款廚師推介。裝潢以流水作主題，融入中國傳統繪畫藝術：涓涓流水般的地氈、半透明水墨畫屏風和獨特的天花燈飾等，顯示出設計者的巧思。

TEL. 3983 0688
2F, Crowne Plaza Kowloon East,
3 Tong Tak Street, Tseung Kwan O
將軍澳唐德街 3號
香港九龍東皇冠假日酒店 2樓
www.crowneplaza.com/kowlooneast

■ PRICE 價錢
Lunch 午膳
set 套餐 $ 168
à la carte 點菜 $ 270-460

Dinner 晚膳
set 套餐 $ 688
à la carte 點菜 $ 270-460

■ OPENING HOURS 營業時間
Lunch 午膳   11:30-14:30 (L.O.)
Weekend and Public Holiday lunch
週末及公眾假期午膳
09:00-15:30 (L.O.)
Dinner 晚膳   18:00-22:30 (L.O.)

Upper Modern Bistro

The name is an amalgam of the street name, the atmosphere and the style of place. It certainly has a fresh, energetic feel with its whites, greys and blues, its cascading 'petals' and its semi-open kitchen. The French cuisine comes with a healthy dose of creativity, in both the preparation and presentation; there are also Asian influences, in dishes such as the Alaskan salmon teriyaki – and an impressive selection of over 30 French cheeses.

純白、銀灰及海藍色的配搭，予人清新和滿有朝氣的感覺，花瓣狀的銀片天花裝飾添了點前衛創新的味道。這兒的法國菜同樣在傳統上滲入了亞洲風味的新元素，如照燒阿拉斯加三文魚，從材料的運用到賣相也頗有創意。還有超過三十款法國芝士任你挑選。

TEL. 2517 0977
6-14 Upper Station Street,
Sheung Wan
上環差館上街 6-14號
www.upper-bistro.com

■ PRICE 價錢
Lunch 午膳
set 套餐 $ 268-348
à la carte 點菜 $ 420-820

Dinner 晚膳
set 套餐 $ 788
à la carte 點菜 $ 420-820

■ OPENING HOURS 營業時間
Lunch 午膳　12:00-14:30 (L.O.)
Dinner 晚膳　18:00-22:30 (L.O.)

VEA

✗✗   ♿ ⛶10 ⛲ ☏🍷

This is where culinary theatrics raise counter dining to new heights. The 8 course menu offers skilfully executed and innovative dishes that use French and modern techniques with Chinese flavour, from sous-vide to smoke guns. Service is slick and smooth and wine matches are well chosen; even the cocktail pairings are worth considering. The name is an amalgam of the two owners' names: Vicky, the chef, 'et' Antonio, who runs the cocktail bar on the floor below.

時尚舒適的VEA座位不多，就座時間限於18:45、19:15、19:45或20:15，食客必須於網上預訂。雄心勃勃的廚師為食客帶來有八道菜的套餐，有創意的食材組合、融合了中法與現代烹調方式，每道菜都呈現出豐富的質感和味道，充分展現廚師的精湛技藝。服務嫻熟精練，覺酒配搭紆續思密想，雞尾酒也值得一試。

TEL. 2711 8639
30F, The Wellington,
198 Wellington Street, Central
中環威靈頓街 198號 The Wellington 30樓
www.vea.hk

■ PRICE 價錢
Dinner 晚膳
set 套餐 $ 1,480

■ OPENING HOURS 營業時間
Dinner 晚膳 17:00-21:30 (L.O.)

■ ANNUAL AND WEEKLY CLOSING 休息日期
Closed Sunday 週日休息

Symbols shown in red indicate particularly
charming establishments 🏠🏠 XxX.

紅色標誌 🏠🏠 XxX 表示酒店和餐館在同級別的
舒適程度中較優秀。

Read 'How to use this guide' for an explanation of our
symbols, classifications and abbreviations.

請細閱「如何使用餐廳／酒店指南」，當中的標誌、分類等簡介
助你掌握使用本指南的訣竅，作出智慧選擇。

Wang Fu (Central)
王府 (中環)

Wang Fu was one of the first shops to open on Wellington Street and its Pekingese dumplings are renowned. Over ten kinds of freshly hand-made dumplings with different fillings are on offer each day. Don't miss the green onion mutton dumpling or the vegetarian dumpling – the tomato and egg dumpling, which is only available after 2pm, is also good. As well as the dumplings and noodles, assorted hot Sichuan dishes are also offered.

王府是威靈頓街最早期開業的水餃店，其北京水餃遠近馳名，供應的餃子款式超過十種，每天均由人手新鮮包製，羊肉京葱餃和花素餃不可不試。除水餃麵食外，還供應多款京式小菜。

TEL. 2121 8006
65 Wellington Street, Central
中環威靈頓街 65號

■ PRICE 價錢
à la carte 點菜 $ 50-100

■ OPENING HOURS 營業時間
11:00-22:00 (L.O.)

■ ANNUAL AND WEEKLY CLOSING 休息日期
Closed 4 days Lunar New Year
農曆新年休息 4 天

HONG KONG 香港

Whisk

Contemporary European cooking techniques and the finest seasonal ingredients from around the world are used here at Whisk to create satisfying dishes with appealing combinations of flavours. Try the tagliolini with Bretagne lobster or suckling pig with pickled vegetables. The restaurant has a relaxed yet comfortable feel; there are over 200 wines available and you can also have drinks on the adjoining terrace.

採用當代歐洲烹調技巧，融合全球時令精選食材的 Whisk，創造出多款獨特菜式，為食客的味覺帶來新享受。推介菜式包括布列塔尼龍蝦意粉和烤乳豬配醃製蔬菜。此店提供超過二百款全球精選佳釀，愛酒之士可與良朋在此品酒談心，在露台享用另有一番風情！

TEL. 2315 5999
5F, The Mira Hotel, 118 Nathan Road, Tsim Sha Tsui
尖沙咀彌敦道 118號 The Mira 5樓
www.themirahotel.com

■ PRICE 價錢
Lunch 午膳
set 套餐 $ 268-398
Dinner 晚膳
à la carte 點菜 $ 900-1,200

■ OPENING HOURS 營業時間
Lunch 午膳   12:00-14:30 (L.O.)
Sunday lunch 週日午膳   12:00-15:00 (L.O.)
Dinner 晚膳   18:30-22:30 (L.O.)

■ ANNUAL AND WEEKLY CLOSING 休息日期
Closed Sunday dinner 週日晚膳休息

Wing Lai Yuen
詠藜園

     🅿 ♿ 🍴12 ☎

The film business glitterati used to flock to the original shop in San Po Kong for the authentic Sichuan Dan Dan noodles. A decade ago the Yeung family moved it to its current address in Whampoa Garden, where the Dan Dan noodles are still the main attraction, although these days you can decide whether or not you want them spicy. Along with other Sichuan dishes are a few Shanghainese specialities too.

新蒲崗原舖吸引了無數影星名人，全為了一嘗正宗四川擔擔麵蜂擁而至。隨着社區的發展，楊氏家族決定把店子遷址到現在的黃埔花園。直至今日擔擔麵仍然是其主打麵食，不過，現在你還可以選擇辣或不辣的湯底。另外，店內同時供應多款川菜和上海美食。

TEL. 2320 6430
Shop 102-105, 1F, Whampoa Plaza,
Site 8, Hung Hom
紅磡黃埔花園第 8 期 1 樓 102-105 號舖

■ PRICE 價錢
Lunch 午膳
à la carte 點菜 $80-120
Dinner 晚膳
à la carte 點菜 $100-180

■ OPENING HOURS 營業時間
Lunch 午膳　11:00-15:30 (L.O.)
Dinner 晚膳　18:00-22:30 (L.O.)

HONG KONG 香港

Wing Wah
永華雲吞麵家

This simple operation has been maintaining high standards for well over 50 years now, the secret being that they do everything from scratch upstairs, making their noodles by hand using bamboo. So proud are they of their skills that there's a photographic display of their craft on the walls. Finest offerings include shrimp wonton and barbecued pork noodle, a coconut milk dessert with honeydew melon and sago, and drinks like sweet herbal tea.

這間麵家營運至今逾五十年，一直堅持在店舖樓上的小工房中，用傳統的竹昇法人工打製麵條，店主對其高水準的麵條深感自豪，牆上貼滿製麵過程的照片。招牌美食包括鮮蝦雲吞麵及炸醬麵等，亦有令人驚喜的蝦子柚皮及自家磨製的合桃露。

TEL. 2527 7476
89 Hennessy Road, Wan Chai
灣仔軒尼詩道 89號

■ PRICE 價錢
à la carte 點菜 $40-150

■ OPENING HOURS 營業時間
12:00-01:30 (L.O.)

■ ANNUAL AND WEEKLY CLOSING 休息日期
Closed 3 days Lunar New Year and Sunday
農曆新年 3 天及週日休息

Wu Kong (Causeway Bay)
滬江 (銅鑼灣)

🍴36 ☎️🍴

The many customers of this Shanghainese restaurant had reason to celebrate its relocation in 2011 to the upper level of Lee Theatre Plaza as it resulted in better views, more space and a nicer environment in which to eat. An experienced kitchen shows its practised hand in specialities such as braised pig's knuckle with brown sauce and honey ham and crispy bean curd in bread. Do try the hairy crab menu in the autumn season.

於2011年搬到利舞臺高層的滬江飯店，為顧客帶來更佳的景觀、更寬敞的空間和更舒適的環境，讓他們更盡情享用美食。廚藝精湛的廚師為顧客炮製多款巧手小菜，如紅燒元蹄和響鈴火腿夾。於秋季期間，肥美的大閘蟹是必吃的時令佳餚。

TEL. 2506 1018
Shop B, 17F, Lee Theatre Plaza,
99 Percival Street, Causeway Bay
銅鑼灣波斯富街99號利舞臺廣場17樓B號舖
www.wukong.com.hk

■ PRICE 價錢
Lunch 午膳
set 套餐 $88
à la carte 點菜 $150-450
Dinner 晚膳
à la carte 點菜 $150-450

■ OPENING HOURS 營業時間
Lunch 午膳 11:45-14:45 (L.O.)
Dinner 晚膳 17:45-22:45 (L.O.)

■ ANNUAL AND WEEKLY CLOSING 休息日期
Closed 3 days Lunar New Year
農曆新年休息3天

SUSHI 壽司

Xuan Sushi
玄鮨

Whilst there are tables in this gracefully decorated and surprisingly spacious dining room, the best place to sit is at the long, wave-shaped counter. From here you can watch the action as the four sushi chefs prepare the omakase menu – they use Niigata rice and two different types of vinegar for the sushi. There are other hot dishes available and many of the ingredients are flown in daily from Japan.

棕色木材與黃銅管的配搭，予人時尚優雅的感覺。壽司吧佔了大部分空間，大廚就在吧枱後為你準備各款美味壽司。這裏的壽司飯是用新潟米按特定比例加入兩種醋煮成，其餘材料均每日由日本新鮮運到。坐在吧枱前享用廚師套餐是最好選擇。此店亦供應燒物及天婦羅等熱食。

TEL. 2537 5555
3F, Parekh House,
61-63 Wyndham Street, Central
中環雲咸街 61-63 號巴力大廈 3 樓

■ PRICE 價錢
Lunch 午膳
set 套餐 $ 300-500
Dinner 晚膳
set 套餐 $ 1,200-2,000

■ OPENING HOURS 營業時間
Lunch 午膳　12:00-14:30 (L.O.)
Dinner 晚膳　18:00-22:30 (L.O.)

■ ANNUAL AND WEEKLY CLOSING 休息日期
Closed Sunday 週日休息

Yan Toh Heen
欣圖軒

Its location on the ground floor of the InterContinental hotel may be somewhat concealed but it's well worth seeking out this elegant Cantonese restaurant and that's not just because of the lovely views of Hong Kong Island. The authentic, carefully prepared specialities include stuffed crab shell with crabmeat; wagyu beef with green peppers, mushrooms and garlic; double-boiled fish maw and sea whelk; and wok-fried lobster with crab roe and milk.

這家優雅的粵菜酒家就在洲際酒店地下，所處位置可能較為隱蔽，但十分值得去尋找，而這裏的魅力，絕不止於能夠觀賞香港島的美景，更因其供應多款精心炮製的傳統粵式佳餚，包括：脆釀鮮蟹蓋、蒜片青尖椒爆和牛、花膠響螺燉湯及龍皇炒鮮奶等。

TEL. 2313 2243
GF, InterContinental Hotel,
18 Salisbury Road, Tsim Sha Tsui
尖沙咀梳士巴利道18號洲際酒店地下
www.hongkong-ic.intercontinental.com

SPECIALITIES TO PRE-ORDER 預訂食物
Braised fish maw with sea cucumber in oyster jus 蠔皇厚花膠扣遼參 / Barbecued whole suckling pig 金陵脆皮乳豬 / Peking duck 北京片皮鴨 / Hangzhou beggar's fortune chicken 杭州富貴雞

■ PRICE 價錢
Lunch 午膳
à la carte 點菜 $350-2,000
Dinner 晚膳
set 套餐 $2,688
à la carte 點菜 $450-2,000

■ OPENING HOURS 營業時間
Lunch 午膳　12:00-14:30 (L.O.)
Sunday & Public Holiday lunch
週日及公眾假期午膳　11:30-15:00 (L.O.)
Dinner 晚膳　18:00-23:00 (L.O.)

Yat Lok
一樂燒鵝

If you're after delicious roast goose then Yat Lok may fit the bill. This family business has been going since 1957 but moved to its current location in 2011. The owner-chef prepares his roast meats using a secret family recipe; his chicken in soy sauce and rose wine is well worth ordering. The place is basic and space limited – you'll be sharing your table with others – but the owner's wife and her team create a pleasant atmosphere.

一樂早於1957年開始營業，其後在2011年遷至現址。每次經過其門前，總會被掛在窗前的燒鵝吸引而垂涎三尺。以家族秘方醃製、經過二十多道工序炮製而成的燒鵝，色香味俱佳，蠻受街坊歡迎，其他食物如玫瑰油雞也做得不錯。

TEL. 2524 3882
34-38 Stanley Street, Central
中環士丹利街 34-38號

■ PRICE 價錢
à la carte 點菜 $60-360

■ OPENING HOURS 營業時間
10:00-21:00 (L.O.)
Sunday & Public Holidays 週日及公眾假期
10:00-17:30 (L.O.)

■ ANNUAL AND WEEKLY CLOSING 休息日期
Closed 3 days Lunar New Year and last Wednesday of each month 農曆新年 3 天及每月最後一個星期三休息

Yat Tung Heen (Jordan)
逸東軒 (佐敦)

One to be filed under 'hidden gems', this Cantonese restaurant makes the best of its hotel basement location through warm tones and soft lighting. The kitchen keeps things traditional in order to highlight the natural flavours of the season's produce. Regulars love the roasted meats and double-boiled soups but other signature dishes include fried chicken with ginger and mandarin peel, and double-boiled pig's lung with fish maw in almond soup.

位處酒店地庫的逸東軒在2017年進行全面裝修。自1990年開業至今,一直為食客帶來沒花巧噱頭的傳統粵菜,扎實的烹調功夫盡顯四時食材真鮮味,燒味、小菜和老火湯深得食客歡迎,招牌菜有花膠杏汁燉白肺、沙薑陳皮生煎雞等,不少人更愛於廂房以鮑魚燕窩套餐宴客。

TEL. 2710 1093
B2F, Eaton Hotel, 380 Nathan Road, Jordan
佐敦彌敦道 380號逸東酒店地庫 2樓

■ PRICE 價錢
Lunch 午膳
set 套餐 $230-600
weekend set 週末套餐 $280-400
à la carte 點菜 $300-600

Dinner 晚膳
set 套餐 $400-780
weekend set 週末套餐 $500-780
à la carte 點菜 $300-600

■ OPENING HOURS 營業時間
Lunch 午膳　11:00-15:30 (L.O.)
Dinner 晚膳　18:00-22:30 (L.O.)

Yau Yuen Siu Tsui
有緣小敘

The owner's wife works alone in this shop, serving authentic Shaanxi dishes and snacks from her hometown, like dumplings and baked buns with meat. The most impressive dish is Biang Biang noodles – these long, flat, handmade noodles come with a spicy chilli sauce and are full of flavour. Other specialities include Shaanxi-style noodles with vegetables and pork in spicy and sour soup, and Shaanxi-style bread with stewed pork.

由原來位於西貢街的小店搬至現址後，環境較為舒適且能招待更多客人。來自陝西的店東太太為食客奉上風味獨特的家鄉小食如哨子麵、肉夾饃等，其中最令人難忘的莫過於Biang Biang麵。這款由人手製作，麵身寬長的麵食配上特製醬料，香辣味濃，令人再三回味。店內還提供多款熱葷小菜。

TEL. 5300 2682
GF, 36 Man Yuen Street, Jordan
佐敦文苑街 36號地下

■ PRICE 價錢
à la carte 點菜 $50-100

■ OPENING HOURS 營業時間
12:00-22:00 (L.O.)

Yè Shanghai (Tsim Sha Tsui)
夜上海 (尖沙咀)

XXX   ⅋ 🅿 ⇶80 ℂ⑂

Drawing not only on Shanghai but also on the neighbouring provinces of Jiangsu and Zhejiang, the cooking here is subtle and expertly balanced. Specialities include sautéed shredded Mandarin fish, baked stuffed crab shell and braised beef ribs with brown sauce. The contemporary décor recalls 1930s Shanghai in its use of dark woods, subdued lighting and semi-private alcoves. This is a busy, sophisticated operation.

這裏的烹調水準專業，技術精湛，不但提供上海菜，還供應江蘇及浙江菜。特色美食包括龍鬚桂魚絲、蟹粉釀蟹蓋及紅燒原條牛肋排。餐廳以當代風格設計，採用昏暗的燈光，深色的木材，加上半私家餐桌，散發着三十年代上海的味道。餐廳生氣勃勃，營運順暢，服務非常周到。

TEL. 2376 3322
6F, Marco Polo Hotel, Harbour City,
3 Canton Road, Tsim Sha Tsui
尖沙咀廣東道 3號海運大廈
馬哥孛羅酒店 6樓
www.elite-concepts.com

SPECIALITIES TO PRE-ORDER 預訂食物
Beggar's chicken 富貴雞

■ PRICE 價錢
Lunch 午膳
à la carte 點菜 $ 150-300
Dinner 晚膳
à la carte 點菜 $ 250-600

■ OPENING HOURS 營業時間
Lunch 午膳 11:30-14:30 (L.O.)
Dinner 晚膳 18:00-22:30 (L.O.)

Yee Tung Heen
怡東軒

The first thing you'll notice is the Chinese ornaments and the second is how well Chinese screens and contemporary lighting go together. This elegant restaurant not only offers traditional Cantonese favourites but also serves specialities of a more creative persuasion. The enthusiastic chef and his team spend much time seeking out the best quality seasonal ingredients, whether that's from local markets or overseas.

踏入怡東酒店內的怡東軒中菜廳,馬上便會給精緻的中式擺設吸引。往內走,會發現四周的中式屏風與現代天花燈,配搭得十分別致。餐廳供應傳統粵菜,廚師及營運團隊充滿熱誠,專程由本地及世界各地搜羅各種高質素及時令食材,時有創新菜式或特別餐單推出。

TEL. 2837 6790
2F, The Excelsior Hotel,
281 Gloucester Road, Causeway Bay
銅鑼灣告士打道 281 號怡東酒店 2 樓

SPECIALITIES TO PRE-ORDER 預訂食物
Baked traditional salt-crusted chicken with
Chinese wine 古法酒香鹽焗雞

■ PRICE 價錢
Lunch 午膳
à la carte 點菜 $ 200-500
Dinner 晚膳
à la carte 點菜 $ 400-800

■ OPENING HOURS 營業時間
Lunch 午膳　12:00-14:30 (L.O.)
Dinner 晚膳　18:00-22:30 (L.O.)

Yin Yue
殷悅

Yin Yue provides a warm and relaxing space; its large windows letting in lots of light and providing great views of Tsuen Wan from its perch on the top floor of a hotel. The cooking is undertaken by an experienced chef who prepares the attractively presented dishes in a traditional but healthy way, using secret recipes, quality ingredients and a lesser amount of oil. Try suckling pig with dried mullet roe, or stir-fried beef with black truffle.

位於酒店頂樓，以淡色系作裝潢的餐廳，格調輕鬆。兩邊的落地玻璃窗除了引入自然光外，還讓你一覽舊社區景色。店內粵菜由富數十年經驗的大廚主理，結合了健康少油的烹調方式與傳統秘方，再配上世界各地食材和日本美學，形味俱佳。推介菜式有用台灣烏魚子製作的烏金麒麟乳豬和黑松露牛柳粒。

TEL. 2409 3182
30F, Panda Hotel, 3 Tsuen Wah Street, Tsuen Wan
新界荃灣荃華街 3 號悅來酒店 30 樓
www.pandahotel.com.hk/en/dining/yinyue

■ PRICE 價錢
Lunch 午膳
à la carte 點菜 $ 120-400
Dinner 晚膳
à la carte 點菜 $ 300-900

■ OPENING HOURS 營業時間
Lunch 午膳　11:00-15:00 (L.O.)
Sunday & Public Holidays lunch
週日及公眾假期午膳　10:00-15:30 (L.O.)
Dinner 晚膳　18:00-22:30 (L.O.)

Ying Jee Club
營致會館

XXX   🍽24 ⚟🍴

Rather than gimmicky promotions, the owner prefer diverting more energy and resources to the freshest ingredients and refining the chef's cooking techniques. Diners are greeted by an elegant and contemporary dining hall adorned by marble tables, velvet seats and metallic trims. The menu is traditionally Cantonese with a touch of finesse. Their signature crispy salted chicken is silky and tender without being overly oily.

沒有花巧和猛烈的宣傳攻勢，只以最新鮮的食材和熟練的烹調技巧為客人奉上傳統而細緻的廣東菜，招牌菜脆香貴妃雞皮脆酥香、肉質嫩滑且不油膩。以翡翠、雲石、絲絨、金屬框等物料作裝潢陳設，感覺典雅時尚。

TEL. 2801 6882
Shop G05, 107-108, Nexxus Building,
41 Connaught Road, Central
中環干諾道中 41號盈置大廈地下 G05及 1樓
107-108號舖
www.yingjeeclub.hk

■ PRICE 價錢
Lunch 午膳
set 套餐 $ 380
à la carte 點菜 $ 300-1,000
Dinner 晚膳
à la carte 點菜 $ 500-1,200

■ OPENING HOURS 營業時間
Lunch 午膳　11:30-15:00 (L.O.)
Dinner 晚膳　18:00-23:00 (L.O.)

CANTONESE 粵菜

Yixin
益新

✕✕   ⊟36 ○⥮

North Point was the original location for this family-run restaurant when it opened in the 1950s. It's moved a few times since then but is now firmly ensconced here in Wan Chai. Run by the 3rd generation of the family, a sense of continuity also comes from the head chef who has been with the company over 50 years! The Cantonese food is traditional, with quite a few Shun Tak dishes; specialities include roasted duck Pipa-style, and smoked pomfret.

早於五十年代於港島區開業，輾轉搬至灣仔現址，現由第三代經營。益新一向以傳統粵菜馳名，餐單上不乏耗功夫製作的懷舊菜式，吸引不少客人在此舉行宴會。琵琶鴨、金錢雞及煙焗鯧魚等都是常客所愛。除了地面的主廳和客房外，地庫還有一個裝潢時尚的餐室。

TEL. 2834 9963
50 Hennessy Road, Wan Chai
灣仔軒尼詩道 50 號

■ PRICE 價錢
Lunch 午膳
à la carte 點菜 $ 150-200
Dinner 晚膳
à la carte 點菜 $ 250-350

■ OPENING HOURS 營業時間
Lunch 午膳　11:30-15:30 (L.O.)
Dinner 晚膳　17:30-22:30 (L.O.)

■ ANNUAL AND WEEKLY CLOSING 休息日期
Closed 2 days Lunar New Year and 1st July lunch 農曆新年 2 天及 7 月 1 日午膳休息

Yuè (Gold Coast)
粵 (黃金海岸)

It's not often one can enjoy Cantonese food surrounded by verdant scenery but here on the ground floor of the Gold Coast hotel that's exactly what you get as this comfortable restaurant looks out onto a delightful garden. The menu includes both traditional and more contemporary dishes and it's worth seeking out the chef's specialities such as barbecued pork and chicken liver with honey, and deep-fried chicken with shrimp paste.

位於黃金海岸酒店的地面層，優雅舒適的室內環境，與落地玻璃窗外的園林景致巧妙地配合起來。選擇豐富的餐單提供傳統懷舊及較創新的粵菜，廚師精選菜式如蜜餞金錢雞和星洲蝦醬炸雞件等，值得一試。邊品嘗美味的廣式點心邊欣賞怡人的園林美景，實在是賞心樂事。

TEL. 2452 8668
LG, Gold Coast Hotel,
1 Castle Peak Road, Gold Coast
黃金海岸青山公路 1 號黃金海岸酒店低層
www.goldcoasthotel.com.hk

■ PRICE 價錢
Lunch 午膳
set 套餐 $ 180
à la carte 點菜 $ 200-500

Dinner 晚膳
set 套餐 $ 280
weekend set 套餐 $ 300
à la carte 點菜 $ 250-700

■ OPENING HOURS 營業時間
Lunch 午膳　11:30-15:15 (L.O.)
Sunday & Public Holiday lunch 週日及公
眾假期午膳　09:00-15:45 (L.O.)
Dinner 晚膳　18:30-22:45 (L.O.)

Yuè (North Point)
粵 (北角)

♿ 🖐 🅿 ▱120 ☎🍴

It may seem like nothing more than a mezzanine area of the City Garden hotel but it's well worth coming up here for the Cantonese food. The experienced chef's respect for the traditions of Cantonese cuisine is clearly demonstrated in dishes like double-boiled jus of almonds with fish maw, fried rice with prawns and barbecue pork, and seared garoupa with layered egg white. There are a number of different sized private rooms.

看起來只是城市花園酒店的間層，並不特別，定讓不少人忽略了這間中菜廳，但絕對值得前來一嘗這兒的粵菜。資深大廚對傳統粵菜的尊重完全反映在其製作的各樣菜式上，例如杏汁花膠燉蹄筋、師傅炒飯和雪嶺紅梅映松露等。餐廳設有不同大小的廂房供各類宴會之用。

TEL. 2806 4918
1F, City Garden Hotel,
9 City Garden Road, North Point
北角城市花園道 9號城市花園酒店 1樓
www.citygarden.com.hk

■ PRICE 價錢
Lunch 午膳
set 套餐 $ 250-300
à la carte 點菜 $ 280-1,300

Dinner 晚膳
set 套餐 $ 468-638
à la carte 點菜 $ 280-1,300

■ OPENING HOURS 營業時間
Lunch 午膳　11:30-14:30 (L.O.)
weekend and Public Holiday lunch
週末及公眾假期午膳　10:30-14:30 (L.O.)
Dinner 晚膳　18:00-22:30 (L.O.)

Yue Kee
裕記

Since its humble beginnings as a tiny countryside joint 60 years ago, this second-generation family business has grown substantially while still retaining its unique flair. Geese are sourced from eight different farms in China to ensure quality and a steady supply. The owner insists on chargrilling the geese, according to his family recipe, for distinctive smokiness, crispy skin and juicy meat. Apart from geese, seafood and stir-fries are also served.

開業59年，從鄉村小店到現在的規模，仍保留着傳統食店風味。現由第二代打理。採用的鵝是從內地八個農場合作伙伴中挑選，確保鵝肉的貨源和質素，店主多年來堅持按家傳秘方以炭火烤製燒鵝，味道獨特且酥香肉嫩。現更增設海鮮及特色小菜，讓食客有更多選擇。

TEL. 2491 0105
9 Sham Hong Road, Sham Tseng
深井深康路 9號
www.yuekee.com.hk

■ PRICE 價錢
à la carte 點菜 $ 150-550

■ OPENING HOURS 營業時間
11:00-23:00 (L.O.)

■ ANNUAL AND WEEKLY CLOSING 休息日期
Closed 3 days Lunar New Year
農曆新年休息 3 天

Yuet Lai Shun
粵來順

Ceiling fans, window grilles, booth seats and faux-marble tables are reminiscent of the good old cha chaan teng in Hong Kong circa 1960s. The décor also chimes with the food it serves – retro Cantonese classics that are well-made and reasonably priced. Chicken poached in honey soy stands out, with juicy velvety meat and well-balanced sauce. Deep-fried shrimp balls with cheese filling and pork lung almond milk soup are among diners' favourites.

吊扇加鐵窗花、帶點茶餐廳味道的雲石方桌卡座，裝潢一如六、七十年代的酒樓，很有老香港風情。與其裝潢一樣，這兒主打的就是懷舊廣東菜。蜂蜜豉油雞，肉質嫩滑，與以蝦膠芝士作餡料的千絲芝心球和生磨杏汁白肺湯同屬招牌菜。

TEL. 2788 3078
Shop 10-12, GF Po Hang Building,
2-8 Dundas Street, Mong Kok
旺角登打士街 2-8號寶亨大廈地下 10-12號舖

SPECIALITIES TO PRE-ORDER 預訂食物
Double-boiled pork lung and almond milk soup 生磨杏汁白肺湯 /Steamed crab roe with glutinous rice in lotus leaf 籠仔荷香糯米蒸羔蟹

■ PRICE 價錢
Lunch 午膳
set 套餐 $ 42-50
à la carte 點菜 $ 100-200
Dinner 晚膳
à la carte 點菜 $ 200-300

■ OPENING HOURS 營業時間
11:30-23:00 (L.O.)

Yung Kee
容記小菜王

✕ 🍴　　　　　　　　　　　　　　♿ 🍽16 ☎🍴

Moved to this new location in 2017, this bustling hawker-style joint attracts crowds who jam its entrance every night. Regulars come for their traditional Cantonese fare including home-style braised pork belly and baked fish tripe omelette in earthenware bowl, both of which are limited in offer. Make sure you book ahead of time and show up on time. Walk-in guests should expect to wait for at least one hour.

由深水埗遷至現址只有數個月，已吸引許多食客每晚在門外輪候，因為他們全是熟客。建議各位預早訂座並切記準時到達，否則或要等候一個小時或以上才能入座。菜館主打傳統粵菜，招牌菜包括家鄉秘製扣肉和家鄉焗魚腸，熟客都知道這兩道菜式皆限量供應。

TEL. 2363 9380
GF & 1F, 123 Prince Edward Road West, Prince Edward
太子太子道西 123號地下及 1樓

SPECIALITIES TO PRE-ORDER 預訂食物
Home-style braised pork belly 家鄉秘製扣肉

■ PRICE 價錢
Lunch 午膳
à la carte 點菜 $ 200-300
Dinner 晚膳
à la carte 點菜 $ 200-300

■ OPENING HOURS 營業時間
Lunch 午膳　11:00-15:00 (L.O.)
Dinner 晚膳　17:30-00:00 (L.O.)

Zenpachi
禪八

⊟ 16　◐❙❙

It's all about sukiyaki and shabu shabu at this Japanese restaurant. The high quality ingredients include Saga beef and assorted seafood from Japan, along with Australian Wagyu. The soup base of the shabu shabu is nicely concentrated and using a paper pot ensures that the stock is never oily. For the sukiyaki, you can choose either Kansai or Kanto style and can either do the cooking yourself or ask the staff to do it for you.

店內餐單毫不複雜，提供日式火鍋及汁燒會席料理，配以佐賀5A和牛、澳洲和牛及各種日本海鮮等食材。火鍋使用日本紙鍋，能吸走油脂和雜質，味道更清鮮。顧客可選擇關東或關西兩種不同做法的汁燒鍋，更可請店員協助烹調。靠窗有數張榻榻米餐桌，適合二人用餐，別具情調。

TEL. 3428 3615
6F, The Toy House, 100 Canton Road,
Tsim Sha Tsui
尖沙咀廣東道100號彩星集團大廈6樓

■ PRICE 價錢
Lunch 午膳
set 套餐 $ 105-750
à la carte 點菜 $ 400-800
Dinner 晚膳
set 套餐 $ 350-980
à la carte 點菜 $ 400-800

■ OPENING HOURS 營業時間
Lunch 午膳　12:00-14:30 (L.O.)
Dinner 晚膳　18:00-22:30 (L.O.)

■ ANNUAL AND WEEKLY CLOSING 休息日期
Closed 2 days Lunar New Year
農曆新年休息2天

The symbol 🕸 denotes a particularly interesting wine list.

🕸 這個標誌表示該餐廳提供一系列優質餐酒。

Enjoy good food without spending a fortune! Look out for the Bib Gourmand symbol 🚲 to find restaurants offering good food at great prices!

既想省錢又想品嘗美食，便要留心注有這個 🚲 車胎人標誌的餐廳，她們提供的是價錢實惠且高質素的美食。

les bonnes étapes

Zhejiang Heen
浙江軒

✕✕　　　　　　　　　🛏16 ◐🍴

At what must be one of the easiest restaurants to find – just look for the huge Zhejiang landscape on the outside of the building – you'll find authentic Zhejiang and Shanghainese specialities made from top quality ingredients, such as smoked fish, shrimps with seaweed, and steamed chou tofu. Run by a Zhejiang Fraternity Association, the dining room is spread over two floors and while it may not be particularly lavish, it is comfortable.

要數最容易找的酒家，這家必定榜上有名，因為它的外牆有一大幅浙江風景圖。你可在這裏品嘗到採用上等食材烹調的傳統浙江及上海美食，如長江燻魚、苔條蝦仁及紹興蒸臭豆腐。這裏由香港浙江省同鄉會聯合會經營，樓高兩層，雖然裝修並个豪華，但感覺十分舒適。

TEL. 2877 9011
1-3F, Kiu Fu Comm Bldg,
300-306 Lockhart Road, Wan Chai
灣仔駱克道 300-306號
橋阜商業大廈 1-3樓
www.zhejiangheen.com

SPECIALITIES TO PRE-ORDER 預訂食物
Crispy deep-fried chicken with 4 treasures
四寶片皮雞 / Braised duck stuffed with 8
treasures 蠔燒八寶鴨

■ PRICE 價錢
Lunch 午膳
à la carte 點菜　$ 160-400
Dinner 晚膳
à la carte 點菜　$ 200-600

■ OPENING HOURS 營業時間
Lunch 午膳　11:00-14:30 (L.O.)
Dinner 晚膳　18:00-22:30 (L.O.)

■ ANNUAL AND WEEKLY CLOSING 休息日期
Closed 3 days Lunar New Year
農曆新年休息 3 天

Street Food 街頭小吃
Popular places for snack food
馳名小食店

🚐 Block 18 Doggie's Noodle 十八座狗仔粉

Fried pork fat noodles.
狗仔粉(豬油渣麵)及豬皮蘿蔔。
$ 20-40   12:00-04:00

MAP 地圖   17/C-2
GF, 27A Ning Po Street, Jordan
佐敦寧波街 27A地下

🚐 Butchers Club

Burgers and duck fat fries.
漢堡包及鴨油薯條。
$ 100-150   12:00-23:00

MAP 地圖   28/A-2
GF, 2 Landale Street, Wan Chai
灣仔蘭杜街 2號

🚐 Chin Sik 千色車仔麵

Choose your own selection of noodles and toppings.
車仔麵。
$ 25-50   11:30-01:00

MAP 地圖   5/B-1
49 Shiu Wo Street, Tsuen Wan
荃灣兆和街 49號

🚌 Fat Boy 第三代肥仔

Octopus and duck's stomach marinated in soy sauce.

墨魚及鴨胗。

$20-40   13:00-23:30 (Mon-Sat
週一至週六)
13:00-21:00 (Sun 週日)

MAP 地圖 19/C-2
3 Hau Fook Street, Tsim Sha Tsui
尖沙咀厚福街 3號

🚌 Fork Eat

Slow cooked local farm chicken, USDA rib steak.

自家農場雞，真空慢煮美國安格斯小牛排。

$100-150   12:00-21:30

MAP 地圖 2/B-2
Shop 10, GF, Yik Fat Building,
11-15 Fung Yau Street North, Yuen Long
元朗鳳琴北街 11-15號益發大廈 10號舖

🚌 Hop Yik Tai 合益泰小食

Rice rolls; fish balls and radish.

豬腸粉、魚蛋、豬皮及蘿蔔。

$10-40   06:30-20:00

MAP 地圖 7/B-2
121 Kweilin Street, Sham Shui Po
深水埗桂林街 121號

🚌 I Love You Dessert Bar

Soufflé pancake.

梳乎厘班戟。

$30-40   15:00-00:00 (Mon-Thu 週一至週四)
15:00-01:00 (Fri 週五)
13:00-01:00 (Sat 週六)
13:00-00:00 (Sun 週日)

MAP 地圖 15/D-3
Shop 3A, GF, Ngai Hing Mansion,
24 Pak Po Street, Mong Kok
旺角白布街 24號藝興大廈地下 3A號舖

Joyful Dessert House

Western desserts like mango Napoleon, pineapple sherbet.

西式甜品如黑糖芭菲、芒果拿破崙及燒菠蘿雪芭。

$ 50-80   15:00-01:00

MAP 地圖　15/D-3
Shop 2-3, 74 Hak Po Street, Mong Kok
旺角黑布街 74號 2-3號舖

Kai Kai 佳佳甜品

Glutinous rice dumplings in ginger sweet soup; stewed papaya with rock sugar.

寧波薑汁湯丸、冰糖燉木瓜。

$ 20-30   12:00-04:00

MAP 地圖　17/C-2
29 Ning Po Street, Jordan
佐敦寧波街 29號

Kei Tsui 奇趣餅家

Cantonese puddings and pastries like Xiaofeng cake and walnut cookies.

雞仔餅、合桃酥及香蕉糕等。

$ 20-40   08:00-20:00

MAP 地圖　15/D-2
135 Fa Yuen Street, Mong Kok
旺角花園街 135號

Kelly's Cope Bop

Korean fried chicken; tteokbokki; kimbap.

韓國炸雞、辣年糕、飯卷。

$ 50-150   11:00-21:00

MAP 地圖　28/B-3
57 Johnston Road, Wan Chai
灣仔莊士敦道 57號

🚐 Keung Kee 強記

Glutinous rice; rice roll and sweet soup.

糯米飯、腸粉及糖水。

$ 20-40   12:00-01:00

MAP 地圖   29/D-2
382 Lockhart Road, Wan Chai
灣仔駱克道 382號

🚐 Kwan Kee Store 坤記糕品

Chinese rice pudding; white sugar cake and black sesame roll.

砵仔糕、芝麻糕、白糖糕、馬蹄糕等。

$ 20-40   08:00-23:00

MAP 地圖   7/B-2
115-117 Fuk Wa Street, Sham Shui Po
深水埗福華街 115-117號

🚐 Lan Ying 蘭英印尼小食

Satay and nasi rendang.

沙爹串燒及巴東牛肉飯。

$ 20-50   11:00-24:00

MAP 地圖   13/D-1
92-94 Fuk Lo Tsun Road, Kowloon City
九龍城福佬村道 92-94號

🚐 Mak Kee 麥記美食

Xiao Lung Bao, pan-fried pork dumplings, pan-fried pork buns and fish balls.

小籠包、鍋貼、生煎包、魚蛋及葱油餅。

$ 30-50   11:00-23:00

MAP 地圖   34/B-2
21-23 Fort Street, North Point
北角堡壘街 21-23號

🚐 Mammy Pancake 媽咪雞蛋仔

Classic street food cooked in a special egg waffle pan.

雞蛋仔。

$ 15-30   12:30-21:00

MAP 地圖   19/C-2
8-12 Carnarvon Road, Tsim Sha Tsui
尖沙咀加拿芬道 8-12號

🚐 Man Kei Cart Noodles 文記車仔麵

Turnip, minced dace, Chinese chive dumpling, beef tendon, pork trotter, pig intestine and chicken wing.

蘿蔔、鯪魚肉、韭菜餃、牛孖筋、豬手、豬大腸、雞中翼。

$ 25-80   11:00-03:30

MAP 地圖   7/B-2
121 Fuk Wing Street, Sham Shui Po
深水埗福榮街 121號

🚐 Owl's

Homemade choux and gelato with different condiments.

手工泡芙及意大利雪糕。

$ 20-60   12:30-22:30

MAP 地圖   19/C-2
GF, 32 Mody Road, Tsim Sha Tsui
尖沙咀麼地道 32號地下

🚐 Soupreme 湯品小棧

Cantonese double-boiled soups like matsutake soup.

粵式燉湯如牛肝菌湯、松茸湯。

$ 30-50   12:00-21:00

MAP 地圖   14/B-3
20 Beech Street, Tai Kwok Tsui
大角咀櫸樹街 20號

🚌 Three Potatoes 叁薯

Baked potatoes, fries and potato hash.

焗薯、炸薯及薯餅。

$ 25-40   12:00-21:00

MAP 地圖   15/C-2
Shop 5, GF, 30-32A Nullah Road, Mong Kok
旺角水渠道 30-32A號地下 5號舖

🚌 Wah Yuan 華園甜品

Cantonese sweet soup.

廣東糖水。

$ 20-40   12:00-00:00

MAP 地圖   8/A-2
GF, 38 Shung Ling Street, San Po Kong
新蒲崗崇齡街 38號地下

HOTELS
酒店

HOTELS IN ORDER OF COMFORT
酒店 — 以舒適程度分類

CLASSIC 古典

Citadines Mercer
馨樂庭尚圜

Those who need the convenience of a Central location but also want a little space should consider Citadines Mercer. The narrow 31 storey building just has 15 standard bedrooms but 40 one-bedroom suites. Ubiquitous beige tones add to the up-to-date feel and rooms come with large writing desks and a host of free extras which include the minibar and local phone calls.

如果你既愛中環的便利，又需要較多私人空間，馨樂庭尚圜服務公寓絕對適合你。建築外形修長，樓高三十一層，只有十五間標準客房，卻有達四十間單人睡房套間。統一的米白色調散發出時尚感覺，房間設有大型書桌和附送多項免費服務，包括免費本地電話服務和迷你酒吧。

TEL. 2922 9988
29 Jervois Street, Sheung Wan
上環蘇杭街 29號
www.citadines.com

RECOMMENDED RESTAURANTS 餐廳推薦
Sushi Shikon 志魂 ✲✲✲ ✗

♦ = $ 1,800-3,200
♦♦ = $ 1,800-3,500
Suites 套房 = $ 2,100-3,500

Rooms 客房 15
Suites 套房 40

City Garden
城市花園

You'll find the City Garden in a largely residential area, a short walk from Fortress Hill MTR. The bedrooms would not necessarily win any design awards but they are fair in both size and price. The Garden Café offers an extensive international buffet; Satay Inn on the basement level provides Asian specialities; and Yuè serves authentic Cantonese dishes.

城市花園酒店坐落於寧靜的住宅區內，與炮台山港鐵站只有咫尺，交通網絡非常便利。除了佔盡港島區的優越地勢外，客房空間充裕且收費合理；附屬的綠茵閣餐廳提供豐富的午、晚市環球美食自助餐，開設在一樓的粵中菜廳則提供傳統廣東佳餚。

TEL. 2887 2888
9 City Garden Road, North Point
北角城市花園道 9 號
www.citygarden.com.hk

RECOMMENDED RESTAURANTS 餐廳推薦
Yuè (North Point) 粵（北角） XX

♂ = $ 2,800-4,200
♂♂ = $ 2,800-4,200
Suites 套房 = $5,900
☕ = $178

Rooms 客房　583
Suites 套房　15

Conrad
港麗

Sitting above the Pacific Place complex is the Conrad, deftly mixing the traditional with the modern. The vast oval lobby showcases Chinese vases and bronze sculptures. Bedrooms are between the 40th and 61st floors, ensuring sweeping views; suites are particularly spacious and have elegant marble bathrooms. An outdoor swimming pool offers an equally dramatic panorama.

酒店位處集購物娛樂於一身的太古廣場之上。寬闊的橢圓形大堂擺放着中式花瓶及銅像，設計融合了傳統和現代元素，優雅而壯麗；寢室設在40至61樓，坐擁遼闊美景，而套房則特別寬敞，設有雲石浴室。室外游泳池讓你飽覽香港全景。

TEL. 2521 3838
Pacific Place, 88 Queensway, Admiralty
金鐘道 88號太古廣場
www.conradhongkong.com

RECOMMENDED RESTAURANTS 餐廳推薦
Golden Leaf 金葉庭　XxX

👤 = $ 2,300-5,300
👥 = $ 2,300-5,300
Suites 套房 = $ 5,200-8,600
☕ = $ 285

Rooms 客房　467
Suites 套房　45

Cordis
康得思

The modern, luminous lobby of this 42-storey glass tower features contemporary Chinese paintings and sculpture – part of the collection of 1,500 pieces that you'll find dotted around the hotel. Good-sized rooms with picture windows come with smart marble bathrooms and nice views. There's a pool on the top floor and an all-day buffet restaurant on the lobby floor.

康得思坐落於行人如鯽的旺角心臟地帶,連接地鐵站和購物商場。琉璃塔般的大樓高42層,不僅有科技發燒友夢寐以求的電子產品,還有超過1,500幅畫作、雕塑與裝置藝術品,是一個中國現代美術展覽館。客房的設計含蓄而時髦,窗外是五光十色的繁華市景;天台設有室外恒溫游泳池,並有多間餐廳供客人選擇。

TEL. 3552 3388
555 Shanghai Street, Mong Kok
旺角上海街555號
www.cordishotels.com/en/hong-kong

RECOMMENDED RESTAURANTS 餐廳推薦
Ming Court 明閣 ❀ XxX

🧍 = $ 1,300-3,500
🧍🧍 = $ 1,300-3,500
Suites 套房 = $ 2,650-4,850
☕ = $ 218

Rooms 客房　640
Suites 套房　29

Crowne Plaza
皇冠假日

Upper level bedrooms at this modern, corporate-minded hotel have the best outlooks, which include views of the Happy Valley racetrack on the south side. All of the bedrooms are decently sized and come with glass-walled bathrooms and impressive extras such as a wide choice of pillows. On the top floor you'll find Club@28: a chic bar with a terrace.

這家精心設計的時尚酒店，高層客房坐擁最美麗的港島景觀，南邊客房可飽覽跑馬地馬場全景。所有房間都寬敞舒適，浴室牆壁以玻璃砌成，擴闊了視覺上的空間，設施應有盡有，包括不同款色的枕頭。酒店頂層有為時尚人士而設的Club@28酒吧，還有小型泳池和健身室。

TEL. 3980 3980
8 Leighton Road, Causeway Bay
銅鑼灣禮頓道 8號
www.cphongkong.com

👤 = $ 2,000-3,500
👥 = $ 2,000-3,500
Suites 套房 = $ 4,800-5,300
☕ = $ 228

Rooms 客房　253
Suites 套房　10

Crowne Plaza Kowloon East
九龍東皇冠假日

A comfortable, well-equipped hotel in a busy commercial district with good transport links. It boasts one of the largest ballrooms around and dining options include a buffet, a Chinese restaurant and an Italian on the roof-top, along with a bar with great views. The contemporary bedrooms are warm and stylish and come with glass-walled bathrooms and a host of extras.

由著名酒店集團管理，坐落於將軍澳鐵路站上蓋，交通便捷。客房設計時尚，色調柔和、簡單的線條和善用空間的設計，平實卻不失優雅。大型多用途宴會廳和會議設施是其一大特色。綠草如茵的露天花園可作婚禮場地。酒店頂層的露天酒吧是一個能讓人放鬆心情的好地方。

TEL. 3983 0388
3 Tong Tak Street, Tseung Kwan O
將軍澳唐德街 3號
www.crowneplaza.com/kowlooneast

RECOMMENDED RESTAURANTS 餐廳推薦
Tze Yuet Heen 紫粵軒 ✕✕

👤 = $ 1,300-1,700
👤👤 = $ 1,300-1,700
Suites 套房 = $ 6,300-6,700
☕ = $ 248

Rooms 客房　354
Suites 套房　5

East
東隅

East is a modern business hotel designed for those who, like the hotel staff, can wear a pair of Converse with their suit. It has an uncluttered lobby, a bright, open plan restaurant serving international cuisine, and a great rooftop terrace bar named 'Sugar', as this was once a sugar factory. Bedrooms are minimalist but well-kept; corner rooms are especially light.

標榜為品味商務酒店。整潔的大堂、時尚的酒吧、提供國際美食的餐廳，加上可觀看迷人維港景色的天台酒吧Sugar──名字靈感源自酒店前身的糖廠，絕對切合你的需要。客房佈置簡約優雅，以大量玻璃與木材塑造出溫暖感覺與品味。位處轉角的客房景觀尤佳。

TEL. 3968 3968
29 Taikoo Shing Road, Taikoo Shing
太古城太古城道 29號
www.east-hongkong.com

♟ = $ 2,800-3,700
♟♟ = $ 2,800-3,700
Suites 套房 = $ 4,300-6,500
☗ = $ 218

Rooms 客房 339
Suites 套房 6

Four Seasons
四季

Four Seasons hotel not only offers some of the most spacious accommodation in Hong Kong but the bedrooms, which have wall-to-wall windows, also feature an impressive array of extras. Choose between a Western style room and one with a more Asian feel; all have large and luxurious bathrooms. The hotel also boasts two bars, two swimming pools and two world class restaurants.

四季酒店與維港毗鄰，景色壯麗，提供香港最寬敞時尚的客房。客房佈置分為現代風格和東方情調兩種，且設有大型豪華浴室。Blue Bar專為享受雞尾酒和現場音樂演奏而設。水療設施令人印象難忘，更設有兩個溫度不同的泳池。舒適的環境與高質素服務兩者俱備。

TEL. 3196 8888
8 Finance Street, Central
中環金融街 8 號
www.fourseasons.com/hongkong

RECOMMENDED RESTAURANTS 餐廳推薦
Caprice ✿✿ ҲxXxX
Lung King Heen 龍景軒 ✿✿✿ ҲxxX

👤 = $ 4,300-8,900
👥 = $ 4,300-8,900
Suites 套房 = $ 9,300-75,000
☕ = $ 330

Rooms 客房 343
Suites 套房 56

Gold Coast
黃金海岸

The beach resort 30 minutes away from the city has undergone a major overhaul. Two-thirds of the rooms were revamped with a few themed around outer space, pirates, princesses and safaris to amuse your little ones. The new ocean-themed play area is also a fun way to burn off energy. Those tying the knot will applaud the indoor garden feel of The Terrace and the solemn grandeur of The Chapel.

酒店三分之二的客房經過翻新，感覺明亮、時尚、舒適。兒童特色主題房間：公主、太空、恐龍、森林等，佈置得色彩繽紛、生動逼真，此外，新增設的鯊魚冒險島，緊張刺激卻有趣。重新設計的婚禮教堂和庭園，是不錯的婚宴場地。毗鄰泳灘，兼有完備的康樂設施和幽美園林，是度假的理想之選。

TEL. 2452 8888
1 Castle Peak Road, Gold Coast
黃金海岸青山公路 1號
www.goldcoasthotel.com.hk

RECOMMENDED RESTAURANTS 餐廳推薦
Yuè (Gold Coast) 粵（黃金海岸）XX

👤 = $ 2,900-4,000
👥 = $ 2,900-4,000
Suites 套房 = $ 5,800-16,000
☕ = $ 238

Rooms 客房 443
Suites 套房 10

Grand Hyatt
君悅

A fixture in Wan Chai since 1989, this hotel comes with a grand lobby and is perfectly located for the Convention and Exhibition Centre. All the bedrooms have been refurbished fairly recently and have opulent bathrooms – the deluxe rooms are the ones with the great harbour views. Along with a large outdoor pool, the hotel offers a wide selection of restaurants and a champagne bar.

這家酒店鄰近香港會議展覽中心，維港兩岸景色盡收於眼底。富麗堂皇的大堂早於1989年酒店開業時便已落成，全面修葺後的客房裝潢更時尚，並設豪華雲石浴室。酒店設有多家餐館，分別提供中外菜式，大型室外泳池可盡情舒展身心。

TEL. 2588 1234
1 Harbour Road, Wan Chai
灣仔港灣道 1號
www.hongkong.grand.hyatt.com

RECOMMENDED RESTAURANTS 餐廳推薦
Grand Hyatt Steakhouse XX
Grissini XXX
One Harbour Road 港灣壹號 XXX

 = $ 2,800-6,000
 = $ 2,800-6,000
Suites 套房 = $ 5,800-88,000
 = $ 318

Rooms 客房 493
Suites 套房 49

Harbour Grand Kowloon
九龍海逸君綽

This shimmering glass structure is right on the waterfront and offers superb views across Victoria Harbour. It boasts a spectacularly grand lobby with an impressive white marble staircase and, although the bedrooms are bright, comfortable and well-equipped, they are sober by comparison to other areas. Do visit the dramatic rooftop pool with its glass walls.

這座位於紅磡海濱、閃閃發亮的玻璃建築物與維港相毗鄰，金碧輝煌的大堂設有白色雲石階梯。房間光潔舒適，設備齊全，相比酒店內其他設施或有點樸實。住客可於天台上的玻璃幕牆泳池內盡情暢泳及享用頂樓健身中心設施和蒸氣浴。

TEL. 2621 3188
20 Tak Fung Street, Whampoa Garden,
Hung Hom
紅磡黃埔花園德豐街 20號
www.harbourgrand.com/kowloon

RECOMMENDED RESTAURANTS 餐廳推薦
Robatayaki 炉端燒 ✗

👤 = $ 2,900-4,200
👥 = $ 3,200-4,500
Suites 套房 = $ 5,800-35,000
☕ = $218

Rooms 客房 468
Suites 套房 87

Harbour Plaza North Point
北角海逸

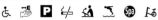

Those doing business in North Point or Quarry Bay will find this hotel a useful address. It's spread over 32 floors and everything feels contemporary, right from the moment you enter the lobby with its unusual water feature. Bedrooms are a fair size and well soundproofed. There are also 180 serviced suites available for long-stay clients (a minimum of one month).

樓高32層的北角海逸酒店地點便利，對在北角或鰂魚涌洽談商務的人士來說，是短暫停留的好住處。大堂水池的設計盡顯時尚氣派。客房寬敞寧靜；大部分房間只有淋浴設備，如需泡浴，須於訂房時提出。酒店另設有180間為長期住客而設的服務式套房，租期最短為一個月。

TEL. 2187 8888
665 King's Road, North Point
北角英皇道665號
www.harbour-plaza.com/northpoint/
Index-en.htm

👤 = $ 2,150-4,150
👥 = $2,250-4,150
Suites 套房 = $ 4,150-6,950
☕ = $ 158

Rooms 客房 638
Suites 套房 76

HONG KONG 香港

Hyatt Regency Sha Tin
沙田凱悅

Just a minute's walk from University Station is this 26 floor hotel, whose large, well-equipped bedrooms have either harbour or mountain views. It makes clever use of neutral colours and natural materials like stone and wood to create a soothing ambience. It's business-orientated during the week; the impressive leisure facilities appeal to families at weekends.

沙田凱悅於2009年開幕,從港鐵大學站前往僅需步行兩分鐘。酒店設計充滿時代感,巧妙運用中性色彩及天然物料如石材及木材製造出柔和融洽的感覺。酒店平日以接待商務旅客為主,到週末則以出色的休閒設施吸引家庭顧客。

TEL. 3723 1234
18 Chak Cheung Street, University Station, Sha Tin
沙田大學站澤祥街18號
www.hongkongshatin.regency.hyatt.com

🕴 = $1,050-2,800
🕴🕴 = $1,050-2,800
Suites 套房 = $2,250-4,000
☕ = $218

Rooms 客房 385
Suites 套房 174

Hyatt Regency Tsim Sha Tsui
尖沙咀凱悅

Occupying floors 3-24 of the impressive K11 skyscraper means that bedrooms here at the Hyatt Regency benefit from impressive views of the city or harbour. The rooms are decorated in a crisp, modern style; anyone choosing the Regency Club level has access to a private lounge. There are dining options galore and an impressive selection of whiskies in the Chin Chin Bar.

尖沙咀凱悅佔據K11摩天大樓的3至24層，並與K11購物藝術館相連，酒店房間能看到城市的繁華景色或醉人的維港景致。房間風格清新時尚，選擇嘉賓軒樓層的住客更可享受專用酒廊服務。酒店提供多種餐飲選擇，請請吧內的威士忌種類之多更是令人歎為觀止。

TEL. 2311 1234
18 Hanoi Road, Tsim Sha Tsui
尖沙咀河內道18號
www.hongkongtsimshatsui.regency.
hyatt.com

RECOMMENDED RESTAURANTS 餐廳推薦
Hugo's 希戈 ✕✕✕

♀ = $2,500-4,200
♀♀ = $2,500-4,200
Suites 套房 = $4,200-22,000
☕ = $228

Rooms 客房 348
Suites 套房 33

HONG KONG 香港

Icon
唯港薈

Rocco Yim, Sir Terence Conran and William Lim were among the celebrated designers brought together to create this chic hotel, which is owned by the Hong Kong Polytechnic University. Its style credentials are clear, from the works by local artists to the modern staircase and 'vertical garden'. Market is a buffet restaurant; formal dining in Above and Beyond.

著名設計師嚴迅奇、泰倫斯・康藍爵士和林偉而等攜手打造出這間香港理工大學名下最新最潮的酒店。它的設計風格鮮明，可欣賞本地藝術家的精彩作品，亦有令人驚歎的現代化樓梯和垂直花園。The Market是廣受歡迎的自助餐廳，天外天則供應傳統粵菜。

TEL. 3400 1000
17 Science Museum Road,
East Tsim Sha Tsui
尖東科學館道 17號
www.hotel-icon.com

RECOMMENDED RESTAURANTS 餐廳推薦
Above & Beyond 天外天　XxX

♟ = $ 2,000-5,000
♟♟ = $ 2,000-5,000
Suites 套房 = $ 4,000-15,000
☕ = $ 218

Rooms 客房　236
Suites 套房　26

Indigo
英迪格

Bordering Tai Yuen Street and its market, so ideally placed for discovering old Hong Kong, Indigo is also a good choice for those who've come to shop – there's even a shopping bag placed in every room! For others, there's always the rooftop bar and infinity pool. The bedrooms come with floor-to-ceiling windows and boast some cute design touches.

這幢外觀獨特的建築物坐落於灣仔商業區及住宅區交界，不光擁有完善的交通網絡，更與有濃厚地區色彩的市集毗鄰，讓你深入了解本區生活脈搏。全部房間設有落地玻璃窗，家具擺設均經過精心設計，設施亦十分齊全，文具、購物袋一應俱全。天台玻璃底泳池，前臨山巒，感覺開揚，是放鬆身心的好地方。

TEL. 3926 3888
246 Queen's Road East, Wan Chai
灣仔皇后大道東 246號
www.hotelindigo.com/hongkong

👤 = $ 1,600-2,600
👥 = $ 1,600-2,600
Suites 套房 = $ 3,500-5,000
☕ = $ 180

Rooms 客房　132
Suites 套房　6

InterContinental
洲際

 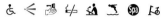

It may be unremarkable from the outside, but this hotel is decidedly impressive once you're in the lobby with its magnificent harbour views. All bedrooms are well-equipped, with spacious marble bathrooms. Relax in either the swimming pool or spa pool, or enjoy a massage in an outside cabana. Options for dining are excellent (see separate entries) and service is exemplary.

踏入富麗堂皇的酒店大堂，望着一流海景，絕對令你印象深刻。客房非常寬敞，淺色調的設計感覺寧靜，更設有寬闊的雲石浴室。你可以在優雅的游泳池或水療池鬆弛身心；戶外的池邊小室內有按摩服務。酒店內的餐飲服務非常出色，服務水準一流。

TEL. 2721 1211
18 Salisbury Road, Tsim Sha Tsui
尖沙咀梳士巴利道 18號
www.intercontinental.com

👤 = $2,000-6,000	
👥 = $2,000-6,000	
Suites 套房 = $3,500-98,000	
☕ = $330	

RECOMMENDED RESTAURANTS 餐廳推薦
Nobu XX
The Steak House Winebar + grill XxX
Yan Toh Heen 欣圖軒 ✿✿ XxxX

Rooms 客房　419
Suites 套房　82

InterContinental Grand Stanford
海景嘉福洲際

After a comprehensive renovation programme, this 18-storey waterfront hotel, which opened back in 1981, is looking much more contemporary in style. The service is good and the bedrooms are a decent size – just be sure to ask for one with a harbour view. There are plenty of dining options and the heated outdoor swimming pool on the roof is nicely secluded.

這幢龐大的臨海建築物樓高18層，建於1981年並剛完成全面翻新工程。翻新後的寢室雅致時尚，因此訂房時謹記要選擇一間有海景並且經過翻新的房間。酒店頂層設有健身室及戶外溫水泳池。酒店內有數間食店供住客選擇。

TEL. 2721 5161
70 Mody Road, East Tsim Sha Tsui
尖восточ麼地道 70號
www.hongkong.intercontinental.com

♟ = $ 3,300-4,600
♟♟ = $ 3,300-4,600
Suites 套房 = $ 7,500-15,000
☕ = $ 248

Rooms 客房   531
Suites 套房   39

Island Shangri-La
港島香格里拉

A vast, intricate Chinese silk painting towers over the glamorous atrium and rises up all of 16 storeys; more sparkle is provided by the dazzling array of chandeliers placed around the hotel. The bedrooms are thoughtfully laid out and comfortable; those rooms on the Horizon Club (52nd to 55th floor) are especially sumptuous and have access to a super rooftop terrace.

延伸至16樓、世上最大幅的中國絲綢畫，筆工細膩、構圖錯綜複雜，散發着迷人魅力，加上金光閃爍的吊燈，五光十色的中庭，令人目眩神馳。樓上是華麗典雅的客房，尤以52至55樓豪華閣樓層的房間為甚，此樓層的住客可使用專屬會客廳和美不勝收的天台庭園。

TEL. 2877 3838
Pacific Place, Supreme Court Road, Admiralty
金鐘法院道太古廣場
www.shangri-la.com/island

RECOMMENDED RESTAURANTS 餐廳推薦
Lobster Bar and Grill 龍蝦吧 XX
Petrus 珀翠 XxXxX
Summer Palace 夏宮 ✿ XxX

🧍 = $ 2,800-5,000
🧍🧍 = $ 2,800-5,000
Suites 套房 = $ 6,800-9,000
☕ = $ 328

Rooms 客房 531
Suites 套房 34

JW Marriott
JW萬豪

Boasting 602 rooms spread over 35 storeys, this business hotel also offers a number of executive floors which have their own discreet lounge and meeting rooms. The bedrooms are functional but up-to-date and there's a pleasant outdoor pool and a well-equipped fitness centre. Dining options include Cantonese and seafood, along with a wine bar and tea room.

以商務住客為主的萬豪酒店樓高三十五層，客房數量達602間。位於頂樓的一列行政套房，附有素雅的休息室和會議室。房間設計富現代感且十分實用。戶外游泳池環境清幽、健身中心設備齊全，還網羅了各地餐飲美食，廣東菜、海鮮、酒吧、茶室等不同類別的餐室任君選擇。

TEL. 2810 8366
Pacific Place, 88 Queensway, Admiralty
金鐘道88號太古廣場
www.jwmarriotthongkong.com

👤 = $2,500-5,000
👥 = $2,500-5,000
Suites 套房 = $5,600-8,500
☕ = $318

Rooms 客房 577
Suites 套房 25

Kowloon Shangri-La
九龍香格里拉

The first thing to strike you will be the size and grandeur of the lobby, with its marble, sparkling chandeliers and tiered water fountain – it is certainly one of the most impressive aspects of this business-orientated hotel. The enthusiastic staff are another great strength. The bedrooms are larger than many of its competitors and come with a subtle Asian theme.

不僅是氣派宏偉的雲石酒店大堂，還是閃爍的吊燈與三層噴泉水池，都令你對這家以商務為主的酒店留下極深刻印象。全部客房都經過重新粉飾，跟其他同級酒店比較更見寬敞，服務水準更是毋庸置疑。最佳的客房採用亞洲風情為主題作裝潢。

TEL. 2721 2111
64 Mody Road, East Tsim Sha Tsui
尖東麼地道 64 號
www.shangri-la.com/kowloon

RECOMMENDED RESTAURANTS 餐廳推薦
Shang Palace 香宮 ❀❀ ⅩⅩⅩⅩ

♦ = $ 2,400-3,700
♦♦ = $ 2,400-4,000
Suites 套房 = $ 4,180-22,080
☕ = $ 275

Rooms 客房   646
Suites 套房   42

Lan Kwai Fong
蘭桂坊

♿ ♿ 🚶 🚴

A hotel which feels part of the local area and mixes Chinese and contemporary furniture, neutral tones and dark wood veneers to create a relaxing environment. Try to secure one of the deluxe corner bedrooms or a suite with a balcony if you want more space; those higher than the 21st floor have the harbour views. Celebrity Cuisine offers accomplished Cantonese food.

融合了中國傳統與現代品味的家具，中性色調及深色木間隔，環境舒適。如果你需要更寬敞的空間，建議預訂轉角位置的豪華客房或附設露台的套房。21樓以上的房間可飽覽維港景色。客人可借用房間內的流動電話，方便在外與朋友聯絡。

TEL. 3650 0000
3 Kau U Fong, Central
中環九如坊 3號
www.lankwaifonghotel.com.hk

RECOMMENDED RESTAURANTS 餐廳推薦
Celebrity Cuisine 名人坊 ❀ ✕✕

🚹 = $ 1,080-2,780
🚻 = $1,080-2,780
Suites 套房 = $ 2,880-6,800
☕ = $ 150

Rooms 客房   157
Suites 套房   5

Lanson Place

This discreet and stylish boutique hotel comes with an air of calm exclusivity and an attractive European-influenced aesthetic. The cool lounge and bar allows the hotel to feel more intimate than the number of bedrooms would suggest. Those rooms come with small kitchenettes and have a clean and bright feel. The hotel is ideally located for those going to HK stadium.

擁有歐洲風格的典雅外觀，Lanson Place能稱為一間時尚精品酒店。古典與現代設計交織出酒店的獨特氣派，室內的藝術作品，營造溫暖寧靜的感覺。客房雅致明亮，設有大型窗戶，多家客房能眺望香港大球場。休閒舒適的休息室與酒吧也是入住期間值得蹓躂的地方。

TEL. 3477 6888
133 Leighton Road, Causeway Bay
銅鑼灣禮頓道 133號
www.lansonplace.com

👤 = $ 1,800-4,000
👥 = $ 1,800-4,000
Suites 套房 = $ 4,800-12,000
☕ = $ 210

Rooms 客房　188
Suites 套房　6

Mandarin Oriental
文華東方

HONG KONG 香港

Having celebrated its 50th birthday in 2013, this iconic hotel continues to update itself while remaining true to its heritage. Bedrooms may not be the largest but are charmingly decorated and are split between Tai Pan-style (woods and browns) and brighter Veranda-style. The spa is a spiritual haven and the dining and bar options are many and varied.

開業超過五十年，營運者在保留其優良傳統之餘，還致力提升其質素。和其他酒店相比，其客房並非最大，但無論是典雅的大班風格或陽台房間的裝潢均非常精緻，附設的水療設施令你如置身樂園；酒店還為客人提供多元化餐飲選擇。

TEL. 2522 0111
5 Connaught Road, Central
中環干諾道中 5號
www.mandarinoriental.com/hongkong

RECOMMENDED RESTAURANTS 餐廳推薦
Man Wah 文華廳 ☼ XxX
Mandarin Grill + Bar
文華扒房 + 酒吧 ☼ XxxX
Pierre ☼☼ XxxX

👤 = $4,000-6,500
👥 = $4,000-6,500
Suites 套房 = $5,500-9,800
☕ = $350

Rooms 客房　434
Suites 套房　67

Metropark (Causeway Bay)
銅鑼灣維景

This 31-storey tower near Victoria is a popular choice for business travellers. Its bedrooms are not that large so it's worth booking one of the executive rooms, many of which have harbour views. The rooftop swimming pool is small but appealing and the views from the fitness centre help you deal with the pain of exercise. Café du Parc offers all-day buffet dining.

酒店大樓樓高三十一層，鄰近維多利亞公園，為商務旅客提供舒適環境及娛樂設施。這兒大部分房間的面積較小，因此選擇面積較大的行政套房絕對物有所值，而大部分房間可看到無敵海景。小型天台游泳池配備水底音樂，設計別出心裁。附設的繽紛維苑餐廳全日均有自助餐供應。

TEL. 2600 1000
148 Tung Lo Wan Road, Causeway Bay
銅鑼灣道 148號
www.metroparkhotel.com

👤 = $ 1,000-3,000
👥 = $1,000-3,000
Suites 套房 = $ 2,500-4,300
☕ = $ 163

Rooms 客房　238
Suites 套房　28

New World Millennium
千禧新世界

The former Nikko hotel is now run by a different management company but little else has changed here. The hotel is known for its comprehensive banqueting and conference rooms and its impressive number of restaurants providing a wide range of different cuisines. The smart bedrooms come with up-to-the-minute comforts. The harbour-front location adds to the appeal.

日航酒店易名後，酒店完善的宴會及會議設施仍然保留，四間提供不同菜式的餐廳仍然為賓客提供多種選擇，令他們樂在其中；優越的海濱地段及設計現代化的智能客房，為顧客帶來舒適享受，上述種種條件均足以令它躋身國際級酒店之列。

TEL. 2739 1111
72 Mody Road, East Tsim Sha Tsui
尖東麼地道 72號
www.newworldmillenniumhotel.com

🧍 = $ 1,500-4,200
🧍🧍 = $ 1,500-4,200
Suites 套房 = $ 3,500-7,700
☕ = $ 295

Rooms 客房　445
Suites 套房　19

Ozo Wesley
遨舍衛蘭軒

You'll find Ozo Wesley sitting pretty between Wan Chai and Admiralty so it's ideally placed whether you're in town for business or just in the mood for shopping and dining. All of the guest rooms are crisply decorated in a bright, fresh and contemporary style and the effective soundproofing ensures a decent night's sleep however busy it is outside.

位於金鐘與灣仔交界，距金鐘的商業金融區只有數分鐘路程，附近的小街道滿佈食店，位置便利，適合商業旅客。大堂設計具時代感。客房均以素色系配搭簡單時尚裝潢，舒適的感覺令你身心放鬆。全部房間都設有大玻璃窗和隔音設備，讓你既能欣賞灣仔的繁華景象又能享受片刻寧靜。

TEL. 2292 3000
22 Hennessy Road, Wan Chai
灣仔軒尼詩道 22號
www.ozohotels.com

= $ 1,250-2,950
= $1,250-2,950
Suites 套房 = $ 2,500-3,800
= $ 145

Rooms 客房 241
Suites 套房 16

Sheraton
喜來登

One of Hong Kong's biggest hotels is a short walk from the Star Ferry Pier so you can expect some great views of Victoria Harbour. These can be best appreciated from the health club's rooftop pool, over a plate of oysters in the wine bar, or from a swish executive room on the 16th or 17th floor. The hotel also has a cigar room, a wine shop and an international café.

位於九龍半島的喜來登是香港最大的酒店之一，只需短短的步行距離便到達天星碼頭。客人可盡覽維多利亞港景色，最佳位置包括健身俱樂部的天台游泳池、16樓及17樓的高級面海行政套房，在蠔酒吧吃蠔時亦可欣賞美景。較為樸實但非常舒適的有雪茄廊、酒鋪和國際咖啡廳。

TEL. 2369 1111
20 Nathan Road, Tsim Sha Tsui
尖沙咀彌敦道20號
www.sheratonhongkonghotel.com

RECOMMENDED RESTAURANTS 餐廳推薦
Celestial Court 天寶閣 ✗✗✗

👤 = $ 4,600-6,200
👥 = $ 4,600-6,400
Suites 套房 = $ 7,500-16,000
🍷 = $ 250

Rooms 客房　691
Suites 套房　91

HONG KONG 香港

The Landmark Mandarin Oriental
置地文華東方

From the personal airport pick-up to the endless spa choices, this is the hotel for those after a little pampering. Not only are the comfortable, smartly designed bedrooms big on luxury and size but they also come with stylish bathrooms attached; these feature either sunken or circular baths. MO is the cool ground floor bar for all-day dining or night time cocktails.

從專人機場接送服務到設備完善的水療設備，置地文華東方讓你盡享尊貴服務。令人讚歎的不光是設計型格獨特、面積達450至600呎的寬敞客房，還有房內豪華時尚的浴室設備，包括巨型下沈式或圓形浴缸。位於地下的MO Bar是解決一日三餐和品嘗雞尾酒的好去處。

TEL. 2132 0188
15 Queen's Road, Central
中環皇后大道中15號
www.mandarinoriental.com/landmark

RECOMMENDED RESTAURANTS 餐廳推薦
Amber ✪✪ ✗✗✗✗

♀ = $ 4,300-6,300
♀♀ = $ 4,300-6,300
Suites 套房 = $ 8,800-18,000
☕ = $ 263

Rooms 客房   97
Suites 套房   12

The Langham
朗廷

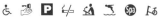

The clamour of Peking Road will seem but a distant memory once you're in the hushed surroundings of this elegant hotel. Its striking lobby, furnished in a classical European style, features some impressive modern art and sculptures, and bedrooms are furnished in a smart, contemporary style. The charm of the hotel is underpinned by modern facilities and attentive service.

進入這棟優雅建築物，讓你立刻忘卻北京道熙來攘往的煩囂。大堂以傳統歐洲風格裝潢，配上當代藝術品及雕塑作點綴，奢華奪目。客房典雅時尚，極具吸引力。迷人之處，盡見於其現代設施及細心周到的服務。

TEL. 2375 1133
8 Peking Road, Tsim Sha Tsui
尖沙咀北京道 8 號
www.langhamhotels.com/hongkong

RECOMMENDED RESTAURANTS 餐廳推薦
Bostonian Seafood and Grill XX
T'ang Court 唐閣 ❀❀❀ XxxX

♦ = $ 2,450-3,800
♦♦ = $2,450-3,800
Suites 套房 = $ 5,400-13,000
🖵 = $ 200

Rooms 客房　471
Suites 套房　27

The Mira

Smallish rooms but they're fitted with glass-clad ensuites, designer furniture and hi-tech gadgets. Rooms with views of Kowloon Park are worth paying extra for. Spa-goers will be thrilled at the newly renovated Heat experience zone in MiraSpa, while conference and event planners may check out the new AV system and LED wall in the updated penthouse ballroom.

房間面積雖不大，但出色的設計彌補了不足，浴室非常現代化；套房裝潢豪華。訂房時不妨要求面向九龍公園的客房。舒適豪華的水療設施值得一讚，其中Heat體驗區經過翻新，服務更完善。重新設計的宴會廳擁有最時尚的音訊設備和巨型入牆顯示屏，適合各種宴會。

TEL. 2368 1111
118 Nathan Road, Tsim Sha Tsui
尖沙咀彌敦道118號
www.themirahotel.com

RECOMMENDED RESTAURANTS 餐廳推薦
Cuisine Cuisine at The Mira
國金軒 (The Mira) 𝄇𝄇𝄇
Whisk 𝄇𝄇

𝄊 = $ 1,500-2,200
𝄊𝄊 = $1,700-2,400
Suites 套房 = $2,500-3,600
☕ = $ 248

Rooms 客房　436
Suites 套房　56

The Peninsula
半島

2013 saw the grande dame of Hong Kong hotels celebrate her 85th birthday, just as the refurbishment of the bedrooms was completed – they now come with a contemporary elegance and clever touch-pad technology. The iconic lobby remains the place for afternoon tea; the spa boasts a Roman-style pool; and a host of dining choices range from the modern to the traditional.

酒店於2013年修葺過後，客房更時尚雅致，房內設備全部透過高科技觸控屏操作。作為酒店標誌的大堂保留原來樣式，供顧客享用下午茶；羅馬式泳池仍然是一貫的迷人；新派菜和傳統菜餐館一應俱全。

TEL. 2920 2888
Salisbury Road, Tsim Sha Tsui
尖沙咀梳士巴利道
www.peninsula.com/hongkong

RECOMMENDED RESTAURANTS 餐廳推薦
Chesa 瑞樵閣 XX
Felix XX
Gaddi's 吉地士 XxxX
Spring Moon 嘉麟樓 ❀ XxX

    = $ 4,180-6,180
    = $ 4,180-6,180
Suites 套房 = $ 7,180-128,000
    = $ 360

Rooms 客房 246
Suites 套房 54

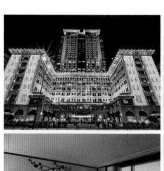

The Pottinger
中環・石板街

　　　　　　　　　　　　　　　　　　　　♿ ✖

Standing in the middle of Central, and on one of Hong Kong's oldest 'stone slab streets', is this elegant and stylish hotel. Its location is celebrated through its collection of iconic and historic photographs taken by award-winning artist Fan Ho. The 68 bedrooms are contemporary and graceful and boast all the amenities the modern traveller expects.

位於有過百年歷史的砵甸乍街(又名石板街)旁邊，故以此命名。斜斜的石板路見證了中環百多年來的故事，也為酒店增添了一分魅力。接待廳雖小卻流露着歐陸優雅格調，共有68間客房，面積適中、設備齊全。位處中環心臟地帶，無論往辦公、飲食、娛樂或乘搭交通工具都非常便利，是商務住宿的理想選擇。

TEL. 2308 3188
21 Stanley Street, Central
中環士丹利街 21號
www.thepottinger.com

RECOMMENDED RESTAURANTS 餐廳推薦
Ta Vie 旅 ✿✿ ✕✕

♟ = $ 1,700-4,800
♟♟ = $1,860-5,800
Suites 套房 = $ 3,900-10,000

Rooms 客房　61
Suites 套房　7

The Ritz-Carlton
麗思卡爾頓

The highest hotel in the world occupies the top 16 floors of Hong Kong's tallest building; to witness first-hand just how high this feels, head up to the cool Ozone bar on the 118th floor – it even comes with an outside terrace! Bedrooms are large and elegant and the suites are equipped with telescopes so guests can keep an eye on what's happening down on earth.

這家酒店佔據了香港最高建築物最頂的16層樓，部分人置身其中可能會感到暈眩。其位於118層的Ozone酒吧設有戶外露台，而游泳池也設於海拔490米高處。酒店客房空間偌大、裝潢高雅，套房中還設有望遠鏡，讓住客居高臨下俯瞰香港景色。

TEL. 2263 2263
International Commerce Centre,
1 Austin Road West, Tsim Sha Tsui
尖沙咀柯士甸道西 1號環球貿易廣場
www.ritzcarlton.com/hongkong

RECOMMENDED RESTAURANTS 餐廳推薦
Tin Lung Heen 天龍軒 ✿✿ XXXX
Tosca ✿ XXXX

† = $ 3,800-11,100
†† = $3,800-11,600
Suites 套房 = $ 6,600-13,900
☕ = $338

Rooms 客房 262
Suites 套房 50

The Royal Garden
帝苑

The two-storey extension in 2016 houses the Sky Tower with 28 suites, and an updated Mediterranean-style Sky Club boasting a rooftop pool, hot tub, gym, sauna and spa. Other rooms have recently been remodelled. Be it city, courtyard or harbour-view, all rooms come with mod cons you'd expect (or not), such as a smartphone for free unlimited calls and data usage.

帝苑酒店最為人樂道的，是中庭內110呎高的繁茂枝葉裝飾，不論住哪一個樓層，沿走廊進入客房時都能俯視庭內景況。客房時尚舒適，附有現代化設備。位於16-19樓的天際套房不光陳設豪華，更坐擁維港兩岸景色。Sky Club內的泳池、水療中心、健身室、桑拿浴室及按摩浴缸，足夠你享受一整天。

TEL. 2721 5215
69 Mody Road, East Tsim Sha Tsui
尖東麼地道 69號
www.rghk.com.hk

RECOMMENDED RESTAURANTS 餐廳推薦
Dong Lai Shun 東來順 XXX

♦ = $ 4,620-9,240
♦♦ = $ 4,620-9,240
Suites 套房 = $ 6,380-75,680
☕ = $ 275

Rooms 客房　396
Suites 套房　54

The Upper House
奕居

Cool and uncluttered, this stylish hotel makes great use of natural materials, art and sculpture to create a calm and relaxing environment for the modern traveller. It also does things a little differently: the checking-in process, for example, happens in your bedroom and not at the front desk. The bedrooms are crisp and neat, with all mod cons carefully concealed.

奕居早已成為潮流人士趨之若鶩的住宿熱點,是一家經過精心設計,細緻豪華的時尚酒店。酒店希望為客人帶來私人居所感覺,住客入住時會給直接帶到房間,服務員將送上飲品,並以平板電腦作簡單登記。寬敞的房間內設衣帽間,瀰漫着平和氣息。六樓設有小花園陽台。

TEL. 2918 1838
Pacific Place, 88 Queensway,
Admiralty
金鐘道 88號太古廣場
www.upperhouse.com

RECOMMENDED RESTAURANTS 餐廳推薦
Café Gray Deluxe XX

👤 = $ 5,200-8,000
👥 = $ 5,200-8,000
Suites 套房 = $ 17,000-25,000
🍵 = $ 280

Rooms 客房 96
Suites 套房 21

MACAU
澳門

RESTAURANTS
餐廳

STARRED RESTAURANTS
星級餐廳

Within this selection, we have highlighted a number of restaurants for their particularly good cooking. When awarding one, two or three Michelin Stars there are a number of factors we consider: the quality and compatibility of the ingredients, the technical skill and flair that goes into their preparation, the clarity and combination of flavours, the value for money and above all, the taste. Equally important is the ability to produce excellent cooking not once but time and time again. Our inspectors make as many visits as necessary, so that you can be sure of the quality and consistency.

A two or three star restaurant has to offer something very special that separates it from the rest. Three stars – our highest award – are given to the very best.

Cuisines in any style of restaurant and of any nationality are eligible for a star. The decoration, service and comfort levels have no bearing on the award.

在這系列的選擇裏，推薦的是食物質素特別出色的餐廳。給予一、二或三粒米芝蓮星時，我們考慮到以下因素：材料的質素和配搭、烹調技巧和特色、氣味濃度和組合、價錢是否相宜及味道層次。同樣重要的是該餐館的食物恆常保持在高水平。閣下對我們的推薦絕對可以放心！我們的評審員會因應需要多次到訪同一家餐館，以確認其食物品質能恆常保持高水準。

二或三星餐廳必有獨特之處，比同類型其他餐廳更出眾。最高評級 – 三星 – 只會給予最好的餐廳。

星級評定不會受到餐廳風格、菜式、裝潢陳設、服務及舒適程度影響。只要烹調技巧出色，食物品質特別優秀，都有機會獲得米芝蓮星星。

❀ ❀ ❀

Exceptional cuisine, worth a special journey.
卓越的烹調，值得專程到訪。

Our highest award is given for the superlative cooking of chefs at the peak of their profession. The ingredients are exemplary, the cooking is elevated to an art form and their dishes are often destined to become classics.

獲得最高級別的餐館，其廚師的烹調技巧卓絕，選材用料堪稱典範，並將烹飪提升至藝術層次，菜式大多會成為經典。

Robuchon au Dôme 天巢法國餐廳	XxXxX	French contemporary 時尚法國菜	394
The Eight 8餐廳	XxxX	Chinese 中國菜	401

Excellent cooking, worth a detour.
烹調出色，不容錯過！

The personality and talent of the chef and their team is evident in the refined, expertly crafted dishes.

主廚的個人風格與烹飪天賦及其團隊的優秀手藝完全反映在精巧味美的菜式上。

Feng Wei Ju 風味居	XxX	Hunanese and Sichuan 湘川菜	368
Golden Flower 京花軒	XxxX	Chinese 中國菜	370
Jade Dragon 譽瓏軒	XxxX	Cantonese 粵菜	376
Mizumi 泓	XxX	Japanese 日本菜	387
The Tasting Room 御膳房	XxxX	French contemporary 時尚法國菜	405

High quality cooking, worth a stop!
優質烹調，不妨一試！

Within their category, these establishments use quality ingredients and serve carefully prepared dishes with distinct flavours.

此名單上的餐館，在同類型餐館中，其食材較具質素，烹調細緻用心、味道出色。

King 帝皇樓	XX	Cantonese 粵菜	379
Lai Heen 麗軒	XxXxX	Cantonese 粵菜	380
8 1/2 Otto e Mezzo - Bombana	XxX	Italian 意大利菜	392
Pearl Dragon 玥龍軒	XxxX	Cantonese 粵菜	393
Shinji by Kanesaka 金坂極上壽司	XX	Sushi 壽司	397
The Golden Peacock 皇雀	XX	Indian 印度菜	402
The Kitchen 大廚	XX	Steakhouse 扒房	403
Tim's Kitchen 桃花源小廚	XxX	Cantonese 粵菜	406
Wing Lei 永利軒	XxxX	Cantonese 粵菜	409
Ying 帝影樓	XxX	Cantonese 粵菜	414
Zi Yat Heen 紫逸軒	XxxX	Cantonese 粵菜	415

BIB GOURMAND RESTAURANTS
車胎人美食推介餐廳

This symbol indicates our inspectors' favourites for good value. These restaurants offer quality cooking for $400 or less (price of a 3 course meal excluding drinks).

必比登標誌表示該餐廳提供具質素且經濟實惠的美食：費用在400元或以下（三道菜但不包括飲品）。

Castiço	X	Portuguese 葡國菜	358
Chan Seng Kei 陳勝記	⁸⫴	Cantonese 粵菜	359
Cheong Kei 祥記	⁸⫴	Noodles 麵食	360
Din Tai Fung (COD) 鼎泰豐 (新濠天地)	X	Shanghainese 滬菜	362
Hou Kong Chi Kei 濠江志記美食	⁸⫴	Cantonese 粵菜	372
IFT Educational Restaurant 旅遊學院教學餐廳	XX	Macanese 澳門菜	373
Lou Kei (Fai Chi Kei) 老記 (筷子基)	⁸⫴	Cantonese 粵菜	382
Luk Kei Noodle 六記粥麵	⁸⫴	Noodles and Congee 粥麵	383
Tou Tou Koi 陶陶居	X	Cantonese 粵菜	407

N : New entry in the guide 新增推介

ᵗᵉ⟋ : Restaurant promoted to a Bib Gourmand or Star 評級有所晉升的餐廳

RESTAURANTS BY AREA
餐廳 — 以地區分類

Coloane 路環

Macau 澳門

ⓝ : New entry in the guide 新增推介

🏃 : Restaurant promoted to a Bib Gourmand or Star 評級有所晉升的餐廳

Lung Wah Tea House 龍華茶樓	ⅠO	🍜	Cantonese 粵菜	384
Mizumi 泓	❀❀	XxX	Japanese 日本菜	387
Naam 灆	ⅠO	XX	Thai 泰國菜	389
Ngao Kei Ka Lei Chon 牛記咖喱美食	ⅠO	🍜	Noodles and Congee 粥麵	390
99 Noodles 99麵	ⅠO	X	Noodles 麵食	391
Robuchon au Dôme 天巢法國餐廳	❀❀❀	XxXxX	French contemporary 時尚法國菜	394
Temptations 品味坊	ⅠO	XX	European 歐陸菜	398
The Eight 8餐廳	❀❀❀	XxX	Chinese 中國菜	401
The Kitchen 大廚	❀	XX	Steakhouse 扒房	403
Tim's Kitchen 桃花源小廚	❀	XxX	Cantonese 粵菜	406
Tou Tou Koi 陶陶居	☺	X	Cantonese 粵菜	407
Vida Rica 御苑	ⅠO	XX	International 國際菜	408
Wing Lei 永利軒	❀	XxXX	Cantonese 粵菜	409
Wong Kung Sio Kung (Rua do Campo) 皇冠小館 (水坑尾街)	ⅠO	🍜	Noodles and Congee 粥麵	411

Taipa 氹仔

Antonio 安東尼奧	ⅠO	XX	Portuguese 葡國菜	351
Aurora 奧羅拉	ⅠO	XxX	Italian 意大利菜	352
Banza 百姓	ⅠO	X	Portuguese 葡國菜	353
Beijing Kitchen 滿堂彩	ⅠO	XX	Chinese 中國菜	354
Bi Ying 碧迎居	ⅠO	X	Chinese 中國菜	355
Canton 喜粵	ⅠO	XxX	Cantonese 粵菜	357
Castiço	☺	X	Portuguese 葡國菜	358
Din Tai Fung (COD) 鼎泰豐 (新濠天地)	☺	X	Shanghainese 滬菜	362
Dragon Portuguese Cuisine (Broadway) 福龍葡國餐 (百老滙)	ⅠO	X	Portuguese 葡國菜	364
Du Hsiao Yueh 度小月	ⅠO	🍜	Taiwanese 台灣菜	365
Dynasty 8 朝	ⅠO	XxX	Cantonese 粵菜	366
Fook Lam Moon 福臨門	ⅠO	XxX	Cantonese 粵菜	369
Jade Dragon 譽瓏軒	❀❀	XxXX	Cantonese 粵菜	376

RESTAURANTS BY CUISINE TYPE
餐廳 — 以菜式分類

Cantonese 粵菜

Canton 喜粵	ⅱ○	XxX	Taipa 氹仔		357
Chan Seng Kei 陳勝記	⊛	吕╟	Coloane 路環		359
Dynasty 8 朝	ⅱ○	XxX	Taipa 氹仔		366
Fook Lam Moon 福臨門	ⅱ○	XxX	Taipa 氹仔		369
Hou Kong Chi Kei 濠江志記美食	⊛	吕╟	Macau 澳門		372
Imperial Court 金殿堂	ⅱ○	XxX	Macau 澳門		375
Jade Dragon 譽瓏軒	⊛⊛	XxxX	Taipa 氹仔		376
Kam Lai Heen 金麗軒	ⅱ○	XX	Macau 澳門		377
King 帝皇樓	⊛	XX	Macau 澳門		379
Lai Heen 麗軒	⊛	XxXxX	Taipa 氹仔		380
Lei Garden 利苑酒家	ⅱ○	XxX	Taipa 氹仔		381
Lou Kei (Fai Chi Kei) 老記 (筷子基)	⊛	吕╟	Macau 澳門		382
Lung Wah Tea House 龍華茶樓	ⅱ○	吕╟	Macau 澳門		384
Pearl Dragon 玥龍軒	⊛	XxxX	Taipa 氹仔		393
San Tou Tou 新陶陶	ⅱ○	X	Taipa 氹仔		395
Tim's Kitchen 桃花源小廚	⊛	XxX	Macau 澳門		406
Tou Tou Koi 陶陶居	⊛	X	Macau 澳門		407
Wing Lei 永利軒	⊛	XxxX	Macau 澳門		409
Ying 帝影樓	⊛	XxX	Taipa 氹仔		414
Zi Yat Heen 紫逸軒	⊛	XxxX	Taipa 氹仔		415

Chinese 中國菜

Beijing Kitchen 滿堂彩	ⅱ○	XX	Taipa 氹仔		354
Bi Ying 碧迎居	ⅱ○	X	Taipa 氹仔		355
Golden Flower 京花軒	⊛⊛	XxxX	Macau 澳門		370
The Eight 8餐廳	⊛⊛⊛	XxxX	Macau 澳門		401

Ⓝ : New entry in the guide 新增推介

ⓝ : Restaurant promoted to a Bib Gourmand or Star 評級有所晉升的餐廳

European 歐陸菜

Temptations 品味坊	ⅰ○	XX	Macau 澳門	398

French 法國菜

The Ritz-Carlton Café 麗思咖啡廳	ⅰ○	XX	Taipa 氹仔	404

French contemporary 時尚法國菜

Robuchon au Dôme 天巢法國餐廳	✿✿✿	XxXxX	Macau 澳門	394
The Tasting Room 御膳房	✿✿	XxxX	Taipa 氹仔	405

Hunanese and Sichuan 湘川菜

Feng Wei Ju 風味居	✿✿	XxX	Macau 澳門	368

Indian 印度菜

The Golden Peacock 皇雀	✿	XX	Taipa 氹仔	402

International 國際菜

Mezza9	ⅰ○	XX	Taipa 氹仔	386
Vida Rica 御苑	ⅰ○	XX	Macau 澳門	408

Italian 意大利菜

Aurora 奧羅拉	ⅰ○	XxX	Taipa 氹仔	352
Don Alfonso 1890 當奧豐素 1890	ⅰ○	XxxX	Macau 澳門	363
Il Teatro 帝雅廷	ⅰ○	XxxX	Macau 澳門	374
8 1/2 Otto e Mezzo - Bombana	✿	XxX	Taipa 氹仔	392
Terrazza 庭園	ⅰ○	XxX	Taipa 氹仔	400

Japanese 日本菜

Mizumi 泓	✿✿	XxX	Macau 澳門	387
Tenmasa 天政	ⅰ○	XX	Taipa 氹仔	399
Yamazato 山里	ⅰ○	XxX	Taipa 氹仔	413

Korean 韓國菜

Myung Ga 名家	ⅰ○	X	Taipa 氹仔	388

Macanese 澳門菜

Café Encore 咖啡廷	Ⅰ○	XX	Macau 澳門	356
IFT Educational Restaurant 旅遊學院教學餐廳	⌂	XX	Macau 澳門	373

Noodles 麵食

Cheong Kei 祥記	⌂	⌐⌐⌐	Macau 澳門	360
99 Noodles 99麵	Ⅰ○	X	Macau 澳門	391

Noodles and Congee 粥麵

Luk Kei Noodle 六記粥麵	⌂	⌐⌐⌐	Macau 澳門	383
Ngao Kei Ka Lei Chon 牛記咖喱美食	ⅠO	⌐⌐⌐	Macau 澳門	390
Wong Kung Sio Kung (Broadway) 皇冠小館 (百老匯)	ⅠO	⌐⌐⌐	Taipa 氹仔	410
Wong Kung Sio Kung (Rua do Campo) 皇冠小館 (水坑尾街)	ⅠO	⌐⌐⌐	Macau 澳門	411

Portuguese 葡國菜

A Lorcha 船屋	ⅠO	X	Macau 澳門	350
Antonio 安東尼奧	ⅠO	XX	Taipa 氹仔	351
Banza 百姓	ⅠO	X	Taipa 氹仔	353
Castiço	⌂	X	Taipa 氹仔	358
Clube Militar de Macau 澳門陸軍俱樂部	ⅠO	XX	Macau 澳門	361
Dragon Portuguese Cuisine (Broadway) 福龍葡國餐 (百老滙)	ⅠO	X	Taipa 氹仔	364
Espaço Lisboa 里斯本地帶	ⅠO	X	Coloane 路環	367
Guincho a Galera 葡國餐廳	ⅠO	XxxX	Macau 澳門	371
Manuel Cozinha Portuguesa 阿曼諾葡國餐	ⅠO	X	Taipa 氹仔	385

Shanghainese 滬菜

Din Tai Fung (COD) 鼎泰豐 (新濠天地)	⌂	X	Taipa 氹仔	362
Shanghai Magic 上海魅影	ⅠO	XX	Taipa 氹仔	396

Singaporean and Malaysian 星馬菜

Katong Corner 加東	ⅈ○	𝖚	Taipa 氹仔	378

Steakhouse 扒房

The Kitchen 大廚	✿	XX	Macau 澳門	403

Sushi 壽司

Shinji by Kanesaka 金坂極上壽司	✿	XX	Taipa 氹仔	397

Taiwanese 台灣菜

Du Hsiao Yueh 度小月	ⅈ○	𝖚	Taipa 氹仔	365

Thai 泰國菜

Naam 灆	ⅈ○	XX	Macau 澳門	389

RESTAURANTS WITH INTERESTING WINE LISTS
供應優質餐酒的餐廳

Aurora 奧羅拉	ⅰ○	XxX	Italian 意大利菜	352
Don Alfonso 1890 當奧豐素 1890	ⅰ○	XxxX	Italian 意大利菜	363
Fook Lam Moon 福臨門	ⅰ○	XxX	Cantonese 粵菜	369
Guincho a Galera 葡國餐廳	ⅰ○	XxxX	Portuguese 葡國菜	371
Imperial Court 金殿堂	ⅰ○	XxX	Cantonese 粵菜	375
Jade Dragon 譽瓏軒	✿✿	XxxX	Cantonese 粵菜	376
8 1/2 Otto e Mezzo - Bombana ✿		XxX	Italian 意大利菜	392
Pearl Dragon 玥龍軒	✿	XxxX	Cantonese 粵菜	393
Robuchon au Dôme 天巢法國餐廳	✿✿✿	XxxxX	French contemporary 時尚法國菜	394
Shanghai Magic 上海魅影	ⅰ○	XX	Shanghainese 滬菜	396
Terrazza 庭園	ⅰ○	XxX	Italian 意大利菜	400
The Eight 8餐廳	✿✿✿	XxxX	Chinese 中國菜	401
The Kitchen 大廚	✿	XX	Steakhouse 扒房	403
The Tasting Room 御膳房	✿✿	XxxX	French contemporary 時尚法國菜	405
Tim's Kitchen 桃花源小廚	✿	XxX	Cantonese 粵菜	406
Wing Lei 永利軒	✿	XxxX	Cantonese 粵菜	409
Ying 帝影樓	✿	XxX	Cantonese 粵菜	414
Zi Yat Heen 紫逸軒	✿	XxxX	Cantonese 粵菜	415

Ⓝ : New entry in the guide 新增推介

ⁿ⁹ : Restaurant promoted to a Bib Gourmand or Star 評級有所晉升的餐廳

STREET FOOD
街頭小吃

MACAU 澳門

A Lorcha
船屋

Business is booming at this friendly Portuguese restaurant and that's not just because it's close to Barra Temple. The owner's mother still holds the most important role here – as head chef – and she makes sure the quality of the food remains high. A charcoal grill in the kitchen is used for the barbecue and grill dishes and carefully prepared specialities include Ameijoas "Bulhão Pato", Arroz de marisco à Portuguesa and Galinha à Africana.

這家位於媽閣廟附近的葡國餐廳，地點便利並非其成功的主要因素，餐廳總廚的要職由東主母親擔任，致力保持食品質素和正宗風味。燒烤菜式全部用炭爐烹調。餐廳精選推介包括欖油香蒜炒鮮蜆、葡式燴海鮮飯及非洲辣雞。

TEL. 2831 3193
289 Rua do Almirante Sergio
河邊新街 289號
www.alorcha.com

■ PRICE 價錢
Lunch 午膳
à la carte 點菜 MOP 200-350
Dinner 晚膳
à la carte 點菜 MOP 200-350

■ OPENING HOURS 營業時間
Lunch 午膳 12:30-14:30 (L.O.)
Dinner 晚膳 18:30-22:30 (L.O.)

■ ANNUAL AND WEEKLY CLOSING 休息日期
Closed Tuesday 週二休息

Antonio
安東尼奧

Antonio is not just the owner – he is the head chef, the creator of the menus and the heart and soul of the restaurant. Customers come for the atmosphere as much as the food; Antonio offers everyone a glass of his own label port at the end of the evening and a musician passes by every night to sing fado. The restaurant occupies a three storey house and has a charming little terrace. The speciality is seafood stew in a copper pot.

安東尼奧現址在離舊店不遠的一座三層高小屋中，餐室主要在地下和二樓，還附有小露台。為了營造歐陸風情，店主選用了葡式瓷磚及皮椅，並飾以古舊的葡國書作。店主的好客熱情和餐單保持不變，晚膳時每位客人會獲贈一杯店主獨家進口的砵酒，並有音樂人獻唱葡國民謠。海鮮燴飯是招牌菜。

TEL. 2899 9998
7 Rua dos Clerigos
氹仔木鐸街 7 號
www.antoniomacau.com

SPECIALITIES TO PRE-ORDER 預訂食物
Cabidela duck rice 血鴨飯 / Portuguese
veal stew 葡萄牙燉牛仔肉

■ PRICE 價錢
set 套餐 MOP 290-400
à la carte 點菜 MOP 350-1,100

■ OPENING HOURS 營業時間
11:30-22:30 (L.O.)

MACAU 澳門

Aurora
奧羅拉

♿ ⟨ 🤚 **P** ⌂12 🚌 ☎⑪ 🗲 ⌂12

Having a drink on the stunning terrace is a must before eating at this contemporary Italian restaurant – it's on the 10th floor of Altira Hotel and provides terrific views of Macau. The restaurant has an elegant and sophisticated feel, which is helped along by the attentive and well-informed staff. There's an open kitchen and also some counter seating; the cuisine is creative and accomplished and there's an attractively priced set menu at lunch.

空間寬敞、設計時尚的奧羅拉位於新濠鋒酒店10樓，落地玻璃窗築成一道有形無色的城牆，將明亮的餐室與只供客人會飲、景色迷人的露台分隔；一到晚上，不論於室內室外均能欣賞到醉人夜色。侍應的服務貼心專注；還可讓侍酒師替你配搭餐點與美酒。午市套餐價錢甚具吸引力。

TEL. 2886 8868
10F, Altira Hotel, Avenida de Kwong Tung, Taipa
氹仔廣東大馬路新濠鋒酒店 10樓
www.altiramacau.com/en/dining/detail/1/aurora

■ PRICE 價錢
Lunch 午膳
set 套餐 MOP 218-398
à la carte 點菜 MOP 550-1,700

Dinner 晚膳
set 套餐 MOP 588-988
à la carte 點菜 MOP 550-1,700

■ OPENING HOURS 營業時間
Lunch 午膳 12:00-14:00 (L.O.)
Dinner 晚膳 18:00-22:30 (L.O.)

■ ANNUAL AND WEEKLY CLOSING 休息日期
Closed Sunday dinner & Monday
週日晚膳及週一休息

Banza
百姓

The Portuguese owner, whose nickname is Banza, visits local markets each morning to decide on the chef's frequently changing specials; fish dishes tend to be the most popular choice among his many regulars. The restaurant lies in the shadow of a huge apartment complex and comes in tones of green and white, with large paintings and a cosy mezzanine seating about six. Banza can also give you advice on his selection of Portuguese wines.

此店以店主的別名命名，他每天早上都會前往市場，為每日精選尋找靈感和挑選食材。眾多美食中以魚類最受歡迎。餐廳坐落於氹仔的大型屋苑內，四周環境寧靜。裝潢以白、綠為主色，掛有大型畫作。Banza還會向你介紹他精選的葡萄牙美酒。

TEL. 2882 1519
Avenida de Kwong Tung, n°s 154A e
154B, Edf. Nam San Garden, Bl. 5, r/c "G"
e "H", Taipa
氹仔廣東大馬路 154A及 154B號
南新花園第 5座地下 G,H座

■ PRICE 價錢
Lunch 午膳
set 套餐 MOP 88
à la carte 點菜 MOP 200-300
Dinner 晚膳
à la carte 點菜 MOP 200-300

■ OPENING HOURS 營業時間
Lunch 午膳　12:00-15.00 (L.O.)
Weekend lunch 週末午膳
12:00-16:00 (L.O.)
Dinner 晚膳　18:30-22:30 (L.O.)

Beijing Kitchen
滿堂彩

  🚽10 ☎️

'Dinner and a show' at Beijing Kitchen means one and the same, as the cooking is divided between four lively show kitchens which will hold your attention. There's a dim sum and noodle area; a duck section with two applewood-fired ovens; a wok station; and a dessert counter whose bounty is well worth leaving room for. Northern China provides many of the specialities. Ask for one of the tables under the birdcages suspended from the ceiling.

這家店子有四個開放式廚房：點心與粉麵區、烤鴨區、明爐小炒區和甜品區；食客在進餐之餘還能欣賞現場「直播」的烹飪表演，稱得上集用膳與娛樂於一身。烤鴨區廚房內懸掛着兩座燃木窯爐，甚具特色，因此絕不能錯過這兒的烤鴨。招牌菜以北方菜為主。建議選擇天花上懸着鳥籠的座位，別有趣味。

TEL. 8868 1930
GF, Grand Hyatt Hotel, City of Dreams,
Estrada do Istmo, Cotai
路氹連貫公路新濠天地君悅酒店地下
www.macau.grand.hyatt.com

■ PRICE 價錢
Lunch 午膳
set 套餐 MOP 200-500
à la carte 點菜 MOP 300-1,400
Dinner 晚膳
set 套餐 MOP 400-800
à la carte 點菜 MOP 300-1,400

■ OPENING HOURS 營業時間
Lunch 午膳 11:30-14:30 (L.O.)
Dinner 晚膳 17:30-23:30 (L.O.)

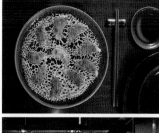

Bi Ying
碧迎居

The name means 'sure win' and it provides the ideal pit-stop if you need a quick break from the gaming tables. It's a buzzy, busy 24-hour operation with its focus on the open kitchen where you can watch noodles being made. The menu offers a culinary journey around China, with plenty of regional specialities, although the wood-roasted dishes are a particular highlight. Finish with one of the desserts made with medicinal herbs.

位處酒店娛樂場所旁的碧迎居，廿四小時提供大江南北美饌，不論你鍾情川式脆椒炒肉蟹、佛跳牆、古法醬燒琵琶鴨，或巧手南北點心，都能盡情滿足口欲。不妨試試其招牌燒味，以靈芝龜靈膏或花旗參冰糖燉官燕作結也不錯。開放式廚房設有果木燒烤爐，食客更有機會觀賞手拉麵條的製作過程。

TEL. 8865 6650
Shop 1182, Level 1,
Casino at Studio City Hotel,
Estrada do Istmo, Cotai
路氹連貫公路新濠影匯娛樂場 1 樓 1182號舖
www.studiocity-macau.com

■ PRICE 價錢
Lunch 午膳
set 套餐 MOP 180-300
à la carte 點菜 MOP 190-1,200
Dinner 晚膳
set 套餐 MOP 300-500
à la carte 點菜 MOP 190-1,200

■ OPENING HOURS 營業時間
24 hours 24 小時

Café Encore
咖啡廷

Café Encore is an elegant restaurant on the ground floor of the Encore hotel. The look is that of a classic European café but one with a strong Italian accent. The menu offers a combination of Macanese and Portuguese cuisine, along with a separate menu of Cantonese dishes, but it is in the Macanese specialities that the kitchen particularly excels. Try dishes like curried crab and baked African chicken.

咖啡廷位於萬利酒店地下，格調高雅。餐廳設計以傳統歐洲餐館裝潢作藍本，並滲入大量意大利藝術元素。菜單以澳門菜與葡國菜為主，另設有粵菜菜單。不過這裏最出色的還是地道澳門菜，例如咖喱蟹與非洲雞。

TEL. 8986 3663
GF, Encore Hotel, Rua Cidade de Sintra, Nape
外港新填海區仙德麗街萬利酒店地下
www.wynnmacau.com

■ PRICE 價錢
set 套餐 MOP 250-400
à la carte 點菜 MOP 160-900

■ OPENING HOURS 營業時間
06:30-23:45 (L.O.)

Canton
喜粵

Modern in design and a deep sensual red in colour, Canton is a stylish restaurant with a sophisticated atmosphere – and is hidden away in a corner of the world's biggest indoor gaming floor. A Kouan-Chiau (gastronomic) version of Cantonese cooking is on offer, with dishes like steamed egg white topped with red birds nest, and deep-fried duck with almond flake in a lime sauce. Popular Sichuan dishes are also available.

喜粵位於全球最大室內娛樂場的一角，採用誘人的深紅色作主調，裝潢時尚。菜單以廣州粵菜如太極芙蓉紅燕及西檸杏香鴨片等為主。此外，店內亦有提供數款四川名菜，讓食客有更多美食選擇。

TEL. 8118 9930
Shop 1018, Casino level,
The Venetian Resort,
Estrada da Baia de N. Senhora da
Esperanca, s/n, The Cotai Strip, Taipa
氹仔路氹金光大道-望德聖母灣大馬路
威尼斯人酒店娛樂場地下 1018號舖
www.venetianmacao.com/restaurants/
signature/canton.html

■ PRICE 價錢
Lunch 午膳
à la carte 點菜 MOP 250-1,000
Dinner 晚膳
à la carte 點菜 MOP 400-1,000

■ OPENING HOURS 營業時間
Lunch 午膳   11:00-15:00 (L.O.)
Dinner 晚膳   18:00-22:00 (L.O.)
Saturday dinner 週六晚膳
18:00-23:00 (L.O.)

PORTUGUESE 葡國菜　　　　　　　　　　MAP 地圖　44/B-1

Castiço

🍴　　　　　　　　　　　　　　　　　　$　☎🍴

Ownership of this simple, unassuming little place with just five tables has now passed down to the owner's girlfriend – though the deceased spirit is honoured in the atmosphere of the restaurant, which is as friendly and as intimate as it ever was. The food is also just as good – the home-style dishes are authentic and carefully prepared, with recommendations being the stewed pork with clams and oven-roasted bacalhau with potatoes.

這家隱藏於氹仔舊城區大街附近的小店陳設簡約樸實，只有五張餐桌。店子由已故葡藉廚師的女友掌廚。從清早到深夜，她就在細小的開放式廚房，以原店主的食譜繼續烹調家庭式葡國美食，店子待客如親人、收費合理的作風貫徹不變，推介菜有豬肉粒炒蜆。

TEL. 2857 6505
65B Rua Direita Carlos Eugénio, Taipa
氹仔施督憲正街 65號 B

■ PRICE 價錢
à la carte 點菜 MOP 130-250

■ OPENING HOURS 營業時間
11:00-22:30 (L.O.)

■ ANNUAL AND WEEKLY CLOSING 休息日期
Closed Thursday 週四休息

Chan Seng Kei
陳勝記

MACAU 澳門

Chan Seng Kei has stood next to the ancient church for over 70 years and is now run by the 3rd generation of the family. It's well known for its traditional Cantonese food, with seafood supplied daily by local fishermen. The signature dish is stewed duck with tangerine peel but, as the cooking process takes more than 10 hours, only a few are available each day. It's a simple, semi open-air restaurant intertwined with several old banyan trees.

坐落舊教堂旁的陳勝記開業至今已傳至第三代，向以傳統粵菜和海鮮菜式馳名。新鮮野生海鮮每天直接從漁民處採購；而製作工序繁複，需烹調十個小時的陳皮鴨是其招牌菜，每天限量供應。半開放式餐室非常樸實，當中數棵樹身粗壯的老榕樹，見證着飯店逾七十載歷史。

TEL. 2888 2021
Rua Caetano No21, Coloane
路環計單奴街 21號

SPECIALITIES TO PRE-ORDER 預訂食物
Stewed duck with tangerine peel
陳皮鴨

■ PRICE 價錢
à la carte 點菜 MOP 150-350

■ OPENING HOURS 營業時間
12:00-22:30 (L.O.)

■ ANNUAL AND WEEKLY CLOSING 休息日期
Closed 2 days Lunar New Year
農曆新年休息 2 天

Cheong Kei
祥記

A family business since the '70s, this tiny noodle shop sticks to its roots and its thin, fine noodles are pressed by bamboo shoots in its own little factory nearby. Their soup uses dried prawns and bonito and is cooked for 8 hours. The noodles with dried shrimp roe are great, but also try the wonton and deep-fried fish ball. Although it's handily placed on Rua de Felicidade, you'll need to weave round shoppers and stalls to get here.

這間家族經營的小麵店於七十年代開業，且在鄰近自設小型廠房製造幼細竹昇麵。湯底以蝦乾和地魚熬製八小時；蝦籽撈麵非試不可，雲吞及鯪魚球亦不容錯過。

TEL. 2857 4310
68 Rua de Felicidade
福隆新街 68號

■ PRICE 價錢
Lunch 午膳
à la carte 點菜 MOP 25-50
Dinner 晚膳
à la carte 點菜 MOP 25-50

■ OPENING HOURS 營業時間
11:30-23:30 (L.O.)

■ ANNUAL AND WEEKLY CLOSING 休息日期
Closed 4 days each month 每月休息 4 天

Clube Militar de Macau
澳門陸軍俱樂部

 ＆ 🍽32 ◐🍴

Built in 1870 for the benefit of army officers, this striking pink-hued building was renovated in 1995 when its restaurant was opened to the public; but sadly the delightful sitting room and bar are reserved for its club members. The room has a charming colonial feel, thanks largely to the echoing teak floorboards, netted windows and ceiling fans. The kitchen focuses on traditional Portuguese flavours and hosts occasional food festivals.

這座最初為澳門陸軍軍官而設的粉紅色建築物建於1870年，在1995年完成翻新，並將餐廳對外開放，惟俱樂部內的雅致大廳及酒吧則只限會員使用。大廳內的柚木地板，配上網紗的大窗及天花板上的吊扇，帶有濃厚的殖民地色彩。俱樂部供應傳統葡萄牙菜式，並會偶爾舉辦美食節。

TEL. 2871 4000
975 Avenida da Praia Grande
南灣大馬路 975號

■ PRICE 價錢
Lunch 午膳
à la carte 點菜 MOP 250-450
Dinner 晚膳
set 套餐 MOP 198
à la carte 點菜 MOP 250-450

■ OPENING HOURS 營業時間
Lunch 午膳　12:30-14:30 (L.O.)
Weekend lunch 週末午膳　12:00-14:30 (L.O.)
Dinner 晚膳　19:00-22:30 (L.O.)

MACAU 澳門

Din Tai Fung (COD)
鼎泰豐（新濠天地）

The second floor of COD plays host to a plethora of casual eateries – and in the corner you'll find this sizeable branch of the international chain. Din Tai Fung is rightly known for its exquisite Xiao Long Bao but also special here is the steamed crab roe and pork dumpling. Other notables from the 70-odd Shanghainese dishes on offer include the excellent braised beef noodle soup. To finish, try the red bean glutinous rice cake.

這家鼎泰豐在澳門的第一間分店，位於新濠天地的蘇豪區內，特高的樓底搭配一貫的雅淨裝潢。菜單包羅逾七十款涼菜、麵食、小炒、湯品及甜點等，焦點自然是玲瓏的小籠包，香濃味美的紅燒牛肉麵會給你不少驚喜，正宗上海甜點如赤豆鬆糕亦不容錯過。

TEL. 8868 7348
Level 2, City of Dreams, Estrada do Istmo, Cotai
路氹連貫公路新濠天地 2樓

■ PRICE 價錢
Lunch 午膳
set 套餐 MOP 120-250
à la carte 點菜 MOP 140-360
Dinner 晚膳
set 套餐 MOP 120-250
à la carte 點菜 MOP 140-360

■ OPENING HOURS 營業時間
11:30-22:15 (L.O.)

Don Alfonso 1890
當奧豐素 1890

XXXX   🛅 ♨ P ⛩8 ☎ 🎋

This opulent dining room features dozens of red Murano chandeliers and a huge fresco of the Italian coast divided into five parts. The somewhat dated feel and bright lights can detract a little from the experience but the Italian cuisine uses well-selected ingredients and flavours are clean and sharp. Service can be almost overly attentive. If you're lucky, you'll be here during one of the owner's quarterly visits when he prepares his own tasting menu.

這家豪華餐室的獨特之處是設有許多紅色穆拉諾穆璃琉璃吊燈，並懸了一幅將意大利海岸分為五個部分的巨型壁畫。古老的風格和明亮的光線配搭令人嚮往，此外，其意大利菜選材不俗，清新味美，服務更是周到得有點超乎常理。如果你運氣不俗，還有機會品嘗店主每季度的特備餐單。

TEL. 8803 7722
3F, Grand Lisboa Hotel,
Avenida de Lisboa
葡京路新葡京酒店 3樓
www.grandlisboahotel.com

■ PRICE 價錢
Lunch 午膳
set 套餐 MOP 330-530
à la carte 點菜 MOP 650-1,500
Dinner 晚膳
set 套餐 MOP 600-1,350
à la carte 點菜 MOP 650-1,500

■ OPENING HOURS 營業時間
Lunch 午膳   12:00-14:30 (L.O.)
Dinner 晚膳   18:30-22:30 (L.O.)

MACAU 澳門

Dragon Portuguese Cuisine (Broadway)
福龍葡國餐 (百老滙)

It may not be the easiest place to find but Dragon Portuguese Cuisine's second branch is a busy spot and attracts a young, lively crowd. The menu sensibly avoids trying to reinvent the wheel and instead focuses on using fresh ingredients in classic dishes. Look out for baked crabmeat or mussels with mozzarella; dishes for two like seafood rice; and their signature baked suckling pig which needs to be ordered two days in advance.

福龍在澳門的第二家分店隱藏在行人如鯽的百老滙大街，若不留神容易錯過。餐廳內以米黃色的牆身飾以澳門為題的油畫，充滿異國風情。其露天用餐位置面向河景，是情侶用餐的上佳選擇。這兒提供多樣的葡國菜式，例如葡式芝士焗蟹蓋和葡萄牙海鮮大燴飯等，葡式烤乳豬更是其招牌菜。

TEL. 8883 1816
Broadway Food Street,
Shop A-G005-G-009, Broadway Macau,
Avenida Marginal Flor de Lotus, Cotai
路氹城蓮花海濱大馬路澳門百老滙
百老滙美食街 A-G005-G009號舖
www.broadwaymacau.com.mo

SPECIALITIES TO PRE-ORDER 預訂食物
Portuguese baked suckling pig 葡式烤乳豬

■ PRICE 價錢
Lunch 午膳
set 套餐 MOP 110-120
weekend set 週末套餐 MOP 110-150
à la carte 點菜 MOP 160-650
Dinner 晚膳
set 套餐 MOP 200-250
à la carte 點菜 MOP 160-650

■ OPENING HOURS 營業時間
Lunch 午膳　12:00-14:45 (L.O.)
Dinner 晚膳　18:00-22:45 (L.O.)

Du Hsiao Yueh
度小月

P　☐8

The name means 'survived a month' and refers to the hardships ensured by fishermen in Tainan during the typhoon season. It was during one such period in 1895 that a fisherman started selling Dan Tzai noodles to make ends meet – and a restaurant was born. Fast forward to today and this branch still specialises in Dan Tzai noodles; it also offers 'three cup chicken' and other Taiwanese dishes like roasted mullet roe and deep-fried oysters.

度小月是台灣知名麵店，其先祖為漁民，他們將無法出海捕魚的季節稱為「小月」，並賣麵維生以度過小月，因廣受歡迎索性轉為賣麵。其招牌擔仔麵以五印醋、蒜蓉和蝦湯炮製，是必選美食。此店除了提供招牌肉燥飯和擔仔麵，還有這裏才供應的三杯雞，而蚵仔酥、現烤烏魚子等傳統台灣美食亦值得一試。

TEL. 8883 1878
Broadway Food Street, Shop A-G014-16,
GF, Broadway Macau,
Avenida Marginal Flor de Lotus, Cotai
路氹城蓮花海濱大馬路澳門百老匯
百老匯美食街地下 A-G014-16號舖

■ PRICE 價錢
Lunch 午膳
set 套餐 MOP 70-90
weekend set 週末套餐 MOP 80-100
à la carte 點菜 MOP 100-250
Dinner 晚膳
set 套餐 MOP 90-100
weekend set 週末套餐 MOP 100-120
à la carte 點菜 MOP 100-250

■ OPENING HOURS 營業時間
11:00-23:45 (L.O.)

CANTONESE 粵菜

Dynasty 8
朝

Old China is celebrated at this sophisticated and professionally run Chinese restaurant within the Conrad hotel. It takes its name and decorative styling from the eight dynasties of ancient China – Qin, Han, Sui, Tang, Song, Yuan, Ming and Qing – which are also used as the names of the private dining rooms. The traditional Cantonese food includes a varied choice of dim sum at lunch and the restaurant boasts an impressive wine cellar.

朝，顧名思義，其名字和室內裝潢意念源自中國古代八個皇朝：秦、漢、隋、唐、宋、元、明、清。雕花木椅、木地板、紅燈籠和中式古典簷篷帶來強烈的中國古風。此店除供應以最新鮮的食材製作的傳統廣東小菜外，午市亦有點心供應，還設有酒窖，適合愛酒人士。

TEL. 8113 8920
Level 1, Conrad Hotel, Estrada do Istmo, s/n, Cotai
路氹連貫公路康萊德酒店 1樓
www.sandscotaicentral.com/restaurants/chinese/dynasty-8.html

■ PRICE 價錢
Lunch 午膳
set 套餐 MOP 688-1,988
à la carte 點菜 MOP 210-820
Dinner 晚膳
set 套餐 MOP 688-1,988
à la carte 點菜 MOP 210-820

■ OPENING HOURS 營業時間
Lunch 午膳   11:00-15:00 (L.O.)
Weekend lunch 週末午膳   10:00-15:00 (L.O.)
Dinner 晚膳   18:00-23:00 (L.O.)

Espaço Lisboa
里斯本地帶

The owner has created a homely 'Lisbon space' within this two-storey house in this Chinese village. The decorative style comes straight out of Portugal, as do the influences behind many of the home-style dishes. Don't miss the presunto pata negra and if you fancy something a little different then try the African chicken from Mozambique with its coconut flavour. Ask for a table on the veranda when the weather is right.

Espaço意謂空間，店主有意在東方這臨海小鎮營造一個充滿葡國情調的空間。不論是鋪地板的石塊、擺設以至烹調用的陶缽，全部從葡國運抵。葡籍廚師用家鄉材料與傳統食譜炮製多款家常菜。源自莫桑比克食譜的非洲雞，啖啖椰汁香，美味無窮；風味絕佳的黑蹄火腿亦不能錯過。

TEL. 2888 2226
Rua das Gaivotas No8, Coloane
路環水鴨街 8 號

SPECIALITIES TO PRE-ORDER 預訂食物
Lobster Rice 龍蝦飯 /Suckling pig (whole)
乳豬

■ PRICE 價錢
Lunch 午膳
à la carte 點菜 MOP 250-500
Dinner 晚膳
à la carte 點菜 MOP 250-500

■ OPENING HOURS 營業時間
Lunch 午膳 12:00-15:00 (L.O.)
Dinner 晚膳 18:30-22:00 (L.O.)
Weekends 週末 12:00-22:30 (L.O.)

■ ANNUAL AND WEEKLY CLOSING 休息日期
Closed Wednesday 週三休息

Feng Wei Ju
風味居

👤 🖐 🍴16 📞

A bright and shiny golden bar is the first thing you notice at this 5th floor restaurant at StarWorld. Gold is certainly used enthusiastically - so much so you may even need to keep your sunglasses on! There are three types of cuisine served: Sichuan, with dishes such as sautéed chicken with peanuts and red chili; Hunanese with specialities like steamed carp fish head; and handmade noodles, which you can watch being made in the open kitchen.

當大紅配上金，整個餐室都給映襯得金光閃爍；紅色就像與餐廳提供的湘川菜互相呼應似的。由剁椒魚頭到宮保雞丁，味道全都鮮辣刺激！此外，還有多款手製麵條和餃子。離開餐廳時你除了一定會帶着飽飽的肚子外，還可能會帶着一雙被金光刺得感到疲累的眼睛。

TEL. 8290 8668
5F, StarWorld Hotel, Avenida da Amizade
友誼大馬路星際酒店 5樓
www.starworldmacau.com

■ PRICE 價錢
Lunch 午膳
set 套餐 MOP 100-180
à la carte 點菜 MOP 300-500
Dinner 晚膳
set 套餐 MOP 190-290
à la carte 點菜 MOP 300-500

■ OPENING HOURS 營業時間
11:00-22:30 (L.O.)

Fook Lam Moon
福臨門

One of the most famous restaurant names in Hong Kong has long been celebrated for its traditional Cantonese menu. It is also known for its clientele of high-rollers and decision makers, so it was perhaps inevitable that a branch would eventually appear in Macau. You'll find local lobster on the menu, along with their famous crispy chicken; many regulars opt for the chicken stuffed with bird's nest – even though it isn't always listed on the menu.

門外懸掛著的一副對聯和橢圓形的水晶吊燈為餐廳營造了別具一格的氣派。福臨門是香港享負盛名的粵菜酒家，熟客都懂得預訂餐牌上沒有的鳳吞燕，當紅炸子雞則是廚師得意之作，此外，選用本地BB龍蝦製作的油泡龍蝦球亦值得一試。食客更可向駐場的專業品酒師請教配搭美酒佳餚的心得。

TEL. 8886 2182
Shop 2008, 2/F, Galaxy Macau,
Coloane-Taipa
路氹城
澳門銀河綜合渡假城 2 樓 2008號舖
www.fooklammoon-grp.com

SPECIALITIES TO PRE-ORDER 預訂食物
Steamed duck stuffed with various fillings
八寶鴨

■ PRICE 價錢
Lunch 午膳
set 套餐 MOP 38-108
à la carte 點菜 MOP 200-500
Dinner 晚膳
set 套餐 MOP 50-2,300
à la carte 點菜 MOP 500-1,000

■ OPENING HOURS 營業時間
Lunch 午膳　11:00-15:00 (L.O.)
Dinner 晚膳　18:00-23:00 (L.O.)

Golden Flower
京花軒

  🚹 ♿ 🖐 **P** 🍽10 🕙🍴

Within the Encore hotel is this elegant and sophisticated restaurant, whose kitchen is noted for its dextrous use of superb ingredients in the preparation of three different cuisines: Sichuan, Lu and Tan – along with a few Cantonese dishes. The room is adorned with the colours of gold and orange and the booths are the prized seats, but wherever you sit you'll receive charming service from the strikingly attired ladies, including the 'tea sommelier'.

京花軒坐落於澳門萬利酒店內，以金色和橙色裝潢，既典雅又獨特。店內設有圓形白色皮卡座，不管安坐何處，都能享受端莊的女侍應的悉心服務，包括「調茶」服務。廚房出色之處，除了選料上乘，還能俐落地烹調出川菜、魯菜、譚家菜三款不同菜系的菜式，同時供應少量廣東菜。

TEL. 8986 3663
GF, Encore Hotel, Rua Cidade de Sintra, Nape
外港新填海區仙德麗街萬利酒店地下
www.wynnmacau.com

■ PRICE 價錢
Weekend lunch 週末午膳
set 套餐 MOP 2,000
à la carte 點菜 MOP 230-2,100

Dinner 晚膳
set 套餐 MOP 450
Weekend set 週末套餐 MOP 2,500
à la carte 點菜 MOP 230-2,500

■ OPENING HOURS 營業時間
Weekend lunch 週末午膳
11:30-14:30 L.O. 14:15
Dinner 晚膳   18:00-22:15 (L.O.)

■ ANNUAL AND WEEKLY CLOSING 休息日期
Closed Monday 週一休息

Guincho a Galera
葡國餐廳

   ♿ ⏱24 ◐ᵢ 🐾

Portuguese 'fine dining' comes to Macau in the form of this branch of Fortaleza do Guincho restaurant in Cascais, near Lisbon. It occupies the room in the Lisboa hotel that was formerly used by Joël Robuchon. The atmosphere is refined, the decoration vivid and the service attentive. The Portuguese food is polished and classical and is occasionally accompanied by subtle French notes; it is also complemented by a very impressive wine list.

來自鄰近里斯本的卡斯凱什，Fortaleza do Guincho餐廳的分店正式登陸澳門，帶來葡式高級餐飲享受。它位處葡京酒店內，餐廳格調高雅，裝潢精緻，服務亦十分周到。它供應的葡式佳餚製作精美、味道正宗，偶爾小會滲入些許法國風味。餐廳還提供種類繁多的美酒。

TEL. 8803 7676
3F, Hotel Lisboa, 2-4 Avenida de Lisboa
葡京路 2-4號葡京酒店 3樓
www.hotelisboa.com

■ PRICE 價錢
Lunch 午膳
set 套餐 MOP 345
à la carte 點菜 MOP 500-1,190
Dinner 晚膳
set 套餐 MOP 600
à la carte 點菜 MOP 500-1,190

■ OPENING HOURS 營業時間
Lunch 午膳　12:00-14:30 (L.O.)
Dinner 晚膳　18:30-22:30 (L.O.)

CANTONESE 粵菜   MAP 地圖 38/B-3

Hou Kong Chi Kei
濠江志記美食

There are a couple of challenges to overcome – it'll take you a while to find this hidden little shop and the environment is not particularly striking – but the satisfying Cantonese dishes, which reflect owner-chef Mr. Chan's great enthusiasim for food, are well worth coming for. Call in advance to reserve the fresh seafood dishes like the steamed crab with sticky rice; also try the barbecued fish and the deep-fried taro fish ball.

要找到這家位置隱蔽的餐廳確是個小小的挑戰，其環境亦非十分出眾；但你所獲得的回報，就是一嘗東主兼廚師陳先生主理的廣式佳餚，並感受他對烹調美食的熱情。個別海鮮美食如蒸糯米蟹飯，需致電預訂；其他推介菜式還有燒魚及香芋炸魚球。

TEL. 2895 3098
GF, Block 3, Lai Hou Gardens, Rua Coelho do Amaral
白鴿巢前地麗豪花園第三座地鋪
佳樂園石級上

SPECIALITIES TO PRE-ORDER 預訂食物
Steamed crab on sticky rice 蒸糯米蟹飯／
Grilled fish or prawns 燒魚或蝦

■ PRICE 價錢
Dinner 晚膳
à la carte 點菜 MOP 100-200

■ OPENING HOURS 營業時間
19:00-23:00 (L.O.)

■ ANNUAL AND WEEKLY CLOSING 休息日期
Closed the 15th & 16th of each month
每月 15 及 16 日休息

IFT Educational Restaurant
旅遊學院教學餐廳

XX   P ⊟12 ◎❢

Being part of the Institute for Tourism Studies means that while the head chef is a professional, most of his brigade and front of house team are students – and the pride they have in their work is palpable. The menu is a mix of European and Macanese dishes – presented in a modern style using herbs from their own garden. There's even the occasional Scandinavian touch (they cure their own salmon). On Friday nights they offer a Macanese buffet.

這家旅遊學院教學餐廳的廚房由專業廚師主理，團隊則由學生組成，供應多款歐陸及澳葡美食。其特色是採用多種自家種植的有機香草和蔬菜作食材，並以廚餘作肥料。非洲雞和乾炒兔治肉碎都是推介菜式，別忘了試試這兒的甜品。團隊友善而專業，是遠離賭場喧囂的用膳好去處。逢周五供應澳葡自助晚餐。

TEL. 8598 3077
Colina de Mong-Há
望廈山
www.ift.edu.mo/pousada

■ PRICE 價錢
Lunch 午膳
set 套餐 MOP 200-300
à la carte 點菜 MOP 260-960

Dinner 晚膳
set 套餐 MOP 350-500
à la carte 點菜 MOP 260-960

■ OPENING HOURS 營業時間
Lunch 午膳   12:30-14:30 (L.O.)
Dinner 晚膳   19:00-22:00 (L.O.)

■ ANNUAL AND WEEKLY CLOSING 休息日期
Closed weekends and Public Holidays
週末及公眾假期休息

ITALIAN 意大利菜

MAP 地圖 40/B-3

Il Teatro
帝雅廷

XXXX

   ♿ ⟨ 🍽 **P** ⊕10 ☎🍴

It's not called 'the theatre' for nothing so be sure to get a window table to catch the song, fire, water and light show that'll bring a smile to your face. In competition for your attention is the food which champions an Italian family-style, albeit with a modern edge and a touch of refinement. Go for the spaghetti with clams or the milk-fed veal chop – and be sure to have the Amedei chocolate soufflé. Service is slick and smooth.

大多數食客到來是為了觀賞噴泉美景，每十數分鐘便會有音樂水柱和激光穿梭表演。因此，記着預訂面向噴泉的座位。這兒主要提供帶現代元素的意大利家庭菜，白酒汁海膽蜆肉幼麵或奶飼牛仔扒伴巴瑪火腿皆不錯，Amedei朱古力梳乎厘不容錯過。年輕的團隊服務殷勤周到。穿涼鞋或無袖汗衫者不准內進。

TEL. 8986 3663
GF, Wynn Hotel, Rua Cidade de Sintra, Nape
外港新填海區仙德麗街永利酒店地下
www.wynnmacau.com

■ PRICE 價錢
Dinner 晚膳
set 套餐 MOP 888
à la carte 點菜 MOP 600-1,000

■ OPENING HOURS 營業時間
17:30-23:00 (L.O.)

■ ANNUAL AND WEEKLY CLOSING 休息日期
Closed Monday 週一休息

Imperial Court
金殿堂

 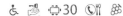

A massive marble pillar with a carved dragon dominates this elegant and contemporary restaurant, which is found on the same floor as the VIP lobby. The kitchen prepares classic Cantonese cuisine, with dishes such as scrambled organic egg whites with sea urchin and crabmeat, which is topped with caviar; braised boneless pork knuckle; and turtle rim in shrimp roe sauce. The impressive wine list includes over 2,000 labels.

金殿堂與貴賓大堂位於同一樓層，龐大的雕龍雲石柱是最矚目之處，設計風格高貴優雅中見時尚。餐廳主要供應廣東美食，如海膽鮮蟹肉炒蛋白及蝦子瑞裙邊扣豬肘等；餐酒選擇逾千種，令人印象深刻。

TEL. 8802 2361
GF, MGM Hotel, Avenida Dr. Sun Yat Sen, Nape
外港新填海區孫逸仙大馬路美高梅酒店地下
www.mgm.mo

■ PRICE 價錢
Lunch 午膳
set 套餐 MOP 188-1,580
weekend set 週末套餐 MOP 1,080-1,580
à la carte 點菜 MOP 200-1,000

Dinner 晚膳
set 套餐 MOP 1,080-1,580
à la carte 點菜 MOP 200-2,000

■ OPENING HOURS 營業時間
Lunch 午膳 11:00-14:30 (L.O.)
Weekend and Public Holiday lunch
週末及公眾假期午膳 10:00-15:00 (L.O.)
Dinner 晚膳 18:00-22:30 (L.O.)

Jade Dragon
譽瓏軒

XXXX

♨40 ⊙❙❙ ❀

Traditional Chinese art, ebony, crystal, gold and silver converge with modern design to form this stunning and eminently comfortable Cantonese restaurant. Equal thought has gone into the details, such as the striking carved jade chopstick holder. The specialities to look out for are goose grilled over lychee wood, and barbecued Ibérico pork. Seafood is also a highlight, along with herbal soups and recipes based on traditional medicine.

譽瓏軒的瑰麗裝潢十分美輪美奐。烏木、金、銀和水晶的運用，揉合了現代設計與中國傳統美學的精髓，透明方柱酒窖、豪華廂房，或是餐桌上的玉雕筷子座，都給人留下深刻印象。食材均是高級用料。按中藥處方熬煮的老火湯和以荔枝柴烤製的燒鵝和黑毛豬叉燒值得一試。

TEL. 8868 2822
Level 2, The Shops at the Boulevard,
City of Dreams, Estrada do Istmo, Cotai
路氹連貫公路新濠天地新濠大道 2樓
www.cityofdreamsmacau.com/en/dining

SPECIALITIES TO PRE-ORDER 預訂食物
Steamed herbal chicken wrap 藥膳紙包雞 /
Whole supreme fish maw 原隻廣肚花膠公

■ PRICE 價錢
Lunch 午膳
set 套餐 MOP 300-1,100
à la carte 點菜 MOP 300-2,000
Dinner 晚膳
set 套餐 MOP 500-1,800
à la carte 點菜 MOP 300-2,000

■ OPENING HOURS 營業時間
Lunch 午膳   11:00-14:30 (L.O.)
Dinner 晚膳   18:00-22:30 (L.O.)

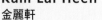

Kam Lai Heen
金麗軒

 ✗✗   ♿ 🅿 ⊟150 ◐⍾

Grand Lapa's Cantonese restaurant is an elegant space, with eye-catching ceiling lights and subtle Chinese design motifs. The longstanding chef and his team prepare traditional Cantonese cuisine which goes down well with their many local Macanese customers. Signature dishes include steamed silver cod in Oolong tea soup, and scallops and soft bean curd soup; it is also worth pre-ordering the Beggar's chicken.

金麗軒位於酒店大堂之上，裝潢並非十分豪華，卻有一種自然的寧靜與優雅。經驗十足的廚師團隊按傳統技法，炮製一系列富澳門特色的粵菜。凍頂銀鱈魚及茶壺豆腐海鮮湯均值得嘗試。

TEL. 8793 3821
1F, Grand Lapa Hotel,
956-1110 Avenida da Amizade, Macau
澳門友誼大馬路 956-1110號
金麗華酒店 1樓
www.grandlapa.com

■ PRICE 價錢
Lunch 午膳
set 套餐 MOP 166
à la carte 點菜 MOP 200-2,300

Dinner 晚膳
set 套餐 MOP 204
à la carte 點菜 MOP 200-2,300

■ OPENING HOURS 營業時間
Lunch 午膳 11:00-15:00 (L.O.)
Dinner 晚膳 18:00-22:00 (L.O.)

■ ANNUAL AND WEEKLY CLOSING 休息日期
Closed Tuesday 週二休息

Katong Corner
加東

In amongst the many Asian brands and local eateries that populate this foodie street is a contemporary yet relaxed dining room serving Singaporean and Malaysian food. The laksa is a must – it's made using a special recipe that delivers complex yet balanced flavours. Another signature dish is the Black Pepper Crab: an aromatic and flavoursome dish where the sweetness of the crab meat works well with the black pepper from Sarawak.

百老匯酒店後面的食街，齊集數十間澳門本土和亞洲食店，實是遊澳旅客的一個新去處！加東提供一系列星馬美食如海南雞和肉骨茶等，當中非試不可的是以重達一公斤的斯里蘭卡肉蟹，加上以沙撈越黑椒所製的黑胡椒炒蟹及湯底加入了蜊蚶、喇沙葉的招牌喇沙。

TEL. 8883 3338
Broadway Food Street, Shop E-G031-G032,
Broadway Macau, Avenida Marginal Flor
de Lotus, Cotai
路氹城蓮花海濱大馬路澳門百老匯
百老匯美食街 E-G031-G032號舖
www.broadwaymacau.com.mo

■ PRICE 價錢
Lunch 午膳
set 套餐 MOP 100-150
weekend set 週末套餐 MOP 100-200
à la carte 點菜 MOP 110-650
Dinner 晚膳
set 套餐 MOP 100-200
weekend set 週末套餐 MOP 100-250
à la carte 點菜 MOP 110-650

■ OPENING HOURS 營業時間
Lunch 午膳　12:00-14:45 (L.O.)
Dinner 晚膳　18:00-22:45 (L.O.)

King
帝皇樓

✗✗　　　　　　　　　　　　　　　P　⇔24　◎↾

MACAU 澳門

Though discreetly tucked away in a commercial building, it hasn't stopped the regular coming for their cantonese dishes. The signature dishes include braised abalone with goose web, and baked chicken with Shaoxing wine; the homemade dim sum also comes highly recommended. Being sufficiently removed from the casinos means the atmosphere is comparatively sedate.

這家隱藏在商業大樓內的餐廳並不顯眼，但卻有不少捧場熟客。此酒家的招牌菜有鵝掌扣吉品鮑魚及花雕焗飛天雞，自製點心亦十分值得一試。酒家位置與各大賭場之間有一段距離，環境較為寧靜。

TEL. 2875 7218
G05-07, GF, AIA Tower,
251A-301 Avenida Commercial de Macau
澳門商業大馬路友邦廣場地下 G05-07

SPECIALITIES TO PRE-ORDER 預訂食物
Whole duck stuffed with eight goodies 八子全鴨 /Steamed crab claw in egg white 蛋白蒸蟹拑 /Deep-fried crab claw with peppered salt white 椒鹽蟹拑

■ PRICE 價錢
Lunch 午膳
à la carte 點菜 MOP 150-300
Dinner 晚膳
à la carte 點菜 MOP 250-500

■ OPENING HOURS 營業時間
Lunch 午膳　11:30-15:30 (L.O.)
Dinner 晚膳　18:00-22:30 (L.O.)

CANTONESE 粵菜　　　　　　　　　　　　MAP 地圖　42/B-2

Lai Heen
麗軒

🏇 🍴 🍴 🍴 🍴 🍴　　　　　　　　🚻 ⟵ 🧼 🅿 ⬚24 ◎🍴

If you're looking to impress then you can't fail with this Cantonese restaurant on the top floor of the Ritz-Carlton hotel. The stunning room is richly decorated and supremely comfortable, as are the numerous private dining rooms which can be opened out and enlarged. The ambition of the kitchen is apparent in the Cantonese specialities – they are presented in a modern way and are a match for the sumptuous surroundings.

麗軒位處麗思卡爾頓酒店51樓，居高臨下，盡賞窗外秀麗景色。富麗堂皇的裝潢與造型時尚精緻的傳統粵菜，同時滿足視覺與味覺的需求。館內設有五間裝飾同樣華美，能隨時將木板牆移開騰出更多空間的私人廂房，適合舉行大小宴會。

TEL. 8886 6742
51F, The Ritz-Carlton, Galaxy, Estrada da Baia da N. Senhora da Esperanca, Cotai
氹仔路望德聖母灣大馬路銀河綜合渡假城
麗思卡爾頓酒店 51樓
www.ritzcarlton.com/macau

■ PRICE 價錢
Lunch 午膳
set 套餐 MOP 400
à la carte 點菜 MOP 280-9,290

Dinner 晚膳
set 套餐 MOP 1,200
à la carte 點菜 MOP 280-9,290

■ OPENING HOURS 營業時間
Lunch 午膳　12:00-14:30 (L.O.)
Weekend lunch 週末午膳
11:30-15:00 (L.O.)
Dinner 晚膳　18:00-22:30 (L.O.)

Lei Garden
利苑酒家

A smart restaurant set amongst the canals of this vast hotel's third floor – arrive by gondola if you wish…Venetian guests predominate here; gamblers mostly give it a miss as it's too far from the gaming tables. Walls of marble provide the backdrop to a comprehensive range of traditional Cantonese dishes which are delivered by an efficient and well-organised team of servers. The best place to be seated is in one of the cosy booths.

餐廳設於三樓，佔據此大型酒店運河旁的位置，雄據地利，顧客可以乘坐貢朵拉前往這兒。由於離賭場較遠，娛樂場玩家通常會光顧其他餐廳，因此這裏的顧客以酒店住客為主。雲石牆壁與傳統廣東菜互相映襯。服務效率非常高。最好的座位是靠近前門的舒適卡位。

TEL. 2882 8689
Shop 855, 3F Grand Canal Shoppes,
The Venetian Resort,
Estrada da Baia de N. Senhora de
Esperança, Taipa
氹仔路望德聖母灣大馬路威尼斯人酒店
大運河購物中心 3樓 855號舖
www.venetianmacao.com

■ PRICE 價錢
Lunch 午膳
à la carte 點菜 MOP 200-1,000
Dinner 晚膳
à la carte 點菜 MOP 250-1,000

■ OPENING HOURS 營業時間
Lunch 午膳　11:30-14:30 (L.O.)
Dinner 晚膳　18:00-22:30 (L.O.)

■ ANNUAL AND WEEKLY CLOSING 休息日期
Closed 3 days Lunar New Year
農曆新年休息 3 天

Lou Kei (Fai Chi Kei)
老記 (筷子基)

If you're looking for a simple, good value supper then Lou Kei may well fit the bill. Granted, it may not be in the centre of town, but every cab driver knows this lively place. It has been renowned for over 20 years for its sizeable selection of tasty noodles, congee and Cantonese dishes; frogs' legs in a clay pot and sea crab congee are both highly recommended. The interior is bright and neat while the service is polite and attentive.

若然你想品嘗價廉物美的美食，老記便是不二之選。儘管餐廳並非位於市中心，但是所有的士司機皆知這間馳名食府的位置。老記二十多年來提供美味粥品麵食及廣東菜式，其田雞腿煲及水蟹粥更備受食客推崇，店內光猛潔淨，侍應親切有禮。

TEL. 2856 9494
Avenida Da Concórdia N, 12R/C E S/L
Loja H
和樂大馬路 12號宏基大廈第 4座 H及 M鋪

■ PRICE 價錢
à la carte 點菜 MOP 120-250

■ OPENING HOURS 營業時間
18:00-05:00 (L.O.)

Luk Kei Noodle
六記粥麵

The second generation owner-chef insists on making his very popular noodles the traditional way: with a bamboo stick. The small menu provides photos of the specialities which include noodles with dried prawn roe; crunchy deep-fried wontons; crispy fish balls with soft centres served with either oyster or soy sauce; and the filling congee with crab. This is a small and busy shop, found on a lively street next to the pier.

第二代店主兼大廚堅持以傳統手法炮製極受歡迎的竹昇麵。小小的餐牌上附有特色食品的照片，包括蝦子撈麵、炸鴛鴦（炸雲吞及米通鯪魚球），還有水蟹粥。這家廣受食客歡迎的小店，就在碼頭旁邊的熱鬧街道上。

TEL. 2855 9627
1-D Travessa da Saudade
沙梨頭仁慕巷 1號 D

■ PRICE 價錢
à la carte 點菜 MOP 40-70

■ OPENING HOURS 營業時間
18:30-02:30 (L.O.)

■ ANNUAL AND WEEKLY CLOSING 休息日期
Closed 4 days Lunar New Year
農曆新年休息 4天

MACAU 澳門

Lung Wah Tea House
龍華茶樓

Little has changed from when this old-style Cantonese tea house, up a flight of stairs, opened in the 1960s: the large clock still works, the boss still uses an abacus to add the bill and you still have to refill your own pot of tea at the boiler. The owner buys fresh produce, including chicken for their most popular dish, from the market across the road. Get here early for the freshly made dim sum.

這家有一列樓梯的傳統廣東茶樓自一九六零年代開業以來，變化不大，古老大鐘依然在擺動，老闆依然用算盤結算帳單，你依然要自行到熱水器前沖茶。店主從對面街市選購新鮮食材烹調美食，包括茶樓名菜油雞。建議早上前來享用新鮮點心。

TEL. 2857 4456
3 Rua Norte do Mercado Aim-Lacerda
提督市北街 3 號

■ PRICE 價錢
à la carte 點菜 MOP 25-140

■ OPENING HOURS 營業時間
07:00-14:00 (L.O.)

■ ANNUAL AND WEEKLY CLOSING 休息日期
Closed 4 days Lunar New Year, 4 days
May and 4 days October 農曆新年、五月
及十月各休息 4 天

Manuel Cozinha Portuguesa
阿曼諾葡國餐

MACAU 澳門

Authenticity and hospitality are what draws customers to this cosy little corner restaurant. Newcomers will find themselves welcomed by the owner-chef just as warmly as if they were regulars. His traditional Portuguese cooking uses quality ingredients and many of the dishes are cooked in the old-fashioned barbecue way. He makes his own cheese and the two specialities of which he is most proud are stewed rabbit, and fried rice with squid ink.

離開氹仔舊城區的熱鬧街道，從施督憲正街向飛能便度街方向走，便會找到位於路口這家小店。在這兒你能吃到美味正宗的葡國菜。葡籍店東兼主廚親切好客。他堅持選用本地和葡國優質食材，且以碳火燒烤食物，還在店內自製芝士。炆兔肉和墨魚汁炒飯是他最引以為傲的菜式。

TEL. 2882 7571
Rua de Femão Mendes Pinto, Nº 90 R/C, Taipa
氹仔飛能便度街 90號

SPECIALITIES TO PRE-ORDER 預訂食物
Roasted piglet "Manuel style" 原隻阿曼諾燒乳豬 / Baked lobster "Manuel style" 阿曼諾焗龍蝦 /Seafood rice 海鮮飯

■ PRICE 價錢
Lunch 午膳
à la carte 點菜 MOP 130-340
Dinner 晚膳
à la carte 點菜 MOP 130-340

■ OPENING HOURS 營業時間
Lunch 午膳 12:00-15:00 (L.O.)
Dinner 晚膳 18:00-22:00 (L.O.)

■ ANNUAL AND WEEKLY CLOSING 休息日期
Closed Wednesday 週三休息

Mezza9

Mezza9 is ideal for those who can never decide on what nationality of cuisine they fancy but who do like a little theatre with their food. The vast and quite striking interior comes with several show kitchens offering an impressive array of different cuisines: you can choose sushi, chargrilled meats, Cantonese wok dishes, Macanese specialities and South Asian noodles. The vaulted wine cellar is the pick of the private rooms.

如果你是嗜吃一族，又經常無法決定享用哪一國的菜式，Mezza9是你理想之選。餐廳面積非常闊落，設有數個開放式廚房，供應多國菜式，包括壽司、烤肉、廣東小炒、澳門特色菜、南亞麵食等。二人套餐分量不少，且能一次過品嘗多國美食。

TEL. 8868 1920
3F, Grand Hyatt Hotel, City of Dreams, Estrada do Istmo, Cotai
路氹連貫公路新濠天地君悦酒店 3樓
www.macau.grand.hyatt.com

■ PRICE 價錢
set 套餐 MOP 539-639

■ OPENING HOURS 營業時間
Dinner 晚膳 18:00-23:00 (L.O.)

Mizumi
泓

🍽 10

The lucky colours of gold and red were incorporated into the latest redecoration – and it's certainly a strikingly bright room now. Three consultants are involved: Chef Shimamiya from Sushi Zen in Hokkaido, Chef Yoshida from Ishigaki Yoshida in Tokyo and Kazuhito Motoyoshi from Tempura Motoyoshi in Tokyo. The fish comes from Tsukiji market in Tokyo; the beef from a private ranch on Ishigaki Island, south of Okinawa. Go for the 'Taste of Mizumi'.

裝修後的餐室，地氈、牆身和裝飾均換上金、紅兩色，加上入門的銅鑄日本摺紙工藝雕塑，奪目且煥然一新。食物方面，不論是魚生、壽司、鐵板燒或天婦羅均選用高質食材，包括每周由日本運到的新鮮海產及精心搜購的沖繩和牛，加上精細的烹調，令人回味無窮。點選泓之風味套餐能一次品嘗各式料理。

TEL. 8986 3663
GF, Wynn Hotel, Rua Cidade de Sintra, Nape
外港新填海區仙德麗街永利酒店地下
www.wynnmacau.com

■ PRICE 價錢
Dinner 晚膳
set 套餐 MOP 1,890
weekend set 週末套餐 MOP 2,890
à la carte 點菜 MOP 350-2,880

■ OPENING HOURS 營業時間
Dinner 晚膳 17:30-23:00 (L.O.)

■ ANNUAL AND WEEKLY CLOSING 休息日期
Closed Tuesday 週二休息

Myung Ga
名家

Many ingredients are imported from Korea to ensure authenticity at this restaurant specialising in Korean classics and BBQ. If you opt for one of the large booths, instead of the cushioned seating on the floor, you'll get your own grill. The family set menu for up to six people is a popular way to sample dishes like homemade kimchi. Along with the contemporary cocktails, you can also try traditional Korean drinks like milky white makgeolli.

名家供應的食材全都是從韓國搜購回來，確保客人吃到原汁原味的韓國菜。食客除了可以以韓國傳統方式，以墊子墊着坐在地上進餐外，還可選擇坐在擁有獨立燒烤爐的卡座上。家庭套餐和自製泡菜非常受歡迎。餐酒選擇豐富，除了新派雞尾酒外，還提供乳白濁酒之類的傳統韓國餐酒。

TEL. 8883 2221
G015, GF East Promenade, Galaxy Hotel,
Estrada da Baia de Nossa Senhora da
Esperança, Cotai
路氹望德聖母灣大馬路
銀河購物大道東地下 G015
www.galaxymacau.com

■ PRICE 價錢
Lunch 午膳
à la carte 點菜 MOP 300-900
Dinner 晚膳
à la carte 點菜 MOP 300-900

■ OPENING HOURS 營業時間
11:00-23:00 (L.O.)

Naam
灌

The name of Grand Lapa's Thai restaurant translates as 'water' which seems appropriate as it overlooks the pool and tropical garden and features a small fountain in the middle of the room, which all add to the calm and peaceful atmosphere. The majority of the kitchen and service teams are Thai and the food is attractively presented and the spicing is well-judged. The menu also features a section of Royal Thai cuisine dishes.

Naam在泰文中是水的意思。餐廳位於泳池旁邊，中央位置設有一口噴泉，天然光線從其頂上透射而下，整個環境寧靜而優雅。這兒的泰國菜味道較為柔諧，更設有一系列的宮廷菜式，友善的泰國侍應亦會給予客人合適的推介。

TEL. 8793 4818
GF, Grand Lapa Hotel,
956-1110 Avenida da Amizade, Macau
澳門友誼大馬路 956-1110號
金麗華酒店地下
www.grandlapa.com

■ PRICE 價錢
Lunch 午膳
set 套餐 MOP 158-198
à la carte 點菜 MOP 350-850
Dinner 晚膳
set 套餐 MOP 260
à la carte 點菜 MOP 350-850

■ OPENING HOURS 營業時間
Lunch 午膳　12:00-14:30 (L.O.)
Dinner 晚膳　18:30-22:30 (L.O.)

■ ANNUAL AND WEEKLY CLOSING 休息日期
Closed Monday 週一休息

Ngao Kei Ka Lei Chon
牛記咖喱美食

Set at the corner of a main road and a narrow street full of industrious little shops. The broken neon lights outside may lessen its appeal but this is a friendly, well-run and well-staffed little noodle shop, with regulars popping in and out throughout the day. Bestsellers are the crab noodles and the crab congee but it's also worth trying the clear soup with beef flank and the spicy chicken or beef curry with noodles.

此店位於大街一角的小巷內，四周的小店均其門如市，常客往來不絕。四周老舊的建築物看似減弱了餐廳的吸引力，但小麵店職員的友善態度和管理有序彌補了這個不足，店內服務令人滿意。最暢銷的美食要算是水蟹、蟹黃炆伊麵和蟹粥，清湯牛腩和椰汁咖喱雞、牛筋麵也值得一試。

TEL. 2895 6129
GF, 1 Rua de Cinco de Outubro
十月初五街 1號地下

■ PRICE 價錢
à la carte 點菜 MOP 40-90

■ OPENING HOURS 營業時間
08:00-01:00 (L.O.)

NOODLES 麵食

MAP 地圖　41/C-3
MACAU 澳門

99 Noodles
99麵

Noodle lovers will need a few visits to this stylish pit-stop at the Encore hotel to work their way through the huge choice of Chinese noodles – there's everything from Beijing la mian to Shanxi knife-shaved, tip-ended and one string noodles, all served with various broths and garnishes, along with specialities from Northern China. The colours of the room are vivid; the jumbo chopsticks on the walls are striking; and the atmosphere's buzzy.

細小的餐室以鮮艷的紅色作主調，牆上懸着一雙雙色彩繽紛的巨型筷子，華麗且充滿活力，與四周的賭場環境風格一致。顧名思義，這裏是嘗麵的好地方：北京拉麵、山西刀削麵、轉盤剔尖及一根麵等多款麵食，配以各式湯底和澆頭，令人食指大動。餃子和北方點心當然也不能錯過。

TEL. 8986 3629
GF, Encore Hotel, Rua Cidade de Sintra, Nape
外港新填海區仙德麗街萬利酒店地下
www.wynnmacau.com

■ PRICE 價錢
set 套餐 MOP 150-250
à la carte 點菜 MOP 200-1,660

■ OPENING HOURS 營業時間
10:00-00:30 (L.O.)

ITALIAN 意大利菜 MAP 地圖 42/B-2

8 1/2 Otto e Mezzo - Bombana

XXX   ♿ 🧼 **P** ⊡12 ⏛ ◐❢ ✿

A handsome, well-dressed Italian restaurant with a striking central cocktail bar – this comfortable, elegant space certainly pays suitable homage to the Hong Kong original. Chef Umberto Bombana sensibly offers virtually the same menu and the wine list is of equal breadth and depth, with a focus on Italian and French wines. The entrance is from the Promenade Shopping Mall of the Galaxy but you can also enter from the lobby of the Ritz-Carlton.

美輪美奐的佈置和奪目的雞尾酒吧，此家位於時尚匯內的8 ½ Otto e Mezzo與香港店一脈相承，同由名廚Bombana帶領，不論是餐牌還是食物風格均與香港店無異。餐酒單羅列的美酒種類豐富，有不少來自意大利及法國的佳釀。此店有兩個入口，分別設在購物區內和麗思卡爾頓酒店大堂內，易於尋找。

TEL. 8886 2169
1F, Galaxy, The Promenade, Shop 1031,
Avenida de Cotai
澳門銀河綜合渡假城 1樓 1031號舖
www.ottoemezzobombana.com

■ PRICE 價錢
Lunch 午膳
weekend set 週末套餐 MOP 880-1,080
à la carte 點菜 MOP 820-1,200

Dinner 晚膳
set 套餐 MOP 1,380-1,580
à la carte 點菜 MOP 820-1,200

■ OPENING HOURS 營業時間
Lunch 午膳　12:00-14:00 (L.O.)
Dinner 晚膳　18:00-22:30 (L.O.)

■ ANNUAL AND WEEKLY CLOSING 休息日期
Closedd Monday to Thursday lunch and Wednesday 週一至週四午膳及週三休息

Pearl Dragon
玥龍軒

❀

MACAU 澳門

🚻 ♿ 🅿 🍽20 📞🍴 🎴

No expense has been spared at this elegant and luxurious Cantonese restaurant on the 2nd floor of Studio City. The menu offers a range of refined Cantonese dishes: soy-braised dishes from the lychee wood barbecue are a speciality. Other highlights are double-boiled chicken soup with matsutake and sea conch; stir-fried lobster with caviar; and seafood rice with fish maw and sea cucumber. The tea counter offers a choice of over 50 premium teas.

這家位於新濠影滙酒店的粵菜餐廳裝潢素雅，但細節中顯心思。香茗選擇逾五十款，酒櫃內放滿陳年佳釀，餐桌上的雕塑、餐具和轉盤皆是著名品牌出品，雍雅豪華。餐單選擇繁多，招牌菜包括果木燒烤和滷水菜式，油泡龍蝦球伴黑魚子和上品海皇泡飯均值得一試。貼心周到的服務，令用餐過程更添美滿。

TEL. 8865 6560
Shop 2111, Level 2, Star Tower,
Studio City Hotel, Estrada do Istmo,
The Cotai Strip, Taipa
路氹連貫公路新濠影滙酒店
巨星匯 2樓 2111號
www.studiocity-macau.com

■ PRICE 價錢
Lunch 午膳
set 套餐 MOP 300-500
à la carte 點菜 MOP 310-1,360

Dinner 晚膳
set 套餐 MOP 500-1,400
à la carte 點菜 MOP 310-1,360

■ OPENING HOURS 營業時間
Lunch 午膳　12:00-15:00 (L.O.)
Weekend lunch
週末午膳　11:00-15:00 (L.O.)
Dinner 晚膳　18:00-23:00 (L.O.)

■ ANNUAL AND WEEKLY CLOSING 休息日期
Closed Tuesday 週二休息

MACAU 澳門

Robuchon au Dôme
天巢法國餐廳

Joël Robuchon's flagship restaurant sits majestically in the dome of the Grand Lisboa hotel, where a striking chandelier competes for your attention with 360° views of Macau. Impeccable service, immaculate table settings and a superb wine list all complement the superlative contemporary cuisine.

Joël Robuchon 的旗艦店位於新葡京酒店內。矚目的大型水晶吊燈和令人屏息的360度澳門全景，餐桌亦佈置得十分細緻，實在是賞心悅目。這兒除了供應優質的當代菜式，還提供超過一萬種餐酒。服務亦很周到。

TEL. 8803 7878
43F, Grand Lisboa Hotel,
Avenida de Lisboa
葡京路新葡京酒店 43樓
www.grandlisboahotel.com

■ PRICE 價錢
Lunch 午膳
set 套餐 MOP 688-888
à la carte 點菜 MOP 970-3,680
Dinner 晚膳
set 套餐 MOP 1,888-2,988
à la carte 點菜 MOP 970-3,680

■ OPENING HOURS 營業時間
Lunch 午膳 12:00-14:30 (L.O.)
Dinner 晚膳 18:30-22:30 (L.O.)

San Tou Tou
新陶陶

Found on a narrow street in the centre of Taipa is this Cantonese restaurant, run by the same family for three generations and now supervised by two brothers. The cooking is very traditional and it is the chicken soup served in very hot clay pots that attracts so many; but there are plenty of other, more affordable, specialities. The restaurant is spread over two floors and the air conditioning is most efficient!

這間家族經營的廣東菜餐廳位於氹仔中心地帶的小巷內，現時由第三代的兩兄弟主理。煮法非常傳統，燉雞湯用砂鍋盛載，吸引大量食客。除此之外，這裏還提供很多價錢相宜的小菜選擇。

TEL. 2882 7065
26 Rua Correia da Silva, Taipa
氹仔告利雅施利華街 26號

SPECIALITIES TO PRE-ORDER 預訂食物
Salt-baked chicken 古法鹽焗雞 / Crispy chicken 脆皮炸子雞

■ PRICE 價錢
Lunch 午膳
à la carte 點菜 MOP 180-550
Dinner 晚膳
à la carte 點菜 MOP 180-550

■ OPENING HOURS 營業時間
Lunch 午膳 11:30-15:00 (L.O.)
Dinner 晚膳 17:30-22:00 (L.O.)

■ ANNUAL AND WEEKLY CLOSING 休息日期
Closed 1 week Lunar New Year, 2 days early May and 2 days early October 農曆新年 7 天、五月初及十月初各休息 2 天

SHANGHAINESE 滬菜

Shanghai Magic
上海魅影

✗✗　　　　　　　　　　　　　　&. **P** ☎️⏹️ 🐝

If you're on the way to the House of Magic by Franz Harary, get yourself in the mood by dining at this theatrically themed restaurant and don't say you haven't been warned – the restaurant has plenty of tricks up its sleeve, include its own gang of magicians who move from table to table. The modern Shanghainese menu is equally appealing, with dishes like hot and sour crab meat soup, or soy-marinated cod fish. Ask for one of the 'birdcage' tables.

想邊用膳邊觀賞魔術表演？這家在新濠影滙酒店魔術劇場旁邊、劇院式瑰麗裝潢的餐廳是最佳選擇。魔術師於餐桌間穿插表演，連侍應也會點小把戲，讓你目不暇給，位於鳥籠的餐桌令人仿若置身舞台。餐單選擇同樣吸引，花雕糟醉雞、蘇式燻銀鱈魚和蟹肉酸辣羹都不錯，午市的點心餐牌叫人感到花多眼亂。

TEL. 8865 6620
Shop 2110, Level 2,
The Boulevard at Studio City Hotel,
Estrada do Istmo, The Cotai Strip, Taipa
路氹連貫公路新濠影滙購物大道 2樓 2110號
www.studiocity-macau.com

■ PRICE 價錢
Lunch 午膳
set 套餐 MOP 150-180
à la carte 點菜 MOP 170-430
Dinner 晚膳
set 套餐 MOP 180-450
à la carte 點菜 MOP 170-430

■ OPENING HOURS 營業時間
Lunch 午膳　12:00-14:30 (L.O.)
Dinner 晚膳　17:30-22:30 (L.O.)

Shinji by Kanesaka
金坂極上壽司

There's a real flavour of Japan at this sushi restaurant, from the kanji characters on the wall to the impressive counter, which uses 220 year old cypress wood. The fish comes from Tokyo's Tsukiji Market; the sushi is relatively small and delicate; and the vinegar is a pale red. Go for the 'Edomae 15 Sushi' menu if you just want sushi; if you'd prefer to start with appetisers and sashimi then choose the 'Wa' or 'Shin' menus.

步入金坂極上壽司，即能感受到濃濃的日本風：由享齡逾二百歲的柏木打造的日式壽司枱、牆上的日本漢字、清一色的日籍服務員，頃刻讓你誤以為自己穿越到了日本。喜歡壽司的你可從「江戶前壽司」挑選心愛的手握紅醋飯壽司，欲先品嘗刺身請從「真」或「和」餐單上挑選從築地市場直接運到的鮮魚。

TEL. 8868 7300
Level 1, Crown Towers, City of Dreams,
Estrada do Istmo, Cotai
路氹連貫公路新濠天地皇冠度假酒店 1 樓
www.cityofdreamsmacau.com/en/
dining/detail/kanesaka

■ PRICE 價錢
Lunch 午膳
set 套餐 MOP 688-1,688
Dinner 晚膳
set 套餐 MOP 1,688-2,988

■ OPENING HOURS 營業時間
Lunch 午膳   12:00-14:30 (L.O.)
Dinner 晚膳   18:00-22:30 (L.O.)

■ ANNUAL AND WEEKLY CLOSING 休息日期
Closed Tuesday lunch and Monday
週二午膳及週一休息

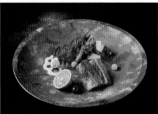

Temptations
品味坊

On the 16th floor atop the StarWorld hotel is a bright, airy restaurant serving a variety of cuisines from a number of European countries – your best bet is to go straight for the Portuguese and Macanese specialities. If you're undecided about dessert, then peek into the kitchen through the window and watch the effort that goes into their creation. This well-run restaurant is ideally suited for those wanting to relax with family or friends.

位於星際酒店16樓，室內設計以時尚簡約線條配合淺棕色調，淡雅輕鬆的環境氣氛與酒店內其他設施或店舖截然不同，讓人眼前一亮。餐廳主要提供歐陸菜和葡國菜，半自助午餐包含多款前菜與甜品及精選燒烤美食，是不錯的休閒聚餐處。食客可透過開放式廚房的玻璃窗觀賞廚師製作甜品的過程。

TEL. 8290 8688
16F, StarWorld Hotel,
Avenida da Amizade
友誼大馬路星際酒店 16樓
www.starworldmacau.com

■ PRICE 價錢
Lunch 午膳
set 套餐 MOP 278
weekend set 週末套餐 MOP 238
à la carte 點菜 MOP 370-750
Dinner 晚膳
set 套餐 MOP 198-480
à la carte 點菜 MOP 370-750

■ OPENING HOURS 營業時間
Lunch 午膳　12:00-14:45 (L.O.)
Dinner 晚膳　18:30-21:45 (L.O.)

Tenmasa
天政

Taipa's own version of Tenmasa, which opened in Tokyo in 1937 and is still going strong, is a charmingly run restaurant that boasts a sushi bar, a tempura counter and a tatami floor, as well as decked walkways leading across golden pebble ponds to private rooms. Sit and watch the chef at work, as he uses quality ingredients to prepare well-balanced dishes. There are a variety of different menus available at lunch.

天政早於1937年在東京開業，至今仍廣受歡迎。澳門的天政設有壽司吧、天婦羅櫃枱及榻榻米地板，也有鋪板走廊、金石水池和私人餐室。食客可安坐座位上，觀看廚師大顯身手，將優質食材炮製成美味菜式。餐廳於午市時段提供多款精選美食。

TEL. 2886 8868
11F, Altira Hotel,
Avenida de Kwong Tung, Taipa
氹仔廣東大馬路新濠鋒酒店11樓
www.altiramacau.com/en/dining/
detail/12/tenmasa

■ PRICE 價錢
Lunch 午膳
set 套餐 MOP 288-1,180
à la carte 點菜 MOP 210-1,010

Dinner 晚膳
set 套餐 MOP 680-1,780
à la carte 點菜 MOP 210-1,010

■ OPENING HOURS 營業時間
Lunch 午膳   12:00-14:15 (L.O.)
Dinner 晚膳   18:00-22:15 (L.O.)

■ ANNUAL AND WEEKLY CLOSING 休息日期
Closed Monday 週一休息

MACAU 澳門

Terrazza
庭園

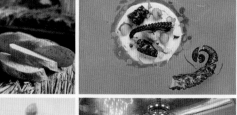

 ᵭ ⬛ **P** 🍽14 ⚜

It is all about relaxation at this large, classically decorated Italian restaurant – thanks largely to the very comfortable chairs and the warm and welcoming service. The menu covers all parts of the country and there's something for everyone, whether you're after a pizza or a more elaborate dish. One thing definitely worth exploring is the wine list. There's a great glass-enclosed private room on the terrace which is surrounded by waterfalls.

古典優雅的設計、柔軟舒適的座椅、友善熱情的服務,讓你身心放鬆。這裏供應的菜式涵蓋意大利全國美食,不論是薄餅或是別的意大利菜,你總能挑選到合心意的美食。最使人驚喜的,是其種類繁多的酒單。露台上的玻璃屋私人廂房給瀑布重重圍著,置身其中猶如身處花果山下的水簾洞,令人嚮往。

TEL. 8883 2221
Shop 201, 2F Galaxy Hotel, Estrada da Baia de Nossa Senhora da Esperanca, Cotai
路氹望德聖母灣大馬路澳門銀河綜合渡假城
銀河酒店 2樓 201號舖
www.galaxymacau.com

■ PRICE 價錢
Dinner 晚膳
set 套餐　MOP 488-988
à la carte 點菜　MOP 550-1,600

■ OPENING HOURS 營業時間
Dinner 晚膳　18:00-22:30 (L.O.)

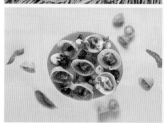

The Eight
8餐廳

✲✲✲

The lavish interior uses the traditional Chinese elements of the goldfish and the number eight to ensure good fortune for all who dine here. The cuisine is a mix of Cantonese and Huaiyang, but the kitchen also adds its own innovative touches to some dishes. Specialities include steamed crab claw with ginger and Chinese wine, and stir-fried lobster with egg, minced pork and black bean. At lunchtime, over 40 kinds of dim sum are served.

豪華的內部裝潢採用了傳統中國元素，如金魚及數目字8，寓意所有到訪的客人都會遇上好運。菜式融合了廣東及淮揚風味，部份美食更滲入了創新點子。推介菜式有薑米酒蒸鮮蟹拑及廣東式炒龍蝦。午餐時段供應逾四十款點心。

TEL. 8803 7788
2F, Grand Lisboa Hotel,
Avenida da Lisboa
葡京路新葡京酒店 2樓
www.grandlisboahotel.com

■ PRICE 價錢
Lunch 午膳
set 套餐 MOP 950-2,500
à la carte 點菜 MOP 310-2,920
Dinner 晚膳
set 套餐 MOP 950-2,500
à la carte 點菜 MOP 310-2,920

■ OPENING HOURS 營業時間
Lunch 午膳　11:30-14:30 (L.O.)
Sunday & Public Holidays lunch
週日及公眾假期午膳　10:00-15:00 (L.O.)
Dinner 晚膳　18:30-22:30 (L.O.)

MACAU 澳門

The Golden Peacock
皇雀

It's in the vast Venetian complex so you may need a map to find this contemporary Indian restaurant – just look out for the bright neon peacock. The chef is a native of Kerala but the menu covers all parts of India. Spices are ground in-house and everything from paneer to pickles is made from scratch. At lunch they offer an extensive buffet; come for dinner and you'll experience dishes that are flamboyant in presentation and rich in flavour.

嚴謹認真的印度主廚會自製各種醬料、乳酪、芝士、腰果蓉等，加上每周由印度空運而到的食材和新鮮研磨的香料，炮製出色香味俱全的印度美食。香濃芒果燒鱈魚咖喱、印式洋蔥燴羊小腿和各款素菜均值得一試。午市供應自助餐，價格相宜。店內陳設簡約時尚，以印度國鳥孔雀作裝飾，具濃濃的印度風情。

TEL. 8118 9696
Shop 1037, 1F The Venetian Resort,
Estrada de Baia de N. Senhora da
Esperanca, Taipa
氹仔路望德聖母灣大馬路威尼斯人酒店
大運河購物中心 1樓 1037號舖
www.venetianmacao.com/restaurants
/signature/golden-peacock.html

■ PRICE 價錢
Lunch 午膳
buffet 自助餐 MOP 188
à la carte 點菜 MOP 230-580
Dinner 晚膳
à la carte 點菜 MOP 230-580

■ OPENING HOURS 營業時間
Lunch 午膳　11:00-15:00 (L.O.)
Dinner 晚膳　18:00-22:30 (L.O.)

The Kitchen
大廚

There's a handsome, masculine feel to this restaurant on the 3rd floor of the Grand Lisboa. It comes with a sushi bar, a salad counter and a live fish tank but the star of the show is undoubtedly the beef. Prime meat from the US, Japan and Australia is cooked on an open flame and you decide which cut you want and in what size. You're guaranteed to find something to go with your steak from the wine list of over 15,000 labels.

將西式扒房、日式壽司吧及海鮮魚缸融匯一室，這裏的設計確是匠心獨具，閃爍的天花燈飾、金牛形酒吧等，都給人留下深刻印象，更讓人難以忘懷的是其美食！食客可在肉櫃挑選來自美國、澳洲及日本等地的頂級牛肉，並選取不同部位與分量，亦可從魚缸中點選新鮮海產。逾萬款餐酒可供選擇。

TEL. 8803 7777
3F, Grand Lisboa Hotel,
Avenida de Lisboa
葡京路新葡京酒店 3樓
www.grandlisboahotel.com

■ PRICE 價錢
Lunch 午膳
set 套餐 MOP 380-580
à la carte 點菜 MOP 540-2,150
Dinner 晚膳
set 套餐 MOP 900-1,400
à la carte 點菜 MOP 540-2,150

■ OPENING HOURS 營業時間
Lunch 午膳　12:00-14:30 (L.O.)
Dinner 晚膳　18:30-22:30 (L.O.)

The Ritz-Carlton Café
麗思咖啡廳

Tiles, mirrors and marble have all been used to great effect to create a chic French brasserie here at the Ritz-Carlton. There's a Tasting menu along with the à la carte and set menus so, whether you're here for a full meal of classic French dishes or a quick bite or afternoon tea after shopping, you'll find there's plenty of choice. You can also expect live music, mime artists and even a caricaturist.

意大利白色雲石地、長長的真皮沙發和圓形雲石面餐桌、典雅的水滴形吊燈、精緻的長鏡，營造出高雅、舒適的環境。來自法國里昂的主廚擅長烹調法國住家菜，許多食客到此是為了品嘗帶有住家風味的法國菜。除了美食，餐廳內每天都有不同的藝術表演如音樂演奏、默劇等演出。

TEL. 8886 6696
GF, The Ritz-Carlton, Galaxy, Estrada da Baia da N. Senhora da Esperanca, Cotai
路氹望德聖母灣大馬路澳門銀河綜合渡假城
麗思卡爾頓酒店地下
www.ritzcarlton.com/macau

■ PRICE 價錢
Lunch 午膳
set 套餐 MOP 250
weekend set 週末套餐 MOP 350
à la carte 點菜 MOP 320-1,480
Dinner 晚膳
set 套餐 MOP 400
weekend set 週末套餐 MOP 500
à la carte 點菜 MOP 320-1,480

■ OPENING HOURS 營業時間
Lunch 午膳　11:30-14:30 (L.O.)
Dinner 晚膳　18:00-22:30 (L.O.)

The Tasting Room
御膳房

XXXX

  👨‍🦽 ≤ 🧼 🍽14 ◎🍴 🔗

MACAU 澳門

If it's privacy you're after, then this discreet, circular-shaped restaurant is the place for you as tables are so far apart you'll barely notice your neighbours. Chef Fabrice Vulin imports most of his premium ingredients directly from France and his cooking is as sophisticated and self-assured as the smartly dressed room itself. Service is formally arranged yet not devoid of personality. There's an excellent value lunch menu offered.

重視私隱的你，大概會喜歡這家經過縝思布置的餐室，因為餐桌與餐桌之間的距離，令你難以留意和接觸鄰桌的客人。廚師Fabrice Vulin從法國直接引入高級材料，加上他細膩而自信的烹調技術，炮製出的菜式一如餐廳的裝潢般講究，服務也同樣經過精心安排。午餐菜單物有所值。

TEL. 8868 6681
3F, Crown Towers, City of Dreams,
Estrada do Istmo, Cotai
路氹連貫公路新濠天地皇冠度假酒店 3樓
www.cityofdreamsmacau.com/en/dining/
detail/tasting-room

■ PRICE 價錢
Lunch 午膳
set 套餐 MOP 398-588
à la carte 點菜 MOP 980-1,500
Dinner 晚膳
set 套餐 MOP 1,588
à la carte 點菜 MOP 980-1,500

■ OPENING HOURS 營業時間
Lunch 午膳　12:00-15:00 (L.O.)
Dinner 晚膳　18:00-22:30 (L.O.)

Tim's Kitchen
桃花源小廚

✗✗✗   ♿ ⊡24 ◐❙ 🎴

Hong Kong foodies make special pilgrimages here and it's easy to see why: the Cantonese dishes may appear quite simple but they are very skilfully prepared. Among the highlights are poached and sliced pork stomach in wasabi sauce, and sweet & sour pork ribs. Do make sure you try the crystal prawn and, during the winter, the tasty snake ragout. The restaurant is decorated with a variety of operatic costumes and photos.

香港食家喜歡專程到此朝聖，原因十分簡單：此食店的廣東菜式看似簡單，卻實在是經過精心巧手炮製。推介菜式包括涼拌爽肚片及京都骨。此外，萬勿錯過玻璃蝦球，而冬天的重點推介則離不開美味的蛇羹。餐廳放滿戲曲照片和戲服裝飾，散發出淡淡的藝術氣息。

TEL. 8803 3682
Shop F25, GF, Hotel Lisboa, East Wing,
2-4 Avenida de Lisboa
葡京路 2-4號葡京酒店東翼地下 F25號舖
www.hotelisboa.com

■ PRICE 價錢
Lunch 午膳
set 套餐 MOP 300
à la carte 點菜 MOP 220-1,360
Dinner 晚膳
set 套餐 MOP 600
à la carte 點菜 MOP 220-1,360

■ OPENING HOURS 營業時間
Lunch 午膳   12:00-14:30 (L.O.)
Dinner 晚膳   18:30-22:30 (L.O.)

Tou Tou Koi
陶陶居

MACAU 澳門

🍴　　　　　　　　　　　　　　　🛋24　📞🍴

As this 80 year old restaurant is always packed, it's vital to book ahead; at the same time why not also pre-order the duck? It's dim sum during the day and Cantonese cuisine at night and among the favourites are deep-fried crab, deep-fried US beef belly and fish from the tank in the dining room. Service is sufficiently swift to accommodate the non-stop flow of customers. A refurbishment has left the restaurant looking much more contemporary.

有八十多年歷史的陶陶居總是賓客如雲，必須訂座，你亦可順道預訂八寶鴨。日間以點心為主，晚上則提供粵菜，受歡迎菜式包括金錢蟹盒和脆皮美國牛坑腩，還有新鮮烹調的海魚。為了應付絡繹不絕的客人，侍應生的工作效率十分高。早上九時開始有早茶供應，吸引不少茶客前來一聚。

TEL. 2857 2629
6-8 Travessa do Mastro
爐石塘巷 6-8號

SPECIALITIES TO PRE-ORDER 預訂食物
Braised duck stuffed with eight treasures
八寶霸王鴨 /Signature deep-fried
dumplings stuffed with pork, shrimp and
crabmeat 鮮蝦金錢蟹盒

■ PRICE 價錢
Lunch 午膳
à la carte 點菜 MOP 100-300
Dinner 晚膳
à la carte 點菜 MOP 250-800

■ OPENING HOURS 營業時間
Lunch 午膳　11:00-15:00 (L.O.)
Dinner 晚膳　17:00-23:15 (L.O.)

Vida Rica
御苑

Dark marble and Asian art combine to create a sophisticated yet relaxing spot here on the second floor of the Mandarin Oriental. The kitchen's plan is to make everyone's life a little richer by covering all bases: the large menu offers international cuisine with a French twist, and even some Cantonese dishes. There's also a simple lunchtime buffet in the bar on the same floor.

坐落於文華東方酒店二樓，裝潢結合深色雲石和亞洲藝術的御苑，營造出既豪華又悠閒的氣氛。它的宗旨，是要做到面面俱圓，令所有顧客的生活都更見豐盛。豐富的菜單羅列多國菜式、法式糕點和廣東經典美食。同一樓層的酒吧，更提供簡便的午市自助餐。

TEL. 8805 8918
2F, Mandarin Oriental Hotel,
945 Avenida Dr. Sun Yat Sen, Nape
外港新填海區孫逸仙大馬路 945號
文華東方酒店 2樓
www.mandarinoriental.com/macau

■ PRICE 價錢
Lunch 午膳
set 套餐 MOP 298-368
à la carte 點菜 MOP 290-2,910
Dinner 晚膳
set 套餐 MOP 488-988
à la carte 點菜 MOP 290-2,910

■ OPENING HOURS 營業時間
Lunch 午膳　12:00-14:30 (L.O.)
Dinner 晚膳　18:00-22:00 (L.O.)

Wing Lei
永利軒

{XXXX}   ♿ 🍽 🅿 💺10 🚇 ☕🍴 🎴

The bright yellow look gives the room an airy feel, while the tassel lamps hanging from the ceiling cast a romantic glow. The centrepiece of the room, however, remains the three-dimensional flying dragon made up of 100,000 sparkling Swarovski crystals. At lunch over 40 dim sum are available, while the à la carte offers a great range of refined Cantonese classics. The 'Signature Menu' is a good way of trying the chef's best dishes.

明亮的黃色裝潢營造出輕鬆悠閒的氣氛，大型燈籠透出浪漫燈光，襯托以十萬片水晶製成的立體飛龍，盡展豪華氣派；舒適寬敞的座椅讓人生出好感。餐廳裝潢一流，服務也親切周到。傳統粵菜，菜式選擇良多，大廚精髓菜譜是一嘗其手藝的最佳選擇。午市的手工點心叫人眼花瞭亂，不妨點選自選點心套餐。

TEL. 8986 3663
GF, Wynn Hotel, Rua Cidade de Sintra, Nape
外港新填海區仙德麗街永利酒店地下
www.wynnmacau.com

■ PRICE 價錢
Lunch 午膳
set 套餐 MOP 210
à la carte 點菜 MOP 200-1,910
Dinner 晚膳
set 套餐 MOP 1,200
à la carte 點菜 MOP 200-1,910

■ OPENING HOURS 營業時間
Lunch 午膳 11:30-14:45 (L.O.)
Sunday and Public Holiday lunch
週日及公眾假期午膳
10:30-14:45 (L.O.)
Dinner 晚膳 18:00-22:45 (L.O.)

MACAU 澳門

Wong Kung Sio Kung (Broadway)
皇冠小館 (百老匯)

If you're looking for a quick bite after watching all the street entertainment on Broadway then try this simple noodle and congee shop. The menu is slightly smaller than the original branch but it still has the same focus on handmade noodles using the traditional bamboo method and served with dried shrimp roe. The congee is smooth and satisfying and has a delicate aftertaste and there are also a few other hot dishes available.

百老匯酒店後面的食街，雲集多間澳門本地知名食店，非常熱鬧。作為本地代表之一，皇冠小館以古法竹竿炮製的彈牙麵配大頭蝦子及以新鮮原隻海蟹及瑤柱熬製的蟹粥馳名。另外還有其他粥麵小食和數款小炒。環境簡樸乾淨。

TEL. 8883 3338
Broadway Food Street, Shop A-G017,
Broadway Macau,
Avenida Marginal Flor de Lotus, Cotai
路氹城蓮花海濱大馬路澳門百老匯
百老匯美食街 A-G017舖
www.broadwaymacau.mo

■ PRICE 價錢
Lunch 午膳
set 套餐 MOP 100-105
à la carte 點菜 MOP 40-600
Dinner 晚膳
set 套餐 MOP 100-110
weekend set 週末套餐 MOP 100-150
à la carte 點菜 MOP 40-600

■ OPENING HOURS 營業時間
11:00-22:45 (L.O.)

Wong Kung Sio Kung (Rua do Campo)
皇冠小館 (水坑尾街)

Owner Mr. Cheng, who is native Macanese, has over 30 years of experience when it comes to making noodles using the traditional bamboo pressing method. His shop opened back in 2000 but such was its popularity that he later expanded into next door. A selection of traditional Cantonese dishes is offered but most come here for the sea crab congee and the bamboo noodles with dried shrimp roe (which is also sold in bottles in the shop).

澳門土生土長的東主鄭先生，已有逾三十年以傳統竹竿手打方法製麵的經驗。餐廳早於2000年開業，大受歡迎下擴充至隔鄰舖位。他的店子提供一系列傳統廣東美食，但慕名而來的食客，通常會點遠近馳名的竹昇蝦子撈麵及海蟹粥。店內亦有出售瓶裝蝦子。

TEL. 2837 2248
308-310A Rua do Campo
水坑尾街 308-310號 A
www.wongkun.com.mo

■ PRICE 價錢
à la carte 點菜 MOP 30-120

■ OPENING HOURS 營業時間
10:00-02:00 (L.O.)

■ ANNUAL AND WEEKLY CLOSING 休息日期
Closed 5 days Lunar New Year
農曆新年休息 5 天

Don't confuse the rating ✗ with the Stars ✿! The first defines comfort and service, while Stars are awarded for the best cuisine.

千萬別混淆了餐具 ✗ 和星星 ✿ 標誌！餐具標誌表示該餐廳的舒適程度和服務質素，而星星代表的是食物質素與味道非常出色而獲授為米芝蓮星級餐廳的餐館。

If you are looking for particularly pleasant accommodation, book a hotel shown in red: 🏠 ... 🏨.

欲享受特別舒適的留宿體驗，請選擇注有此 🏠 …… 🏨 紅色酒店標誌的推介酒店。

Yamazato
山里

Hotel Okura's flagship restaurant proves that, with a few contemporary flourishes, minimalism can also be warm and welcoming. It's located on the 28th floor and its large windows provide diners with pleasant views of the gardens of Galaxy Macau. A wide range of Japanese cuisines is offered, from tempura to grilled dishes and even shabu shabu; sashimi is a highlight and there's also a little sushi bar at the side of the restaurant.

除了壽司和刺身兩款主打食物外，山里還供應各式日本料理：懷石料理小菜、天婦羅、燒物、日本火鍋……大概你能想到的菜式都能在這兒品嘗。杳莆色的牆身、時尚的水晶吊燈和淺啡色的木製家具，瑰麗雅致，巨幅玻璃窗讓你盡賞動人園景。

TEL. 8883 5127
28F, Hotel Okura Macau, Galaxy,
Avenida Marginal Flor de Lotus, Cotai
路氹城蓮花海濱大馬路澳門銀河綜合渡假城
大倉酒店 28樓
www.hotelokuramacau.com

■ PRICE 價錢
Lunch 午膳
set 套餐 MOP 280-580
à la carte 點菜 MOP 290-1,140

Dinner 晚膳
set 套餐 MOP 1,280-1,580
à la carte 點菜 MOP 290-1,140

■ OPENING HOURS 營業時間
Lunch 午膳   12:00-14:30 (L.O.)
Dinner 晚膳   17:30-21:30 (L.O.)

■ ANNUAL AND WEEKLY CLOSING 休息日期
Closed Monday
週一休息

Ying
帝影樓

XXX   ♿ ≤ 🖐 P ⇌16 📞🍴 🎍

It's not just the breathtaking views looking north to Macau that set this restaurant apart – the beautifully styled interior has been designed with taste and verve; the beaded curtains, which feature gold cranes and crystal trees, are particularly striking. The Cantonese dishes are prepared with contemporary twists and much flair. Try the deep-fried crispy chicken with lemon sauce, and lobster Cantonese style.

帝影樓北望海港及澳門繁華景色，環境宜人。餐廳設計品味獨特，風格絢麗；珠簾上飾有金鶴和水晶樹圖案，使裝潢更添神采。餐廳的粵菜融入了新口味，大廚的烹調技藝精湛。專業的服務態度令人賓至如歸。值得一試的有檸香脆皮雞和粵式炒龍蝦。

TEL. 2886 8868
11F, Altira Hotel,
Avenida de Kwong Tung, Taipa
氹仔廣東大馬路新濠鋒酒店 11樓
www.altiramacau.com/en/dining/
detail/15/ying

■ PRICE 價錢
Lunch 午膳
set 套餐 MOP 150-1,700
à la carte 點菜 MOP 220-1,390
Dinner 晚膳
set 套餐 MOP 200-1,700
à la carte 點菜 MOP 220-1,390

■ OPENING HOURS 營業時間
Lunch 午膳   11:00-15:00 (L.O.)
Dinner 晚膳   18:00-22:30 (L.O.)

Zi Yat Heen
紫逸軒

     ✤ 🖐 **P** 🍽24 🐾

With a large glass-enclosed wine cellar at its centre, Zi Yat Heen is an elegant yet intimate restaurant, located within the Four Seasons Hotel Macau. By using first rate ingredients and minimal amounts of seasoning, the chef prepares a traditional Cantonese menu but one that is lighter and fresher tasting. Interesting creations include the baked lamb chops with coffee sauce, while a more traditional dish would be pigeon with Yunnan ham.

地方寬敞，格調高雅的紫逸軒位於四季酒店一樓，正中位置設有巨型玻璃餐酒庫。廚帥烹調傳統菜式時採用最新鮮的食材與最少的調味料，炮製出更鮮味清新的粵菜。有趣創意菜式包括咖啡汁焗羊排，較傳統的選擇有酥香雲腿伴鴿脯。

TEL. 2881 8888
GF, Four Seasons Hotel, Estrada da Baia de N. Senhora da Esperanca, s/n, The Cotai Strip, Taipa
氹仔路氹金光大道望德聖母灣大馬路
四季酒店地下
www.fourseasons.com/macau

■ PRICE 價錢
Lunch 午膳
set 套餐 MOP 1,488-2,388
à la carte 點菜 MOP 290-5,010
Dinner 晚膳
set 套餐 MOP 1,488-2,388
à la carte 點菜 MOP 290-5,010

■ OPENING HOURS 營業時間
Lunch 午膳   12:00-14:15 (L.O.)
Dinner 晚膳   18:00-22:15 (L.O.)

Street Food 街頭小吃
Popular places for snack food
馳名小食店

🚃 Chong Shing 昌盛

Cantonese steamed buns.
粵式包點。
MOP 10-20   07:00-20:00

MAP 地圖 38/B-2
GF, 11 rua de Tome Pires, Macau
澳門新橋道咩啤利士街 11 號地下

🚃 Fong Kei 晃記餅家

Almond cake; egg rolls.
杏仁餅及蛋捲。
MOP 30-50   10:00-20:00

MAP 地圖 44/B-2
14 Rua do Cunha, Taipa
氹仔官也街 14號

🚃 KIKA

Japanese Gelato.
日本雪糕。
MOP 30-50   10:00-22:00

MAP 地圖 38/B-3
Trav. Se 11A r/c, Macau
澳門大堂巷 11A號

🚍 Lei Ka Choi 李家菜

Cantonese snacks such as duck's blood soup, wontons and noodles.

鴨血、炸雲吞及魚球麵。

MOP 30-90   11:00-01:00

MAP 地圖 42/B-3
Shop E-G028, Broadway Macau, Cotai
路氹城澳門百老匯 E-G028號舖

🚍 Lemon Cello 檸檬車露

Gelato.

意大利雪糕。

MOP 30-50   12.00-23.00

MAP 地圖 38/B-3
Trav. Se 11r/c, Macau
澳門大堂巷 11號

🚍 Lord Stow's Bakery 安德魯餅店

Portuguese egg tart.

葡撻。

MOP 20-30   07:00-22:00

MAP 地圖 45/A-1
1 Rua do Tassara, Coloane
路環撻沙街 1號

🚍 Mok Yee Kei 莫義記

Durian ice cream; mango ice cream.

榴槤雪糕及芒果雪糕。

MOP 25-70   09:00-22:30

MAP 地圖 44/B-2
9 Rua do Cunha, Taipa
氹仔官也街 9號

417

Looking for a taste of local life? Check out our top street food picks.

到哪兒尋找本土特色小食？請翻閱本年度的街頭小吃推介。

Enjoy good food without spending a fortune! Look out for the Bib Gourmand symbol ⊛ to find restaurants offering good food at great prices!

既想省錢又想品嘗美食，便要留心注有這個 ⊛ 車胎人標誌的餐廳，她們提供的是價錢實惠且高質素的美食。

🚌 Neng Meng Wang 檸檬王

Preserved fruits.

甘草檸檬、川貝陳皮、檸汁薑。

MOP 10-35　　09:00-21:00 (Mon-Fri 週一
　　　　　　　至五)
　　　　　　　13:00-21:00 (Sat-Sun 週末)

MAP 地圖　38/B-3
GF, Lai Hou Garden,
Rua Coelho do Amaral, Macau
澳門白鴿巢前地麗豪花園平台

🚌 Sun Ying Kei 新英記

Pork chop buns.

豬扒包。

MOP 20-40　　　　　　07:30-17:30
　　　　　　　　　　　Closed Sunday
　　　　　　　　　　　週日休息

MAP 地圖　38/B-2
GF, 2B Rua da Alegria do Patane, Macau
澳門沙梨頭惠愛街 2B地下

🚌 Ving Kei 榮記荳腐

Tofu products and noodles.

豆腐、豆腐花及麵食。

MOP 20-40　　　　　　08:00-18:30

MAP 地圖　38/B-3
GF, 47 Rua da Tercena, Macau
澳門果欄街 47號地下

🚌 Yi Shun 義順鮮奶

Fresh milk custard; milk custard with ginger juice.

雙皮燉奶、薑汁撞奶。

MOP 30-40　　　　　　11:00-21:00

MAP 地圖　38/A-3
381 Avenida de Almeida Ribeiro, Macau
澳門新馬路 381號

HOTELS
酒店

HOTELS IN ORDER OF COMFORT
酒店 — 以舒適程度分類

Altira
新濠鋒

High quality design, a serene atmosphere and wondrous peninsula views produce something quite spectacular here. Guests arrive at the stylish lobby on the 38th floor and the luxury feel is enhanced by a super lounge and terrace on the same level. Bedrooms face the sea and merge tranquil tones with a contemporary feel. There's also a great spa and a pool-with-a-view.

酒店設計獨特，舒適典雅，位置優越，澳門半島的環迴美景盡入眼簾。38樓的大堂時尚尊貴，同層的天宮備有室內酒廊及露天陽台，豪華瑰麗。客房位於較高的樓層，海景一望無際，寧靜的環境與現代設計相互交織，氣派超凡。顧客享用附設的豪華水療設施時可飽覽美景。

TEL. 2886 8888
Avenida de Kwong Tung, Taipa
氹仔廣東大馬路
www.altiramacau.com

RECOMMENDED RESTAURANTS 餐廳推薦
Aurora 奧羅拉 XxX
Tenmasa 天政 XX
Ying 帝影樓 ✿ XxX

🛉 = MOP 2,688-6,988
🛉🛉 = MOP 2,688-7,188
Suites 套房 = MOP 9,388-32,988
☕ = MOP 298

Rooms 客房   152
Suites 套房   32

Banyan Tree
悅榕莊

Forming part of Galaxy Macau, this luxurious resort comprises 246 suites, as well as 10 villas which come with their own private gardens and swimming pools. The very comfortable bedrooms all have large baths set by the window and the array of services includes a state-of-the-art spa – the biggest in the group. Guests enjoy full access to all of Galaxy's facilities.

作為路氹城澳門銀河綜合渡假城的一部分及毗鄰澳門國際機場，澳門悅榕莊共有246間套房和10間擁有私人花園和泳池的別墅。所有寬敞套房內均設有私人悅心池，酒店提供一系列貼心服務，當中包括集團最大及最頂級的水療中心。住客更可享用銀河綜合渡假城內所有設施。

TEL. 8883 6001
Galaxy Macau, Avenida Marginal Flor
de Lotus, Cotai
路氹城蓮花海濱大馬路澳門銀河綜合渡假城
www.banyantree.com/en/cn-china-macau

Suites 套房 = MOP 2,399-16,888
Villas 別墅 = MOP 30,888-88,888

Suites 套房　246
Villas 別墅　10

Conrad
康萊德

The largest of all the Conrad hotels is on the Cotai Strip and its guests have access to an abundance of shopping, gaming, dining and entertainment opportunities. The Himalayan and Chinese inspired décor creates a relaxing environment; anyone requiring extra stress reduction should book a restorative session in one of the ten treatment rooms in the luxurious spa.

坐落於路氹金光大道上的康萊德，是全球規模最大的酒店，這裏有為數不少的購物、賭博、餐飲及娛樂場所。陳設靈感取材自喜瑪拉雅和中國地區，感覺悠閒舒適。豪華水療中心內設有十間套房，客人可盡情享受水療服務，令壓力和疲勞一掃而空。客房空間寬敞，設計時尚。

TEL. 2882 9000
Estrada do Istmo, s/n, Cotai
路氹連貫公路
www.conradmacao.com

RECOMMENDED RESTAURANTS 餐廳推薦
Dynasty 8 朝 ※※※

 = MOP 1,698-6,098
 = MOP 1,948-6,348
Suites 套房 = MOP 2,548-6,948
 = MOP 208

Rooms 客房　430
Suites 套房　224

Encore
萬利

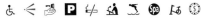

For VIPs wanting an even more exclusive resort experience than the Wynn, there is Encore – their luxury brand. The word 'standard' certainly does not apply here as the choice is between suites or villas, all of which are lavishly decorated. You also get an exceptional spa offering bespoke treatments and Bar Cristal: as small as a jewellery box and just as precious.

欲享受比永利更獨特尊貴的服務，可考慮同集團旗下更豪華的萬利。酒店提供豪華套房及渡假別墅，兩者均以紅色與金色裝潢，特顯富麗堂皇。貴賓級水療中心為你提供度身訂造的療程，酒店內的Bar Cristal一如其名，像珠寶盒般嬌小高貴。賭場內附設多間貴賓娛樂房。

TEL. 2888 9966
Rua Cidade de Sintra, Nape
外港新填海區仙德麗街
www.wynnmacau.com

Suites 套房 – MOP 4,400 22,000
☕ = MOP 160

Suites 套房 414

RECOMMENDED RESTAURANTS 餐廳推薦
Café Encore 咖啡廷 XX
Golden Flower 京花軒 ✿✿ XxxX
99 Noodles 99 麵 X

427

Four Seasons
四季

The luxurious Four Seasons fuses East and West by blending Colonial Portuguese style with Chinese traditions. The lobby acts as a living room, with its fireplace, Portuguese lanterns and Chinese lacquer screens. The hotel also has a luxury shopping mall and connects to The Venetian and Plaza Casino. If you want peace, simply escape to the spa or one of the five pools and the charming garden.

2008年開幕的四季酒店融合了東西方元素，將殖民地時代的葡萄牙風格與中國傳統融為一體。大堂設有壁爐、葡國燈籠和中國雕漆屏風，猶如置身家中客廳。酒店設有豪華購物商場，直通威尼斯人酒店及百利沙娛樂場。想離開五光十色稍作喘息，可享用酒店的水療設備和五個泳池，還有迷人的花園。

TEL. 2881 8888
Estrada da Baia de N. Senhora da Esperanca, s/n, The Cotai Strip, Taipa
氹仔路氹金光大道望德聖母灣大馬路
www.fourseasons.com/macau

† = MOP 2,088-10,888
†† = MOP 2,088-10,888
Suites 套房 = MOP 4,088-64,588
☕ = MOP 258

Rooms 客房　192
Suites 套房　84

RECOMMENDED RESTAURANTS 餐廳推薦
Zi Yat Heen 紫逸軒 ❀ XxxX

428

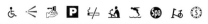
Galaxy
銀河

The striking exterior of Galaxy is one of the most recognisable landmarks of Taipa. The guestrooms are very spacious and impressively well equipped. Another of the attractions of the hotel is its 2,000sqm artificial beach and the world's largest wave pool; there also are cinemas and assorted restaurants. It's just a few minutes' walk from the Old Town.

外觀金碧輝煌的銀河渡假城是氹仔的新地標。作為渡假城內三間酒店之一，銀河酒店予人國際化的印象。每間客房都裝潢時尚、空間寬敞、設備齊全兼現代化。最吸引的設施是佔地2000平方米的人造沙灘及大型衝浪泳池。戲院和餐飲設施一應俱全，與舊城區只有一條馬路之隔，便於觀光購物。

TEL. 2888 0888
Estrada da Baia de N. Senhora da Esperanca, s/n, The Cotai Strip, Taipa
路氹望德聖母灣大馬路
www.galaxymacau.com

RECOMMENDED RESTAURANTS 餐廳推薦
Myung Ga 名家 ✗
Terrazza 庭園 ✗✗✗

♦ = MOP 1,298-4998
♦♦ = MOP 1,498-5,198
Suites 套房 = MOP 2,298-5,998
☐ = MOP 148

Rooms 客房 1307
Suites 套房 142

Grand Hyatt
君悅

With its striking 22m ceiling and fabulous artwork, the lobby sets the tone – the droplets appear to be falling from a cloud. The contemporary bedrooms are split between two towers. Along with contemporary and luxurious suites, the Grand Club on the top floor provides a dining service where customers can order any kind of cuisine they choose.

君悅酒店的大堂設計獨特，從22米天花上空墜下的吊飾，配合藝術設計營造出水珠從雲層落下再匯聚一起的壯觀景象。設計時尚的房間分佈在兩棟大樓內。位於頂層的嘉賓軒裝潢高雅，有多間貴賓廂房，按客人喜好提供不同餐飲服務，是舉辦私人商務聚會的理想場地。

TEL. 8868 1234
City of Dreams, Estrada do Istmo, Cotai
路氹連貫公路新濠天地
www.macau.grand.hyatt.com

RECOMMENDED RESTAURANTS 餐廳推薦
Beijing Kitchen 滿堂彩 ✗✗
mezza9 ✗✗

👤 = MOP 1,499-5,499
👤👤 = MOP 1,749-5,749
Suites 套房 = MOP 1,799-5,799
☕ = MOP 258

Rooms 客房   503
Suites 套房   288

Grand Lapa
金麗華

Plenty of Portuguese character and a relaxing, peaceful atmosphere set this hotel apart. There is also a lovely tropical garden behind the main building, along with a swimming pool and spa. Bedrooms come with large windows and face either the harbour or the city – ask for one with a balcony on floors 16-18. Prices are reasonable and the staff are eager to please.

於1984年建成，是澳門早期的豪華酒店之一。大堂面貌多年來改變不大，頗富葡國色彩且有一種寧靜優雅的感覺。房間裝潢並不時髦，然方正寬敞，16至18樓的客房更設有露台可觀賞海景。大樓後的熱帶園林邊設有水療中心及露天泳池，是澳門鬧市中少有的幽閒設施。

TEL. 2856 7888
956-1110 Avenida da Amizade, Macau
澳門友誼大馬路 956-1110號
www.grandlapa.com

RECOMMENDED RESTAURANTS 餐廳推薦
Kam Lai Heen 金麗軒 XX
Naam 灆 XX

♦ = MOP 3,000-4,200
♦♦ = MOP 3,000-4,200
Suites 套房 = MOP 6,300-28,000
☕ = MOP 198

Rooms 客房 388
Suites 套房 28

Grand Lisboa
新葡京

Impossible to miss, the Grand Lisboa can be seen from miles away with its eye-popping, brightly-lit lotus design atop a shining diamond. Opulent soundproofed bedrooms feature Asian paintings, and offer grand sea or city vistas. If you have a corner room or a suite, you'll get the added bonus of a sauna; if you have neither, you can make use of the sumptuous spa.

2008年12月開幕的新葡京外形像一片耀目的黃蓮葉,坐落於一顆閃爍的鑽石之上,遠處可見。客房隔音設備完善,擁有典型的棕色牆壁、紅色扶手椅和亞洲油畫,並坐擁豪華海景或澳門的秀麗風光。角位客房及套房設有桑拿設施,其他客房亦可享用豪華的水療設施。

TEL. 2828 3838
Avenida de Lisboa
葡京路
www.grandlisboahotel.com

♦ = MOP 2,400-3,200
♦♦ = MOP 2,400-3,200
Suites 套房 = MOP 4,480-48,000
☕ = MOP 150

Rooms 客房 331
Suites 套房 50

RECOMMENDED RESTAURANTS 餐廳推薦
Don Alfonso 1890 當奧豐素 1890 ХххХ
Robuchon au Dôme
天巢法國餐廳 ✿✿✿ ХхххХ
The Eight 8 餐廳 ✿✿✿ ХххХ
The Kitchen 大厨 ✿ ХХ

JW Marriott
JW萬豪

A soaring lobby forms the centrepiece of this impressive hotel within Galaxy Macau. The Grand Ballroom can host up to 1,600 and the hotel offers every service you'd expect in a resort. The well-equipped bedrooms may lack a little personality but they make up for it in square footage. Restaurants include the contemporary 'Urban Kitchen' with its international buffet.

宏偉的酒店大堂和完備的休閒設施如水療按摩及健身中心等服務，令你怦然心動！偌大的客房裝潢風格一致，設備齊全，雖稱不上別致，卻不失明亮整潔。酒店內的大宴會廳能容納千六人，不論是大型私人宴會或業務交流會議，都不愁找不到場地。設計時尚雅致的名廚都匯提供早、午、晚國際自助餐。

TEL. 8886 6888
Galaxy, Estrada da Baia da Nossa Senhora da Esperança, Cotai
路氹望德聖母灣大馬路澳門銀河綜合渡假城
www.jwmarriottmacau.com

🧍	= MOP 1,388-5,000
🧍🧍	= MOP 1,588-5,300
Suites 套房	= MOP 3,088-13,000
☕	= MOP 208

Rooms 客房　944
Suites 套房　71

Lisboa
葡京

Thanks largely to its 1970s style façade, The Lisboa sports a relatively sober look for Macau, and so stands in stark contrast to the glitzier Grand Lisboa. There are ten types of guestroom available and the decoration is a mix of Chinese and Portuguese styles; it's worth asking for a Royal Tower room, as these are larger and more luxurious than those in the east wing.

仍然保留着七十年代外觀的葡京酒店,帶出澳門較為樸實的一面,與閃閃生輝的新葡京酒店可謂相映成趣。酒店共有十種客房,其陳設融合了中葡兩國的風格與特色;當中尊尚客房比東翼的客房更大更豪華。酒店設有多家餐廳,提供多國菜式。

TEL. 2888 3888
2-4 Avenida de Lisboa
葡京路 2-4 號
www.hotelisboa.com

RECOMMENDED RESTAURANTS 餐廳推薦
Guincho a Galera 葡國餐廳　XxxX
Tim's Kitchen 桃花源小廚　❀　XxX

👤 = MOP 1,180-1,980
👥 = MOP 1,180-1,980
Suites 套房 = MOP 3,780-23,880
☕ = MOP 140

Rooms 客房　826
Suites 套房　50

Mandarin Oriental
文華東方

The Mandarin Oriental is a non-gaming hotel but that's not the only reason it stands out – it is also a model of taste and discretion. Local artists' work adds a sense of locale to the bedrooms which come in muted, contemporary tones and offer great views – even from the tub! Those in search of further relaxation can choose between a very serene spa and a slick bar.

於2010年開業的澳門文華東方，除了不經營賭場外，更是品味的典範。本地藝術家的創作，為色調柔和時尚的客房添上韻味，即使在浴室裏也能欣賞醉人景觀。想進一步放鬆身心，可到幽靜的水療中心或雅致的酒吧。此外，服務質素保持極高水準。

TEL. 8805 8888
945, Avenida Dr. Sun Yat Sen, Nape
外港新填海區孫逸仙大馬路945號
www.mandarinoriental.com/macau

RECOMMENDED RESTAURANTS 餐廳推薦
Vida Rica 御苑 XX

🛉 = MOP 1,888-5,000
🛉🛉 = MOP 1,888-5,000
Suites 套房 = MOP 3,288-9,300
☕ = MOP 251

Rooms 客房　186
Suites 套房　27

MACAU 澳門

MGM
美高梅

Its iconic, wave-like exterior makes MGM one of Macau's more instantly recognisable hotels. The interior is pretty eye-catching too: topped by a vast glass ceiling, the Grande Praça covers over 1,000 square metres and is where you'll find an assortment of bars and restaurants. Spread over 35 floors, bedrooms are suitably luxurious and have glass-walled bathrooms.

標誌性的波浪形建築設計讓美高梅成為澳門最矚目酒店之一。店內設計同樣出色：巨型玻璃天幕下的天幕廣場佔地逾一千平方米，設有多間酒吧和餐廳。如果看膩了浮華的裝潢，不妨前往恬靜的水療中心。酒店有35層，客房華麗得恰到好處，景觀優美，浴室採用玻璃間隔，感覺寬敞。

TEL. 8802 8888
Avenida Dr. Sun Yat Sen, Nape
外港新填海區孫逸仙大馬路
www.mgm.mo

RECOMMENDED RESTAURANTS 餐廳推薦
Imperial Court 金殿堂 ✕✕✕

♟ = MOP 1,688-6,000
♟♟ = MOP 1,688-6,000
Suites 套房 = MOP 3,488-18,000
☕ = MOP 190

Rooms 客房　483
Suites 套房　99

Okura
大倉

Looking for sanctuary from the outside world? Try this tasteful, discreet and elegant hotel, which is part of Galaxy Macau resort. Charming staff provide excellent service; bedrooms are up-to-the-minute; and all suites have private saunas and steam showers. Dining options include Japanese and international fare.

裝修典雅與品味並重的大倉酒店讓賓客感覺如遠離了凡塵的一切。身穿日本和服的服務員服務親切貼心，時尚的酒店客房寬敞舒適，套房內設有私人桑拿及蒸氣浴。

TEL. 8883 8883
Galaxy, Avenida Marginal Flor de
Lotus, Cotai
路氹城蓮花海濱大馬路澳門銀河綜合渡假城
www.hotelokuramacau.com

RECOMMENDED RESTAURANTS 餐廳推薦
Yamazato 山里 ҲxҲ

👤 = MOP 1,498-4,998
👥 = MOP 1,498-4,998
Suites 套房 = MOP 2,698-6,498
🛏 = MOP 190

Rooms 客房　429
Suites 套房　59

MACAU 澳門

Pousada de Mong-Há
望廈迎賓館

  🚻 **P** 🚭 🏄 🛶

A very good value hotel with a distinct difference – it is run by the Institute for Tourism Studies, so you will be welcomed at the desk by students learning their trade. The hotel benefits from a very peaceful position, away from the casinos and surrounded by a lovely garden. Its bedrooms may not be big but they are quiet and come with some nice Asian touches.

這家與眾不同的超值賓館由旅遊學院營運，因此全部服務員由學院的學生擔任，為你悉心服務。它位處寧靜的望廈山半山腰，遠離娛樂場的煩囂，更給可愛的花園重重圍繞。客房地方不算大，不過環境寧靜，設計帶有亞洲風格。教學餐廳是品嘗澳門美食的好去處。

TEL. 2851 5222
Colina de Mong-Há
望廈山
www.ift.edu.mo/pousada

RECOMMENDED RESTAURANTS 餐廳推薦
IFT Educational Restaurant
旅遊學院教學餐廳 🍴 XX

🛏 = MOP 700-1,300
🛏🛏 = MOP 700-1,300
Suites 套房 = MOP 1,300-1,800
☕ = MOP 140

Rooms 客房 16
Suites 套房 4

Sheraton
喜來登

Currently the biggest hotel in Macau, Sheraton Macau forms part of the resort complex of Sands Cotai Central and is connected to a huge shopping mall. Needless to say, the facilities are comprehensive and include a varied choice of restaurant, three outdoor pools with private cabanas and an impressive spa. There are Family suites and special amenities for children.

作為全澳門最大規模、位於金沙城中心的喜來登酒店，連接大型購物商場，便於閒逛購物。酒店內設備亦相當完善：設有數間餐館、三個戶外泳池及舒適的水療設施，吃喝玩樂與休憩，一網打盡。酒店還設有家庭套房和兒童遊樂設施，適合一家大小住宿。

TEL. 2880 2000
Estrada do Istmo. s/n, The Cotai Strip, Taipa
路氹路氹連貫公路
www.sheratongrandmacao.com

👤 = MOP 1,088-5,838
👥 = MOP 1,088-5,838
Suites 套房 = MOP 1,888-21,838
☕ = MOP 288

Rooms 客房　3,640
Suites 套房　361

St. Regis
瑞吉

Starwood are relative newcomers to Macau but their very comfortable St. Regis hotel is a worthy addition to the Cotai Strip. The spacious bedrooms, on floors 8-37, have good views and are well-appointed in an understated, contemporary style; they have floor to ceiling windows and white marble bathrooms. The Manor restaurant offers a wide-ranging international menu.

這家Starwood麾下的酒店位於路氹金光大道，地點優越。1樓的雅舍餐廳明亮而富現代氣息，可品嘗各式國際菜餚美饌。客房位處8-37樓，寬敞時尚的室內陳設透着點點東方韻味，配上落地玻璃窗，予人舒適靜謐之感，記着預訂能眺望金光大道美景的房間。水療中心的寶石按摩讓人感官愉悅。

TEL. 2882 8898
Estrada do Istmo, s/n, The Cotai Strip, Taipa
路氹路氹連貫公路
www.stregismacao.com

♦ = MOP 1,888-7,338
♦♦ = MOP 1,888-7,338
Suites 套房 = MOP 2,988-8,738
☕ = MOP 248

Rooms 客房　278
Suites 套房　122

StarWorld
星際

Opened in 2006, StarWorld Macau is a comfortable, well-managed hotel in a good location. Its bedrooms are bright and contemporary and the bathrooms are smart and well-equipped. Along with various restaurants and assorted gaming, the hotel also offers comprehensive entertainment and leisure facilities and these include a bar with live music every night.

在2006年開業的星際酒店地點便利之餘，亦是一間管理完善的酒店。光猛的房間設計風格前衛，時髦的浴室設施相當完備。除了各式餐館和娛樂場所外，酒店內還附設各種休閒設施，例如每天晚上都有現場音樂演奏的酒吧。

TEL. 2838 3838
Rua Cidade de Sintra, n. 338
仙德麗街 338號
www.starworldmacau.com

RECOMMENDED RESTAURANTS 餐廳推薦
Feng Wei Ju 風味居 ✿✿ ✕✕✕
Temptations 品味坊 ✕✕

♦ = MOP 1,460-2,360
♦♦ = MOP 1,460-2,360
Suites 套房 = MOP 2,920-4,720
☕ = MOP 98

Rooms 客房 465
Suites 套房 40

MACAU 澳門

Studio City
新濠影滙

Even by Macau standards, this immense, art deco styled hotel made quite a statement when it opened in 2015. It aims to offer the complete leisure experience and that means extensive gaming facilities, a 5,000 seater arena, a 4D Batman experience, a magic show, shopping malls, spas, numerous restaurants and a nightclub! Bedrooms have floor to ceiling windows and good views.

這家耗資逾三十億美元興建、裝飾派藝術風格的酒店於2015年開業,目標是提供一站式的綜合娛樂,設有娛樂場、大型表演場地、4D影院、購物商場、水療中心等等,還有號稱高度冠絕全球、達130米的8字形摩天輪,讓你流連忘返。時尚而設備完善的客房分佈於兩幢大樓內,落地玻璃窗外是金光大道的醉人景致。

TEL. 8865 6868
Estrada do Istmo, The Cotai Strip, Taipa
路氹連貫公路
www.studiocity-macau.com

RECOMMENDED RESTAURANTS 餐廳推薦
Bi Ying 碧迎居 ✗
Pearl Dragon 玥龍軒 ۞ ✗✗✗✗
Shanghai Magic 上海魅影 ✗✗

🛉 = MOP 871-6,588
🛉🛉 = MOP 871-6,588
Suites 套房 = MOP 4,711-30,888
☕ = MOP 238

Rooms 客房 1,525
Suites 套房 75

The Parisian
巴黎人

Building a half-scale recreation of the Eiffel Tower in front of your hotel is certainly one way of getting it noticed. Opened in 2016, the hotel's interior also makes much of French history – the reception area is inspired by Louis XIV. Bedrooms, in contrast, are more neutral in tone. Dining options include La Chine, a fusion restaurant within the replica Eiffel Tower.

在酒店外重塑一個只有半個規模的艾菲爾鐵塔，絕對有助吸引遊客的焦點。於2016年開業的巴黎人酒店，裝潢帶有路易十四時期的巴洛克風格，客房的布置卻較為素淨。位於酒店外的仿艾菲爾鐵塔內的餐廳，供應自助餐、法國菜或多國菜的都有，不妨挑一間坐下來，邊享用餐點邊欣賞窗外景色。

TEL. 2882 8833
Estrada do Istmo, Lote 3, Cotai Strip
路氹金光大道連貫公路
www.parisianmacao.com

♂ = MOP 1,298-1,798
♂♀ = MOP 1,548-2,048
Suites 套房 = MOP 2,148-2,648
🛏 = MOP 208

Rooms 客房　2,420
Suites 套房　98

The Ritz-Carlton
麗思卡爾頓

All bedrooms are suites at the exclusive Ritz-Carlton hotel, which is located on the upper floors at Galaxy Macau. They are impeccably dressed and come with particularly luxurious marble bathrooms. They also provide great views of Cotai, as does the outdoor pool. Along with a state-of-the-art spa is an elegant bar and stylish, very comfortable lounges.

講究的裝潢、精緻的藝術擺設、舒適的座椅，甫踏進設在51樓的接待處，心已給溶化！風格典雅的套房除了設有舒適奢華的大理石浴室外，還能俯瞰欣賞銀河渡假村景觀或遠眺市內風光。與接待處同層的麗思酒廊設計優雅，且能飽覽氹仔景致，是與摯愛親朋把酒談心的好地方。

TEL. 8886 6868
Galaxy, Estrada da Baia da Nossa
Senhora da Esperança, Cotai
路氹城望德聖母灣大馬路
澳門銀河綜合渡假城
www.ritzcarlton.com/macau

Suites 套房 = MOP 3,088-24,888

Suites 套房　236

RECOMMENDED RESTAURANTS 餐廳推薦
Lai Heen 麗軒 ✿ XXXXX
The Ritz-Carlton Café 麗思咖啡廳 XX

The Venetian
威尼斯人

One thing you'll need at Asia's largest integrated resort is a map to find your way around. Expect vast shopping malls and even canals with singing gondoliers; there are frescoes, colonnades and sculptures everywhere – it's easy to get caught up in the sheer scale and exuberance of it all. Identikit luxury is assured in a towering bedroom skyscraper with 3,000 rooms.

你需要一張地圖才能環遊這間全亞洲最大型綜合渡假酒店！在這裏你會找到大型購物商場，更有貢多拉船夫一邊掌船一邊唱歌。遍佈各處的壁畫、柱廊和雕塑裝飾，具規模且色彩繽紛，令人目不暇給。高聳的摩天大樓設有三千間套房，全部房間都很寬敞。

TEL. 2882 8888
Estrada da Baia de N. Senhora da Esperanca, s/n, The Cotai Strip, Taipa
氹仔路氹金光大道望德聖母灣大馬路
www.venetianmacao.com

Suites 套房 = MOP 1,300-3,000
☕ = MOP 200

Suites 套房 3,000

RECOMMENDED RESTAURANTS 餐廳推薦
Canton 喜粵 ✗✗✗
The Golden Peacock 皇雀 ✿ ✗✗

Wynn
永利

The Wynn's easy-on-the-eye curving glass façade is enhanced with a lake and dancing fountains, while the classically luxurious interior includes Murano glass chandeliers, plush carpets and much marble. An attractively landscaped oasis pool forms the centrepiece to corridors lined with famous retail names. Comfortable bedrooms display a considerable degree of taste.

弧形的玻璃外牆十分奪目，更設有表演湖及噴水池。酒店內部散發着經典豪華氣息：穆拉諾穆璃玻璃吊燈、豪華的地毯，觸目所及皆是大理石。走廊中心設有一個造型迷人的綠洲池，而兩旁滿是名店。客房融合了傳統與現代兩種設計風格，盡顯卓越品味。其吉祥樹同樣令你印象深刻。

TEL. 2888 9966
Rua Cidade de Sintra, Nape
外港新填海區仙德麗街
www.wynnmacau.com

RECOMMENDED RESTAURANTS 餐廳推薦
Il Teatro 帝雅廷 XxxX
Mizumi 泓 ✿✿ XxX
Wing Lei 永利軒 ✿ XxxX

♙ = MOP 1,888-13,500
♙♙ = MOP 1,888-13,500
Suites 套房 = MOP 3,988-17,000
🍽 = MOP 210

Rooms 客房   460
Suites 套房   134

Wynn Palace
永利皇宮

Opened in 2016, with a striking flower motif and impressive pieces of art scattered around the vast hotel. Luxurious bedrooms are uncluttered, large and bright, with a Mandarin, Peacock or Gold theme; the caramel-coloured suites are also impressive. There's a host of dining choices, from noodles to steaks; show kitchens are a feature of several of the restaurants.

於2016年開業，以上萬朵花卉製作的巨型花卉雕塑、隨處可見的藝術作品，寬敞的酒店，典雅高貴。以橙、孔雀和金作主題陳設的豪華客房感覺整潔、寬敞及明亮，橙棕色作主調的套房尤為使人印象深刻。酒店內餐廳種類很廣，從簡單的麵食到高級的牛扒，一應俱全，開放式廚房似乎是這裏的餐廳特色。

TEL. 8889 8889
Avenida da Nave Desportiva, Cotai
路氹體育館大馬路
www.wynnpalace.com

♦ = MOP 1,888-3,188
♦♦ = MOP 1,888-3,188
Suites 套房 = MOP 3,500-20,000
☕ = MOP 220

Rooms 客房　845
Suites 套房　861

MAPS
地圖

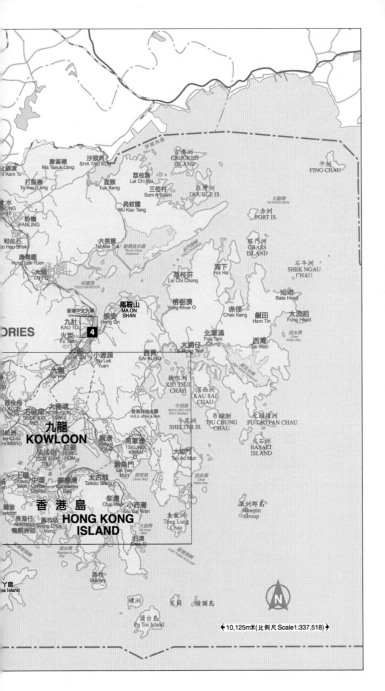

馬鞍山 MA ON SHAN

九肚 KAU TO

火炭 Fo Tam

4

沙田 SHA TIN

小瀝源 Siu Lek Yuen

西貢 SAI KUNG

大網仔 Tai Mong Tsai

北潭涌 Pak Tam Chung

西灣 Sai Wan

大浪咀 Fung Head

鹹田 Ham Tin

赤徑 Chek Keng

榕樹澳 Yung Shue O

荔枝莊 Lai Chi Chong

海下 Hoi Ha

石牛洲 SHEK NGAU CHAU

短咀 Bate Head

GRASS ISLAND 塔門洲

赤洲 PORT IS.

大鵬灣 TAI PANG WAN

平洲 PING CHAU

CROOKED ISLAND 吉澳洲

往灣洲 DOUBLE IS.

三椏村 Sam A Tsuen

烏蛟騰 Wu Kau Tang

荔枝窩 Lai Chi Wo

鹿頸 Luk Keng

沙頭角 SHA TAU KOK

麻雀嶺 Ma Tseuk Leng

打鼓嶺 Ta Kwu Ling

大美督 Tai Mei Tuk

船灣淡水湖 Plover Cove Reservoir

大埔 TAI PO

大埔滘 Tai Po Kau

粉嶺 FANLING

聯和墟 Luen Wo Hui

上水 SHEUNG SHUI

和合石 Wo Hop Shek

麻雀嶺 Ma Kam To

小瀝源 Siu Lek Yuen

九龍坑 KAU TO

香港中文大學 Chinese Univ. of H.K.

馬料水 Ma Liu Shui

火炭 Fo Tam

KIU TSUI CHAU 橋咀洲

滘西洲 KAU SAI CHAU

牛耳海 NDAU MEI HOI (Port Shelter)

牛尾洲 SHELTER IS.

吊鐘洲 TIU CHUNG CHAU

火石洲 FU TAU FAN CHAU

BASALT ISLAND 伙石洲

香港科技大學 H.K.U. of Sci.&Tech.

九龍塘 KOWLOON TONG

石硤尾 SHEK KIP MEI

九龍 KOWLOON

紅磡 HUNG HOM

觀塘 KWUN TONG

將軍澳 TSEUNG KWAN O

藍田 Lam Tin

鯉魚門 Lei Yue Mun

大坳門 Tai Au Mun

西貢 Junk Bay 清水灣

大廟灣 Joss House Bay

油麻地 Yau Ma Tei

尖沙咀 TSIM SHA TSUI

上環 Sheung Wan

中環 Central District

銅鑼灣 Causeway Bay

太古城 Taikoo Shing

柴灣 Chai Wan

小西灣 Siu Sai Wan

香港島 HONG KONG ISLAND

灣仔 Wan Chai

香港仔 Aberdeen

黃竹坑 Wong Chuk Hang

鴨脷洲 Ap Lei Chau

深水灣 Repulse Bay

淺水灣 Repulse Bay

赤柱 Stanley

東龍洲 Tung Lung Chau

藍塘海峽 LAI TONG HOI HAP

清水灣 Clear Water Bay

TERRITORIES

九龍 ... KOWLOON

蒲台島 Po Toi Island

果洲 ... 橫瀾島

擔杆群島 Ninepin Group

N

←10,125米(比例尺 Scale 1:337,518)→

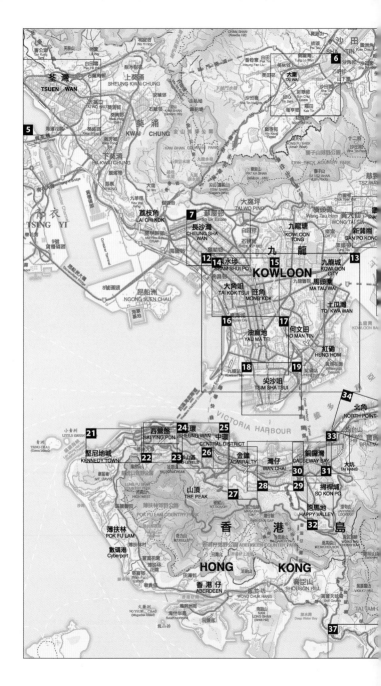

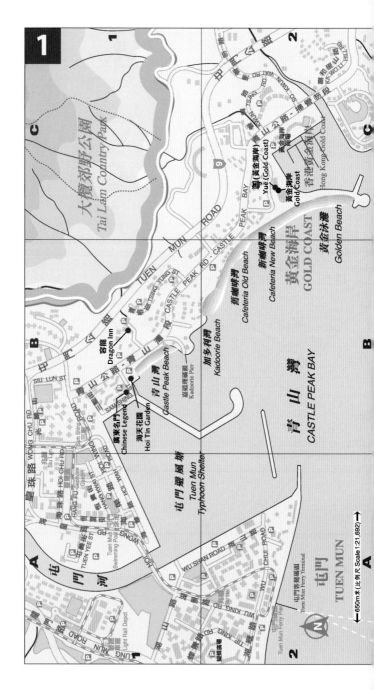

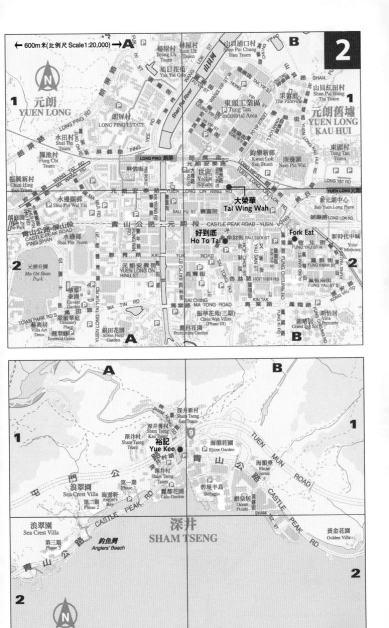

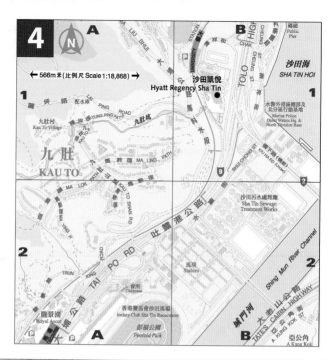

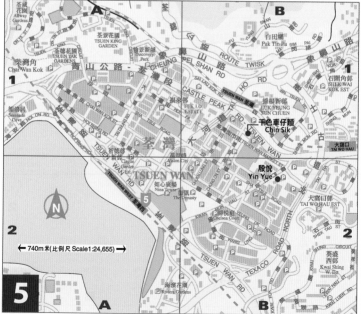

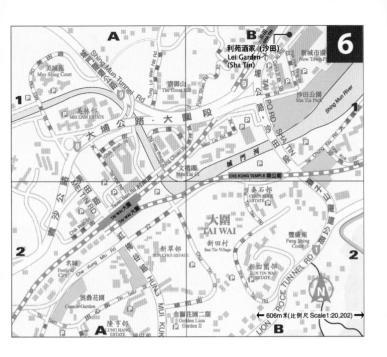

利苑酒家 (沙田)
Lei Garden
(Sha Tin)

坤記竹昇麵 (長沙灣)
Kwan Kee Bamboo Noodles
(Cheung Sha Wan)

劉森記麵家 (福榮街)
Lau Sum Kee
(Fuk Wing Street)

文記車仔麵
Man Kei Cart Noodles

泰潮
Thai Chiu

坤記糕品
Kwan Kee Store

合益泰小食
Hop Yik Tai

添好運 (深水埗)
Tim Ho Wan
(Sham Shui Po)

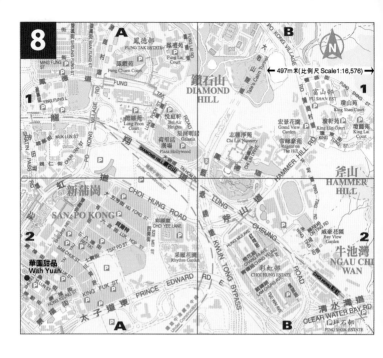

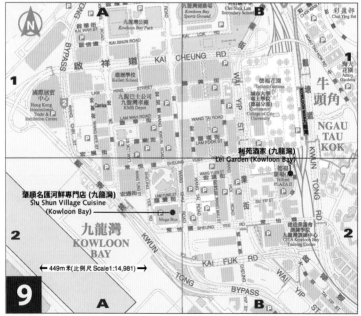

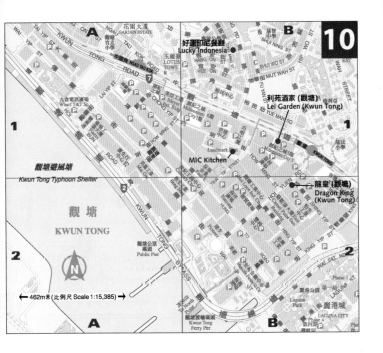

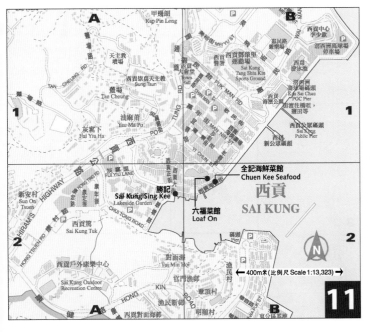

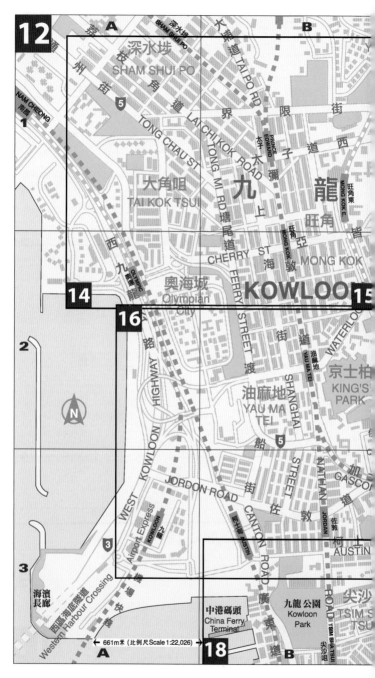

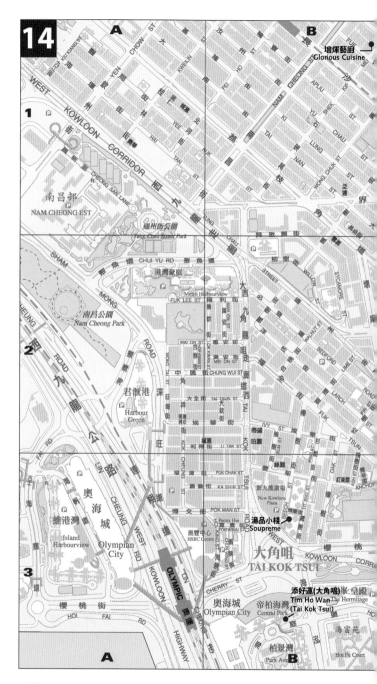

增煇藝廚
Glorious Cuisine

WEST KOWLOON CORRIDOR 西九龍走廊

南昌邨
NAM CHEONG EST

通州街公園
Tung Chau Street Park

SHAM MONG ROAD 深旺道

深旺道

南昌公園
Nam Cheong Park

CHUI YU RD 翠魚道

港灣豪庭
Metro Harbourview
FUK LEE ST 福利街
福安街 WAN ON ST
WAI ON ST 惠安街
美安街 MEI ON ST
中匯街 CHUNG WUI ST
大全街 TAI TSUEN ST
祥利街
埃華街
利棠街 LI TAK ST

君滙港
Harbour
Green

深旺道

奧海城
維港灣
Island
Harbourview
Olympian
City

LIN CHEUNG RD 連翔道

FUK CHAK ST 福澤街
KA SHIN ST 嘉善街

帝盛酒店

新九龍廣場
New Kowloon
Plaza

POK MAN ST 博文街

渣豐中心
HSBC CENTRE

湯品小棧
Soupreme

大角咀
TAI KOK TSUI

KOWLOON CORRIDOR 櫻桃

OLYMPIC 奧運

CHERRY ST 櫻桃街

奧海城
Olympian City

帝柏海灣
Central Park

添好運(大角咀)
Tim Ho Wan
(Tai Kok Tsui)

峯皇殿
The Hermitage

櫻桃街
HOI FAI 海輝

柏景灣
Park Ave

海富苑
Hoi Fu Court

聚興家
Ju Xing Home

蘭苑饊館
Lan Yuen Chee Koon

界限街遊樂場
Boundary Street
Recreation Ground

旺角大球場
Mong Kok Stadium

花墟市場
Flower Market

旺角警署
Mong Kok
Police Station

帝京
Royal Plaza

阿純山東餃子
Chun Shandong Dumpling

叁薯
Three potatoes

容記小菜王
Yung Kee

鳳城 (旺角)
Fung Shing (Mong Kok)

新世紀廣場
Grand Century
Place

旺角
MONG KOK

奇趣餅家
Kei Tsui

利苑酒家 (旺角)
Lei Garden (Mong Kok)

明閣
Ming Court

泉章居 (旺角)
Chuen Cheung Kui
(Mong Kok)

康得思
Cordis

I Love You Dessert Bar

Joyful Dessert House

好旺角麵家(花園街)
Good Hope Noodle (Fa Yuen Street)

C · D

1

2

3

NA

15

278米 (比例尺 Scale 1:9,260)

463

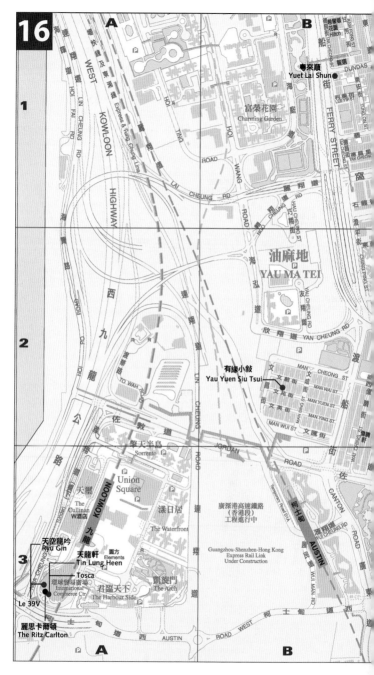

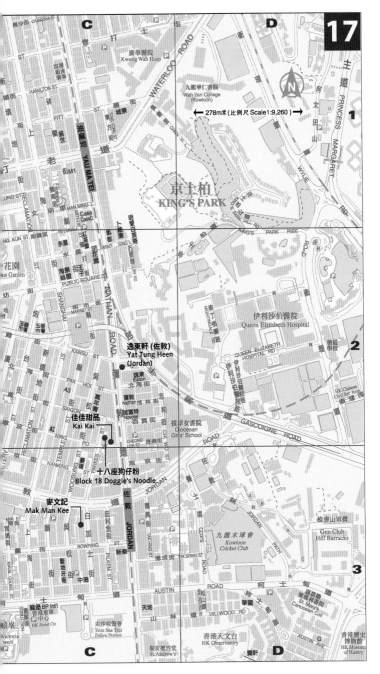

廣華醫院
Kwong Wah Hosp

WATERLOO ROAD

九龍華仁書院
Wah Yan College
(Kowloon)

PRINCESS MARGARET RD.

← 278m米 (比例尺 Scale1:9,260) →

油麻地
YAU MA TEI

京士柏
KING'S PARK

KING'S PARK RISE

KING'S PARK ROAD

伊利沙伯醫院
Queen Elizabeth Hospital

QUEEN ELIZABETH HOSPITAL RD.

HK Chinese Civil Ser. Sci.

NATHAN ROAD

PUBLIC SQUARE ST.

MARKET ST.

SHANGHAI ST.

KANSU ST.

逸東軒 (佐敦)
Yat Tung Heen
(Jordan)

PAK HOI ST.

SAIGON ST.

Eaton

Nathan 彌敦酒店

Novotel

GASCOIGNE ROAD

Diocesan
Girls' School

佳佳甜品
Kai Kai

NING ST.

TEMPLE ST.

WOOSUNG ST.

PARKES ST.

CHEONG LOK ST.

NANKING ST.

十八座狗仔粉
Block 18 Doggie's Noodle

JORDAN ROAD

JORDAN ROAD

COX'S ROAD

KOWLOON PATH

燒會山軍營
Gun Club
Hill Barracks

麥文記
Mak Man Kee

BOWRING ST.

PILKEM ST.

九龍木球會
Kowloon
Cricket Club

AUSTIN ROAD

AUSTIN ROAD

聖瑪利書院
St. Mary's
Canossian Coll.

龍堡 BP Int'l
HK Scout Ctr

尖沙咀警署
Tsim Sha Tsui
Police Station

St. Andrew's

香港天文台
HK Observatory

AUSTIN AVE.

香港歷史博物館
HK Museum
of History

18

柯士甸道 WUI MAN RD
區民道

CANTON ROAD

KWUN CHUNG ST
SHANGHAI ST
TEMPLE ST
PARKES ST

新樂 shamrock 恆豐 Prudential
PILKEM ST 白加士街
彌敦道 AU

聖地 San Diego

避風塘興記
Hing Kee
天地

AUSTIN RD W 柯士甸道西

廣東道

龍堡 BP Intl
龍堡國際賓館
港景洲 Scout Path
HK Scout Ctr
P

尖沙咀警署
Tsim Sha Tsui
Police Station

The Victoria Towers

1

聖安娜 St.Anne

富豪 (尖沙咀)
Fu Ho (Tsim Sha Tsui)

中港城
China HK City

室內體育館
Sports Centre

九龍公園游泳池
新同樂 (尖沙咀)
Sun Tung Lok (Tsim Sha Tsui)

翠亨邨 (尖沙咀)
Tsui Hang Village (TST)

棧話
語言
Landmark
Centre
Piece

栢麗購物大道
Park Lane Shopper's Boulevard

國金軒 (The Mira)
Cuisine Cuisine at The Mira
Whisk

The M

豪泰太平洋
Royal Pacific

九龍公園
Kowloon Park

The M

China Ferry Terminal
中港客運碼頭

海港城

Gateway
港威大廈

香港文物探知館
HK Heritage
Discovery Centre

香港太子
Prince HK

禪八
Zenpachi

KOWLOON PARK

清真寺
Jamia Masjid
Islamic Centre

唐人館 (海港城)
China Tang (Harbour City)

Sushi Tokami

鼎泰豐 (新港中心)
Din Tai Fung (Silvercord)

(北座)
環球金融
中心 (南座)
World Finance
Centre

HAIPHONG

新港中心
Silvercord

九龍太平洋會

海港城

廣東道
CANTON ROAD

海防道
HAIPHONG RD

2

阿一海景飯店
Ah Yat Harbour View

T'ang Court
唐閣

Bostonian
Seafood
and Grill

世界商業中心
World Comm
Centre

新世紀廣場力寶太陽廣場
New T & T Centre
Lippo Sun Plaza

朗廷
The Langham

漆咸 (尖沙咀)
Qi (Tsim Sha Tsui)

Épure

HARBOUR
CITY

GATEWAY BOULEVARD

海洋中心
Ocean
Centre

北京道
PEKING RD

御寶軒
Imperial Treasure

北京道
Peking Rd

海利公寓
Hullett

夜上海 (尖沙咀)
Yè Shanghai
(Tsim Sha Tsui)

青年會
YMCA of
HK

半島
The Peninsula

海運大廈
Marco Polo HK
P

馬哥孛羅香港
Marco Polo HK

Ocean Terminal
海運大廈

星光行
Star House

瑞樵閣
Chesa
Felix

吉地士
Gaddi's

香港太空館
HK Space Museum

嘉麟樓
Spring Moon

香港藝術館
HK Museum of Art

3

旅客諮詢中心
Visitor Info Centre

往中環
To Central
天星碼頭
Star Ferry Pier

香港文化中心
HK Cultural Centre

鐘樓
Clock
Tower

往灣仔
To Wan Chai

九龍公眾碼頭
Kowloon Public Pier

尖沙咀
TSIM SHA TSUI

N

← 250m米 (比例尺 Scale 1:8,333) →

A
B

466

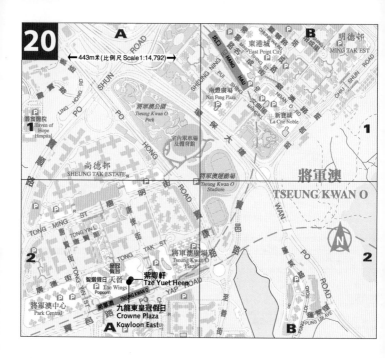

443m米(比例尺 Scale 1:14,792)

A

B

SHUN ROAD

LING PO ROAD

靈寶路

SHEUNG NING ROUT

城名路

HANG MAU

坑口

MING TAK
明名路

東港城
East Point City

明德邨
MING TAK EST

CHIU SHUN ROAD

NGAN O ROAD
銀澳路

南豐廣場
Nan Fung Plaza

新寶城
La Cité Noble

將軍澳公園
Tseung Kwan O
Park

靈寶醫院
Haven of
Hope
Hospital

1

寶康路
PO HONG ROAD

室內單車場
及醫育館

尚德邨
SHEUNG TAK ESTATE

將軍澳運動場
Tseung Kwan O
Stadium

將軍澳
TSEUNG KWAN O

將軍澳

TSEUNG KWAN O

1

TONG MING ST
唐明街

TONG YIN L
唐賢里

MING TAK ST
明德街

寶邑路
PO WAN ROAD

寶寧路

將軍澳座場路
Tseung Kwan O
Plaza

将軍澳座場
Tseung Kwan O
Plaza

N

2

TONG MING ST

TONG YIN ST
唐賢街

TONG YAP ROAD
唐業路

TSEUNG KWAN O

PO NING
寶寧路

POPUNG LEUNG
蓬瀛里

2

智選假日天譽
The Wings
Popcorn

紫悅軒
Tze Yuet Heen

將軍澳中心
Park Central

九龍東皇冠假日
Crowne Plaza
Kowloon East

A

B

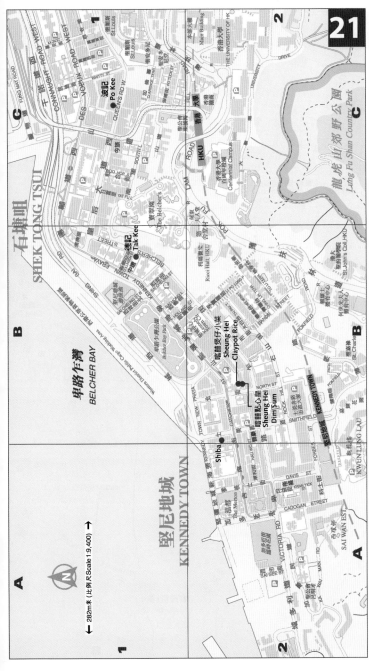

石塘咀 SHEK TONG TSUI

堅尼地城 KENNEDY TOWN

卑路乍灣 BELCHER BAY

龍虎山郊野公園 Lung Fu Shan Country Park

香港大學 THE UNIVERSITY OF HK

波記 Po Kee

德記 Tak Kee

嚐囍煲仔小菜 Sheung Hei Claypot Rice

嚐囍點心皇 Sheung Hei Dim Sum

Shiba

← 282米(比例尺Scale 1:9,400) →

A

B

干諾道 西

高樂花園 Connaught Garden

港島太平洋

萬怡 Courtyard

西港中心

朝光街

西 ROAD WEST

華貴品 Plus

西區警署

奇靈里 CHUNG CHING ST

石棧里

正街

西營盤 SAI YING PUN

DES VOEUX

WEST

華大 品 Plus

西安里

SALON L

紅茶館

皇后

水街 WATER ST

ROAD

西 安里

西興隆里

三多里 SAM TO L

西華里

第 街 Western Garden

第一街

正街

第二街

德輔道里家坡里

薯�‧湘門第 (西環) Café Hunan (Western District)

QUEEN'S

福祉坊

HUK SAU L 鹹魚里

譚里 TAM L

福滿里

CR

WESTERN

THIRD ST

第三

街

聖類斯 St. Louis

由義街

第

扶 林 道

薄

巴依 Ba Yi

POK FU LAM L

玫瑰里 ROSE LANE

餘樂里 YU LOK L

長安里

Kaum Fish School

高

英記麵家 Eng Kee Noodle Shop

西營盤

聖士提反堂 St. Stephen's

PU LAM KU YAN L

般

聖保羅書院 St. Paul's College

HING HON RD

S T

英皇書院 King's College

請坐 Qing Zuo

YING WA TER

西寧街

本部大樓 Main Building

般咸道

BONHAM

ROAD

聖士提反里 STEPHEN'S LANE

香港大學 THE UNIVERSITY OF HK

美術博物館

光浪台

HON TON RD

港鐵博道

巴內頓道

BABINGTON PATH

羅便臣

屋蘭士

聖嘉勒

地質博物館

R

巴內頓道 BABINGTON PATH

柏立基學院 Robert Black College

R

旭

龢

道

UNIVERSITY DRIVE

R R

R

KOTE WALL

千

龢

道

ROAD

PO

龍虎山 環境教育中心

餘

旭

RD

資珊道1號 No.1 Po Shan Rd

寶

珊

道

A

HATTON

R

R

R

R

B

CONNAUGHT ROAD WEST

WILMER ST

華樂庭

鹹魚街東

德 輔 道 西

桂香街 MUI FONG ST

梅芳街

華麗海景

坤記煲仔小菜
an Kee Claypot Rice

峰 Crest

匯 PUN

威利蔴街

皇后大道西

邊 街

TSZ MI ALLEY
紫薇街

SUTHERLAND

ST

蓮香居
Lin Heung Kui

宜必思
Ibis

修遜街

皇后街

KO SHING ST

QUEEN ST

帝后華庭

SING ST

蘇杭街

德星里

高陞街

PAN KWAI LANE

和興西街 WO FUNG ST

貴桂里

西關

殷豐街 FAT HING ST

CHUEN LANE

NG FUK LANE
五福里

菲臘
牙科醫院
Philip
Dental Hosp.

贊育醫院
Tsan Yuk Hosp

西營盤
賽馬會分料
Tsan Yuk Hosp

新

樂善堂
樂餅坊

ST

郭興里

EASTERN

元勝里

HIGH ST

WEST

STREET 高

香港佐治五世紀念公園
KING GEORGE V
MEMORIAL PARK

西營盤社區
綜合大樓
Community
Complex

殷威道
官立

柏

般

道

道

聖公會
聖馬太

HOSPITAL ROAD

COLLEGE VIEW

商廈坊

東華醫院
Tung Wah
Hospital

寶源坊
PO YUEN LANE

PO YAN ST

太
平

HOLLYWOOD RD

普仁街

善慶
好萊塢

差館上街

太平山街 TAI PING SHAN ST

POY EE ST

普慶坊

居賢坊

WA NING

卜公花園
Blake
Garden

HOSPITAL ROAD

普義坊

和合街

東街

HILLIER ST

荷李活道

CENTERBK

PO HING FONG

BONHAM ROAD

士

道

聖士提反
St. Stephen's
女子中學
Girls' College

PARK RD

ROAD

LYTTELTON

OAKLANDS AVE

ROAD

BREEZY P

CAINE RD

SEYMOUR RD

臣道

瑞麟

ROBINSON

ROAD

帝豪閣
Imperial Court

羅便臣道

ROBINSON

ROAD

CONDUIT

ROAD

聯邦花苑
Realty Gardens

干德道

半山區
MID-LEVELS

N

SHAN ROAD

← 168m米 (比例尺Scale 1:5,587) →

上環
SHEUNG WAN

2

3

471

SERVICES STREET

消防處滅鄉島、
HK I, L & Marine
Fire Command HQs
西滅防

中港道
CHUNG KONG ROAD

海傍分隔智路

Hong Kong
Heliport
香港直升機場

HK-MACAU FERRY TERMINAL
港澳碼頭

1 ONNAUGHT RD W 干諾道西

NEW MARKET ST 新街市街

信德中心
Shun Tak Ctr

招商局大廈
China Merchants
Tower

林士街
多層停車場

宜必思

WING LOK ST

永安中心
Wing On
Centre

Queen's
皇后大
帝后華廈

西港城
Western
Market

中
干
諾
道

上環 SHEUNG WAN

QUEEN'S RD W

陳勤記鹵鵝飯店(上環)
Chan Kan Kee Chiu Chow
(Sheung Wan)

上
環

尚文富德

LOK KU

桃花源小廚
Tim's Kitchen

荷李活道公園
Hollywood Road Park

SHEUNG WAN

新園興記
Sun Yuen Hing Kee

志魂
Sushi Shikon

Upper Modern Bistro

尚園
The Mercer

Moon Thai

Sushi
Wadatsumi

Frantzén's Kitchen

大班樓
The Chairman

Vea

麵鮮醬油房周月(中環)
Shugetsu Ramen
(Central)

Bibo

九記
Kau Kee

文武廟
Man Mo
Temple

Cocotte

名人坊
Celebrity Cuisine

2

卜公花園
Blake
Garden

Aberdeen
Street Social

蘭桂坊
Lan Kwai Fong

香港醫學博物館
HK Museum of
Medical Sciences

一宝
Ippoh

太平伙
Da Ping Huo

英華女學校
Ying Wah
Girls' Sch

香港花園
HK Garden

美麗邨
Merry Terr

Belon

Ohel Leah
Synagogue

羅便臣道
Robinson
Place

Le Souk

富景花園
Scenic Heights

Tate

Buxey Lodge

承德山莊
Scenecliff

藝蘭苑
Arts Mansion

康威園
Conway
Mansion

康苑
Cliffview
Mansions

清真
禮拜堂
Jamia Mosque

嘉諾撒聖心
商學書院
Sacred Heart Canossian
College of Commerce

3

CONDUIT ROAD

ROBINSON ROAD

全景大廈
Panorama

嘉兆臺
The Grand
Panorama

A

B

1號碼頭 Pier 1

2號碼頭 Pier 2
往坪洲 To Peng Island

3號碼頭 Pier 3
往愉景灣 To Discovery Bay

4號碼頭 Pier 4
往梅窩 To Mui Wo / To So Kwu Wan

5號碼頭 Pier 5
往長洲 To Cheung Chau

6號碼頭 Pier 6
往坪洲 To Mui Wo

7號碼頭 Pier 7
往尖沙咀 To Tsim Sha Tsui

Caprice
龍景軒
Lung King Heen

中環碼頭 Central Pier

天星碼頭 Star Ferry Pier

MAN KWONG ST

MAN PO ST

MAN KAT ST

MAN CHIU ST

光 街

民 寶 街

民 耀 街

金 融 街

Pier 9 政府合署 – 國際商業信貸銀行
Harbour Building
海港政府大樓

四季
Four Seasons

FINANCE ST

香港站 停車場
IFC Mall
國際金融中心商場
Intern'l Finance Ctr

國際金融中心二期
Two International
Finance Centre

利苑酒家 (國際金融中心)
Lei Garden (IFC)

正斗粥麵專家 (國際金融中心)
Tasty (IFC)

1

GILMAN ST

JUBILEE ST

中環中心 P
The Center

MAN CHEUNG ST

香港 HONG KONG

MAN YIU ST

民 祥 街

民 豐 街

營致會館
Ying Jee Club

IFC Mall

HARBOUR VIEW ST

QUEEN VICTORIA ST

Central Market
中環街市

MAN YEE LANE
萬宜里

POTTINGER ST
砵典乍街

LI YUEN ST WEST

LI YUEN ST EAST

26

STANLEY ST

WELLINGTON ST

THEATRE LANE

交易廣場
Exchange
Square

翠玉軒
The Square

郵政總局
General Post Office

格林大廈
Jardine House

怡和大廈

文華廳
Man Wah

CONNAUGHT PLACE

砵丁渣甸大廈

2

Des Voeux Rd C
德輔道中

文華扒房+酒吧
Mandarin Grill + Bar
Pierre

文華東方
Mandarin Oriental

4

CONNAUGHT RD C

香港上海匯豐銀行大廈
HK Club

唐人館
(中環)
China Tang
(Central)

CIAK

CENTRAL 中環中

遮打大廈
Chater House

CEN TRA

8½ Otto e Mezzo - Bombana

北京樓 (中環)
Peking Garden (Central)

CHATER RD

Chater Garden
遮打花園

ABERDEEN ST

WYNDHAM ST

LAN KWAI FONG
蘭桂坊

DUDDELL ST
都爹利街

Arcane

柏屋
Kashiwaya

ON

都爹利會館
Duddell's

Beefbar

置地文華東方
The Landmark
Mandarin Oriental

L'Atelier de
Joël Robuchon

Amber

PEDDER ST

QUEEN'S ROAD

遮打道

歷山大廈
Alexandra House

太子大廈
Prince's
Building

會所大廈

HSBC Main
Building
香港上海匯豐銀行

中國銀行大廈
Bank of China
Building

中國銀行
Bank of China

遮打花園

Statue
Square
皇后像廣場

立法會大樓
Legislative
Council
Building

JACKSON RD

Jackson Rd

3

ARBUTHNOT RD
亞畢諾道

醫香公所

港中醫院

港保良局

Church
Guest Hse

CENTRAL
BATTERY
中區軍營

QUEEN'S
ROAD

遮打道

中區政府合署
Central Govt Offices

終審法院
Court of Final
Appeal

政府總部
HESAP Govt HQ

長江集團中心
Cheung Kong
Center

C

ALBANY RD

BATTERY PATH
炮台里

St John's
Cathedral
聖約翰座堂

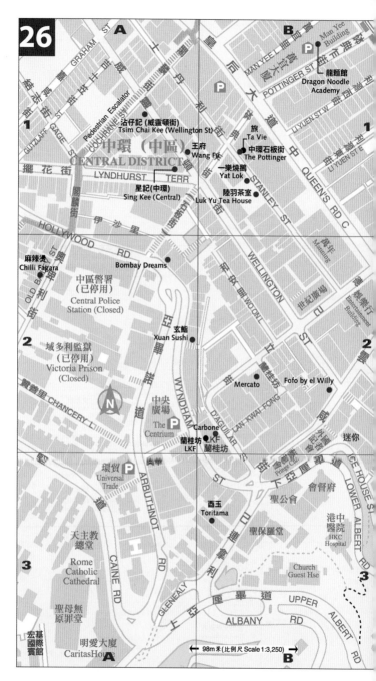

GRAHAM ST　A

B　Man Yee Building

古
咸
大
街

沾仔記 (威靈頓街)
Tsim Chai Kee (Wellington St)

Pedestrian Escalator

COCHRANE ST

GUTZLAFF ST

GAGE ST

攏花街

中環 (中區)
CENTRAL DISTRICT

LYNDHURST　TERR

星記(中環)
Sing Kee (Central)

閣麟街

伊沙里

HOLLYWOOD　RD

麻辣燙
Chilli Fagara

OLD BAILEY ST

中區警署
(已停用)
Central Police
Station (Closed)

域多利監獄
(已停用)
Victoria Prison
(Closed)

贊善里 CHANCERY

Bombay Dreams

WYNDHAM

中央
廣場
The
Centrium

N

環貿
Universal
Trade

ARBUTHNOT

CAINE RD

天主教
總堂
Rome
Catholic
Cathedral

聖母無
原罪堂

宏基
國際
賓館

明愛大廈
Caritas House

A

MAN YEE L

POTTINGER ST

龍麵館
Dragon Noodle
Academy

LIYUEN ST W

QUEEN'S RD C

LIYUEN ST E

旅
Ta Vie

中環石板街
The Pottinger

一樂燒鵝
Yat Lok

STANLEY ST

陸羽茶室
Luk Yu Tea House

WELLINGTON

WO ON L

Manning

世紀廣場

Entertainment Building

玄鮨
Xuan Sushi

Mercato

LAN KWAI FONG

Fofo by el Willy

D'AGUILAR

Carbone
LKF
LKF
蘭桂坊
蘭桂坊

迷你

STREET

Prince C.

聖公會

會督府

LOWER ALBERT

ICE HOUSE ST

西玉
Toritama

聖保羅堂

港中
醫院
HKC
Hospital

Church
Guest Hse

GLENEALY

畢　道

ALBANY　RD

UPPER ALBERT RD

← 98m米 (比例尺 Scale 1:3,250) →

B

金鐘
ADMIRALTY

PLA Berth

EDINBURGH PLACE

大會堂
CITY HALL

龍和道

中西區海濱長廊
Central & Western District Promenade

干諾道中

中環頂舊
Central
Barracks

行政長官
辦公室

LUNG WO ROAD

龍和道

立法會綜合大樓
Legislative
Council
Complex

分域碼頭
Fenwick Pier

CHATER RD

和記大廈
Hutchison
House

美國
銀行中心
Bank of
America
Tower

LAMBETH
WALK

香港特別行政區
政府總部
Hong Kong SAR
Central Government
Offices

中倍大廈
Cigic Tower

紅十字會
總部
HK Red Cross
Headquarters

HARCOURT

ROAD

夏慤道

美利大廈
Murray
Building

力寶大廈 II
力寶中心
Lippo Tw II
Lippo Centre
Lippo Tw I
力寶大廈 I

金鐘
ADMIRALTY

金鐘

MTR
Construction Site
港鐵工地

Caine House

警政大廈
Arsenal House

警察總部
Police Headquarters

中銀大廈
Bank of China
Tower

花旗銀行廣場
Citibank Plaza

茶具文物館
Museum of
Tea Ware

高等法院
High Court

金鐘廊
Queensway
Plaza

DRAKE ST

金鐘
花園

夏慤花園
Harcourt Garden
(臨時封閉)

警政大廈東翼
Arsenal House
East Wing

香港公園
HONG KONG PARK

KC Lo Gallery

金鐘道
政府合署
Queensway
Govt Offices

ADMIRALTY

QUEENSWAY

金鐘道

花園廣場

港島香格里拉
Island Shangri-La

太古廣場
PACIFIC PLACE

港麗
Conrad

JW Marriott
Upper House

Café Gray Deluxe

龍蝦吧
Lobster Bar and Grill

Conrad Hotel

奕居
The Upper House

珀翠
Petrus

英國文化協會
British
Council

萬豪
JW Marriott

夏宮
Summer Palace

英國
總領事館
British
Consulate

金葉庭
Golden Leaf

中國外交部
駐港特派員公署

Island School

港燈中心
HK Electric Co

KENNEDY

Magazine
Gap
Towers

馬己仙
Magazine
Heights

MAGAZINE GAP ROAD

寶雲道花園

PEAK ROAD

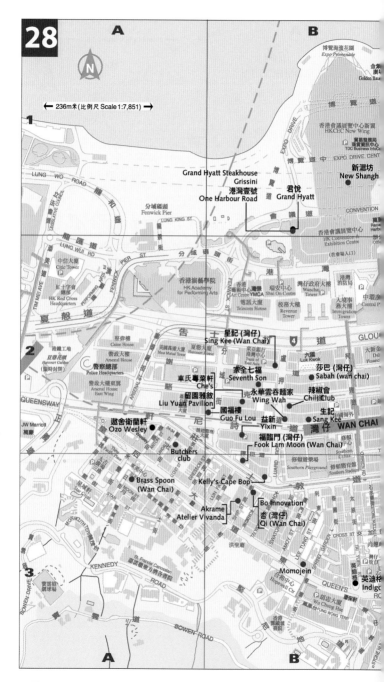

A   B

← 236米 (比例尺 Scale 1:7,851) →

博覽海濱花園
Expo Promenade

金紫荊廣場
Golden Bau

香港會議展覽中心新翼
HKCEC New Wing

軍器廠街電訊
TDC Business InfoCe

新滬坊
New Shangh

LUNG WO ROAD

Grand Hyatt Steakhouse
Grissini

港灣壹號
One Harbour Road

君悅
Grand Hyatt

分域碼頭
Fenwick Pier

LUNG KING ST.

香港會議展覽中心
Hong Kong Convention &
Exhibition Centre
(在會所入口)

中信大廈
Citic Tower

TIM MEI AVE

紅十字會
HK Red Cross
Headquarters

夏愨道

香港演藝學院
HK Academy
for Performing Arts

灣景
Art Centre YMCA

瑞安中心
Shun On Centre

灣仔政府大樓
Wanchai
Tower

港灣
灣仔消防局

電訊大廈
Telecom House

稅務大樓
Revenue
Tower

入境事
務大樓
Immigration
Tower

中港城
Central P

GLOU

大嫁

大新金
Dah Finance

QUEENSWAY

港鐵工地
夏愨花園
(臨時封閉)

警察總部
Police Headquarters

軍器廠東翼
Arsenal House
East Wing

佳仁樓
Caine House

夏慤大樓
Harcourt House

美國萬通大廈
Mass Mutual Tower

星記 (灣仔)
Sing Kee (Wan Chai)

東亞銀行
港灣軒行
Bank of
East Asia

六國
Luk Kwok

莎巴 (灣仔)
Sabah (wan chai)

車氏粵菜軒
Che's

家全七福
Seventh Son

永華雲吞麵家
Wing Wah

辣椒會
Chili Club

留園雅敘
Liu Yuan Pavilion

囻福樓
Guo Fu Lou

益新
Yixin

生記
Sang Kee

JW Marriott

遨舍衛蘭軒
Ozo Wesley

Butchers
club

福臨門 (灣仔)
Fook Lam Moon (Wan Chai)

修頓遊樂場
Southorn Playground 修頓球場
Southorn Stadium

Brass Spoon
(Wan Chai)

Kelly's Cape Bop

Akrame
Atelier Vivanda

Bo Innovation

杏 (灣仔)
Qi (Wan Chai)

WAN CHAI

CROSS ST

Star Street
Terrace

洪聖廟

KENNEDY ROAD

St. Francis' Canossian
嘉諾撒聖方濟各書院

Momojein

英迪格
Indigc

QUEEN'S

胡忠大廈
Wu Chung Ho

FUNG WONG TERR.

香港
國際進出貿
易學院

寶雲道
運動場

BOWEN DRIVE

BOWEN ROAD

A   B

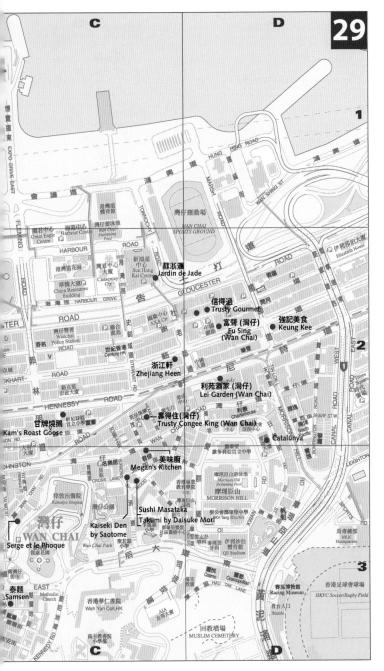

1

博覽道東
EXPO DRIVE EAST

會議道
FLEMING

興興道
HUNG HING ROAD

MARSH ROAD

灣仔運動場
WAN CHAI
SPORTS GROUND

WAN SHING ST

伊利莎伯大廈
Elizabeth House

廈景中心
Great Eagle
Centre

海港中心
Harbour Centre

HARBOUR ROAD

港灣道鷹鵡館

灣仔游泳池
Wan Chai
Swimming Pool

TONNOCHY ROAD

告士打道
GLOUCESTER

ROAD

蘇浙滙
Jardin de Jade

2

港灣花園

華潤大廈
China Resources
Building

HARBOUR DRIVE

新鴻基中心
Sun Hung
Kai Centre

金鐘
Causeway
Cvz

信得過
Trusty Gourmet

強記美食
Keung Kee

ROAD

灣仔警署
Wanchai
Police Station

STEWART RD

富聲 (灣仔)
Fu Sing
(Wan Chai)

CROSS STREET

ROAD

世紀香港
Century HK

浙江軒
Zhejiang Heen

利苑酒家 (灣仔)
Lei Garden (Wan Chai)

EAST

SHARP ST W.

HENNESSY

甘牌燒鵝
Kam's Roast Goose

靠得住 (灣仔)
Trusty Congee King (Wan Chai)

MORRISON HILL

CANAL ROAD

Catalunya

SPORTS

JOHNSTON

美味廚
Megan's Kitchen

CROSS LANE

摩理臣山游泳池
Morrison Hill
Swimming Pool

摩理臣山
MORRISON HILL

KWAN

LEIGHTON

馬會總部
HKFC
Headquarters

偉教治醫院
Ruttonjee Hospital

灣仔
WAN CHAI

灣仔公園

Sushi Masataka
Takumi by Daisuke Mori

Kaiseki Den
by Saotome

Wan Chai Park

Serge et le Phoque

SK Tang Shiu Kin

QB Stadium
伊利莎伯
體育館
QB Stadium

Oi

3

EAST

Methodist
Church

香港華仁書院
Wah Yan Coll, HK

皇后大道
HAU TAK LANE

Cosmo
Cosmopolitan

賽馬博物館
Racing Museum

香港足球會球場
HKFC Soccer/Rugby Field

泰麵
Samsen

AIA
友邦廣場

回教墳場
MUSLIM CEMETERY

跑道入口
Stands

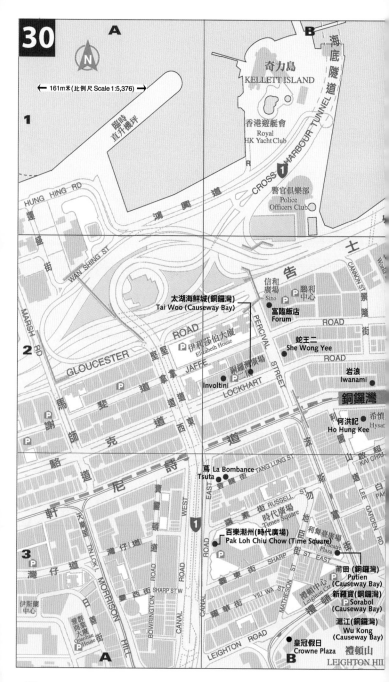

30

A　　　B

← 161m米(比例尺 Scale 1:5,376) →

奇力島
KELLETT ISLAND

海底隧道

香港遊艇會
Royal
HK Yacht Club

臨時
直升機坪

HUNG HING RD
鴻興道

CROSS HARBOUR TUNNEL

警官俱樂部
Police
Officers Club

WAN SHING ST

信和廣場
Sino

鵬利中心

太湖海鮮城(銅鑼灣)
Tai Woo (Causeway Bay)

富臨飯店
Forum

告

ROAD

PERCIVAL STREET

蛇王二
She Wong Yee

ROAD

CANNON ST

MARSH RD
馬師道

GLOUCESTER ROAD

伊利莎伯大廈
Elizabeth House

JAFFE

Involtini

LOCKHART

銅鑼灣廣場

岩浪
Iwanami

銅鑼灣

何洪記
Ho Hung Kee

希慎
Hysar

利

KAI CHIU

LEE GARDEN RD

告士打道

駱克道

謝斐道

軒尼詩道

TANG LUNG ST

La Bombance
Tsuta 蔦

RUSSELL ST

時代廣場
Times Square

百樂潮州(時代廣場)
Pak Loh Chiu Chow (Time Square)

EAST

CANAL ROAD

利舞臺廣場
Plaza

ST EAST

Theatre

莆田(銅鑼灣)
Putien
(Causeway Bay)

新羅寶(銅鑼灣)
Sorabol
(Causeway Bay)

渼江(銅鑼灣)
Wu Kong
(Causeway Bay)

MORRISON HILL

灣仔道

TIN LOK L

BOWRINGTON ROAD

SHARP ST W

CANAL ROAD

YIU WA ST

MATHESON

禮頓中心
Leighton Ctr

伊斯蘭
中心

香業
商業
大廈
Guardian
House

皇冠假日
Crowne Plaza

LEIGHTON ROAD

禮頓山
LEIGHTON HILL

478

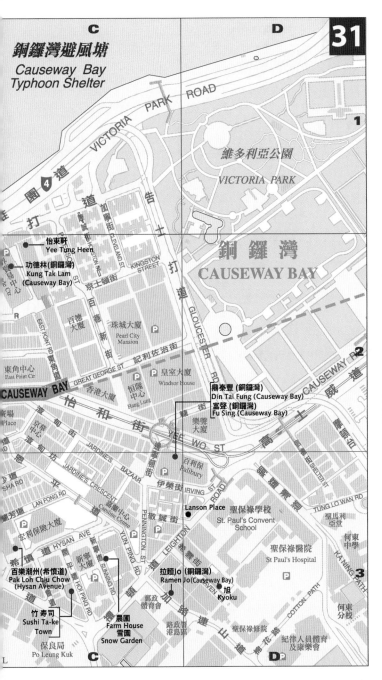

銅鑼灣避風塘
Causeway Bay
Typhoon Shelter

維多利亞公園
VICTORIA PARK

銅鑼灣
CAUSEWAY BAY

VICTORIA PARK ROAD

怡東軒
Yee Tung Heen

功德林 (銅鑼灣)
Kung Tak Lam
(Causeway Bay)

珠城大廈
Pearl City
Mansion

East Point Ctr
東角中心

CAUSEWAY BAY

鼎泰豐 (銅鑼灣)
Din Tai Fung (Causeway Bay)

富聲 (銅鑼灣)
Fu Sing (Causeway Bay)

皇室大廈
Windsor House

百利保
Palibury

Lanson Place

聖保祿學校
St. Paul's Convent
School

聖保祿醫院
St Paul's Hospital

何東
中學

百樂潮州 (希慎道)
Pak Loh Chiu Chow
(Hysan Avenue)

拉麵Jo (銅鑼灣)
Ramen Jo(Causeway Bay)

旭
Kyoku

竹 寿司
Sushi Ta-ke
Town

農圃
Farm House

雪園
Snow Garden

何東
分校

保良局
Po Leung Kuk

紀律人員體育
及康樂會

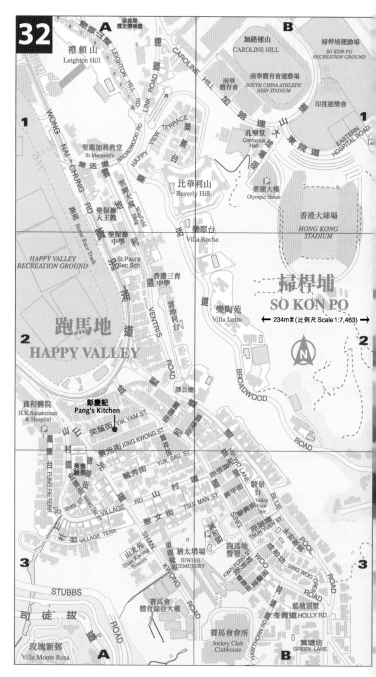

礼頓山
Leighton Hill

保良局
歷史博物館

LEIGHTON HILL LINK ROAD

CAROLINE HILL ROAD

加路連山
CAROLINE HILL

掃桿埔運動場
SO KON PO
RECREATION GROUND

南華
體育會

南華體育會運動場
SOUTH CHINA ATHLETIC
ASSN STADIUM

印度遊樂會

WONG NAI CHUNG RD.

BROADWOOD RD

聖馬加利教堂
St Margaret's

HAPPY VIEW TERRACE

樂景台

大球場道

孔聖堂
Confucius
Hall

EASTERN HOSPITAL ROAD

樂活道

雲地利大廈
Winfield
Bldg

比華利山
Beverly Hill

奧運大樓
Olympic House

香港大球場
HONG KONG
STADIUM

Horse Race Track

聖保祿
天主教

聖保祿
中學
St.Paul's
Sec Sch

黃泥涌道

樂翠台
Villa Rocha

香港三育
中學

HAPPY VALLEY
RECREATION GROUND

VENTRIS ROAD

活道

樂陶苑
Villa Lotto

掃桿埔
SO KON PO

← 234m米(比例尺 Scale 1:7,463) →

雲地利台

跑馬地
HAPPY VALLEY

成和道

N

BROADWOOD ROAD

源遠街

養和醫院
H.K.Sanatorium
& Hospital

彭慶記
Pang's Kitchen

YIK YAM ST

景光街

KING KWONG ST

毓秀街

YUK SAU ST

協和街

禧和里

HIP WO LANE

堅道

棉花路

古翠園

駿景台
Valley
View
Terr

山村台 FUNG FAI TERR

蘭芳道

奕蔭街

書館街

SHIN IN ST

WANG IN ST

SHAN KWONG ROAD

村

VILLAGE RD

山村道

景輝街

YUK SAU ST

TSUI MAN ST

聚文街

棉登徑

蘭杜街

晉源街

昇平街

聯興街

BLUE POOL ROAD

祥和里

禮和里

祥興里

TSUN YUEN ST

永光里

VILLAGE TERR

山光苑
Shan Kwong
Towers

東蓮覺苑

猶太墳場
JEWISH
CEMETERY

跑馬地
警署

奕廬

KWAI FONG ST

成康里

光明臺

成和坊

SING WOO ROAD

HAWTHORN RD

WOO

樂和里

荷和里

SING WOO CRES

藍塘別墅

冬青道 HOLLY RD

STUBBS ROAD

司徒拔道

玫瑰新邨
Villa Monte Rosa

賽馬會
體育綜合大樓

賽馬會會所
Jockey Club
Clubhouse

奕蔭坊
GREEN LANE

← 200m米 (比例尺 Scale 1:6,667) →

N

銅鑼灣
避風塘
Causeway
Bay
Typhoon
Shelter

富澤花園
Fortress Garden

COMFORT TERR

MERLIN ST

SHELL ST

Sushi Mori
Tomoaki

蜆殼街

JUPITER ST
水星街

SUP

英
皇
道

KING'S

FORTRESS
HILL
炮台山

富
澤
山
房

TEMPLE
RD

Belilios
Pub.Sch
庇理羅士女子

東院李潤田
Lee Ching Dea
Mem.Coll

1

WATSON RD
屈地道

MERCURY ST
水星街

WHITFIELD
威非路道

ELECTRIC
RD
電氣道

GORDON RD
歌頓道

WING HING ST
永興街

皇悦

盛捷

TSING FUNG ST
清風街

TIN
HAU
天

蒙特梭利
Montessori

VICTORIA PARK RD 維園道

LAU LI ST
琉璃街

琉璃街

宜室

HING FAT ST
興發街

YACHT ST
帆船街

帆船街

石記厨房
Shek Kee Kitchen

海景
Hotel

LAU SIN ST

新東方台

維多利亞公園
VICTORIA PARK

維園
游泳池
Victoria Park
Swimming Pool

留仙街

華姐清湯腩 (天后)
Sister wah (Tin Hau)

栢景臺
Park Towers

天后

TIN HAU

DRAGON
ROAD
摩頓臺

NEW EASTERN
TERR
新東方台

2

銅鑼灣
CAUSEWAY BAY

CAUSEWAY RD

銅鑼灣維景
Metropark (Causeway Bay)

銅
鑼
灣

Metropark
銅鑼灣
維景
Hotel

KING
RD
近

皇仁書院
Queen's College

IM Teppanyaki & Wine

DRAGON TERR 摩頓臺

LEE
RD

維
多
利
亞

MORETON
TERR

DRAGON PATH 大坑道

銅鑼灣運動場
Causeway Bay
Sports Ground

中華遊樂會
Chinese Recreation Club
Sports Ground

LIN FA KUNG
ST EAST

LAI TAK
TSUEN
RD

3

香港中央
圖書館
Central Library

TUNG LO WAN
TERR
銅鑼灣臺

TUNG LO WAN RD

SCHOOL ST

FIRST LANE

KING ST

SECOND LANE

WARREN ST

SUN CHUN ST

LAI TAK
TSUEN
RD

R

LAI TAK
TSUEN
RD

拔
萃
道

聖保祿醫院 東
t Paul's Hospital 院

何東中學
Hotung

豪園
FONTANA GARDENS

KA NING PATH
何東分校

COTTON PATH
棉花路

大坑道

TAI HANG
RD

TAI HANG
大坑

WUN SHA
ST

ILLUMINATION
TERR

B

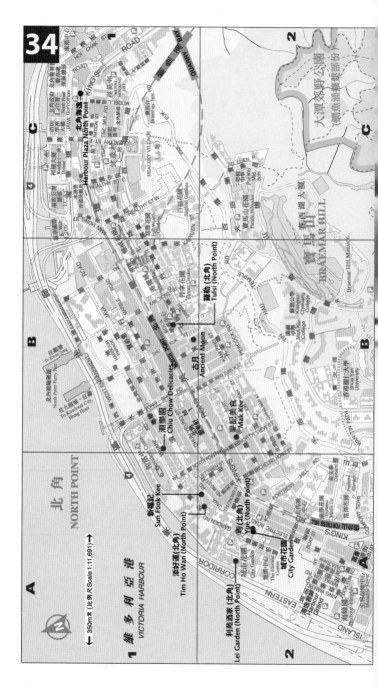

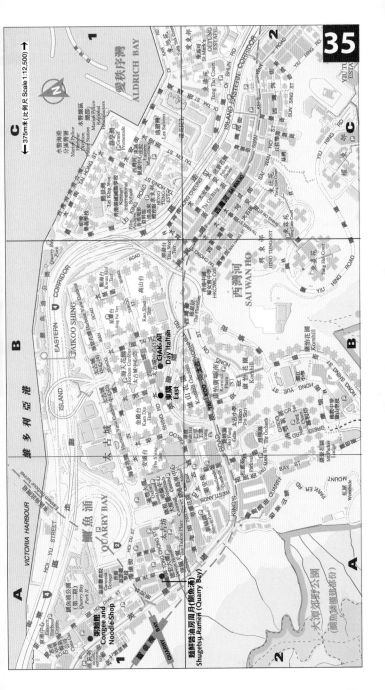

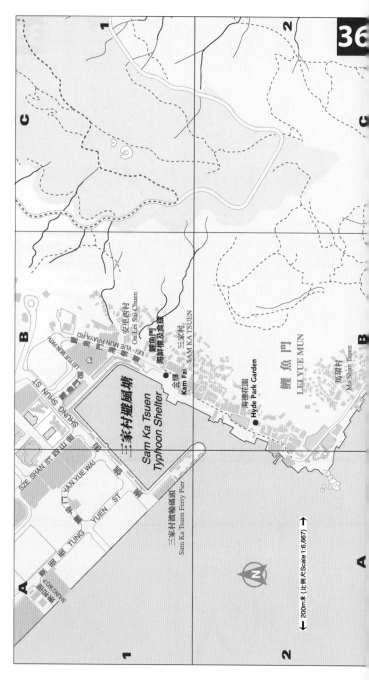

安里西村
On Lei Sai Chuen

油塘西村
鯉魚門海鮮艇及菜園
YUE MUN PRAYA RD

鯉魚門海鮮舫及菜園

三家村
SAM KA TSUEN

金輝
Kam Fai

海德花園
Hyde Park Garden

鯉魚門
LEI YUE MUN

馬環村
Ma Shan Tsuen

三家村避風塘
Sam Ka Tsuen Typhoon Shelter

LEI YUE MUN PATH

SHUNG SHUN ST

SZE SHAN ST 四山街

仁宇園圍 YAN YUE WAI

東源街 TUNG YUEN ST

崇和路 SHUNG WO RD

三家村渡輪碼頭
Sam Ka Tsuen Ferry Pier

← 200m米 (比例尺 Scale 1:6,667) →

484

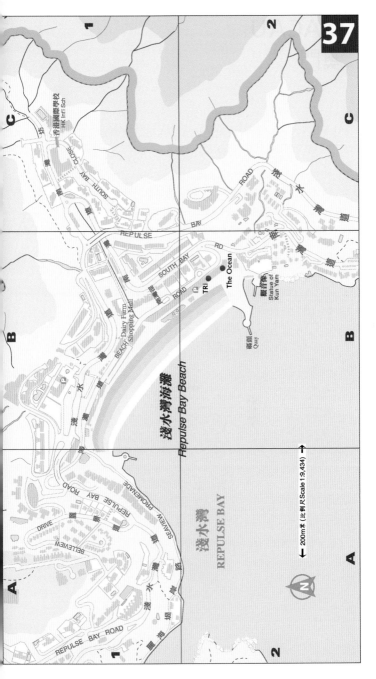

香港國際學校
HK Int'l Sch

SOUTH BAY CLOSE

REPULSE BAY

淺水灣道 ROAD

SOUTH BAY ROAD

Dairy Farm
Shopping Mall

TRi
The Ocean

觀音像
Statue of
Kun Yam

碼頭
Quay

淺水灣海灘
Repulse Bay Beach

REPULSE BAY PROMENADE

SEAVIEW DRIVE
BELLEVIEW

REPULSE BAY ROAD

淺水灣
REPULSE BAY

← 200米 (比例尺 Scale 1:9,434) →

REPULSE BAY ROAD 淺海灣道

MACAU
澳門

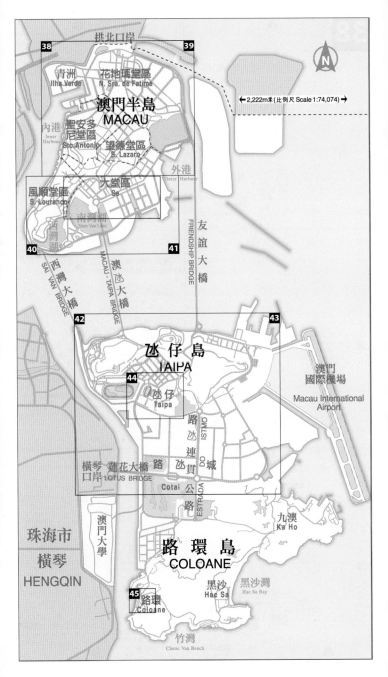

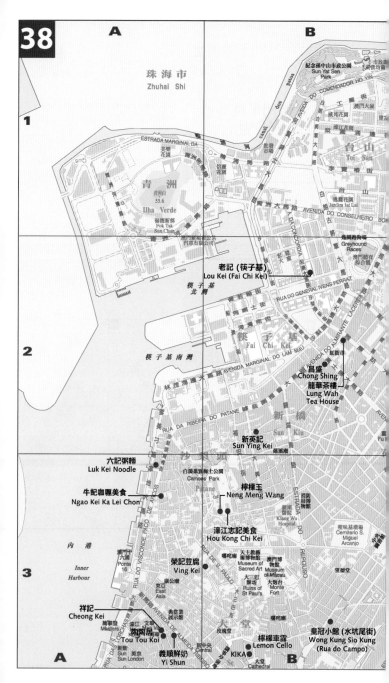

老記 (筷子基)
Lou Kei (Fai Chi Kei)

昌盛
Chong Shing

龍華茶樓
Lung Wah Tea House

新英記
Sun Ying Kei

六記粥麵
Luk Kei Noodle

牛記咖喱美食
Ngao Kei Ka Lei Chon

檸檬王
Neng Meng Wang

濠江志記美食
Hou Kong Chi Kei

榮記荳腐
Ving Kei

祥記
Cheong Kei

陶陶居
Tou Tou Koi

義順鮮奶
Yi Shun

檸檬車露
Lemon Cello

KIKA

皇冠小館 (水坑尾街)
Wong Kung Sio Kung
(Rua do Campo)

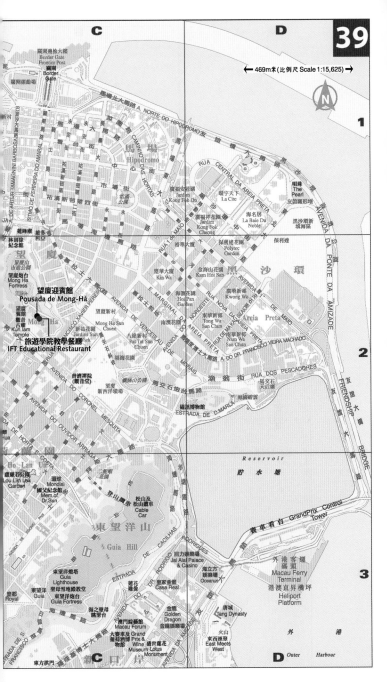

← 469m米 (比例尺 Scale 1:15,625) →

N

1

關閘通檢大樓
Border Gate
Frontier Post
關閘
Border
Gate

賽馬會大馬路 A. NORTE DO HIPODROMO 友

CAMINHO DAS HORTAS

馬場
Hipodromo

RUA CENTRAL DA AREIA PRETA

明珠
The Pearl
友誼圓形墟

廣祖女媧廟
Jardim
Kong Fok On

頤宇天下
La Cité

AVENIDA DA PONTE DA AMIZADE

廣福祥花園
Jardim
Kong Fok Cheong

海名居
La Baie Du
Noble

黑沙環新
填海區

林則徐
紀念館

望廈山
市政公園

保利達花園
Polytec
Garden

保利達

望廈炮台
Mong Ha
Fortress

蓮峰大廟
Kin Wa

金海山花園
Kam Hoi San

黑　沙　環

望廈迎賓館
Posada de Mong-Há

望廈
城隍廟
觀音
古廟
Kun Iam
Temple

望廈新村
Mong Ha Sun
Chuen

海濱新邨
Hou Pan
Garden

廣華新邨
Kwong Wa

AVENIDA DE VENCESLAU

E. MARGINAL DA

NORDESTE DA

AVENIDA DE MAIO

旅遊學院教學餐廳
IFT Educational Restaurant

新祐漢花園
Jardins Sun
Fat

八總廟村
Fat Tat Sun
Chuen

南澳花園
Nam Pan

東望洋新邨
Tong Wa &
Nam Wa
San Chun

祐漢新村
Nam Wa
San Chun

黑沙環
Areia Preta

AVENIDA DA

普濟禪院
(觀音堂)

福海花園

鏡海山公園

望廈
新西墳場

漁翁街 RUA DOS PESCADORES

陽文石
天后廟

AVENIDA DO OUVIDOR ARRIAGA

AVENIDA DO CORONEL MESQUITA

筷交石墳場馬路

藝園博物館

通訊博物館

ESTRADA DE D.MARIA

N
O
R
T
E

何連
環圓
Ho Lan
Un Un

盧廉若公園
Lou Lim Iok
Garden

二龍喉
花園

Reservoir
貯水塘

FRIENDSHIP BRIDGE

東望洋山
S'Guia Hill

環圓
Mondial

國父紀念館
Mem. of
Dr. Sun

登山纜車
松山及
松山纜車
Cable
Car

賽車看台 GrandPrix Control
Tower

DE CACILHAS

RODRIGUES

東望洋燈塔
Guia
Lighthouse

回力娛樂場
Jai Alai Palace
& Casino

外港客運
碼頭
Macau Ferry
Terminal

東望洋
Guia

聖母雪地殿教堂
東望洋炮台
Guia Fortress

海立方
娛樂場
Oceanus

港澳直昇機坪
Heliport
Platform

3

DE RODRIGO DE RODRIGO

皇家金都
Casa Real

ESTRADA

皇家
Royal

海之聖母
瞭望台

唐城
Tang Dynasty

火山
AVENIDA DA

金龍
Golden
Dragon

AVENIDA

澳門綜藝館
Macau Forum

大賽車及
葡萄酒博
物館
Museum Lotus
Monument

金蓮花廣場
金蓮娛樂場

外　港

東西匯聚
East Meets
West

外港拱門

新口岸
C

D
Outer　Harbour

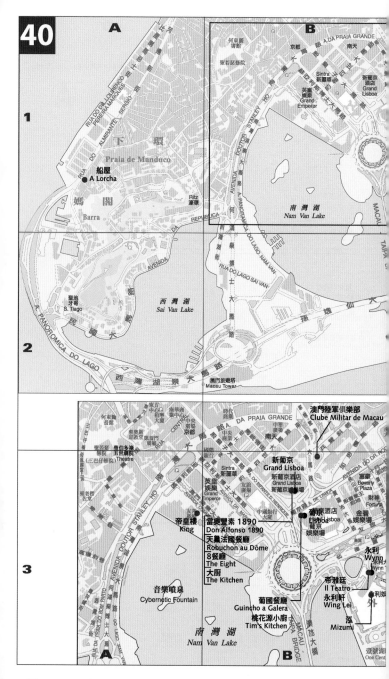

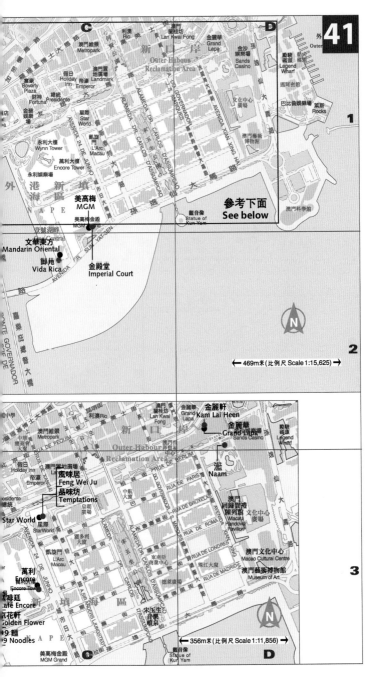

外港 Outer

新口岸 Outer Haboour Reclamation Area

利澳 Rio
Lan Kwai Fong
金麗華 Grand Lapa

澳門維景 Metropark

金沙娛樂場 Sands Casino

豪華酒店 Legend Wharf

巴比倫娛樂場
澳斯 Rocks

假日 Holiday Inn
帝濠 Emperor
總統 Presidente

文化中心 廣場

萬豪 Beverly Plaza
財神 Fortuna

永利大堡 Wynn Tower

星際 Star World

L'Arc Macau

萬利大堡 Encore Tower

永利娛樂場 Wynn

外港新填海區 N A P E

美高梅 MGM

美高梅金殿 MGM Grand

澳門藝術博物館

參考下面
See below

澳門科學館

中區 Central

文華東方
Mandarin Oriental

金殿堂
Imperial Court

御苑
Vida Rica

←469m米(比例尺 Scale 1:15,625)→

澳門維景 Metropark

利澳 Rio
Lan Kwai Fong
金麗華 Grand Lapa

金麗軒 Kam Lai Heen

金麗華 Grand Lapa

金沙娛樂場 Sands Casino

豪華酒店 Legend Wharf

新口岸 Outer Haboour Reclamation Area

假日 Holiday Inn
帝濠 Emperor

風味居 Feng Wei Ju

品味坊 Temptations

藍 Naam

澳門回歸賀禮陳列館 文化中心 廣場 Macau Handover Pavilion

星際 Star World StarWorld

L'Arc Macau

澳門文化中心

澳門藝術博物館 Museum of Art

萬利 Encore

咖啡廷 Cafe Encore

京花軒 Golden Flower

99麵 99 Noodles

美高梅金殿 MGM Grand

N A P E 新填海區

宋玉生生 廣場

觀音像 Statue of Kun Yam

←356m米(比例尺 Scale 1:11,856)→

D

← 627m米(比例尺 Scale 1:20,909) →

N

澳氹大橋
Macau-Taipa Bridge

西灣大橋
Sai Van Bridge

西灣大橋

海洋大馬路
Est dos Sete Tanques

花園大馬路
海洋
會所

迷仔雕塑
Taipa
Monument

110.8
小潭山

海洋花園
Avenida da

奧羅拉
Aurora
天政
Tenmasa
帝影樓
Ying

中伯泰海軍

將軍馬路

觀音岩
University of N

澳門大學

王府
Imperial Palace

麗景灣
Regency

新濠鋒
Altira

新濠鋒

菩提禪院
Pou Tai Un
Monastery

玫瑰山莊

迷仔炮臺

柯維納馬路
Est Governador Albano Oliveira

澳門賽馬會
Macau Jockey Club

賽馬場
Macau Jockey Club

百姓
Banza

君怡
Grandview

四面佛
Four-Faces
Buddha

澳門
運動場
Stadium &
Aquatic Centre

氹仔村
Taipa
Village

奧林匹克
游泳館
Stadium &
Aquatic Centre

路氹連貫公路 Estrada da Baía

銀河
Galaxy

Hou

山里
Yamazato

萬豪
JW Marriott

大倉
Okura

皇庭
海景
Pousada
Marina Infante

悅榕莊
Banyan Tree

銀河渡假城
Galaxy Macau

福臨門
Fook Lam Moon
8 1/2 Otto e Mezzo

麗絲卡爾頓
The Ritz-Carlton

麗軒
Lai Heen

珠 海 市
ZHU HAI CITY

百老匯 Broadway

福龍葡國餐 (百老匯)
Dragon Portuguese Cuisine (Broadway)

麗思咖啡廳
The Ritz-Carlton café

度小月
Du Hsiao Yueh

Avenida de Cotai

橫琴
Hengqin

加東
Katong Corner

路

李家菜
Lei Ka Choi

皇冠小館(百老匯)
Wong Kung Sio Kung (Broadway)

人工濕地

橫琴口岸
Hengqin Port

蓮花大橋
Lotus Bridge

ESTRADA FLOR DE

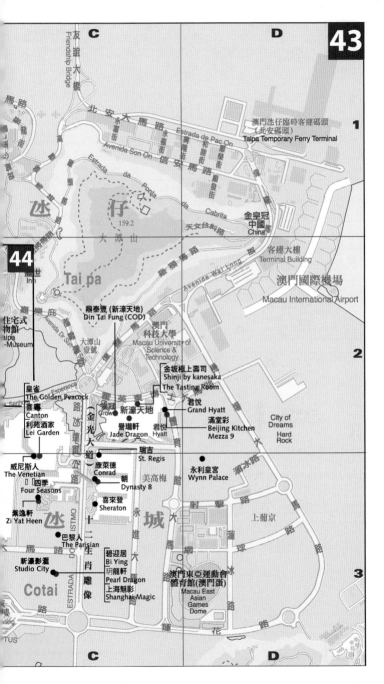

友誼大橋
Friendship Bridge

馬路

北安大馬路
Estrada de Pac On

永安馬路

澳門氹仔臨時客運碼頭
（北安碼頭）
Taipa Temporary Ferry Terminal

Avenida Son On

氹

仔

Estrada da Ponta da Cabrita

天文台斜路

金皇冠
中國
China

159.2

大潭山

客運大樓
Terminal Building

Tai pa

澳門國際機場
Macau International Airport

Avenida Wai Long

住宅式
物館
Taipa
-Museum

鼎泰豐 (新濠天地)
Din Tai Fung (COD)

澳門
科技大學
Macau University of
Science &
Technology

大潭山壹號

皇雀
The Golden Peacock

喜臨
Canton

利苑酒家
Lei Garden

新濠天地
Crown

金坂極上壽司
Shinji by kanesaka

The Tasting Room

君悅
Grand Hyatt

譽瓏軒
Jade Dragon

君悦
Hyatt

滿堂彩
Beijing Kitchen
Mezza 9

City of
Dreams
Hard Rock

瑞吉
St. Regis

康萊德
Conrad

威尼斯人
The Venetian

四季
Four Seasons

朝
Dynasty 8

美高梅

永利皇宮
Wynn Palace

紫逸軒
Zi Yat Heen

氹

喜來登
Sheraton

城

上葡京

巴黎人
The Parisian

新濠影滙
Studio City

碧迎居
Bi Ying
玥龍軒
Pearl Dragon
上海魅影
Shanghai Magic

澳門東亞運動會
體育館(澳門蛋)
Macau East
Asian
Games
Dome

Cotai

44

Chaves
君怡
Grandview

澳門賽馬場
Macau Jockey Club

澳門運動場
Eetadio De Macau

奧林匹克游泳館
Piscina Olimpica De Macau

澳門三育
Escola Secundaria Sam Yuk

AVENIDA DE GUIMARAES

RUA DE BRAGANCA

AVENIDA OLIMPICA

阿曼諾葡國餐
Manuel Cozinha Portuguesa

盛世酒店
Inn

晃記餅家
Fong kei

Castiço

安東尼奧
Antonio

莫義記
Mok Yee Kei

迭仔住宅式博物館
Taipa Houses-Museum

新陶陶
San Tou Tou

銀河
Galaxy

名家
Myung Ga

庭園
Terrazza

銀河
Galaxy

迭仔市區
TAIPA TOWN

◀━ 325m米 (比例尺 Scale 1:10,850) ━▶

里斯本地帶
Espaço Lisboa

RUA DOS NAVEGANTES

ESTRADA DO CAMPO

ESTRADA DE CHEOC VAN

安德魯餅店
Lord Stow's Bakery

陳勝記
Chan Seng Kei

RUA DA CORDOARIA

A. DE CINCO DE OUTUBRO

路環市區
COLOANE TOWN

◀━ 157m米 (比例尺 Scale 1:5,220) ━▶

45

494

PICTURE COPYRIGHT
圖片版權

58 - Aberdeen Street Social/Michelin, 59 - Above & Beyond, 60 - Michelin, 61 - Ah Yat Harbour View, 62 - Akrame, 63 - Amber, 64 - Michelin, 65 - Arcane, 66 - Atelier Vivanda/Michelin, 67 - Michelin, 68 - Beefbar, 69 - Belon, 70 - Bibo, 71 - Bo Innovation, 72 - Bombay Dreams/Michelin, 73 - Bostonian Seafood and Grill, 74 - Brass Spoon/Michelin, 75 - Café Gray Deluxe/Michelin, 76 - Michelin, 77 - Caprice, 78 - Michelin, 79 - Celebrity Cuisine, 80 - Celestial Court, 81 – 82, Michelin, 83 - Chesa/Michelin, 84 – 85, Michelin, 86 - China Tang (Central), 87 - Michelin, 88 - Chinese Legend, 89 - Chiuchow Delicacies, 90 – 91, Michelin, 92 - CIAK - All Day Italian, 93 - CIAK - In The Kitchen, 94 - Cocotte/Michelin, 95 - Come-Into Chiu Chow/Michelin, 96 - Michelin, 97 - Cuisine Cuisine at The Mira, 98 - Michelin, 99 - Din Tai Fung/Michelin, 100 - Din Tai Fung, 101 - Dong Lai Shun, 102 - Dragon Inn/Michelin, 103 - Dragon King/Michelin, 104 - Dragon Noodles Academy, 105 - Duddell's, 106 - Michelin, 107 - Épure, 108 - Michelin, 109 - Felix, 110 - Fish School, 111 - Fofo by el Willy/Michelin, 112 - Fook Lam Moon (Wan Chai), 113 - Forum, 114 - Frantzén's Kitchen, 115 - Fu Ho (Tsim Sha Tsui)/Michelin, 116 – 118, Michelin, 119 - Gaddi's, 120 - Glorious Cuisine, 121 - Golden Leaf, 122 - Michelin, 123 - Grand Hyatt Steakhouse, 124 - Grissini, 125 - Guo Fu Lou, 126 - Michelin, 127 - Ho Hung Kee, 128 – 129, Michelin, 130 - Hugo's, 131 - Michelin, 132 - IM Teppanyaki & Wine/Michelin, 133 - Imperial Treasure Fine Chinese Cuisine, 134 - Involtini/Michelin, 135 - Ippoh, 136 - Iwanami, 137 - Jardin de Jade, 138 - Michelin, 139 - Kaiseki Den by Saotome, 140 - Michelin, 141 - Kam's Roast Goose/Michelin, 142 - Kashiwaya, 143 - Michelin, 144 - Kaum, 145 - Michelin, 146 - Kwan Kee Bamboo Noodle/Michelin, 147 - Michelin, 148 - Kyoku, 149 - La Bombance, 150 - Michelin, 151 - L'Atelier de Joël Robuchon, 152 – 153, Michelin, 154 - Le 39V, 155 - Lei Garden/Michelin, 156 - Lei Garden, 157 - Lei Garden/Michelin, 158 - Lei Garden (Mong Kok), 159 - Michelin, 160 - Lei Garden (Sha Tin), 161 - Lei Garden (Wan Chai), 162 – 163, Michelin, 164 - Loaf On/Michelin, 165 - Lobster Bar and Grill, 166 – 167, Michelin, 168 - Lung King Heen , 169 - Michelin, 170 - Man Wah, 171 - Mandarin Grill + Bar, 172 - Megan's Kitchen/Michelin, 173 - Michelin, 174 - MIC Kitchen, 175 - Ming Court, 177 - Momojein, 178 - Moon Thai/Michelin, 179 - New Shanghai/Michelin, 180 - Michelin, 181 - Nobu, 182 - On, 183 - One Harbour Road, 184 - 8 1/2 Otto e Mezzo - Bombana/Michelin, 185 - Pak Loh Chiu Chow/Michelin, 186 - Pak Loh Chiu Chow (Times Square)/Michelin, 187 - Michelin, 188 - Peking Garden , 189 - Petrus, 190 - Pierre, 191 - Michelin, 192 - Putien/Michelin, 193 - Qi (Tsim Sha Tsui), 194 - Qi/Michelin, 195 - Qīao Cuisine, 196 - Qing Zuo, 197 - Michelin, 198 - Rech, 199 - Robatayaki, 200 - Ryu Gin, 201 - Michelin, 202 - Sai Kung Sing Kee, 203 - Samsen, 204 - Michelin, 205 - Serge et le phoque/Michelin, 206 - Seventh Son, 207 - Shang Palace/Michelin, 208 – 212, Michelin, 213 - Shugetsu Ramen/Michelin, 214 - Shugetsu Ramen/Michelin, 215 – 217, Michelin, 218 - Snow Garden/Michelin, 219 - Sorabol(Causeway Bay)/Michelin , 220 - Spring Moon, 221 - Summer Palace, 222 - Michelin, 223 - Sun Tung Lok (Tsim Sha Tsui)/Michelin, 224 - Michelin, 225 - Sushi Masataka , 226 - Sushi Mori Tomoaki/Michelin, 227 –

NOTES
備註

NOTES
備註

NOTES
備註

Michelin Travel Partner
Société par actions simplifiées au capital de 11 288 880 €
27 Cours de L'Ile Seguin - 92100 Boulogne Billancourt (France)
R.C.S. Nanterre 433 677 721

© **Michelin Travel Partner, All rights reversed**
Dépot légal Novembre 2017

Printed in China: October 2017

No part of this publication may be reproduced in any form without the prior permission of the publisher.

Although the information in this guide was believed by the authors and publisher to be accurate and current at the time of publication, they cannot accept responsibility for any inconvenience, loss or injury sustained by any person relying on information or advice contained in this guide. Things change over time and travellers should take steps to verify and confirm information, especially time sensitive information related to prices, hours of operation and availability.

E-mail : michelinguide.hongkong-macau@michelin.com

Maps : (C) 2017 Cartographic data Universal Publications, Ltd / Michelin
Printing and Binding: Book Partners China Ltd.

WINE ADVOCATE

Welcome to RobertParker.com!

For more than 38 years,
Robert Parker Wine Advocate has established
itself as the independent fine wine guide on the
international scene and is seen today as
the most influential wine review globally.

Receive the WINE ADVOCATE bi-monthly digital
review and access over 10 years of archives with a
fully searchable database of 285,000 tasting notes,
scores, articles and reviews.

Enjoy the member's benefits brought to you by our
Global Membership Programme that will reward
you with special gourmet and wine experiences
offered by our retail and F&B partners, and provide
you a privileged access to our worldwide series of
events *"Matter of Taste"*.

To activate your free one-year online membership
(valued at USD99) to The Wine Advocate and
MICHELIN guide Singapore, simply use the code
below and register on RobertParker.com and
guide.michelin.sg.

MGHKMUJTeSe

PARTNERS OF THE 2018 MICHELIN GUIDE HONG KONG MACAU

Title Partner
Melco Resorts & Entertainment Limited

Official Cars
Mercedes-AMG

Official Water
evian & Badoit

Official Beer
Tiger

Exclusive Champagne (Macau)
Mumm

Exclusive Cognac (Macau)
Martell